D0732831

SISTERS OF HEAVEN

China's Barnstorming Aviatrixes:
Modernity, Feminism, and Popular Imagination
in Asia and the West

Patti Gully

LONG RIVER PRESS
San Francisco

Copyright © 2008 Patti Gully
All rights reserved

Published in the United States of America by:

Long River Press
360 Swift Avenue, Suite 48
South San Francisco, CA 94080
www.longriverpress.com
Editor: Chris Robyn
Book and cover design: Nathan Grover
No part of this book may be reproduced
without written permission of the publisher.

Printed in the U.S.A.
10 9 8 7 6 5 4 3 2 1

ISBN: 978-1-59265-075-0

Library of Congress Cataloging-in-Publication Data

Gully, Patti.
   Sisters of heaven : China's barnstorming aviatrixes : modernity, feminism, and
popular imagination in Asia and the West / Patti Gully.
        p. cm.
   Includes bibliographical references and index.
   ISBN 978-1-59265-075-0 (hardcover)
   1. Women air pilots--China--Biography. 2. Air pilots--China--Biography. 3. Aero-
nautics--China--History--20th century. 4. China--Social life and customs--History--
20th century. 5. East and West. I. Title.
   TL539.G85 2007
   629.13092'251--dc22

                                                                           2006034177

For Guy

TABLE OF CONTENTS

ACKNOWLEDGMENTS ix

LIST OF ILLUSTRATIONS
    (Part I) Hilda Yan: Life of the Heart xiii
    (Part II) Li Xiaqing: Profile of a Legend xv
    (Part III) Zheng Hanying: Uneasy Spirit xvii

LIST OF MAPS xix

INTRODUCTION 1

PART I

HILDA YAN (李霞卿): LIFE OF THE HEART

1. Prologue 10
2. Liberal Strains 11
3. Life under the Soviet Star 24
4. Sexual Slavery & the League of Nations 35
5. A War of Resistance 43
6. Aid to China 54
7. May Day 62
8. American Bureau for Medical Aid to China 71
9. Return to the Far East 77
10. "Coming of Age of the Entire Human Race" 84
11. John Gifford Male   127 90
12. Endings 99
13. Epilogue 102

PART II

LI XIAQING (李霞卿): PROFILE OF A LEGEND

14. Introduction 116
15. Revolutionary to the Core 117
16. Star of the Silver Screen 126
17. "Isn't flying the top of everything?" 136
18. Return to China 144
19. Return to the New World 161
20. Flying Down to Rio 233 177
21. Relief Wings & United China Relief 183
22. South America Reprised 197
23. Blue Skies 201

PART III

ZHENG HANYING (郑汉英): UNEASY SPIRIT

24. Introduction 228
25. Origins 229
26. Wings for China 236
27. Romance… and Unforeseen Consequences 257
28. Zheng Takes Vancouver 264
29. Commissioning 273
30. Crossing Canada 285
31. Gathering Shadows 297
32. Postscript 301

APPENDIX

1. Hilda Yan's Participation in the League of Nations, as Documented in the Minutes of the Meetings: 313

First Committee (5th Meeting), September 19, 1935
Fifth Committee (4th Meeting), September 18, 1937
Fifth Committee (8th Meeting), September 25, 1937

2.   Minxin Films of Li Dandan (Li Xiaqing)   317

GLOSSARY   319

CHRONOLOGY   325

ENDNOTES   335

BIBLIOGRAPHY   375

INDEX   385

·

ACKNOWLEDGEMENTS

It is an honor to acknowledge my indebtedness to the following individuals and organizations without whose aid this project never would have been completed.

For her assistance with the story of Hilda Yan, I would like to express my deepest appreciation to Kim C. Wilson Owen, who, as director of the Autauga Prattville Public Library, Prattville, AL, was extraordinarily generous with her time and resources and was instrumental in helping me get started with the story of Ms Yan's life. I am also grateful to Sandra Scott and Aimee E. Brown of Smith College; Dr. Robert M. Gully, Royal Inland Hospital, Kamloops, BC; Blandine Blukacz-Louisfert, Chief Archivist, UNOG Registry, Records and Archives Unit, United Nations, Geneva; and Bernhardine E. Pejovic League of Nation Archivist, Geneva, Harold K. Everett, of the Federal Aviation Administration in Oklahoma City, OK; Kate de Courcy, Manuscripts Librarian at the Auckland City Library, David Exley and Frank Male of New Zealand. The daughters of the late New Zealand poet, A.R.D. Fairburn, were extremely gracious and generous with their time and remembrances of Ms Yan, and I am deeply grateful to Corin Fairburn Bass, Dinah Holman and Janis Fairburn.

For their assistance with the story of Li Xiaqing, I wish to thank Linda (Hsu) Wei of Oakland, CA; Patricia Lee, veteran aviatrix of Toronto, ON; Tad Bennicoff, Special Collections Assistant, Seeley G. Mudd Manuscript Library, Princeton University, NJ; Blaise Morand, president, Pilotes de glaciers et de montagne, l'Association Genevoise de l'Aéro-Club de Suisse, Geneva, Switzerland; John Houser, retired aero engineer, and John D. Furbay, Director of Finance, Aeronca, Inc., Middletown, OH; Bill Larsen, aviation enthusiast and historian; Dr. Judy Yung, professor of American Studies, University of California, Santa Cruz, CA; Linda K. Smith, Archives Specialist, Eisenhower Library, Abilene, KS; Law Kar, programmer, Hong Kong Film Archive, Hong Kong; Choi Kai-kwong, filmmaker, Hong Kong; Captain Moon Chin, retired professional air pilot of Hillsborough, CA; Danny Lee, retired wartime aircraft mechanic of Vancouver, BC; Sister Gilberte Painchaud, Provinical Animateur of the Sisters of the Child Jesus in Canada, Vancouver, BC; Paul Oelkrug, Senior Curator of Special Collections, McDermott Library, the University of Texas at Dallas, and

Dr. and Mrs. Wen Hsiang-lai of St Petersburg, FL. Jean-Claude Cailliez, Swiss aviation historian of Meyrin, Switzerland, was extremely generous with his information, and I also wish to thank him for his insights, encouragement, and the promotion of Ms. Li's story through the splendid website and journal that celebrate Geneva's aviation pioneers, *Pionnair-GE.com* and *La Feuille Volante*.

The list of those who helped me with the story of Zheng Hanying is a long one. I am grateful for the assistance of the late Madame Song Meiling, and Dr. C.J. Chen, representative of Taipei Economic and Cultural Representative Office in Washington, D.C. The contributions of Cliff Dunnaway and Ian D. Johnson, both of the Hong Kong Historical Aircraft Association, were of paramount importance to my research, and I also very much appreciate the friendly assistance of the following individuals: Larry Y. Wong, curator, Chinese Canadian Military Museum, Vancouver, BC; Dr. Henry Yu, Chinese Canadian Historical Society, Vancouver, BC; How Lee, president, Chinese Canadian Military Museum Society, Vancouver, BC; Steve Evans and Peter Olivieri, Aero Club of British Columbia; Robert Morrison, president, Canadian Military Remembrance Society (CMRS), Burnaby, BC; Colin Macgregor Stevens, manager, and Kelly Stewart, archivist, of Irving House/New Westminster Museum and Archives, New Westminster, BC; Michael DesMazes, RCAF historian; Tom O. Moore, Jr., CNAC history preservationist at cnac.org; Thierry Montigneaux of the Fédération Aéronautique Internationale; Sylvie Grondin, technicienne en gestion de documents et archives, Hôtel-de-Ville, Montréal, PQ; Hogan Loh, Hong Kong Aviation Club, Hong Kong, China; Barry Rolfe, Royal Aero Club, London, UK; Marquise Tessier and Ragnhild Milewski, National Film Board of Canada; Peter Chen, Director, Information Division, Taipei Economic & Cultural Office, Vancouver, BC; B.L. Riddle, Librarian, Royal Aeronautical Society, London, UK; David Walker, Strathcroix, St Andrew's, NB; Terry Hadley, Manager of Communications, Vancouver Board of Trade, Vancouver, BC; Lynn Waller, archivist, City of Richmond Archives, Richmond, BC; Bev Tallon, photo archivist/editor, Western Canada Aviation Museum, Winnipeg, MB; and Paul Lasewicz of the IBM Corporate Archives. I am most grateful to Maurice Guibord, Museum Programs Coordinator of the Burnaby Village Museum, who has worked to ensure the achievements of Flt. Lt. Zheng receive proper recognition.

The staff and collections of the following archives, libraries and organizations have been of invaluable assistance to me: Burnaby Public Library, Bob Prittie Branch, Burnaby, BC; Oceanview Cemetery, Burnaby, BC; City of Vancouver Archives, Vancouver, BC; City of Richmond Archives, Richmond, BC; British Columbia Archives, Victoria, BC; National Library of Canada, Ottawa, ON; University of British Columbia Libraries, Vancouver, BC; Vancouver Public Library, Vancouver, BC; Bibliothèque de Université Laval, Ville de Québec, PQ; Library of Congress, Washington, D.C.; Seeley G. Mudd Manuscript Library, Princeton University, Princeton, NJ; Auckland City Libraries, Auckland, NJ; San Francisco Public Libraries, San Francisco, CA; University of Washington Libraries, Seattle, WA; Alabama Department of Archives, Montgomery, AL; Salt Lake City Libraries, Salt Lake City, UT; Philadelphia Public Libraries, Philadelphia, PN; the Manuscripts and Archives division of Yale University Library, New Haven, CT; Hong Kong Public Libraries, Hong Kong, China; and the Shanghai Library Institute of Technical Information, Shanghai, China.

I must reserve my deepest thanks for the following individuals who gave me their utmost assistance.

Ronald K. Chen, J.D., of New Jersey, was remarkably forthcoming with memories and photographs of his grandmother, Hilda Yaqing Yan. His colorful and beautifully etched recollections of Ms. Yan gave me a vibrant impression of her free-spirited individuality. Dr. Doreen Chen, Hilda's daughter, was also kind enough to share her memories with me, and I am most grateful for her generosity and patience.

Pax Cheng, son of Li Xiaqing, and his wife Susan, graciously welcomed me into their home in Hercules, California, and put at my complete disposal the incredible archive of Ms. Li's papers, photographs and ephemera that had been safely buried underground in Hong Kong for decades, without which the bulk of her amazing story would have remained untold. Through his father, Zheng Baifeng, Mr. Cheng is also related to the aviatrix, Zheng Hanying, and although he had no knowledge of the young flyer, he was able to share with me many recollections of his grand aunt, the astonishing Dr. Zheng Yuxiu, who was undoubtedly the most formidable influence in the lives of so many young people, and in particular, that of her niece, Flight-Lieutenant Zheng.

Although I was only partly successful in tracking down the family of Zheng Hanying, I am extremely grateful to Mrs. Peggy (Wong) Lee of Vancouver, BC, who vividly remembered Ms. Zheng and was able to supply me with much information that otherwise would have remained unknown to me. Mr. Leigh Seto, the son of Ms. Zheng's estranged lover, Wilfred, was kind enough to share with me what he knew of Ms. Zheng's involvement in his family's history, and he generously contributed photos of his father and stepsister.

I wish to thank the remarkably munificent Ms. Renée Lym Robertson of San Francisco, CA for her role as facilitator and resource person *par excellence*, and for her unceasing efforts to preserve Chinese aviation history; Captain Albert Mah of Montréal, PQ, now deceased, and his brother, Captain Cedric Mah of Edmonton, AB, both former pilots of the China National Aviation Corporation, for sharing their intimate knowledge of aviation and wartime China; Michael Alderton of Katoomba, Australia, for his serendipitous photocopying; the principal, teachers and young pupils of Champlain Heights' Pui Ying Chinese School for the things they teach me and the friendship they give me; and the late Guan Zhongren, educator and aviation historian of Enping, Guangdong, for his support and belief in this project. I am most grateful for the principled example and sustenance (mental, physical and spiritual) of my dear friends, Drs. Roderick and Bernice Wong, and for the constant supervision of Kevin Kowal. Rosie and A.O. Gully have kept me on my toes. Dr. Wendy Yin-han Lam also has my heart-felt thanks for helping me to keep my head above water for the duration. I am forever indebted to the late Garth and Anne Pickell for their undying love and encouragement. I would like to thank my editor, Chris Robyn of Long River Press, for his patience, enthusiasm and excellent advice. And I could never have hoped to complete this task without the unfailing assistance of Mr. Angelo Xie, who, with enormous generosity of spirit, provided me with the encouragement I required, as well as fastidious translations of materials from Chinese into English. Without his help, I could not have done justice to this project.

LIST OF ILLUSTRATIONS

Part I: HILDA YAN: LIFE OF THE HEART

Figure

1. Emerging butterfly: Hilda Yan poses in sinuous *qipao*, Shanghai. (R.K. Chen)
2. A portrait of Hilda Yan Chen from the *North-China Herald*, May 22, 1935.
3. News photo of actress Hu Die aboard the *s.s. Sever* en route to the Soviet Union with Hilda and Ambassador Yan. (*Dian ying hua bao*, no. 23)
4. Hilda's uncle, Dr. Yan Huiqing, China's Ambassador to the U.S.S.R. (Author's collection)
5. First edition of *China illustrated*, a newsletter published by Geneva's Bibliothèque Sino-Internationale, highlights the work of the Chinese embassy and the visit of Hu Die to the Soviet Union. (Author's collection)
6. A 1940s portrait of Hilda Yan wearing her favorite Chinese gown. (R.K. Chen)
7. Yan Family portrait. Back row (l-r): Hilda's son, William Chen; brother, William Yan; sister, Dorothy Lieu; Hilda; brother, Victor Yan. Front row (l-r): Hilda's mother, Chow Siu-ying; father, Dr. Yan Fuqing, daughter, Doreen Chen. (R.K. Chen)
8. Delegates to the Nine Power Conference, Brussels, Nov. 1937. Front row, from left: Hilda Yan, Liang Long, Jin Wensi, Guo Taiqi, Gu Weijun (Wellington Koo), Qian Tai, Hu Shize, Yang Guansheng, & unknown. (R.K. Chen)
9. Hon. Dr. Wang Zhengting, China's ambassador to the United States (1937-38) in the Twin Oaks embassy library. (Author's collection)
10. Hilda wins her wings at Roosevelt Field, November 1938. (Author's collection)
11. First day of China aid tour, with Li Xiaqing, right, and Stinson NC-17174 at Philadelphia's Camden Airport, March 1939. (Family of Li Xiaqing)
12. Hilda receiving floral tributes at Philadelphia. (Family of Li Xiaqing)
13. Capt. Roscoe Turner delivers "Spirit of New China" Porterfield 35W to Hilda. (Author's collection)
14. Hilda Yan, ready for takeoff, April 1939. (R.K. Chen)
15. Hilda's proposed 6,500-mile itinerary, spring 1939. (Family of Li Xiaqing)
16. Publicity postcard of "Girl Pilot on Mercy Flight," Miss Hilda Yan. (R.K. Chen)
17. Hilda's upended Porterfield in Prattville, AL, May 1, 1939. Photos of her

accident were flashed to news agencies around the world. (Author's collection)

18. Telegram dispatched by Prattville doctor to Li Xiaqing advising her of Hilda's crash injuries. (Family of Li Xiaqing)

19. Newspaper cartoon relating to Hilda's accident. (*Montgomery Advertiser*, May 10, 1939)

20. Birmingham newspaper shows heightened awareness of Sino-Japanese conflict after Hilda's airplane crash in Alabama. (*Birmingham Age Herald*, May 3, 1939)

21. Hilda Yan (2nd from left) meets Li Xiaqing at the completion of the latter's air tour, June 1939. Bishop Yubin is at far right. (Family of Li Xiaqing)

22. Col. Theodore Roosevelt, Jr., sponsored Hilda's flying tour and coordinated Bowl of Rice parties on behalf of Chinese civilian refugees. (Author's collection)

23. Hilda Yan represents China at high level diplomatic meetings in the U.S., early 1940s. (R.K. Chen)

24. Program cover for New York's 1939 Bowl of Rice party featured a starving child depicted by artist Jiang Zhaohe. (Author's collection)

25. Hilda Yan and Li Xiaqing are listed as members of the 1939 Bowl of Rice Ball's Executive Committee (Author's collection)

26. Chinese delegation at Dumbarton Oaks, September 29, 1944. From left: Dr. Wei Daoming, Chinese Ambassador to the U.S.; Dr. Wellington Koo, Chinese Ambassador to the Court of St. James; Foreign Minister, H.H. Kong, China; Cordell Hull, U.S. Secretary of State; Lord Halifax, British Ambassador to the U.S.; Sir Edward Cadogan, Britain's Under Secretary of State; and Edward Stettinius, U.S. Under Secretary of State. (Author's collection)

27. Dr. T.V. Song, brother of Madame Chiang Kai-shek and the purported lover of Hilda Yan. (*China Journal,* June 1939)

28. On May 1, 1945, China is one of 46 nations represented at an assembly of the San Francisco Conference. Delegates occupy the ground floor of the Opera House, while the media is in the diamond horseshoe, and spectators crowd the two upper balconies. (Author's collection)

29. Hilda serves as liaison officer of the U.N.'s Department of Public Information in her office at the Lake Success site, circa 1948. (R.K. Chen)

30. Advertisement for Hilda's 1946 address on the Bahá'í faith encapsulates her busy career, March 1946.

31. Hilda, far right, and her husband, John Male, second from left, with unknown companions. (John Male Archives, Special Collections, Auckland City Libraries).

Part II: LI XIAQING: PROFILE OF A LEGEND

Figure
1. Postcard of fetching child movie star, Li Dandan (Li Xiaqing), age 14. (Author's collection)
2. A scene from the 1927 Minxin production *Romance of the Western Chamber (Xi Xiang Ji)* starring Li Dandan, left, and Lin Chuchu. (Author's collection)
3. Xiaqing's fans in China were cheered to see a photo of the former actress and her 15-day-old son, Pax, in a popular magazine. (*Liang You*, no. 65)
4. Pioneering aviator, François Durafour, in his Caudron-G3 (F-ABDO), likely the 'shaky' war surplus biplane in which Li Xiaqing made her first flight. The passenger sat between the pilot and the control panel. (Jean-Claude Cailliez)
5. Aerial view of Geneva's Cointrin airfield in 1933, the year Li Xiaqing took flying lessons. Geneva and the Alps are to the left, the Jura Mountains to the right. (Jean-Claude Cailliez)
6. As a member of Geneva's flying club, Li Xiaqing poses with Tiger-Moth c/n 5041, 1934. (Family of Li Xiaqing)
7. Li Xiaqing's Brevet II, awarded by Aéro-Club de Suisse, 1935. She was the first woman to fly in Geneva. (Family of Li Xiaqing)
8. Li Xiaqing is rushed to hospital after an emergency parachute into San Francisco Bay on May 15, 1935. (Family of Li Xiaqing)
9. Li Xiaqing poses with the Navy's amphibious Loening OL-8 that rescued her from San Francisco Bay. (Family of Li Xiaqing)
10. Students of the all-Chinese Shanghai Flying School, 1936. Li Xiaqing was the only female instructor. Many of these students became the first wartime pilots in the Chinese Air Force, and were among the first to die.
11. Architect's rendering of Shanghai's biplane-shaped Aviation League HQ. (Author's collection)
12. Xiaqing prepares to teach flight at Longhua airfield, 1936. (Author's collection)
13. Yang Jinxun, Xiaqing's sole woman flying student at the Shanghai Flying Club, 1936. (Author's collection)
14. Li Xiaqing posing with Eurasia Aviation Corporation's Junkers JU/52 tri-motor during her flying tour of China, January 1937. (Family of Li Xiaqing)
15. Xiaqing waits for fog to clear before flying a SWAC single-engine Stinson as a volunteer transport pilot in Guangdong, Spring, 1937. (Family of Li Xiaqing)

16. Enjoying the crowd's adulation at Longhua after becoming the first Chinese woman to do stunt flying in China, October 24, 1936. (Author's collection)
17. Xiaqing, center, in Shanghai with friends, actress Anna May Wong, left, & designer Zhang Qianying (Hélène Tsang), right. (Family of Li Xiaqing)
18. At Downey, CA, in the cockpit of a Vultee aircraft with test pilot, Gil Clark, whom Xiaqing met in China aboard Madame Chiang Kai-shek's private plane. December 16, 1938. (Author's collection)
19. Xiaqing, left, and Zhang Qianying beside the wreckage of CNAC's DC-2 *Kweilin*, first civilian aircraft downed by enemy action. (Family of Li Xiaqing)
20. Li Xiaqing's tentative itinerary for her "Tour of the United States," 1939. (Family of Li Xiaqing)
21. A postcard issued to publicize Miss Li's 1939 tour of the USA. (Author's collection)
22. Xiaqing in a White S-125 (NX 16791). The fuselage is decorated with a flying tiger and an exhortation to "Move Boldly Forward." (Family of Li Xiaqing)
23. Dorothy Lamour exchanges her trademark sarong for Xiaqing's *qipao* in this publicity shot for Paramount Studios. (*Film Fun,* Nov. 1939)
24. Striking an alluring pose in Miss Lamour's sarong for a *Disputed Passage* publicity photo. (*Film Fun,* Nov. 1939)
25. Program issued by Shanghai's Rialto Theater in September 1940 to publicize *Disputed Passage.* Li Xiaqing played an aviatrix. (Author's collection)
26. Touching down in the *Spirit of New China*, Stinson SR-9B (NC-17174), at Vancouver, Canada, May 1939. (Author's collection)
27. On arrival in Vancouver, Xiaqing meets excited fans. (Author's collection)
28. Waving to well-wishers, 1939. (Family of Li Xiaqing)
29. Greeted by China's Consul in New York, Dr. Yu Junji, at end of her 1939 American tour. (Family of Li Xiaqing)
30. Li Xiaqing makes adjustments to the Lycoming engine of Stinson SR-9B. (Joseph Gervais Papers, McDermott Library, University of Texas at Dallas)
31. Publicity photo of Li Xiaqing. (Joseph Gervais Papers, McDermott Library, University of Texas at Dallas)
32. Miss Li completed her 1939 U.S. tour in this Stinson Racer SR-5E (NC-13865). (Author's collection)
33. On tour in South America, Xiaqing meets Peruvian president, Manuel Prado y Ugarteche, at an evening reception in Lima, 1940. (Family of Li

Xiaqing)
34. Xiaqing, far left, posing with actresses Rosalind Russell, Jane Withers & Mary Pickford at a Hollywood relief benefit, October 1940. (Author's collection)
35. En route to a Red Cross rally in Toronto via American Airline's Flagship, Xiaqing confesses to Captain Ralph Dodson, "I wish I could fly one of these ships," September 1941. (Author's collection)
36. Going for a test flight in United China Relief's Aeronca Super Chief, NC 36631, September 1941. (Courtesy Aeronca Inc.)
37. Li Xiaqing immortalized on a bubble gum card, 1943. (Author's collection)
38. Comic book features Li Xiaqing "Flying for Victory," 1943. (Author's collection)
39. Xiaqing's 1944 visa photo shows her diamond airplane brooch, one of the jewels used as security for her 1939 tour of America. (Family of Li Xiaqing)
40. Li Xiaqing's post-war certificate of flying competency, Hong Kong, 1950. (Family of Li Xiaqing)

Part III: ZHENG HANYING: UNEASY SPIRIT

Figure
1. Press portrait of Jessie Zheng in her flying togs. (*Vancouver Daily Province*)
2. Jessie's formidable aunt and mentor to a generation of Chinese women, Dr. Zheng Yuxiu. (Courtesy, League of Nations Archive, UNOG Library)
3. Advertisement for Hong Kong's Far East Flying Training School.
4. Newspaper article announcing that Jessie has been summoned to serve her country. The squares and x's are code for "resist the enemy." (*Xiang Gang Gong Shang Ri Bao*, Aug. 21, 1937).
5. Anti-Japanese protesters show support for Madame Chiang Kai-shek and the Generalissimo, represented here by giant papier-mâché figures, October 1938. (Author's collection)
6. News article and photo of Jessie in Hong Kong newspaper, *Da Gong Bao*, June 2, 1939.
7. Wilfred Seto. (Leigh Seto)
8. Jessie poses as Chinese consulate attaché. (*Vancouver Sun*, July 8, 1942)
9. Wearing the wings of the Chinese Air Force and China shoulder insignia. (*Forward*, courtesy, Vancouver Board of Trade)
10. Flying Seven club logo. Its members all had brooches bearing this insignia. (Author's collection)

11. Flying Seven club, circa late 1930s, showing original members. From left: Jean Pike, Tosca Trasolini, Betsy Flaherty, Alma Gaudreau Gilbert, Elianne Roberge, Margaret Fane and Rolie Moore. (Photo credit: Shirley Render Collection, Western Canada Aviation Museum)
12. The Aeronca LC CF-BAT belonging to Gilbert's Aero Service at Vancouver Airport. (City of Richmond Archives photo, 1997 5 56)
13. Wearing an air force wings patch on her flying coveralls, Jessie poses with the Aeronca 'BAT' at Vancouver Airport. (*Vancouver Daily Province*)
14. An aerial view of Vancouver's harbor and North Shore mountains as they would have appeared when Jessie went aloft. (Author's collection)
15. Nightlife in Vancouver's vibrant Chinatown, 1940s.
16. Jessie patterned her oratorical style after Madame Chiang Kai-shek, seen here on her 1943 tour of America. (from *First Lady of China,* courtesy, IBM Corporate Archives)
17. A receipt for donations to the Vancouver Chinatown branch of the Chinese War Refugees Relief Commission of Canada. (Author's collection)
18. Hon. Dr. Hu Shi, China's Ambassador to the USA (1938-1942), arrived in Vancouver on a goodwill tour in February 1942. (Author's collection)
19. Jessie flew to Eastern Canada via Trans-Canada Airlines' 3-year-old transcontinental service. This timetable shows the scheduled stops.
20. At the christening of the first made-in-Canada Catalina, Montréal, December 1942. (*Canadian Aviation,* January 1943)
21. Only female member of Canada's Chinese consular corps poses with Vickers test pilot, E.C.W. Dobbin. (*Canadian Aviation,* January 1943*)*
22. Jessie's visit to Montréal's City Hall on December 23, 1942 is commemorated by her signature in the *Livre d'or.* (Les Archives de Montréal, SVM1 S12 D2)
23. Enjoying *yum cha* in Toronto's Chinatown. (*Toronto Daily Star,* February 4, 1943)
24. Jessie takes an RCAF Avro for a test flight at Malton airport, Toronto. (*Toronto Daily Star,* February 4, 1943)
25. Jessie's uncle, Ambassador Wei Daoming, far left, and aunt, Zheng Yuxiu, far right, assisted Madame Chiang Kai-shek on her 1943 U.S. tour. Behind Chiang is her nephew, L.K. Kong. (from *First Lady of China,* courtesy, IBM Corporate Archives)
26. Jessie's obituary in Vancouver's *Chinese Times.* (*Chinese Times,* September 10, 1943)
27. Jessie's daughter, Beverley Ann Seto, aged about 5 years. (Leigh Seto*)*
28. Military funeral for Flt.-Lt. Zheng Hanying. (*Vancouver News-Herald,* September 13, 1943)

MAPS

Page 20 China in 1936-1937, showing Li Xiaqing's flights.

Page 21 Hilda Yan's Proposed Tour of the Eastern United States, March-June 1939; with inset, Hilda Yan's Accident, Prattville, Alabama, May 1, 1939.

Page 22 Li Xiaqing's Proposed Tour of the United States, March-June, 1939.

Page 23 Proposed Tour of the Caribbean, Central & South America by Li Xiaqing, 1940.

Page 24 Tour of the Caribbean, Central & South America byLi Xiaqing, 1944.

Page 25 Trans-Canada Air Lines Route Map.

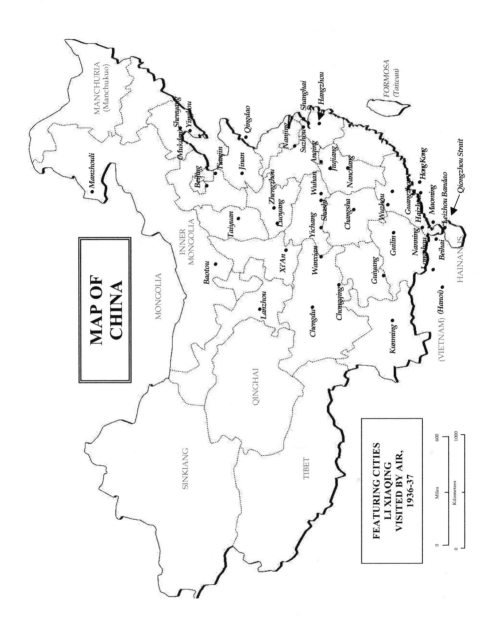

MAP OF
CHINA

FEATURING CITIES
LI XIAQING
VISITED BY AIR,
1936-37

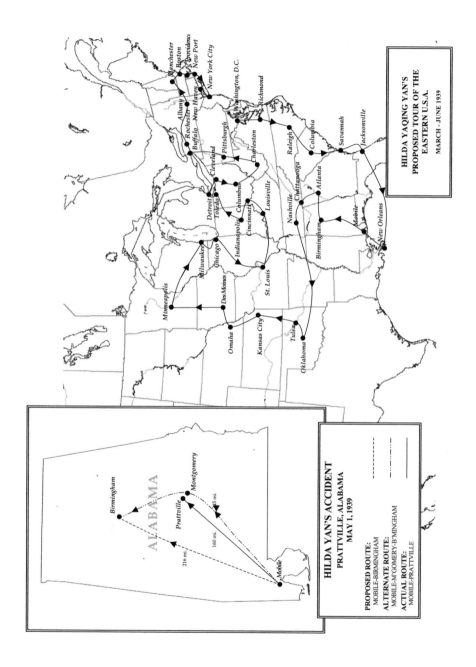

HILDA YAQING YAN'S
PROPOSED TOUR OF THE
EASTERN U.S.A.
MARCH - JUNE 1939

HILDA YAN'S ACCIDENT
PRATTVILLE, ALABAMA
MAY 1, 1939

PROPOSED ROUTE:
MOBILE-BIRMINGHAM

ALTERNATE ROUTE:
MOBILE-M'GOMERY-B'MINGHAM

ACTUAL ROUTE:
MOBILE-PRATTVILLE

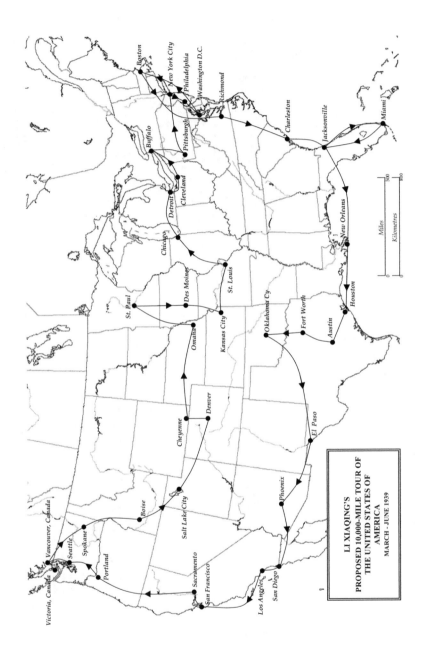

LI XIAQING'S
PROPOSED 10,000-MILE TOUR OF
THE UNITED STATES OF
AMERICA
MARCH - JUNE 1939

Proposed Tour
of the
**CARIBBEAN,
CENTRAL
&
SOUTH AMERICA**
by
LI XIAQING
- 1940 -

FLIGHTS VIA
COMMERCIAL CARRIER

Pan-Am Airways ⟶

Cruzeiro do Sul ----➤

Vía Aérea ·-·-·➤

KLM ·········➤

Tour of the

CARIBBEAN,
CENTRAL
&
SOUTH AMERICA
by

LI XIAQING

- 1944 -

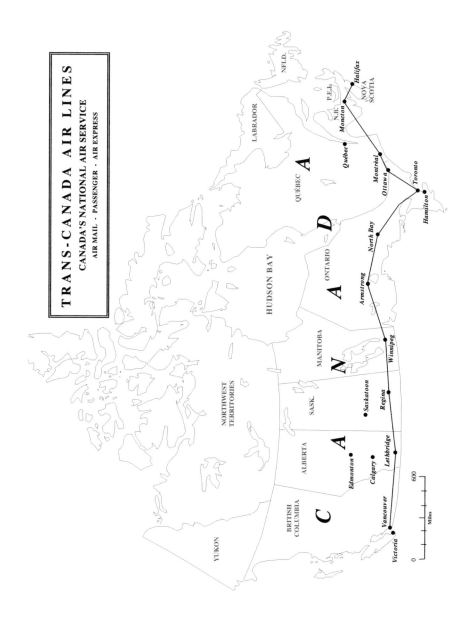

INTRODUCTION

During the Han dynasty some two thousand years ago, there lived three men who came from different backgrounds and different clans, but they were motivated by a common ambition—to save their country from corruption and lawlessness. Together, they met in a peach garden and swore the following oath: "Though we three have different surnames, today we swear brotherhood. We will work as one for our common cause, to save our nation, and for this we are willing to die. If any breaks this pledge, may he suffer eternal perdition. Heaven be our witness!" Their fervent promise became known as the Peach Garden Oath, and their spirit of service to country has fired the patriotism of generations of Chinese.

Fast forward to the twentieth century when China was convulsed by what would become the bloodiest conflict in its five thousand year history. On July 7, 1937, this ancient land was overrun by Emperor Hirohito's Imperial forces. The Japanese military juggernaut, vastly superior to its unprepared Chinese counterpart, crushed all that fell into its path. Cut off from supplies and sources of revenue, China was in genuine danger of losing its very sovereignty when, at its darkest hour, three women stepped forward to offer their services to their country. Like the men who swore the Peach Garden Oath, they came from different families and backgrounds, but they each nourished the same lofty goal—to do their utmost to save the nation from catastrophe. They were wealthy and well-educated, aristocratic and beautiful... and they were aviatrixes. Their names were Hilda Yan Yaqing (颜雅清), Li Xiaqing (李霞卿) and Jessie Zheng Hanying (郑汉英).

At a time when few Chinese women could drive a car, and many of their class and breeding 'wore idleness on their flowing sleeves,' these pioneers became air pilots to serve their country. Like the founder of the Chinese Republic, Dr. Sun Yat-sen, they firmly believed that aviation could save the nation, and by their audacity and daring—not to mention flying expertise—they hoped for nothing less than to help alter the course of the war. To accomplish this, they were willing to die.

Initially, they envisioned themselves as fighter pilots going into aerial action against the enemy, and were dismayed when their government denied them that privilege. But they were only temporarily disheartened; they cast about for other ways to help. The war had created a refugee problem of Homeric proportions. Tens of millions had been rendered homeless or wounded, and vast sums of money were needed for their care and rehabilitation. The women saw their chance. Individually and together, they conceived a plan that was bold, imaginative and breathtaking in scope. The resources and support their homeland so desperately required abounded overseas, and these intrepid women resolved to lay siege to those riches in the West. As solo flying ambassadresses of goodwill, and through countless long-distance mercy flights and public appearances, they would win for their country the precious commodities it needed to survive. They would show the gentle, but determined, face of China to those with little knowledge of the East.

Yet for all their single-minded vision, these women were temperamentally very different: Yan Yaqing, passionate patriot, sophisticated, keenly intelligent, a romantic idealist restlessly searching for the cause that would fulfill her life; Li Xiaqing, wealthy and gutsy, tomboyish yet womanly, eager to serve her country with a *noblesse* that would honor the reputation of her fabled ancestors; Zheng Hanying, patrician feminist, intensely private and fragile of body, yet stubborn, driven, and hard as a diamond. Their exploits would have been remarkable in any era and in any culture, but are particularly noteworthy considering their origins in a China where unlettered, bound-footed women were still far from uncommon. As Li Xiaqing declared to one astonished Western admirer, "I come here to let the world know that, not only can a Chinese woman walk on the ground, she can even fly through the air."

They were not the first Chinese women nationals to become air pilots. Since the 1920s, a smattering of spirited *xin nü xing,* or 'modern women,' had taken to the skies, and others of their race and sex had also gone aloft in America, but it was only these three 'action heroines' who chose to parlay their flying abilities abroad to China's benefit. To enhance their accomplishment of this task, each woman brought with her an exceptional set of skills and life experiences, not to mention the example of her forbears. Without exception, each was the product of an extraordinary upbringing.

Shanghai native, Yan Yaqing, found all the mentors she needed at home. Most of the members of her family, it seems, had dedicated their lives to the service of their fellow countrymen. Her father, Dr. Yan Fuqing, one of the first Chinese to bring Western medicine to the Far East, was the wartime director of the National Health Administration, and her uncle, Dr. Yan Huiqing, was five times premier of China and ambassador to the Soviet Union. In 1935, Yan Yaqing began her professional life in the service of China as her nation's only female representative to the League of Nations. After the Japanese invaded her homeland and diplomacy failed to resolve the conflict, she took up flight training in New York, and when she won her wings, embarked on her flying tour of the United States to win friends and funds for the refugees and orphans of China. This expedition ended in disaster when her plane crashed in the state of Alabama, but despite her extraordinary courage and her many contributions to the war effort, Yan Yaqing is largely unknown in China.

Li Xiaqing's immediate family was intimately involved in the Revolution of 1911, and she was raised with the notion of duty to China. When she was just fourteen years old, she took her first job as a movie actress and, using the name Li Dandan, swiftly rose to the top of her profession. She later became fascinated by aviation, which she came to regard as an important tool in the defense of her homeland. Upon completion of her flight studies in Switzerland and America, she returned to her homeland where she was hailed as China's First Lady of the Air. Li Xiaqing gave breathtaking aerobatic exhibitions throughout China to draw attention to the importance and safety of flight. After the Japanese invasion, and with her nation's official blessing, she went to America to commence her heroic flying tours of North and South America. Logging tens of thousands of miles of solo flight, she made countless public appearances and earned many thousands of dollars for the relief of her people. Of the three women pilots, she is the only one to enjoy a measure of fame today, even occupying a niche in Beijing's Hall of Honor, yet she is mistakenly believed to have died a martyr's death in a wartime plane crash. In truth, she lived on for almost sixty years after her reported demise.

Zheng Hanying's family were also deeply involved with Dr. Sun's uprising. Her aunt was the revolutionary feminist lawyer and parliamentarian, Dr. Zheng Yuxiu, one of the most influential figures in the history of China. Young Hanying was unavoidably influenced by her illustrious relative, and, like her aunt, she attended the University of the Sorbonne in Paris where she earned a degree in law. She was focused on joining the foreign service until the Japanese began to threaten her homeland. With a view to serving her nation, she took flying lessons at the Far East Flying Training School in Hong Kong, a Royal Air Force-approved flight academy, where, in 1938, she became the first Chinese woman to win her wings in the Colony. Generalissimo Chiang Kai-shek, commander of China's Nationalist forces, was so impressed with her flying abilities that he granted her a commission in the Chinese Air Force. She was its only woman officer. As a member of her nation's military, and a representative of the foreign service, Flight-Lieutenant Zheng became the first Chinese woman to be dispatched to Canada in an official capacity, and she soon augmented her impressive credentials by embarking on a cross-country winter tour to raise Canadian awareness of China's refugees and orphans. However, in the midst of her mission and at the height of her success, she died in Vancouver. She was only twenty-eight years old. Such was her popularity that she was given a military funeral by the Royal Canadian Air Force, and her coffin was carried through the streets of the city. And yet, in China, she is forgotten by those to whom she dedicated her life.

Before they traveled to North America to raise funds for the war effort, one of the women's most important tasks was the promotion of aviation among their fellow countrymen. It was a tough sell. The first man to fly in China's skies was a Frenchman, René Vallon, and he took Shanghai by storm when he flew along its celebrated Bund in February 1911. But a few months later, he also became China's first aero casualty when his Sommer biplane crashed at the Shanghai Race Course during a race meet. After the aviator's lifeless body was carted off the field and the plane's wreckage removed, the band played on and the afternoon's festivities recommenced. Aviation had abruptly lost its appeal, and the concept would be shelved for several years thereafter. Despite the vulnerability of China's air space to Japan's growing imperialist ambitions, and regardless of the vast land's suitability for the establishment of air travel, many areas of which were not served by rail or roadway, plane flight was perceived as unsafe and unnatural, and it was not until the 1930s that the general populace gradually grew to have a grudging admiration of the aircraft's capabilities.

Women's involvement in air travel did a great deal to consolidate that admiration.

Song Meiling (Madame Chiang Kai-shek) was one of those who touted the advantages of aviation at every opportunity. In the early 'thirties, she had experienced its benefits firsthand, accompanying her husband on many of his political flights throughout China to visit remote mountainous areas that were otherwise only accessible after many weeks of grueling and dangerous travel by sedan chair. Madame Chiang recalled one such flight that took them to an area rarely visited by the outside world. She reported that it was like entering a time capsule. The mountain women were dressed and wore their hair in the style of her grandmother. For their part, the women stared at the stylish First Lady as if she had come from the moon. The local officials who met them (when they had recovered from their astonishment at finding the Generalissimo in their midst) were readily persuaded to lend China's leader their allegiance, his face-to-face contact having won their support like nothing else could have done.

Encounters like these helped to fire Madame Chiang's support of air travel. As a keen advocate of women's empowerment, Song Meiling was also delighted to learn that the Misses Yan, Li and Zheng were taking a leadership role in aviation. She knew and applauded each of them, and was happy to back their expeditions abroad, thus guaranteeing their success from the outset.

However, despite the air women's sincere and immense exertions, it is difficult to know if the bulk of the dollars they raised actually made it through to the tragic souls they were representing—the refugees, the wounded and, most especially, the orphaned children. It is likely that, in the beginning at least, when intentions were pure and hopes were high, the money was dispatched directly to those whom it was intended to help. But as the war progressed, and unbelievably huge sums began to pour into China relief coffers—funds that were just as rapidly being gobbled up by rocketing inflation—unscrupulous aid officials could not resist exchanging these dollars on the black market and making handsome profits for themselves. The pilfering is thought to have been widespread and later extended to the rifling of official American government aid to China.[1] Sterling Seagrave's tell-all book on the culpability of certain members of the Song family, whom the author targets as the chief offenders in this free-for-all embezzlement scheme, encapsulates their *modus operandi*: "The [Song] family would serve as the courtiers, the handmaidens, and the compradors. They would set the terms, carry the moneybags, keep the accounting ledgers, and be responsible for identifying all enemies and villains. America's role would be to provide the funds. In return for their money, Americans would be in charge of feeling virtuous."[2]

Certainly, if the corruption were as widespread as it was rumored to be, one might say that the strenuous efforts of the three aviatrixes were tarnished by association; worse, that through their earnest appeals, they were touting for the bagmen. However, if the product of their labors did, in the end, help to line the pockets of the rich at the expense of the unfortunate, the three women themselves were no less the dupes of fraud, having committed themselves, body and soul, to the succor of their fellow countrymen.

In their personal lives, the women were not above criticism, and exposure of their frailties might have made for juicy reading at the time, but no such news items ever appeared in the press. The war took center stage, and during an evenly-matched conflict that could be won or lost on propaganda, every hero was needed; investigative journalism of the voyeur variety was one of the luxuries that would have to be foregone until the peace was won. So it was little known that, in spite of the conspicuous fame and public honors these pilot celebrities enjoyed, they were often lonely, and their relationships with the men in their lives were stormy. The public understood them to be single women while, in fact, each of them had intimate relationships with men and had given birth, but the very attributes that guaranteed their excellence as aviators—independence, willpower, stubbornness—became the very traits that caused these relationships to collapse. Rather than salvage the situation by concentrating on their children, they chose instead to serve China, abandoning their offspring (with mixed results) to *amahs* or to the care of their families for the duration. Many months passed before they saw their youngsters again. While it was not unusual for upper class Chinese women to distance themselves from the physical raising of their children, this immoderate detachment was out of the ordinary. Perhaps the root of these women's atypical behavior on several levels may be ascribed to their long exposure to Western culture and education which, while it fostered a progressiveness of thought, seems to have been at the core of many of the problems that bedeviled them.

Although born in China, they spent most of their formative years abroad, and were unavoidably influenced by this contact, but while they learned to become thoroughly at home in the West, they remained, at their hearts' core, essentially Chinese, and beneath the veneer of Occidental modernity that they affected were embedded the ancient Confucian principles they had imbibed since their birth. This dichotomy of East and West created a sort of schism in their souls, and much of the conflict they experienced in their personal lives was probably related to this duality. By leaving their husbands and children—a new-fangled expediency which, until that time, had been largely unknown in China—they were going against the grain and clashing harshly with the venerable Eastern notion of respect for family. The women gained their freedom, but in so doing, they cut themselves off at the knees. Adrift, and with the very foundations of their existence askew, they took refuge in another Confucian imperative—duty to country—and into this ideal they poured everything they had.

From New York to New Orleans, Vancouver to Valparaiso, San Francisco to Salt Lake City, these sisters of heaven literally brought the East to the West and attracted untold numbers of supporters to their nation's cause. Theirs is a story of hard work and determination, of setting large goals and working towards them with courage and tenacity. They stumbled many times on their roads to the fulfillment of that promise, encountering in the process joy and tragedy, victory and death, but they never gave up. Like the men who swore the oath in the peach garden, they kept their sacred promise to China.

PART I

HILDA YAN YAQING 颜雅清: LIFE OF THE HEART

Background is your sense of civility, righteousness and humility. Backbone is the guts, courage and strength to hold your chin up and continue in the face of peril, prejudice and disaster. Both combine to formulate finesse and fortitude in the feminine development of a lady.

—Harper Lee, To Kill a Mockingbird

1. PROLOGUE

In 1936, when Hilda Yan announced that she would learn to fly for China, it is unlikely that she raised many eyebrows among her friends and relatives. They had long grown accustomed to expecting the unexpected from this free-spirited—some would say eccentric—young woman. Unusually gifted, bright and vivacious, Hilda seemed in perpetual quest of that certain something to fulfill her life, and fulfillment would only be possible if she were serving humanity with every fiber of her being.

In repose, her face sometimes held the saddened expression of the disappointed romantic, and her languid eyes, a world-weary, 'come hither' look that could be taken for sensuality. Her male admirers were legion. But when she laughed—and this was often—her smile was generous and dimpled, and her warmth and quick humor attracted a wide circle of devoted friends. She absorbed conversations and events around her with ease and thereby accrued a great deal of information on a wide variety of subjects; she was valued for her wit and intelligent banter. Hilda could be imperious, but her sense of authority derived, not only from her distinguished family's position in society, but also from her exquisite manners, and from always knowing the right thing to do. Certain obligations devolve upon a lady, and her sense of duty to those less fortunate was ingrained and, in many ways, dominated her life.

Broadminded, original, and outgoing, her restless search for meaning and contentment led her down a variety of unconventional paths. More than once her life choices caused much concern—and emotional pain—to those who loved her (Hilda's divorces brought the world crashing down, not only on her ex-husbands, but also on her children and extended family), and certainly her dream to become an aviatrix on China's behalf was perhaps one of the most unusual and risky of all. Had they known that their fears for her safety would be horribly realized, her family likely would have done more to discourage her from this goal. Not that it would have made a difference. Hilda embraced projects of own her choosing with obsessive enthusiasm, and, as she believed that only aviation could save China from annihilation, there was nothing whatever that could have dissuaded her from her mission.

2. LIBERAL STRAINS

Hilda was well born and her antecedents impeccable. The line of the Yan family was reputed to have descended from the illustrious Yan Zi (514-483 BCE), a favorite pupil of Confucius. Master Yan was renowned as a man of great learning and a rigorous teacher whose instruction was earnestly sought by those who desired illumination. His proud descendents were only slightly less eminent. Skipping forward some two thousand years, one of his direct ancestors (who was destined to be Hilda's great-grandfather) was born in Xiamen, Fujian province. While he was yet a child, the boy was evacuated to Shanghai during the Taiping Rebellion of the 1850s, and he grew to manhood in that same city where he later married and raised a family. Thus the Yan clan began its long and fruitful association with the great metropolis of Shanghai. This elder Yan's two sons were named Yan Yongjing and Yan Zujing, and he impressed upon them both the vital importance of a good education. Yielding to their father's admonitions, the boys went abroad to receive their learning in the West.

Yan Yongjing and Yan Zujing (the latter would become Hilda's grandfather) both attended Ohio's Kenyon College, and, before returning to China, were numbered among the small and curious delegation of overseas Chinese who, along with Kenyon's entire student body, joined the army and went off to fight in the American Civil War on the side of the Union. After their stint in the military, and upon completion of their education, both young men returned to China as devout Christians with a heartfelt appreciation for Western culture. They married, raised families and became pastors of the Episcopalian church.

However, tragedy struck when Yan Zujing suddenly died. His children— three sons and two daughters—were still quite young when this misfortune befell them, but luckily, the heartbreak of his passing was ameliorated by the generosity of his brother who absorbed the orphaned offspring into his own family. Although Yan Yongjing had six children of his own, he took seriously his role as surrogate parent and raised his brother's brood as if they were his own.

Yan Yongjing was an excellent mentor to his adopted family. A civic-minded individual, he was committed to the establishment of Western education in China, and became one of those responsible for the founding of the legendary St. John's College (later University) in Shanghai. From 1879 onwards, he began to solicit funds for its construction and was instrumental in its inauguration. The college invited him to join its staff and teach mathematics. His role expanded, and he also held classes in natural philosophy, thereby becoming the first Chinese to introduce Western ethics to the land of Confucius. In 1887, he became pastor of the Episcopal Church of Our Savior, a position he held until his death.

Hilda's father, Yan Fuqing, was one of Yan Zujing's sons whose education was subsidized by his adoptive father. Due to Yan Yongjing's generosity, the young man was able to attend St. John's Medical School where he trained as a physician. Upon his graduation in 1903, he left at once for South Africa where he served as a medical officer to the Chinese work gangs that labored in the diamond mines. His responsibilities were many and arduous, and his working conditions difficult, but he was so beloved by his deeply grateful patients that they awarded him a commemorative gold medal for his good offices. Nevertheless, Yan's professional experiences in South Africa gave him an appreciation of the inadequacy of his medical knowledge, and he yearned to hone his expertise.

Shortly thereafter, Yan Fuqing returned to China and married an educated woman named Chow Siu-ying. With the support of his bride, he made a life-changing decision to apply for entry into the School of Medicine at America's Yale University. His application was accepted. Soon after Yan Fuqing commenced his first year of training, his wife gave birth to their first child, a daughter, in Jiangwan, the Chinese district of Shanghai, on January 17, possibly 1906, by the Gregorian calendar.[1] As the lives of the young parents revolved around Yan Fuqing's studies in the United States, they named the infant Yaqing, the first syllable of which paid tribute to the famed university from which her father hoped to earn his medical degree. She was also baptized with the Christian name Hilda, meaning 'protector' or 'warrior woman.'

The newborn Hilda Yaqing Yan was born into a feudal nation ruled by the all-powerful Qing dynasty, and for the first five years of her life, she was a tiny subject of the mighty Dragon Throne. Her parents, however, held a broader view of her destiny. True, she was Chinese, but she was also a citizen of the world, and they recognized no restrictive boundaries of creed, religion or race that might serve to crimp her aspirations or destiny. They prayed she would mature to lead a rewarding and useful life as a servant of humanity.

In fact, the family into which Hilda had been born was one where higher education, dedication to China, an appreciation of Western culture, and a predilection for just plain hard work, were *leitmotifs* that directed all their lives and would inform her own. She would fulfill her parents' prayers for her future, and mature to inherit her mother's good-natured personality, flair for cooking and easy propensity for entertaining. She would also become a dear friend and companion to her loving father, and one with whom she could communicate on an intellectual level. Following in his footsteps, she would move with ease in the wider world and have an appreciation of all peoples and their cultures.

Yan Fuqing was attending classes at Yale and not at all enjoying his studies overseas. He was perpetually cold, broke and hungry, and his struggle to master the English and Latin medical vocabulary exhausted him. More than once, he came close to quitting, but as a medical student at one of America's most esteemed institutes of learning, he knew he was enormously privileged and had been granted a unique opportunity to absorb Western learning and culture. His homeland and his family were counting on him to excel. Yan Fuqing persevered, and in 1909, he won his heart's desire. He graduated *summa cum laude* and became the first Asian to obtain a medical doctorate degree from Yale University. His scholastic performance had been so impressive that Yale invited him to accept a position on staff, but he humbly refused the offer. It was his dream to serve China. With his knowledge still deficient in those areas that were relevant to Asian practice, Dr. Yan sailed to Britain where entered the University of Liverpool and earned a degree in tropical medicine (D.T.M.). He also made a concentrated tour of Europe to investigate hospital systems in Berlin, Vienna and Paris with a view to applying their administrative practices to the health care bureaucracies of China. Finally, in 1910, he returned to his native land. Well-versed in the specialties of surgery, infectious diseases and hospital administration, he was filled with zeal to bring all he had learned of Western medicine to the East.

In fact, he and his brothers, all of whom had studied abroad, returned home thoroughly Westernized (all but the eldest of them having cut off their queues), and family and friends who met their ships were initially taken aback to see the young men arrayed in three-piece suits and homburg hats.[2] The brothers made themselves even more conspicuous by importing the bicycles they had used to pedal around their Western campuses. Hitherto, this mode of conveyance had been largely unknown in China, and the Yan brothers became credited as being among those considered responsible for introducing this now quintessentially Chinese vehicle to their homeland.

Thus Hilda was raised in a household that looked neither wholly to the East nor wholly to the West, but was imbued with the best of both cultures. In her growth to maturity, she took for granted the pursuit of excellence, surrounded as she was by greatness in the members of her own family. Her father, one of the first Chinese to bring Western medicine to the East, was to spend his life founding and directing medical colleges throughout China. A respected researcher, teacher and administrator, ultimately the National Health Administration would call upon him to become its wartime director. Hilda's beloved uncle, Yan Huiqing, known in the West as Dr. W.W. (William) Yen, was no less distinguished. Chosen five times to be Premier of his country, he became one of the most respected diplomats of the twentieth century, serving as China's Foreign Minister to the United States, and as Ambassador to the U.S.S.R. Another of Hilda's uncles, Yan Deqing or Dr. Strong Yen, held a doctorate in engineering from Pennsylvania's Lehigh University. He developed huge sections of China's vital rail system, a network of steel that, in the absence of roads and before introduction of commercial aviation, provided the only viable form of transportation and the only thread that knit together the huge and unwieldy nation.

Not surprisingly, these remarkable brothers became known as 'The Three Outstanding Yans.' In addition to acumen in their chosen fields, they gave unstintingly of themselves to volunteer organizations and to the betterment of their fellow-citizens. Unavoidably influenced by her family's charitable inclinations, Hilda came to regard voluntarism as one of the privileges and responsibilities of her advantaged upbringing.

When Yan Fuqing returned to China in 1910, he accepted a position as surgeon for the treatment of infectious diseases at Yale-in-China's Changsha mission hospital in Xiang (Hunan) province. His family joined him in the city where, until 1926, he would base his work. Changsha was centrally located on the banks of the Xiang River in the fertile 'rice bowl of China.' The city itself was an important and ancient trade center, site of the governor's office, or *yamen*, and ringed by forbidding stone walls. Significantly, the main gate of this capital city was blocked up with rubble, a sinister metaphor that was intended to symbolize Changsha's anti-foreign sentiments. The introduction of Western medicine into this hostile environment was fraught with difficulties, and Dr. Yan had to employ all his diplomatic arts to work even-handedly between the American Yale scholars who operated the hospital, and the local Chinese officials who mistrusted the intentions of the foreign imperialists in their midst. As a practitioner of both Eastern and Western medicine, Yan was responsible for making the notion of newfangled foreign methods of treatment more palatable to his fellow countrymen.

In 1911, the neighboring province of Hubei summoned Hilda's father to deal with a deadly outbreak of bubonic plague. This dread disease was threatening to spread throughout central China via the rail lines. Yan Fuqing arrived just in time to stem its proliferation, and when the crisis was over, he was credited with saving thousands of lives. He returned to his family in the fall of that year, but by that time, the country had lurched into the grip of the Revolution. Rebels converged on Changsha by rail and, while a large battle was pitched outside the mighty walls of the city, an insurrection raged within. Laborers stormed the gates that had protected the city for centuries and overran the governor's *yamen*. For a time, they even instituted their own short-lived regime. In the aftermath of the gory campaigns that ultimately led to the fall of the Emperor and the introduction of the Republic, Dr. Yan's skills as a Western-trained physician were invaluable. He patched up the combatants and helped to organize Red Cross work to aid the victims of war throughout the province.

While her father was practicing medicine in the field, Hilda remained safe in the care of her mother. She was only six years old when she ceased to be a subject of the Qing Dynasty and became a citizen of the Republic. She was as yet unable to appreciate the opportunities that would be hers as a young woman growing to maturity in the re-born land of China, but a decade later, she would be at the forefront of those who would benefit from its new freedoms, and would work to increase their parameters.

The Yan family had expanded, and Hilda was presented with two brothers—Victor and William. Meanwhile, under the auspices of Yale-in-China and the Xiang provincial Government, her father became deeply occupied in his efforts to establish the Xiangya Medical School ('Xiang' stood for Hunan Province, and 'ya' for Yale), and it was during this period that Hilda's younger sister, Dorothy, was born. Dorothy was given the name Xiangya to reflect her father's intense involvement with the Yale-in-China project.

In 1916, Yan Fuqing resolved to work towards a Certificate in Public Health. He was accepted to enter the program at Harvard Medical School in Boston, and on this trip overseas, he took his family with him. The long odyssey was a landmark event in young Hilda's life. She experienced the first of many significant journeys she would make in her lifetime (she was to take at least two sea voyages around the world, and fly over the land masses of five continents), and the expedition instilled in her a love for the romance and adventure of travel. Even more thrilling was their destination—America!—a country she already admired through her father's descriptions of his schooling there.

Upon their arrival on the American East coast, Hilda's parents enrolled her at Rye Seminary, a genteel private boarding school for young ladies located in Rye, New York. Although Rye was a fashionable village of some four thousand souls that prided itself on its long history, colonial architecture and ancestral oaks, her parents likely chose the facility, not for the refinement of its surroundings, but because it prided itself in placing equal emphasis on academic excellence, community service and compassion for others. The fact that at least two of the school's pupils hailed from Shanghai and were available to lend moral support to their young daughter may also have influenced their choice.[3]

Within a year, Yan Fuqing had earned his public health certificate and the family returned to China. Consistent with her parent's high regard for education, Hilda was sent to Shanghai to board at the prestigious McTyeire School for girls, located in those days on Hankow Road. It was a private institute of learning originally founded by the Methodist mission to educate the daughters of American businessmen living and working in China. The school's teachers were foreign and its orientation Western, but its doors were open to the offspring of the Chinese elite. One of its greatest promoters was Charlie Song, the legendary tycoon who had been ordained in his youth by Bishop Holland McTyeire, the prelate for whom the school had been named. The institute quickly became the *alma mater* of China's most prominent young women, perhaps the most famous of whom were the Song sisters: Ailing, Qingling, and Meiling, the irrepressible daughters of Charlie Song who one day would be known to history as Mesdames H.H. Kong, Sun Yat-sen, and Chiang Kai-shek respectively.

Hilda's acumen—and her social consciousness—flowered in the hot house atmosphere fostered by the school, and its promotion of Christian principles shored up the foundations of her inbred Confucian notions of compassion and community outreach.

However, in 1922, she was obliged to leave McTyeire when her father embarked on his next great learning adventure. Yan Fuqing had resolved to improve public health through clinical medicine and he applied to enter the public health program offered by the Harvard Medical School. His application was accepted, and when he sailed for America, his family accompanied him once more. While Dr. Yan attended university, his family was installed at New Haven, Connecticut, and Hilda was enrolled for the summer session at Walnut Hill School in Natick, Massachusetts. While the school's academic standards were excellent, Hilda was not altogether content; buoyed by the confidence instilled in her by her stint at McTyeire, she nourished ambitious plans for her immediate future.

Without informing her parents, the precocious teenager sat for an entrance exam for Smith College, an institute of higher learning located at Northampton, Massachusetts that had educated the leading daughters of America since 1871. She performed so well on the exam that, in the fall of 1922, Smith accepted her as a cultural exchange student. At just sixteen years of age, Hilda became the youngest Chinese ever accorded this honor. Enrolled as a member of the 'Class of 1926,' she majored in History and merged almost seamlessly into the institute's world of bloomers and bluestockings.

While still a freshman, Hilda applied to join the prestigious Smith College Dramatic Association. This active group produced plays, not only at the college, but also at the Northampton Municipal Theater where it staged two productions a year. The public nature of these performances shone a spotlight on Smith's reputation, and because school pride dictated that the productions be of excellent quality, gaining admission to the select drama association was no easy task. Prospective applicants were closely tested and obliged to perform well in competitive trials that showcased their talents in acting, business, costuming, publicity and dramaturgy. Despite her youth, Hilda managed to fulfill all these requirements and was made a member of the team.[4] Unconsciously or not, she had chosen to participate in a field of endeavor that would lay an excellent foundation for her future work on the world stage.

In addition to acquiring a solid education at Smith, Hilda also came to be imbued with the ideals traditionally cherished by the college—a concern for women's rights, and an acknowledgment of the correlation that existed between higher education and the promotion of world order and human dignity. These principles overlaid the lessons she had already imbibed at McTyeire and further informed her growth to maturity. They would underpin all future endeavors she would undertake on behalf of her fellow human beings.

In 1924, Hilda was obliged to leave Smith College without completing her degree. Her father had received his certificate from Harvard, and he was ready to return home. Characteristically, Yan Fuqing would not go back to China until he had squeezed every opportunity out of his time overseas, so he gathered up his family and sailed to Europe to investigate the current state of continental medical education. While Dr. Yan visited the faculties of medicine in the major capitals, his offspring cultivated an appreciation of the various countries they visited.

When Hilda and her family finally returned to Chinese soil, they settled once again in Changsha where Yan Fuqing applied his newfound knowledge to the educational facilities at the Xiangya medical school. For her part, Hilda was anxious to complete her bachelor's degree and lost no time enrolling in the academic section of the Yale-in-China institute, fondly known as Yali, that her father had helped to establish in Changsha.[5] Due to the unsettled political situation in China, the contrast between the atmospheres at Smith and Yali could not have been more marked, and in the days leading up to her graduation in June 1925, Hilda became involved in a remarkable contretemps.

Shortly before the end of term, students on campus marshaled a movement that opposed foreign involvement in the nation's affairs. Anti-foreign feeling had run rife throughout China for many years, but these sentiments had recently come to a head. There was much hard feeling against the so-called "unequal treaties" that ceded generous territorial rights to American, British, German, French and Portuguese interests in China while leaving the Chinese government in a state of near-bankruptcy as it continued to pay reparations to the West. At an emergency meeting of the Student Union, the academic section of the school determined that only a bold political act would draw attention to the sincerity of their grievances. They voted that the American president of the school, Dr. Edward H. Hume, must die. They also passed the sentence of death on all other foreigners in Changsha, but because Dr. Hume occupied the most prominent position, the students decided he should be the first to meet his Maker.

Hilda learned of this drastic verdict and went at once to Dr. Hume's office where she informed the startled academic, "You are to be shot at dawn."

Dr. Hume, known by his Chinese name, Hu Mei, had arrived in Changsha in 1905, and had worked alongside Hilda's father for many years. In his eyes, his old colleague's daughter was "a charming girl, one of the most gifted students on the campus"... and a very credible witness. He did not for one moment doubt the veracity of her statement, or the seriousness of his position. Thanks to Hilda's intervention, and with Yan Fuqing's help, Dr. Hume was able to take immediate steps to protect himself and his staff. The next day he had the satisfaction of witnessing a steady stream of the students' parents arriving at school to chastise their wayward children and insist that henceforth they pay less attention to politics and more to their studies.[6]

In his memoirs, Dr. Hume describes the graduation ceremonies held just one week after the student uprising. "As I handed out the college diplomas," he recalled, "I caught the eye of the attractive young senior who had brought me the news of possible trouble. As she bowed and received her diploma, there was just the suggestion of a smile on her face."[7]

Remarkably, Hilda was only nineteen when she received that diploma. Graduating with a Bachelor of Arts degree, she completed the four-year program in just three years, majoring in psychology. She received excellent grades, earning six credits in her major, and three each in sociology, chemistry and physiology. She took her first job in the Admissions Office of the Xiang-Yale Hospital, and in her spare time, made use of her training in psychology and sociology by doing, as she described it, "a little amateur volunteer social work after hours or during lunch hour."[8] She discovered that she very much enjoyed helping people.

She had no sooner begun her new job, however, when the political situation in Changsha became untenable and all foreigners were forced to flee for their lives. Having been inextricably involved with the foreign community, Dr. Yan was also at risk, and he decamped with his wife and children to Beijing where he worked briefly at the Union Medical College. A short time later, he shepherded his family back home to Shanghai, and it was here, in his home city, that Yan Fuqing was galvanized to begin one of the most important projects in his career, the organization of the Shanghai Medical College.

For her part, Hilda was delighted to return to the energetic metropolis where she was enthusiastically received by her many friends in the foreign and Chinese communities. She had been well educated both abroad and at home, and was equipped with all the refinements expected of any gentlewoman in any society. Always stylishly turned out, she dressed simply, but elegantly, and, despite her years in the West, she wore with pride the long and sinuous *qipao* that both demonstrated her allegiance to Chinese culture, and also admirably suited her height and slim build. She accessorized her outfits with bold, chunky jewelry, often of antique Chinese design, but she sometimes wore none at all, and few other adornments. She didn't need them. In a city of attractive women, she was considered one of the beauties of Shanghai, and the splendor of her dark eyes and flashing smile captivated many admirers, but her charm and loveliness were as nothing compared to her sharp intelligence, verve and daring.

However, her outward appearance of self-possession and relaxed demeanor belied a passionate and restless nature. She longed to follow her family's example and be of significant use to her country. Instead, she did what other young women of her generation were doing. She got married.

On June 2, 1927, Hilda was joined in holy matrimony to an extraordinary young man who had been selected for her by her father. His name was Chen Bingzhang, known to his Western friends as P.T. Chen, and he possessed many qualities that Yan Fuqing believed would make him an ideal choice for his kinetic daughter.

20

Born at Amoy, Fukien on October 22, 1899, Chen was a brilliant scholar whose education had been extensive and his accomplishments meteoric. In 1921, upon acquiring a Bachelor of Arts degree in Political Science at Shanghai's St. John's University, he worked as an instructor at his *alma mater* before journeying to America to augment his education. Chen attended Princeton University where earned a Master's degree in Political Science in 1924. He stayed on for another year as a Princeton Graduate Scholar, and then, on a Sterling Scholarship, he transferred to Yale University where he served as President of the Chinese Student's Alliance in the U.S.A. In 1927, Chen returned to China and immediately established himself as dean and professor of the Political Science Department at National Jinan University. He also took on a position as assistant professor of English at National Central University. As if this were not enough, in his spare time he was a part-time journalist with an eye on a career in Government.

P.T. Chen was an intellectual, and he was also mild-mannered and grounded—a contemplative figure rather than a man of action—and Hilda's father felt that these attributes would be the perfect foil to his daughter's impetuous character. For his part, Chen rejoiced that he was being joined to one of the most prominent families in Shanghai, and to one of the city's loveliest women. Elegant, learned, and a brilliant hostess and housekeeper, his bride was ideally suited to support him in his career, and her intelligence and refinement would communicate themselves to their future offspring.

The P.T. Chens quickly became one of Shanghai's brightest young couples, much sought-after invitees at the almost daily social functions for which the city was justly famous. P.T. basked in the almost universal celebration of his wife's charm and accomplishments, and Hilda was equally proud of her husband's fine mind and brilliant future.

No social gathering was complete without the presence of Mrs. P.T. Chen, and she became a favorite of Sir Victor Sassoon, the British multi-millionaire and prime developer of the city's celebrated Bund who, despite his vast wealth, was something of a pariah amongst his fellow expatriates in Shanghai because he was a Jew. Partly to avenge himself, Sassoon threw the city's most glittering and lavish parties and he invited those who snubbed him—as well as notable native *taipans* and their women—to enjoy his hospitality. Traditionally the Chinese, no matter how exalted their social positions, had been excluded at upper class foreign gatherings, but Sassoon's innovation gradually changed the pattern, and by the early 1930s, social mixing of the races was the norm in Shanghai. Hilda and her husband were among the most desirable of his invitees. Sassoon was noted for his wicked sense of fun, and to the vast delight of his friends, he often threw 'theme parties.' One such memorable event required his guests to arrive dressed as school children and to play childish games, such as 'Ring around the Roses' and 'Musical Chairs.' To everyone's surprise, Sassoon appeared at his own party majestically arrayed as head master, replete with mortar board, and he took advantage of his lofty status by beating with a birch cane all the naughty 'children' who came within reach. Hilda entered into the rowdy spirit of the evening by wearing overalls and a saucy school cap. It is not known if she, too, received a whipping, but the effect of her costume was reported to be charming.

P.T. continued to fulfill the promise he had early shown as a prize-winning orator and a renowned wordsmith. In 1928, he put these skills to use when he helped to found and edit the *China Critic* journal. Concurrently, he served as contributing editor of the American-owned newspaper, the *China Weekly Review*, and he wrote several learned articles and major papers on national finance. These brought him to prominence and helped him to win a coveted post; he received an appointment as secretary in the Nationalist Government's Ministry of Finance where he was invited to serve as tax commissioner. Soon he came to be regarded by many as one of the builders of the New China, and he was widely considered to have a brilliant future in Government.

Meanwhile, Hilda made her own tangible contribution to the New China. On July 18, 1928, while the temperatures soared to record highs and the oppressive Shanghai heat caused coolies to collapse in the streets, Hilda went into labor and gave birth to the young couple's first-born child, a son. They named him William, both for Hilda's brother and for her distinguished statesman uncle, William Huiqing Yan.

As her husband's star continued to rise, Hilda became involved in several women's organizations, including the National Child Welfare League and the Shanghai Chinese Women's Club.[9] Women's service clubs were a recent phenomenon in China, an innovation imported from the West by foreign women living in Shanghai. In the Confucian manner, Chinese wives and mothers had traditionally focused on the myriad details of daily life within their own family circles, but by the 1920s, Shanghai's most prominent society ladies broke the mould and became enthusiastic clubwomen. Many diamond-studded galas were associated with their fund-raising activities. Hilda participated in the convening of these events, and, on behalf of the Women's Club, was involved in supporting free beds in hospitals and the furnishing and sustaining of local schools for hundreds of needy children.

She also served on the board of the Young Women's Christian Association of Shanghai. In the 1930s, the Shanghai Y was labeled a hotbed of radicalism because it held night school classes for female laborers and taught literacy to women from the lowest levels of society. The association was also judged guilty of attempting to raise the consciousness of these downtrodden young women by awakening in them a sense of their own dignity. For these reasons, conservatives suspiciously regarded the YWCA as an ally of the Communist movement. While the Y based its activities on the teachings of Christ, and not Mao Zedong, it was true that some of its members did go on to become Communist activists, the most prominent of whom was the notorious Jiang Qing, Mao's third wife and the future ringleader of the dreaded Gang of Four.[10] Ironically, in the 1960s, the Gang of Four would be responsible for the unwarranted persecution of Hilda's distinguished father. However, Hilda paid little heed to the aspersions cast on the Y. Like the rest of her family, she was working for the betterment of the Chinese people and not in the interest of any political group, either Communist or Nationalist.

Some four years after the birth of their son, the Chens were blessed with a second child, a daughter, Doreen, born on April 10, 1932, and it was shortly thereafter that P.T. was promoted to the position of Personal Secretary to the Nationalist Minister of Finance, Dr. H.H. Kong, brother-in-law of Generalissimo Chiang Kai-shek.[11]

All of Hilda's menfolk were accomplishing large tasks. While her husband was consumed with his writing and his increasingly important responsibilities at the Ministry, her father was lionized for the yeoman's work he had undertaken to found the Shanghai Medical College, for which he personally and painstakingly had collected funds to make the school a reality.[12] Meanwhile,

Hilda's uncle, Huiqing, was also winning kudos since his appointment in 1933 to the post of Ambassador to the Soviet Union. China and Russia had been on the brink of war, but Yan Huiqing exerted himself to the utmost to achieve a rapprochement between the two governments, and, in the end, success attended his efforts when war was averted. The National Government heaped praise on Yan, declaring that it was only through his good work that peace had been maintained.

Hilda was a busy homemaker, mother, clubwoman and socialite, but the responsibilities that filled her days seemed relatively insubstantial, and she was restless. Possessed with fully as much intelligence and initiative as the rest of her dynamic family, she felt herself capable of great things and yearned to do more. The ongoing threats against Chinese sovereignty made by the Empire of Japan, including the attack on China in 1931 and the 'Shanghai Incident' of 1932, had whipped Hilda's patriotism to a high pitch. Passionately committed to her nation and its people, she was attracted to a career in the diplomatic world where many of her friends already represented China in the great capitals of Europe. If she were involved with the foreign service, her interest in the issues of world order and the dignity of all mankind would have an outlet. Through her uncle, she was poised to have an opportunity to enter this heady milieu.

3. LIFE UNDER THE SOVIET STAR

When China and the Soviet Union had been on the brink of war, Yan Huiqing's intense efforts had helped to avert the crisis, thus earning for him the gratitude of the people of China, but Yan himself had been too overcome with nervous fatigue to appreciate the compliments that showered down upon him. Of a highly-strung disposition to begin with, he collapsed from exhaustion.

Upon his recovery, and on the advice of his doctor, he tendered his resignation as Ambassador, but to his dismay, the foreign office refused to accept it. His superiors argued that the country was yet in mortal danger of outright war, and his utmost efforts were still required to ensure that the peace did not evaporate. Yan wearily agreed to stay on, but increasingly, he came to dread life in Moscow. The challenge of existing under the Red Star during the 1930s was daunting. Many food stuffs and essential items were simply unavailable, and the paranoia of the dictator Stalin resulted in the purges that became the infamous hallmark of the decade. The dreaded knock on the door in the middle of the night, the disappearance of old friends and acquaintances into camps—or worse—and the ever-present anxiety of wondering when and where the axe would fall created an atmosphere of perpetual gloom. Although the diplomatic community was little physically affected by the social climate that existed, nevertheless it was infected by the malaise that permeated Russia.

To make matters worse, by 1935, Yan's wife was unable, or unwilling, to accompany him to Moscow. Her absence would be a serious handicap. The arduous, but imperative, social duties of an ambassador were generally shared by his spouse, who was responsible for entertaining and the smooth running of the Embassy.

On February 16, 1935, Yan Huiqing traveled by train from Nanjing to Shanghai to bid goodbye to his family before returning to Russia, and his brother Fuqing and niece Hilda were on the station platform to greet him.[1] Huiqing was delighted to see them both. Knowing of Hilda's interest in the diplomatic community, he had an important proposal to make. He needed a hostess, and he knew Hilda wanted to enter the foreign service. If she were to accompany him to Moscow to serve as his chatelaine, they would both be well served. He cautioned that the appointment was no sinecure—throwing protocol-laden banquets and tending to VIPs were constants in the life of an Embassy hostess, and she would be required to be on the job for anywhere from one to two years—but if she wished to tackle it, the experience would prove a solid grounding for her aspirations to the diplomatic life. It would also provide a once-in-a-lifetime opportunity to meet the leading statesmen of Europe. He asked her to sleep on the idea.

The next day, Hilda announced she had made her decision. She agreed to accompany Yan Huiqing to the Soviet Union.

The fact that Hilda was willing to leave her husband and two small children for such an extended period suggests that she was almost desperate in her need to escape the life she was living. The vast steppes of Russia were an alluring metaphor for the freedom she craved from the banality of her existence as a society matron. Of course, there was opposition to the notion—even her aunt, Huiqing's wife, objected to Hilda's decision—but in the end, all protests were unavailing.[2] After a whirlwind of preparations, in just three days Hilda was packed and ready to go. The *North-China Daily News* trumpeted her decision and reported with pride that she was to be "the first Chinese lady, other than the wives of diplomats, to act as official hostess of an Embassy, and as China's 'first lady' in Russia is expected to preside with her usual distinction and charm."[3]

Dr. W.W. Yan knew that he would very much require Hilda's "distinction and charm" on this expedition. He and his niece would be accompanied on their journey into the Soviet heartland by a large and unwieldy entourage of some forty persons, the foremost of whom were two of the greatest stars in the Chinese entertainment industry, Dr. Mei Lanfang and Miss Hu Die, popularly known as Butterfly Wu.

Dr. Mei was China's top female impersonator, and he had entranced audiences around the world with his performances in the traditional Chinese theater where, as in Shakespeare's day, the roles of women were played by men. Invited by the Soviet Government to demonstrate his art in Moscow, Dr. Mei would be traveling with a party of some twenty-five actors and musicians of the Beijing Opera, as well as theater educators and dramatists. The alluring Miss Butterfly Wu was a leading cinematic actress who had won international acclaim for her film work in the 1920s and '30s, and she was going to Russia in her own right. In addition, several delegates of the Chinese film industry, who intended to attend the upcoming Moscow Film Festival, were also part of the company.[4] These traveling members of the entertainment community hoped to bring the magic of the Chinese dramatic arts to Russian audiences and so augment the ties of culture and understanding between the two nations.

Not to be outdone, even Dr. W.W. Yan announced he would be journeying to Russia with his own retinue; Yan's personal physician and several staff members of the Embassy would accompany him and his niece to Moscow.[5]

On February 20, 1935, Hilda and her uncle joined their excited traveling companions at the China Merchants' Lower Wharf preparatory to boarding the *s.s. Sever*. The *Sever* was a Russian freighter especially chartered and outfitted by the Soviets to convey their honored guests to the port city of Vladivostok where they would disembark and then climb aboard the legendary Trans-Siberian Express bound for Moscow.

Shanghai was overcast and chilly on the day of departure, and the women huddled in furs, but despite the inclement weather, it seemed that fully half of the city was at the docks to wish them well—a special phalanx of police had to be dispatched to control the ensuing traffic jam. The crush of well-wishers, including Hilda's husband and parents, all crammed aboard the *Sever,* making movement in the ship's passages impossible, but everyone was eager to bless this endeavor that promised to do so much to improve shaky Sino-Soviet relations. Finally the order was given to weigh anchor, and the guests scurried off down the gangplank calling out their goodbyes. The ship pulled away from the quayside, and it was the beginning of a new life for Hilda. As the company slowly steamed down the Huangpu to the open sea, she found it strange to recall that, just days before, she had worn fancy dress and danced with her husband at the Chinese Women's Club Ball.

Four days later, the *s.s. Sever* hove into Vladivostok harbor in a thick fog, and its passengers debarked. They were in for a bit of a letdown. The Yans and their company found the town to be woefully decrepit, and this put a damper on their excited anticipation, but they were warmly received, and the hospitality they encountered there was duplicated many times over during the remainder of their expedition through the heart of the Soviet Union. Before setting off to Moscow, Hilda and her uncle got to work almost immediately, making a side trip on official consular business to the Siberian cities of Khabarovsk and Chita. A couple of days later, they were rejoined by the others who caught up with them by train. Then they all clambered aboard the Trans-Siberian Express and settled in for the long ride across the frosty landscape to the nation's capital.[6]

On March 12, the fabled train pulled into Moscow's Yaroslavsky Station where Wu Nanru, the China's Embassy trusty counselor, was waiting to greet them. Wu was not alone. He was surrounded by a large and eager contingent of the Soviet press that pushed forward as the Chinese delegation alighted from the train. The object of their excited interest was neither Ambassador Yan nor his young niece, but rather Mei Lanfang, the famous actor. Dr. Mei's reputation as the foremost exponent of his art had preceded his arrival, and all of Moscow was anxious to know more about him. The Chinese delegation was enormously gratified by the positive attention that was being showered on its most famous artist, and relieved to learn that all the expense and fuss associated with bringing this extravagant traveling road show to Russia was already paying handsome dividends.

Hilda and her uncle climbed into the surprisingly modest car reserved for the Ambassador and were chauffeured to the legation sector. Another visitor to Moscow in the early months of 1935 described this same car ride through the city's streets. "Large, drab crowds, unsmiling, poorly dressed and ill-fed by our standards, went disinterestedly on their way. The weather, the streets, the people, all seemed grey, sad and unending."[7]

Hilda's first view of the Soviet capital was likely just as unprepossessing, but she was cheered by the sight of the Chinese Embassy, her home from home for the duration. It was an impressive structure. Once the spacious mansion of a Russian nobleman who had fled to the West at the outbreak of the Revolution, the Embassy was located on a gracious, tree-lined street and recently had been restored to its original splendor. To reflect the culture of the nation it represented, its interiors were newly furnished with *chinoiserie* of the highest caliber—plush carpets, porcelains, lanterns, and furniture of *hongmu* wood—and was possessed of several rooms that were ideal for the entertaining of guests on a large scale. In particular, one hall had a seating capacity of a hundred and sixty. Upon viewing it, Hilda and her uncle decided that this chamber would be ideal for the presentation of the upcoming Chinese opera performance, and it was here that they ordered a stage to be erected for the purpose.

Exactly one week after Hilda's arrival in the Soviet capital, the great day finally arrived, and at 5 o'clock on March 19, 1935, she began her professional life as chatelaine of the Chinese Embassy. Flanked by her uncle, she warmly received her distinguished guests—members of the Diplomatic Corps, renowned Russian writers, dramatists, movie directors, members of the press and sundry exotic artists in flamboyant dress—all of whom had flocked to the Embassy to witness the art of Mei Lanfang. Hilda entertained them to high tea, and then she and her uncle led them into the great hall to enjoy the dramatic spectacle. At their first sight of the carved wooden panels and embroidered silk hangings that embellished the stage settings, the audience gasped with delight, but this was as nothing compared to the performances of Mei Lanfang and his troupe.

The spectacle surpassed everyone's expectations. Next day, and for every day following, the Russian press was full of unstinting praise for the realism of the actors' art, the gaudy extravagance of the costumes and set decorations, and the fantastic weirdness of the music. After his opening night at the Embassy, Dr. Mei gave ten sold-out performances for the Russian people at the Moscow Music Hall where his nightly audiences included all the greats of Soviet culture. Prokofiev, Brecht, Gorky, and Eisenstein were just a few of those who witnessed the magic of his act and later claimed to have found their own art renewed by the inspiration they received at these performances.

Seated in the special theater box reserved for the Diplomatic Corps, Hilda and her uncle attended with glowing pride every one of Dr. Mei's performances. Afterwards, they invited their diplomatic colleagues back to the Embassy for late-night dinners, and it was at these glittering soirees that Hilda played the charming hostess to perfection, a talent she had honed at her mother's knee. It was also at these dinners that the beauteous Butterfly Wu demonstrated her art. Although Miss Wu did not participate in the Chinese opera, and in fact did not perform in public while she was in Russia, most evenings she could be prevailed upon to sing after dinner for the Embassy guests, and she captivated them with her loveliness and talent. For those who could not get enough of the charming Butterfly, they could also view her work at the Moscow International Film Festival that was being held in the city.[8]

At the end of March, the opera and cinematic troupes finally bade farewell to the Yans, moving on from the capital to conquer excited crowds in Leningrad and Europe. Hilda and her uncle finally had the Embassy to themselves, but they had little time to put up their feet before two large figures on the international stage arrived in Moscow to conduct high level talks with the Soviets. They were Britain's Lord Privy Seal, Sir Anthony Eden (destined one day to be Prime Minister of the United Kingdom) and France's Foreign Minister, Pierre Laval (three times Prime Minister of France, and fated to be executed postwar as a Vichy supporter). The previous summer, Adolf Hitler had become Führer of Germany, and, in a series of worrying developments, had renounced the Treaty of Versailles and re-established mandatory military service, and on behalf of their governments, both Eden and Laval were anxious to discuss the disturbing implications of the German rearmament. While these distinguished statesmen were in Moscow on their vital mission, they were always assured of a warm and relaxed welcome at the Chinese Embassy where Hilda and her uncle entertained them privately many times during their month-long sojourn. The animated Chinese Ambassador loved to hold forth and amuse his guests. Clad in immaculately tailored English tweeds, and with the light glinting off his horn-rimmed glasses, he punctuated his remarks with the stem of his pipe while Hilda graciously poured tea and passed the cake tray, interjecting from time to time her own cogent and well-considered observations. They made an excellent team.

By late April, Hilda and her uncle had more free time to themselves, and together they set out to enjoy the splendors of Russia—the galleries, museums, and theaters. They also toured as many of the old Orthodox churches, now sadly neglected, as they could, marveling at their stolid, yet whimsical, architecture. They browsed through antique shops where they scooped up many bargains—beautifully bound old books pawned by impoverished aristocrats, icons, porcelains, jewelry, paintings and other knick-knacks. In the evening, there was no shortage of invitations as the various embassies took turns inviting their diplomatic corps colleagues to dinner. The Yans particularly enjoyed being the guests of the U.S. Ambassador, W.C. Bullitt, who treated them to private screenings of the latest American films. Hilda's uncle was a keen fan of the cinema, and, when in Shanghai, was apt to go out to the movies at least twice a week.

When she was not entertaining or being entertained, Hilda paid tribute to her Soviet hosts by studying their language, and soon she had a working knowledge of the Russian tongue. This facility served her well when, in conjunction with embassy work, she had occasion to meet high Russian functionaries, the most notable of whom was the supreme leader of the Soviet Union, Joseph Stalin.

Perhaps Hilda's greatest learning came from listening to her uncle. Yan Huiqing was one of the most respected statesmen in the world, and she could not have absorbed diplomacy and statecraft from a better qualified teacher. As a committed internationalist, Yan instilled in his niece the importance of communications in human relations, and was scornful of those who practiced isolationism.

"They have clung to the old idea of the world's separation into compartments," he indignantly observed, "where in one part of the world, people could live in comfort and tranquility, while in the other, upheavals and catastrophes prevailed. The first European War which should have taught an unforgettable lesson in these things failed in the end to do so, and the great democracies, having turned over to their other side, went to sleep again."[9]

His views fully accorded with Hilda's own, and augmented her burgeoning internationalist outlook.

On May 4, 1935, Hilda received two months wages as an Embassy staff member. Although materially she lacked for nothing, she pocketed this pay packet with great satisfaction. She had worked hard and actually earned the money, but more importantly, this ability to fill her own rice bowl was a precious symbol of her growing independence. In mid-June, when her uncle forwarded a list of his staff members to the Ministry of Foreign Affairs, Hilda's name was on it. No longer just an Embassy hostess, she had won her spurs as a *bona fide* diplomatic representative of her country.[10] To celebrate her success, on June 17, Embassy counselor Wu Nanru held a banquet in Hilda's honor. The gathering was also an opportunity for her colleagues to bid her farewell for the summer. She would be spending a working holiday with friends in Europe before taking up her duties at the League of Nations headquarters in Geneva.

In August, Yan Huiqing received official instructions from the Waijiaobu to attend the 16th Ordinary Session of the Assembly of the League of Nations that was to be convened from September 9 to October 11, 1935. The League, precursor to the United Nations, had opened its offices in Geneva in 1919, and since 1920, China had sent a delegation to attend its assemblies. On August 24, Hilda traveled to Geneva ahead of her uncle, and was at the station to meet him when his train arrived ten days later. Yan Huiqing found his niece joyous and radiant. She was in her element. The League was the first institution in the history of the world that sought to benefit the whole of humanity, and Hilda, ardent idealist, was a part of it. Distinguished representatives of many nations had begun to converge on the city by the lake, many of them wearing native dress, and Geneva was vibrant with their energy. The League of Nations had always cherished a vision that, through its democratic assemblies, a fresh humanism would be born for all peoples. This desire coincided exactly with

Hilda's dream.

In the circular issued to the attending delegates, the name 'Madame Hilda Yan Chen' was listed among the Chinese representatives to the League, and she bore the official title of *conseiller technique*, or 'expert.' She also had the honor of being the only woman delegate on the Chinese team. Her addition to the roster was no hollow inclusion. She had important ideas to present to the world representatives.

On September 19, Madame Yan Chen gave her maiden speech to the League of Nations, addressing the fifth meeting of the First Committee, a body that was assigned the task of examining constitutional and legal questions.[11] The meeting had been convened to discuss the status of women throughout the world, and Hilda's immediate intent was to clear up any antiquated misconceptions the committee might have with regard to women's rights in China, "a country," she declared, "reputed to be one of the oldest and most conservative" in the world.

In an elegant and lengthy address, Hilda took pains to point out that China's reputation for fusty conservatism was not entirely warranted. The new civil code of laws, introduced five years before, had been drawn up in accordance with the principle of equality for women that had been resolved upon by the National Congress of 1927. The four cornerstones of this principle were equality of rights between men and women, women's equal right to inherit property, equality of freedom in contracting and dissolving marriage, and the 'same work, same pay' principle for women workers. She haughtily observed that the supposedly more liberal countries of Europe and America had made no comparable legal provision for their women citizens, and accordingly, she had a word of advice for the men of the West. Give your women legal equality willingly and in good spirit, she warned, or have it taken from you.[12] She also recommended that the League officially take up the important issue of the status of women. Her brusque remarks made headlines in the Far East.

"Give women a chance of half a say in the world and we might see better things," she was quoted as saying. "The present state could not be worse."[13]

Hilda's first speech to the Committee was noteworthy on two counts. It demonstrated that she had worked closely with, and received input from, the formidable feminist lawyer, Dr. Zheng Yuxiu, former delegate to the League of Nations and a member of the commission that had written the very laws of female equality of which Hilda was so proud.[14] Secondly, it also established that Hilda could deliver presentations that were not only informative, but also feisty and verging on the impertinent. There was little likelihood that those who heard the premiere address of China's latest representative to the League would soon forget the speaker, or her message.

Before the Session was officially over, Yan Huiqing left Geneva to attend another meeting in Frankfurt, and normally, as her uncle's aide, Hilda would have accompanied him, but she was busy in her own right and was obliged to remain and complete her work on the committee. On October 6, she attended a League of Nations plenary session with senior Chinese delegate, Hu Shize (Victor Hoo).[15] The charming Hu had much in common with Hilda. In addition to his being an old friend and colleague of her uncle, he had spent his youth in Russia, and cherished a deep regard for the Soviet Union and its people. He also fluently spoke the elegant, pre-Revolutionary language of that country. In the biography of her father, Hu's daughter recalls that his knowledge of Russian "occasionally had its drawbacks, as when Victor and his friend W.W. [Yan] went to the theater in Geneva and overheard a Russian lady behind them whisper to her companion: 'I like Chinese men but these are two of the ugliest I have ever seen.' Victor got his own back during the interval when she pulled out a cigarette and, stepping forward to light it, Victor was able to make a comment in perfect Russian."[16]

Hu was a lady's man and always had an eye for a lovely woman; it is likely that he appreciated Hilda's extraordinary intelligence and beauty.

Yan Huiqing was back in Moscow when Hilda returned to Russia in late October, but she found her uncle in a dispirited frame of mind. He had grown increasingly weary of trying to accomplish anything of value in the Soviet Union, finding roadblocks and prevarication at every turn, and he longed for an opportunity to lay down his burden. Yan resolved to retire from service the following spring when he entered his sixtieth year. In anticipation, he decided to return to Paris and London to confer with his colleagues just one last time before he left the world stage. He departed by train shortly after Christmas, and Hilda hurried to join him in London in the New Year of 1936.

As it was his last hurrah, Yan Huiqing and his niece decided to savor to the full all the delights of the English capital, and they played at being tourists in the great city. Taking time out for a little shopping—Hilda helped her uncle buy a new rug—they also attended the must-see show of the year, the celebrated International Exhibition of Chinese Art at Burlington House. Sponsored by the Royal Academy, the exhibit included superb pieces from the Imperial Collection of the Forbidden City never before seen in the West.

The exhibition received a wide attendance, and the splendor of Chinese artistry was the talk of the town. Hilda and Huiqing nearly burst with pride at the brilliant impact their culture was making on Europe.

It was also a time for introspection. Hilda had lived abroad and apart from her husband for almost one year, and she had come to the fateful decision that she must bring her marriage to P.T. to an end. She was doing the most meaningful and exciting work of her life, and her old responsibilities as wife were anathema to her. However, despite her country's renowned laws of equality, the very ones of which Hilda had bragged to the League of Nations committee, divorce was still relatively uncommon in Chinese society, and the notion of a wife and mother divorcing her husband was even more so. Her worried uncle was caught in the middle, but he did what he could to help all parties involved. On March 8, 1936, he sent a letter to P.T.'s boss, Dr. H.H. Kong, presumably to warn him of the coming separation. The next day, he exercised his clout with the Foreign Office by writing to request that a place be found for Hilda to work at the League of Nations Secretariat.

Hilda herself was not idle; she informed her family that she was commencing divorce proceedings from London. This prompted her father and estranged husband to fire off a joint telegram of woe to Yan Huiqing, but there was little the elder statesman could do to halt the seemingly inexorable disintegration of the marriage. Indeed, by the time he received the telegram from Shanghai, his niece had apparently already signed the papers that formally signified her intent to divorce.[17]

By April, Yan Huiqing's health suffered a complete breakdown, and he retired to a sanatorium in Berlin to regain his vigor. He was diagnosed as suffering from 'nervous prostration' apparently brought on by over-exertion, unhealthy surroundings and mental worries. It is likely that those 'mental worries' included considerable concern for the fate of his niece and her husband, of whom he was genuinely fond and proud, during this crisis in their personal lives. He traveled to Italy, where he rested in the mountains at Merano, and then slowly returned to China, arriving back in Shanghai in June 1936 at which time he once more formally tendered his resignation from the ambassadorship.

4. SEXUAL SLAVERY & THE LEAGUE OF NATIONS

A city already renowned for its sybaritic social life, Shanghai in the sizzling summer of 1936 was notable for the zeal with which its inhabitants took their entertainments. As if some prescience told them the dark clouds of war gathering on the horizon meant that the party was almost over, the residents of Sin City dedicated themselves to their pleasures as never before. House parties were thrown at a moment's notice for anyone arriving in the city—or departing—and in the cool of the evening, women in flowery chiffons or crisp organdies strolled arm-in-arm with their menfolk through scented, moon-lit gardens, attended by houseboys who obligingly trotted after them with refreshment-laden silver salvers. American film star Anna May Wong typified the decadent glamour of that season. She was holidaying in Shanghai, and for the duration of her layover, the celebrity siren's presence in the city was yet another ideal excuse for non-stop partying by the city's rich and famous.

Hilda arrived back in Shanghai in that summer to end all summers. She had shed her married title, and was known no longer as Mrs. P.T. Chen. As if with a magic wand, her past marriage was waved away and she became once again the vivacious Miss Hilda Yan. Reinvented, she threw herself enthusiastically into the summer's social whirl, attending a Chinese Women's Club garden party in a superb chartreuse *qipao*, and then later appearing on the arm of her father at a benefit for the blind. She made a head-turning solo turnout at the annual members' party of the Husi Club, and convened a going-away party for noted author, Lin Yutang and his family. Hilda's ex-husband likewise refused to sit home and mope, and he was no less active. Despite the fierce heat of summer, P.T. was spotted about town entertaining two women friends at the Sunya Restaurant, and later dining with a party at a restaurant on Nanjing Road. He was also observed dancing on the Sky Terrace of the Park Hotel. Hilda countered by attending a showy birthday party for the Count René d'Anjou.

At mid-summer, Miss Hilda Yan officially announced that she had obtained a government job, and would be leaving soon for Nanjing, the nation's capital. This revelation occasioned a fresh round of parties thrown by her friends to celebrate her success. Although the new position meant she would be deserting her family yet again, at least this time she would be thousands of miles nearer to home. On most Fridays, she could book a sleeper on the night train from Nanjing and arrive fresh in Shanghai the next morning. Should she feel the need to travel more quickly, the China National Aviation Corporation had recently connected the two cities with a speedy hour-and-a-half flying service. The news that she had been assigned relatively close to Shanghai was well received by her parents who were helping to care for her children. Her busy father was almost wholly occupied by his efforts to prepare the new National Medical College of Shanghai for its scheduled opening in late summer.

Meanwhile, the Foreign Office granted Yan Huiqing his long-desired wish and finally allowed him to retire from his position as Ambassador to the Soviet Union. The Executive Yuan named his successor as Jiang Tingfu. In view of her past service in Moscow, Hilda was invited to attend a splashy send-off party for Dr. and Mrs. Jiang (the long guest list of VIPs included P.T., as well as actress Anna May Wong), and a few weeks later, she was among those present at Shanghai's dockside to bid farewell to the new Ambassador-designate as he set sail for the Soviet Union on the *s.s. Sever*. It had been over a year and a half since she herself had stood on the deck of that same ship and waved goodbye to her friends and family, and she paused to reflect on the significant changes that had transformed her life since that day, the joys and tumults she had experienced. She had ruthlessly fought for her independence, clashed with her family, and shed her husband. She had effectively taken on a new career, learned to move with ease in the capitals of Europe, and rubbed shoulders with titans of world politics.

She little knew, as she stood waving on the quayside, that her life and sensibilities would undergo yet another revolution that very afternoon—a shake-up that would cause her to take yet another dramatic fork in the road of her life.

Generalissimo Chiang Kai-shek was entering his fiftieth year on October 31, 1936, and the entire nation was galvanized to help him celebrate this milestone with considerable pizzazz. The threat of outright war with Japan had been an omnipresent possibility since 1931, and by this late date, Chinese fears of imminent attack were escalating. The need for an effective air force received much publicity, and the populace was gradually beginning to grow more air-minded. Now on the eve of war, all of China was being urged to contribute funds to be used towards the purchase of aircraft that would be presented to Chiang for his birthday. The people of Shanghai dug deep and raised enough money to acquire ten new Curtiss Hawk 111-type pursuit aircraft. The formal presentation would be made a week before the Generalissimo's birthday, and although the leader himself would not be in attendance, the naming ceremony and dedication of the planes would take place in the presence of the proud citizens of Shanghai.

On the day of the event, a massive crowd arrived at the city's Longhua airfield to witness the christening of the ten aircraft and to enjoy the scheduled air show. Directly adjacent to the airfield, the most prominent members of Shanghai society gathered on a central, flag-festooned platform. Seated among these luminaries were Miss Hilda Yan and her mother.

One of the highlights of that afternoon's extravaganza was an aerobatic display by China's foremost aviatrix, Li Xiaqing, who had recently returned from America where she had undergone training as a professional pilot. Her flawless flying performance on that day caused a sensation. Every young person in the audience who witnessed the courageous aerobatic feats of the young woman pilot wanted nothing more than to learn to fly like the intrepid Miss Li. When the aviatrix made a dangerous power dive over the viewing platform, Hilda was no exception, and she, too, lost her heart to aviation. More than this, she knew that an expanded air power would be the key to saving China from her enemy.

Shortly after this event, Hilda had an official meeting with Miss Li. The two women were already acquainted and discovered they had much in common. They had both lived in Geneva (Xiaqing was resident there while her husband had served with the League of Nations), and they were both mothers of two young children, having each given birth to a boy and a girl. Even more surprisingly, within weeks of each other, they both had taken controversial steps to divorce their husbands. They were also daring, passionate and strong-willed women who were willing to die for China if need be.

After a series of close discussions, they hammered out a bold plan for the creation of a special club or association, the purpose of which would be to encourage young women to enter the field of aviation. All who wished to become air pilots would be welcome to join. Over the next few weeks, Hilda and Xiaqing continued to fine-tune their program, the general aim of which was to make their fellow countrymen more airminded. But they were realistic. They knew their plans would be difficult to achieve without a great deal of money and powerful support.[1]

While Hilda did not abandon her decision to study aviation, she was unable to devote much time to it. For the moment, her increasingly successful professional life took center stage. In January 1937, shortly after her sister, Dorothy, announced her upcoming marriage to Franklin Lieu, Hilda made an important announcement of her own. She was pleased to reveal that the Chinese National Government had appointed her to a special commission being dispatched to the League of Nations in Geneva. China had decided to increase the number of experts sitting with the official Chinese delegation to the League, and one of the six fields of research it intended to support included Public Health.[2] Hilda was allocated to this specialty. In particular, she was assigned the responsibility of investigating the trafficking of young women and even children. Since the 1920s, the League had labored to eradicate white slavery, but this vile crime was still a serious international problem, particularly in the Far East, and Hilda was thrilled to have an opportunity of tackling the issue. She was already involved with the International YWCA and the National Child Welfare Association, the latter a consortium of children's charities headquartered on Shanghai's Kiaochow Road, and had intimate knowledge of the scope of the crisis. With solid experience in the field and international connections, she was ideally suited for the job. She anticipated that this new assignment would keep her away from home for one year.[3]

Not wishing to steal her sister's thunder, she did not announce her appointment until shortly before she was scheduled to depart Shanghai, and accordingly she was obliged to turn down the many invitations of her friends who clambered to fête her at the last minute. However, one intimate luncheon that she was pleased to attend was thrown in her honor by an old family acquaintance, the Italian Commander Genaro Cioppa, aboard the two-funnel gunboat under his command, the *Ermanno Carlotto*. This unusual party venue was made even more so by the fact that the ship, bristling with armaments, was in dry dock at the time.[4] Hilda attended the luncheon in the company of her friend, the celebrated Shanghai dress designer, Miss Zhang Qianying (Hélène Tsing-ying Tsang), whose father was a longtime member of the foreign service.

In mid-January, buoyed by the best wishes of a score of friends who gathered at the Shanghai waterfront to see her off, Hilda boarded the *s.s. Tjiba-dak,* a ship of the Java-China-Japan line, and once more steamed off down the Huangpu to what she hoped would be a fulfilling and worthwhile career. With considerable fanfare, a Shanghai newspaper predicted that she embodied all the elements necessary for success. "A radiant personality," the article enthused, "Miss [Yan] explodes the ancient axiom that intelligence cannot go hand in hand with beauty. A more fitting 'ambassadress' could not have been chosen."[5]

On this lengthy journey to the now-familiar city of Geneva, Hilda would combine business with pleasure. She not only intended to indulge her passion for travel, but she would begin her new work almost immediately by attending an important meeting of the League of Nations in Bandoeng, Java. In response to a resolution adopted by Council on October 10, 1936, the Government of the Netherlands offered to host the meeting entitled, 'The Conference of Central Authorities of Eastern Countries on the Traffic of Women and Children, February 3-15, 1937.'[6] Hilda's fellow-delegates included consular officials and representatives from around the world, and she herself attended the meeting both as a technical advisor representing the Chinese Government, and as a private delegate of the National Child Welfare Association.[7]

Hilda and her colleagues were booked into the palm-shaded Hotel Preanger, a gracious hostelry dedicated to comfortable hospitality in the heart of Bandoeng, but they were not lulled into a passive stupor by the relaxing beauty of their exotic surroundings; they knuckled down to serious work. Although China had outlawed prostitution, the foreign concessions and international settlements within her boundaries had not. The traffic of women and children flourished within these enclaves and spilled over into the prohibited zones. In her maiden speech to the conference, delivered on February 4, Hilda reported on the need for the appointment of an officer to liaise between China and these various areas. If there could be any doubt about the extent of the trafficking problem, the next day she shored up her argument with cold figures that documented a bad situation gone completely out of control. She declared that dancing schools, massage parlors, Turkish baths, and even employment bureaus were known to act as panderers of desperate young women who were forced to sell themselves through economic necessity.[8] She made particular note of dispossessed and vulnerable Russian refugees who streamed into China and typically fell into the clutches of white slavers. Most of these women were doomed to a life of degradation, disease and early death, but, as she optimistically observed, this tragic outcome was not inevitable. She pointed out that those who had been given an opportunity to educate themselves, or enter into business, had been able to avoid the trap of enslavement. Hilda urged the League to finance vocational schools, relief homes and business loans for the support of these unfortunate young women.

By the end of the conference, the delegates had amassed a lengthy list of motions, including a recommendation to create a special Bureau of the League of Nations in the East "to receive regular reports from all participating countries in regard to traffic in women and children."[9] It is likely that Hilda would have played a seminal role in the organization and operation of this proposed bureau. However, in the chaos that attended the outbreak of the Sino-Japanese hostilities just five months after the adjournment of the meeting, most of the recommendations of the conference were eventually consigned to the oblivion of forgotten issues.

When the conference adjourned, Hilda retreated to the nearby island of Bali in the company of fellow-delegate, Miss Jeanne Bayly Perkins, the popular Shanghai-based secretary of the International YWCA.[10] The two women were friends through their work at the Shanghai Y and after the rigors of the Bandoeng conference, they were ready for a relaxing vacation. They thoroughly investigated Bali and then began their leisurely progress to Europe by sea and land, sailing first to Columbo, and then to the mainland of India where they embarked on a two-week train journey from east to west, stopping off at all the usual tourist destinations along the way. From their terminus at Bombay, they boarded a ship and sailed west to the Gulf of Aden, up the Red Sea, and through the Suez Canal to Cairo where they viewed the ancient glories of Egypt. Then they set off to visit the Mediterranean civilizations of Palestine and Greece.

In Italy, the two friends parted, Miss Perkins sailing home to America, and Hilda lingering on in Italy where she visited her many Italian friends in the diplomatic service. Ever the internationalist, Hilda's extended vacation only consolidated her love for the myriad cultures of the earth.[11] She visited Naples where buggies jostled with limousines along the seafront, and lobsters could be cheaply bought in the outdoor markets by the Bay. Tantalizingly, the white vapor cloud rising from the peak of neighboring Mount Vesuvius was clearly visible from the city, and its dangerous majesty proved an irresistible magnet to Hilda. The volcano was temperamental in the 1930s, but in the company of a mountain guide, she climbed as near to the steaming top as she dared. Decades later, when her young grandson was working on a school volcano project, she was able to recall for him how her guide had picked up a warm and malleable piece of lava near the summit and pressed a lira into its soft exterior before presenting it to her as a souvenir ashtray.

Hilda spent considerable time in Rome researching Italy's child welfare program, but she had not forgotten her commitment to help save China through aviation. It was during this busy period that she also took her first formal flying lessons at Littoria airport. Under the tutelage of pilot teacher Signor Briondi, the skills and knowledge of flight she acquired were relatively rudimentary, but she was in Rome long enough to make some solo flights and earn a flying license. The experience would prove a good grounding for the advanced training she would soon receive in America.

In April 1937, she took up temporary residence in Geneva, and, as Mademoiselle Hilda Yan, she made her report to the annual meeting of the Traffic in Women and Children Welfare Committee, specifically referring to the resolutions of the Bandoeng conference. At this particular assembly, the Committee was re-organized, and a Permanent Standing Sub-Committee was formed. Appointed to this sub-committee was her friend and her uncle's diplomatic colleague, the urbane Hu Shize. An old hand in Geneva, he was well-accustomed to advising his younger colleagues how to side-step the lurking minefields of international politics.

However, while she was living the life of a sophisticated and independent diplomatic attaché abroad, Hilda's family back home was wracked with concern for her welfare. Her uncle, Yan Huiqing, had returned to Shanghai, and at the urgent request of Hilda's father, paid an immediate visit to Yan Fuqing's home. There was a flap on. Hilda was intending to be married again, and Fuqing was anxious to discuss his daughter's wedding plans with his brother. When Huiqing returned home that evening, he confided the surprising news to his diary, but provided no details of this unexpected development, nor did he mention the name of the prospective groom. Hilda's decision appears to have been met with a singular lack of enthusiasm. "This matter is very strange," her uncle cryptically observed.[12] Fortunately, considering the concern occasioned by the proposed union, no marriage took place.

Just one month later, Hilda and her ex-husband, P.T. Chen, were unavoidably thrown together for several weeks. They were both members of the large Chinese delegation dispatched to London to celebrate the coronation of George VI and his consort Elizabeth, scheduled to take place on May 12, 1937. P.T. had been appointed official secretary of this Special Mission to Britain. Aside from the delegates' stated intention of celebrating the crowning of the new king and queen, they also had an ancillary agenda. While abroad, they planned to seek financial aid to assist China in the realization of her five-year plan for economic reconstruction, hence P.T.'s close involvement.

The delegation was composed of the most important financial figures in China, and was headed up by P.T.'s immediate boss, Dr. H.H. Kong, who was accompanied by a traveling party of twenty-three prominent dignitaries.[13] To mark the occasion, and to confer additional splendor on the delegates, the members of this Special Mission were decorated by their government prior to departure. P.T. was awarded the Order of Brilliant Jade, Fifth Class. He was, at the time, secretary of the Central Bank of China.

Upon their arrival in London, the delegates were joined by other nationals stationed in the consulates of Europe, and, as a member of the unofficial Chinese delegation, Hilda was also called upon to travel to England and participate in the many special celebrations that were associated with the coronation. One of these festivities required her attendance at a reception held in Buckingham Palace, and on this splendid occasion, Hilda wore a superb Chinese gown created by her friend, the dress designer Zhang Qianying.

Although only ten representatives of China were actually allowed into Westminster Abbey to witness the crowning of the royal couple, the unofficial delegates had an opportunity to view the parade.[14] They were lucky enough to be assigned covered viewing stands ideally situated directly opposite Buckingham Palace, and they enjoyed a more informal day. Hilda and her colleagues took their places in the flag-draped stands under graying skies and watched with fascination the start of the procession as the King and Queen set forth to the Abbey in the glittering State Coach. After the procession had passed the platform, the delegates returned to their hotel for a convivial gathering while they listened to a live radio broadcast of the coronation. When they heard that the Abbey ceremony was drawing to a close, they dashed back to their places at the viewing stands just in time to catch the Royal couple, now resplendent in the jewels of state, returning to the Palace in their horse-drawn coach of gold.

The members of the Chinese delegation found themselves infected by the fairy tale pageantry of the proceedings and the sincere jubilation of the British people, and they cheered the royal couple as loudly as their neighbors. They were also impressed by the orderly and good-tempered behavior of the millions who massed to watch the parade. For the rest of her life, Hilda would remember the colors and pomp attending that day, and would rejoice at having been present on such a historic occasion.

5. A WAR OF RESISTANCE

On July 7, 1937, Japanese troops clashed with Chinese forces at Marco Polo Bridge, also known as Lugouqiao, near Beijing, and the fighting quickly spread to other parts of China. This was the beginning of what would become the bitter Second Sino-Japanese war and the War of Resistance against Japan that would drag on for eight interminable years, ultimately merging into the global conflict known as World War II. China had been steeling herself to meet this contingency ever since the Mukden Incident of 1931, which precipitated the Japanese invasion of Manchuria. Nevertheless, she found herself woefully unprepared to confront the vastly superior Imperial forces that rolled over her land with such impunity.

Although China boasted the largest population on earth (numbering about four hundred fifty million), and no shortage of patriots, both men and women, willing to defend her to the death, her military was poorly trained and ill-equipped. Her air force was almost non-existent. China's Ministry of Information stated that, at the outset of the war, China had two hundred aircraft versus some five hundred Japanese planes. Later, it was discovered that the statistics were even more ill-favored; the enemy probably had between eight hundred and one thousand aircraft, while China had slightly more than one hundred planes in working order.[1]

As a sharp counterpoint to the commencement of outright hostilities, one week after this conflict began, Hilda's sister, Dorothy, was married to Franklin Lieu at St. John's University Pro-Cathedral.[2] The warfare had not yet reached Shanghai, and the celebration of the young couple's union occasioned what was possibly one of the last grand private parties to be held in that city in the twentieth century. The numbers of those who arrived to witness the nuptials were so vast that the church was filled to overflowing, and latecomers were obliged to gather on the grassy verge outside the doors. The color and scent of thousands of flowers filled the aisles and nave of the church, and excess baskets of blossoms tumbled out of the cathedral to be banked against the entire width of the outside walls. The bride entered the church on the arm of her father wearing a dress designed by Miss Zhang Qianying, the fashion designer friend of the Yan sisters, and was preceded by two small flower girls in green gowns who strewed the aisle with rose petals tossed from silver baskets.[3] One of these young charmers was Hilda's daughter, Doreen Chen.

In order to accommodate the three thousand guests invited to his daughter's wedding, Dr. Yan Fuqing secured the New Asia Hotel for the reception. The ballroom where the newlyweds greeted their guests was thickly hung with red silk banners bearing the names of those who sent their blessings. Most notably, these names included those of Generalissimo and Madame Chiang Kai-shek, the H.H. Kongs and the T.V. Songs, as well as hundreds of others who represented the elite of China's diplomatic, medical and financial communities. Hilda was still in Europe doing research work on the welfare of women and children and was unable to attend.

Just three weeks later, on August 9, the pleasant memories of this extravaganza receded abruptly when the conflict arrived on the very doorstep of Shanghai. The killing of two Japanese marines at the Chinese military airfield of Hungjao, ten miles south-west of Shanghai, prompted a Japanese invasion of the city proper. Thousands of miles away in Europe, Hilda read, with helpless horror, the ghastly news accounts of the bombing and carnage visited on her hometown. More than ever, she was motivated to work unceasingly for China, and, once more, the importance of promoting aviation figured largely in her thoughts.

This notion was underscored by the unbelievable events of August 14, 1937—a day appropriately dubbed 'Bloody Saturday'—that witnessed a botched attack by the Chinese Air Force on the Japanese warship *Idzumo*. This cruiser was docked in Shanghai on the Huangpu River next to the Japanese Consulate, and was widely considered to be the enemy's military headquarters. The cause of the ensuing disaster is debated to this day, but initial reports indicate that the tragically inexperienced Chinese pilots who were dispatched to blow up the ship missed their target and mistakenly dropped their bombs on the civilian crowds who milled below in Shanghai's busy shopping district. Over seventeen hundred persons were killed, and even more suffered appalling injuries. China's air capabilities were proven to be embarrassingly and horribly amateur.

Meanwhile in Geneva, the Chinese delegates were enormously busy working to secure peace for their homeland. Hilda raced to prepare for the League of Nations' Eighteenth Ordinary Session of the Assembly, held from September 13 to October 6, 1937. Reflecting the urgency of the situation, the contingent of delegates, led by Dr. Wellington Koo and buttressed by his most distinguished colleagues, was the largest ever dispatched by China to a session of the League. Adding even greater urgency to the situation, the same day that the Assembly opened, Shanghai was subjected to a severe bombing raid, and the impressive new Civic Center complex in Jiangwan, symbol of Shanghai pride and so recently completed, was obliterated. With long faces and fire in their hearts, China's delegates gathered to fulfill their responsibilities.

With considerable difficulty, Hilda set aside her own worries over the war to concentrate on her specialized duties as a League delegate. At a discussion of the First Commission regarding the status of women, she once more spoke out strongly on behalf of her sex. The League was considering a revision of its Covenant, and she and four other nation members joined forces to urge that amendments be made to the revision that would provide equal parliamentary voting rights to both men and women. The team's contribution to this issue was reported to be 'outstanding.'[4]

Then she changed gears, and, as a member of the Fifth Committee that convened to consider humanitarian questions, she made a presentation regarding her sexual slavery portfolio.[5] On September 18, Hilda endorsed the recommendations put forth at the conference she had attended in Bandoeng, specifically the creation of an Eastern Bureau to deal with the traffic of women and children, and she optimistically recommended that it be established in Shanghai.[6]

Unfortunately, with every day that passed, the establishment of this bureau seemed less likely. Most of the news coming out of China was uniformly bad. Nevertheless, Hilda and many others had faith that the League of Nations might somehow save the situation, especially when the eloquent and esteemed Dr. Koo rose to address the Assembly and condemn Japan's aggression. Hilda and some two dozen of her colleagues packed this meeting to lend as much support to China's presentation as possible. At this session, held over two days from October 5-6, there was a breakthrough when the League finally agreed to lift the embargo, which, since 1927, had disallowed the importation of military materiel into China. This significant victory gave the Nationalist Government the green light it needed to purchase the aircraft and munitions that would finally allow the Chinese to mount a decent defense.

Another ray of hope was afforded by the League of Nations Nine Power Conference held in Brussels from November 3-24, 1937. Unfortunately, a sticking point involved a difficulty in law—neither Japan nor China had actually declared war on each other—and this technicality caused an additional complication. One observer described the Byzantine dilemma faced by the League: "If the League acts, it must inquire and report upon the conflict, and the facts are such that it must decide that Japan has committed aggression. Upon such a report, Japan will declare war; and the other countries will have to recognize belligerent rights, for this is not a pseudo-civil war as is the Spanish, but an international war. Belligerent rights mean that Japan can stop and search ships and cut off all supplies from China."[7]

The conference delegates were unwilling to hamstring China, but they were also loath to involve the world in another war, so they took no action. In addition, the meeting had been convened to commence negotiations intended to terminate the conflict, but Japan refused to participate and did not send any delegates. The talks collapsed.

This debacle only served to emasculate the League and to leave China twisting helplessly in the wind. Even while the meeting was in progress, Japanese troops were humiliating Shanghai, and Mussolini was signing an Anticomintern Pact with Emperor Hirohito of Japan. By association, Italy was now an enemy of China, an unhappy dilemma for Hilda, the internationalist, who had so many Italian friends and loved the Mediterranean nation so well. She nostalgically remembered the lovely farewell party held in her honor just one year ago by Commander Cioppa. Incredibly, he and her other dear Italian friends were now 'the enemy.'

With the occupation of Shanghai, most of Hilda's family temporarily relocated to Hong Kong. Her uncle Huiqing, one of the thousands who evacuated to the safety of the British colony, noted the overcrowding in Hong Kong during this period and made a typically wry observation:

"It was sarcastically declared that, when the Manchu Emperor ceded the island to the British, he had the premonition that a century later it would serve as a place of refuge for his subjects exposed to the perils of war!"[8]

By late fall, Hilda had also moved on. In December 1937, she quit Europe for America and arrived in New York by steamer. She maintained constant communications with her family in Hong Kong, and sent them the surprising news that she was applying for a U.S. flying license. Ambitiously, she told them she intended to fly a plane back to China for active service. Her family may have been apprehensive to learn of her plans, but their anxiety was tempered with pride in her patriotic commitment and courage. They transmitted her news to the press. The American media was also intrigued by the startling goal of the newly-arrived Chinese national, and a photo of Hilda looking skyward while togged in her flying gear appeared in a number of newspapers. She took pains to justify her interest in aviation.

"There is a need for such training in China," she observed. "We have a big job ahead of us."[9]

And it was getting bigger. The Japanese military had managed to advance so rapidly into China that the Nationalist Government resolved to move its capital from Nanjing (Nanking) to Chongqing (Chungking), a mountain city located deep within the nation's heartland. The move came none too soon. In December 1937, less than a month after the relocation, Nanjing fell to the invader and lay victim to the shameful attack on its citizenry known to history as the Rape of Nanjing.

As the New Year of 1938 began, the outlook for her native land was bleak, but Hilda was heartened by the knowledge that this would be the year that she would learn in earnest to fly for China. On January 29, just two days before the commencement of the Chinese Year of the Tiger, the U.S. Bureau of Air Commerce saw fit to issue Miss Hilda Yan with Student Pilot's Certificate number 40165.[10] On her application form, Hilda gave her weight as one hundred and thirty pounds (she would shed ten of these over the busy course of the next year), and her height as sixty-seven inches in heels. As she was accustomed to doing, she casually shaved several years off her age, declaring she was born in 1910.

Hilda chose to take flying lessons with the reputable Safair Flying Services ('The Leading Flying School of the East') operating out of Hangar B at the now long-defunct Roosevelt Field complex in Mineola on New York's Long Island.[11] If Hilda sought inspiration from her surroundings, she had come to the right place. The busy airfield had been witness to many firsts in aviation, including Charles Lindbergh's departure on his solo trans-Atlantic flight in 1927, and this benchmark may have added a fillip to Hilda's own ambitions. Safair's Private Pilot's Course cost a little more than $700 and promised the neophyte flyer some twenty or more hours of solo and dual flying for a total of forty hours. Training would also include instruction in loops, rolls, half rolls, vertical banks, pylon figure-eights, strange-field landings and wingovers. Faced with the prospect of this daunting itinerary, no doubt Hilda was glad of her previous training, however rudimentary, in Italy. She also requested instruction in military flying. At this point, she fully expected that she might be ordered to return to China as a flying instructor for the Chinese Air Force, or even as an operational pilot. If called upon to do so, she was fully prepared to do her part by flying bombers against the enemy.

"And why not?" she demanded. "Women can operate a plane just as well as men... I am not rich, but we had a home. It was destroyed. Even our trees were burnt down. But thank God there is a central unified government in China now to which all classes are devoted."[12]

Driven by an obsessive desire to serve her people, Hilda was almost hyperkinetic during this period, and over the next eleven months, she divided her time between New York and Washington, D.C. After studying the minutiae of flight training at Roosevelt Field under the instruction of experienced pilot teacher, O.P. Hebert, she would commute to the nation's capital where the Chinese Embassy, Twin Oaks, served as her home base.[13] Dr. Wang Zhengting (Thomas C.T. Wang) was in residence there as Ambassador, and Hilda soon became close friends with the entire family, including the daughters, Yoeh, An-fu and An-hsiu. The residence was a cozy, almost dowdy, Victorian mansion sited on a rambling estate that had once belonged to the family of Alexander Graham Bell's wife, but its chief attraction for Hilda was its impressive library, a flower-filled room comfortably furnished with overstuffed easy chairs, lace antimacassars, and most importantly, ceiling-high shelves full of carefully catalogued books on every subject.

With its many embassies and diplomatic corps, Washington, D.C. recalled the political and social atmosphere of Geneva, but the added presence of the coterie that surrounded the American president and his staff spiked the capital with a special allure. Senate and House representatives vied with Ambassadors and career diplomats to throw the showiest festivities and entertainments. 'At homes' and tea parties were daily occurrences, and the hostess who managed to lure the greatest number of dignitaries, or better still, the wife of the president or vice-president, to her social gathering was considered to have scored a tremendous coup.

Despite the almost constant round of revelries, it was no easy task for an outsider to penetrate D.C.'s jealously guarded upper echelons, and yet, Hilda encountered no bars to her acceptance. She arrived in Washington in January 1938; a month later, the city lay at her feet, and the *Washington Post* was reporting that that Miss Hilda Yan "is the center of interest wherever she appears."[14] Of especial fascination was Hilda's splendid ambition to serve her beleaguered nation as an air pilot. In no time, there were few luncheons and dinner parties convened in the capital that did not include the remarkable Miss Yan as a valued and unusual guest.[15]

Washington's residents were surprised to discover that the pretty Chinese aviatrix was not merely a lovely visual advertisement for China's cause; she also had an important mission to fulfill. Building on the research she had first undertaken in Europe, she informed them that she had come to America to study methods of social welfare at the national Department of Labor. Under Miss Katherine F. Lenroot of the Children's Bureau, Hilda was already hard at work exploring the various means by which children could receive the best possible physical and emotional care in their formative years, and her findings would be taken under advisement by the appropriate section of the Chinese government. Washington society ladies were favorably impressed by Miss Yan's keen dedication to her assignment and by her deep knowledge of the subject. However, they would have been surprised to learn that the sophisticated Chinese intellectual had offspring of her own, and, despite her apparent concern for the wellbeing of all children, had chosen to have very little involvement in their care and rearing. Although Hilda's absence in the lives of her own youngsters was ironic, she seemed to be unaware of the incongruity. Rather, she considered her investigations to be fascinating and progressive.

"I started studying the Children's Bureau," she explained, "went from there to the Women's Bureau and have found both so interesting I'd like to have months to spend learning more about them."[16]

By exerting herself to improve the lot of others, Hilda seemed to be compensating, subconsciously or not, for the deficiencies in her own mothering.

Hilda's vast experience of hostessing at countless grand gatherings in Shanghai and Moscow made her the ideal guest at the Embassy, and she provided invaluable support for the Wangs at their many social gatherings. On one snowy afternoon in February 1938, the Ambassador and his daughters entertained at tea in honor of Paul Yubin, Bishop of Nanjing, who had just arrived in Washington to raise support for Chinese war refugees.[17] Standing in the receiving line at the Bishop's side, Hilda helped the Wangs to welcome their guests, and soon the party was in full swing. Representatives of Spain, South Africa, and the Soviet Union mingled with their counterparts from Dominica, Chile and Bulgaria. As dusk descended and great flakes of snow began to fall, travel to the Embassy became increasingly difficult, but still the visitors continued to arrive. Then suddenly the heavy blanket of snow caused a power outage. Abrupt darkness fell on the Embassy, and momentarily, the bright conversation was stilled. Unperturbed by this contingency, Hilda called for tall candles to be lit and the guests stayed on, enchanted by the soft illumination and the charming, antique courtesy of their hosts.

When Washington society discovered that Hilda had seen diplomatic corps service in London, Paris, Rome, Berlin and Copenhagen, and had won renown for her effective orations on Geneva's world stage, she was deluged with requests to speak to special interest groups throughout the city. In her addresses to the Chevy Chase Women's Club and the women students of the National School of Law, she had the full attention of her audiences as she read aloud several clauses of the 1927 Tanaka Memorial. She claimed they verified Japanese aspirations to world domination, and this thesis was supported by the dastardly work of Japanese agents who were presently hard at work in India, and even America, endeavoring to persuade minority races of color to unite with them against their white oppressors. In addition, she declared, Japan's repeated overtures to Mexico demonstrated that, ready or not, the seemingly distant conflict in the Far East would soon impact the peace and security of the United States.

On May 16, 1938, peace and security were very much on the minds of the fifteen hundred souls who gathered at a rally convened by the American League for Peace and Democracy at Washington's Rialto Theatre. On China's behalf, Hilda spoke in hawk-like tones and told the crowd, "If China wants to preserve her democratic principles and national existence, she must defend them diligently and fearlessly."[18] She was joined onstage by Haru Matsui, an intellectual Japanese peace activist who fearlessly spoke out in opposition to her homeland's aggression against China. Together, the two women announced that they were contemplating a lecturing air tour of America to promote a boycott of Japan.[19]

In a more frivolous vein, Hilda took time out to model Chinese garments at a fashion show in aid of her country's war refugees. She created a sensation when she appeared on stage in a white satin Chinese dress, her shoulders draped with a fur cape of snow white ermine. The next day, photographic proof of her alluring beauty appeared on the front pages of newspapers across America.[20] The next month, she made sartorial headlines yet again when she was spotted at a large tea party convened at D.C.'s Congressional Club. Mrs. John Nance Garner, wife of the American vice-president, was also in attendance, but it was aviatrix Miss Hilda Yan, wearing a mustard yellow hat and a silver fox fur cape, who stole the spotlight.

Her escalating popularity was reflected by her burgeoning engagement calendar. Although the volume of her speaking appointments increased apace, she was never short of new material for her speeches; she simply augmented them with the latest health statistics dispatched by her father.

"Right now the food supplies are dangerously low," she warned, "with only enough to last another six weeks in certain areas." She also pointed out that the war was no respecter of persons. "Thousands of refugees are without clothes, shoes or homes—rich and poor alike."[21]

Hilda asked for American solidarity with these unfortunate refugees, and urged women to boycott the purchase of silk hosiery loomed by Japanese mills. "Wear lisle for a while, it's the style," she quipped, but it was a hard sell. One of the popular jokes making the rounds asked the question, "What happens to girls who wear lisle hose?" The flat answer was, "Nothing."

In the midst of all this busyness, it is difficult to know when Hilda found time to practice her flying. In constant demand as a speaker, she was barely able to choreograph her public engagements, let alone dedicate herself to the study of aviation principles. On one occasion, due to her participation in a radio broadcast and a vital conference on world peace on the same afternoon, she was obliged at the last minute to back out of a third engagement, a function to which she had been invited as guest of honor. Still the invitations kept on coming. By the end of May 1938, she was beholden to so many persons and organizations in Washington that she decided to return their hospitality all at once by hosting a large reception at the Mayflower Hotel. Shimmering in an ivory silk *qipao* garnished with a corsage of sweet-scented white gardenias, Hilda stood tall and slim at the entrance and personally greeted each of her two hundred invited guests. They included prominent representatives of the House, Senate, diplomatic corps, and armed forces, but among the most important of her invitees were members of the Friends of China association who were offering to sponsor her contemplated flying lecture tour of America. Mrs. Henry Cabot Lodge was one of the more influential members of that committee's executive body.[22]

In addition to the many radio interviews and speeches she made on China's behalf in the nation's capital, Hilda also spent considerable time in New York City, where she became involved with a number of service organizations, notably the Order of the Eastern Star and the American branch of the University Women's Club. One of the more topical societies she chose to support was the Chinese Women's Relief Association of New York whose headquarters was located at 5 East 57th Street. In September 1937, the relief association ramped up its activities and became a magnet for competent Chinese nationals in the city who were anxious to 'do their bit' for the home country.[23] In February 1938, this involved organizing a loan exhibition of Chinese art treasures culled from the personal collections of American women. Acknowledging her organizational efficiency, the association elected Hilda as vice-president in April of that year. She served on the board with several women who were old friends from Shanghai, including the artist, Mai-Mai Sze, daughter of the former Washington ambassador, Dr. Alfred Sze, and Mrs. Xu Zhaodui (Mrs. Frank Co Tui), wife of the prominent physician founder of the American Bureau of Medical Aid to China (ABMAC). The ABMAC was an organization with which Hilda was to become increasingly involved.

Back in the Far East, despite the hostilities that ravaged their country and the myriad war-related duties that claimed their attention, members of the Yan family continued to be concerned for Hilda's welfare. In early March 1938, her uncle Huiqing made a special visit to Fuqing's home to talk about Hilda, and the next day, his concern remained so great that he continued the conversation with his brother by post.[24] Were the brothers once more fretting about her social life, or did they worry about the potential perils associated with her flying training which, when combined with her hectic schedule, held considerable potential for disaster? It is possible they thought that she might make a rather poor aviator. A notoriously alarming driver (her grandson recalls that his parents refused to let him ride as a passenger in any automobile operated by Hilda), there was no reason to expect that her flying skills would be much better.[25]

Throughout the war, Hilda kept in touch with her family, and in April, her uncle was able to confide to his diary that his niece had a new admirer.[26] Unfortunately, he offers no clue as to the identity of this individual. Hilda's new passion for flight animated her person and made her more attractive than usual.

By the fall of 1938, she still gave as her official address the Chinese Embassy in Washington, D.C., but in fact, Hilda's passion for the study of aviation had caused her to take quarters at 109 14th Street in Garden City. This address was a mere mile and a half from Roosevelt Field, but worlds away from the mad social whirl of New York and Washington. Within earshot of the busy airport, and just minutes from her flying lessons, the roar of aircraft overhead served as a constant reminder of her objective. Applying herself to the grindstone of flight theory, she intensified her dedication to her studies.

Her perseverance paid off. On November 10, 1938, Hilda graduated from Private Ground School, and, five days later, received certification that she had also graduated from the Private Pilot's Flight Course at the Flying School Division of Safair, Inc. Miss Hilda Yaqing Yan was entitled to all the rights and privileges pertaining to graduation. Not only had she passed her exams, she had done a splendid job. Her flying grade was 80%, as was her score in Civil Air Regulations, and she received 90% on her navigation and meteorology tests. By the end of the course, she had flown twenty-five dual and twenty-one solo hours in at least two different aircraft, the company's Fleet Trainer and the Curtiss-Wright Sedan. Commemorating the event, the local newspapers printed a photo of Hilda, appropriately helmeted and goggled, in its social pages. She had achieved her goal and was now a fully fledged aviatrix, chaffing at the bit to serve her country.

6. AID TO CHINA

By 1939, in the face of ongoing incursions by the Japanese, the gigantic problems associated with Chinese war refugees and their relief had become acute. Literally millions of persons had been displaced by the war, and the twin scourges of disease and famine were omnipresent. As usual, Hilda's family was at the forefront of those who labored to ease the suffering. When the Japanese invaded Shanghai in August 1937, her father, Dr. Yan Fuqing, had initiated a school that mobilized teachers, students, and health personnel in the formation of a medical ambulance corps, and he personally rushed to the front and rear areas of the conflict to serve those in distress. For his stellar organizational capabilities, he was made the city's Rescue/Defense Committee director, as well as head of the Chinese Red Cross. With his vast experience in managing the war effort on the medical front, which included his work during the Revolution and the violent warlord period that succeeded it, he was the logical choice to oversee the Nation's health during the emergency, and in 1938, he was appointed Chief Minister of the National Government's Health Bureau.

This was an unenviable task in wartime, but Dr. Yan was ever the able administrator and energetic perfectionist, and it is difficult to imagine a more appropriate person for the job. That same year, his brother Yan Huiqing, who had served as president of the Red Cross Society of China in 1924, was appointed chairman of the International Red Cross in Shanghai. His long years in the foreign service, and his wide acquaintance with highly-placed individuals in governments around the world, guaranteed his ability to make valuable contributions to the workings of that organization at the time of its utmost need.[1] Remarkably, then, the two brothers served concurrently as the top administrators of the nation's foremost health and relief agencies at one of the most critical junctures in China's recorded history.

In April 1938, a National Relief Commission was established, and it had as its mission the succor of refugees from war-stricken zones, as well as their placement in productive enterprises in those districts not yet touched by the conflict. This scheme eventually evolved into the famous 'Resistance and Reconstruction' program whereby civilians, universities, and industries were removed from war-torn areas and transported into the interior under cover of the military. The relocation of millions of people required the establishment of many costly way-stations and hospitals *en route*. Meanwhile, representatives were dispatched ahead of the evacuees to examine potential areas of re-settlement, and money was allocated to those areas so that the refugees could more readily establish their new farms and businesses.

Of course, many were not so lucky. Air raids and enemy incursions resulted in the deaths of hundreds of thousands of civilians. Even more were left alive, but grievously wounded. Medical relief for these persons entailed vast expense and a huge bureaucracy. However, another enemy proved to be just as omnipotent as the Japanese. In an effort to halt the enemy's incursion, in 1938, the Yellow River, Huang He, was diverted, but while this drastic expediency only served to slow Japanese progress, its deadly waters killed more than nine hundred thousand Chinese and rendered many millions more homeless. The dispatch of relief units to the flood-stricken areas proved to be costly. In August of 1937, $30,000 was appropriated specifically for relief work; exactly one year later, the amount had ballooned to $3,450,000 with no end in sight.[2]

With her infrastructure in tatters, there was only one way for China to levy sufficient funds to cover these run-away costs. Money had to be sought overseas. Hilda was already abroad, had many influential friends, and was well-placed to help raise these vital dollars. The War Refugees Relief Committee assisted those who had been relocated to the interior and was perhaps the most important of the vital groups that operated under the wider umbrella of the National Relief Committee. Its supreme representative in the United States was the Vicar Apostolic of Nanjing, Bishop Paul Yubin, an important figure with whom Hilda was now well-acquainted, having worked with him on many important Washington committees. The Bishop recognized the powerful gifts of oratory that the charismatic Miss Yan possessed, and he lay siege, urging her to apply her considerable talent and energies to his organization. For her part, Hilda did not need much persuading. Already sold on the committee's goals, and confident in the Bishop's integrity, she agreed to work on his behalf. Soon she would receive assistance from the famed Chinese woman pilot, Li Xiaqing.

In late October 1938, Miss Li, China's so-called 'First Aviatrix,' arrived in San Francisco just as Hilda was approaching the end of her flight training, and in the New Year of 1939, Li Xiaqing flew to New York to meet with Hilda and plot a complicated and ambitious scheme to raise support for Bishop Yubin's refugees. Planning to acquire two light aircraft, the two women determined that, between them, they could fly to all the prominent cities of the United States. Their combined flights would amount to over fifteen thousand air miles and many dangerous and wearying weeks of travel, but in the end, their barnstorming tour of America would highlight the extent of China's suffering and raise the vitally needed funds.

If nothing else, the women could consider their odyssey a success if they were able to convince the U.S. to stop supplying Japan with fuel and steel, materiel that the enemy immediately converted into armaments for use against China. They could also warn America, as Hilda had already been doing, that the Imperialist forces were not likely to confine their attentions to the Far East alone; it was inevitable that other Pacific Rim nations—including the United States—would one day fall prey to their depredations. Chongqing had already dispatched continuous delegations of bureaucrats to petition the American public, but they met with little tangible success. Hilda and Xiaqing confidently hoped that this same message, delivered by lovely and cultured women descending from the sky in brightly-colored aircraft, would receive a wider and more receptive audience.

Their ambitious project required fastidious advance planning. The women needed, and were granted, permission from the U.S. Government to carry out their appeal, and they also requested, and received, the assistance of the State Department in securing aircraft *pro bono* for their temporary use. Famed American aviatrix, Jacqueline Cochran, was deputized to act as a go-between.

With the diligence of generals planning a battle, Xiaqing and Hilda drew up an itinerary of the cities they could not afford to miss, and armed with navigational charts, they calculated the distances they could fly easily and safely at one go. Estimating their dates of arrival and departure, they liaised with the Relief for China organizations (by this time, they could be found in almost every city in the United States) to arrange for halls to be booked and publicity to be broadcast in advance of their appearance. Li Xiaqing, whose aeronautical career already included flights that spanned the length and breadth of China, was elected to fly the longer distances; her tour would take in almost every state in the Union and would wind up in mid-June. Hilda's itinerary required that she visit even more cities than her colleague, but her tour would be confined to relatively short jaunts in the eastern states of America only, and would amount to some 6,500 miles compared to Miss Li's more than 10,000-mile journey. Hilda expected to return to New York City on the last day of July 1939.

The women each prepared a slick press package for distribution to representatives of the media. Li Xiaqing was billed as 'China's First Woman of the Air' and Hilda was dubbed 'China's Amelia Earhart' (The latter was perhaps an unfortunate comparison considering it was just two years since the famous woman pilot had gone missing somewhere over the Pacific and was presumed dead). To lend additional legitimacy to their appeal on behalf of refugees, the aviatrixes secured the sponsorship of several prominent and well-respected Americans. The list of those who were persuaded to support the tour was impressive, and included Colonel and Mrs. Theodore Roosevelt Jr., Helen Keller, Postmaster-General James Farley, beautician Elizabeth Arden, actor Douglas Fairbanks, author Fanny Hurst, eminent journalists William Allen White and John Kieran, aviatrix Jacqueline Cochran, philanthropist Mrs. C.H. Wang, and the glamorous wife of China's ambassador to France, Madame Wellington Koo.

As the prime object of the tour was to raise funds to assist the refugees, additional respectability was conferred by the involvement of the two highly esteemed churchmen, His Excellency Paul Yubin, Archbishop of Nanjing, and Monsignor Barry O'Toole, professor and president of the Fujen Catholic University in Beijing. While Bishop Yu was director of the committee, Father O'Toole was its secretary-treasurer. Rather than accept contributions themselves, for reasons of safety the women would request that China sympathizers forward their donations directly to Father O'Toole in Washington, D.C., who, in turn, guaranteed the direct transfer of these monies to the National Relief Commission in Chongqing.

Hilda and Xiaqing successfully secured two light monoplanes for their tours, one from Walter Beech, the Kansas aircraft manufacturer, and the other from the Porterfield Aircraft Corporation. After taking off and flying their separate ways, the women decided that their barnstorming whirl should close in New York City. This final destination was no idle choice. The entire planet was focused on the great metropolis that was playing host to the 1939 World's Fair.

Early in the morning of March 23, 1939, Hilda Yan and Li Xiaqing arrived at Floyd Bennett airfield in a state of high excitement. The tedious planning stages were over, and their great American tour was about to begin. As yet, they had only one aircraft at their disposal, a Stinson Reliant SR-9B monoplane (NC-17174). It had been donated for Miss Li's use, and sat waiting on the tarmac, a gleaming dragon reposing in the sunshine, resplendent in its new paint job of red with yellow trim. Its name, *Spirit of New China,* was boldly painted on the aircraft's doors and underwings, and reflected the vitality and courage of the two modern Chinese representatives who were embarking on this risky venture for the benefit of their countrymen.

Li Xiaqing, the vastly more experienced pilot, deferred to her newly graduated colleague, and Hilda was elected to take the left-hand seat. She was now razor thin, testament both to the intensity of her war efforts, and to her worry for loved ones back home. The women were casually dressed for this first leg of their journey, Li Xiaqing in trousers and a three-quarter length coat, and Hilda in her usual flying gear—a fur-collared bomber jacket, brown leather helmet, silk scarf and goggles. Hilda throttled up the engine, taxied off down the runway, and lifted off into the waiting blue sky. And so their odyssey began.

Their first port of call, Philadelphia, was less than a hundred miles away, and their flight to that city was uneventful. They landed across the river from the metropolitan area at Camden airfield. The publicity machine had already ground into action, and they were met by the press and an enthusiastic welcoming committee that buried the women in huge bouquets of flowers, the first of many fragrant tributes they would receive over the course of the tour.

The next day, they took off for Washington, D.C., nerve center of the War Refugees Relief Committee, and a city already in thrall to Hilda's sophistication and intelligence. As she landed and taxied to the apron, Hilda could see the tall figure of Bishop Yubin looming over the welcoming delegation. Everyone on the committee was doing his best for the homeland, but these women had taken their commitment to the Chinese people to a new level, and the Bishop was anxious to be there in person to demonstrate his pride in their courage and devotion. Garlanded with roses when they emerged from the cockpit, the two women positioned themselves beside the *Spirit of New China* on this, their second flying day on the job, and smiled self-consciously for news photographers. Garnering publicity would be an important part of their responsibilities and they were resigned, but not yet accustomed, to the spotlight's glare. In the midst of this extravagant attention, they were determined never to forget the plight of the thirty million suffering refugees they were representing.

That evening, Bishop Yubin hosted a gala dinner in the women's honor at the popular Chinese Lantern Restaurant near Washington's Union Station. The Bishop was a large and impressive-looking man, and a well-known figure in China and America. He liked to credit his athletic build to the hearty diet of meat and wheat that he enjoyed while growing up in his native Manchuria. He was currently on his own lecture tour of America on behalf of the War Refugees Relief Committee, and having carefully planned his return to the capital to coincide with the flyers' arrival, he now hosted his guests with jovial enthusiasm. As the incoming pilot of the *Spirit of New China*, Hilda blushingly occupied center stage that night. Other guests at this celebratory feast included the tour's treasurer, Father Barry O'Toole, the Twin Oaks Embassy staff, overseas Chinese dignitaries and Washington news reporters.

Over the next few days, the women continued to fly together to nearby cities on behalf of the refugees until Hilda's own plane finally arrived by special delivery. On April 3, 1939, it was flown into Washington airport by the eminent American aviator, Colonel Roscoe Turner. The celebrated daredevil pilot, who held a clutch of racing titles and was one of the most famous flyers in the world, touched down wearing his trademark military-looking outfit—a peaked cap and battered leather trench coat. The notion of arranging for this flamboyant pilot to deliver the plane and present it personally to Hilda was a brilliant publicity coup, and virtually guaranteed extensive coverage of the event. While the flashbulbs of press cameramen popped enthusiastically, the delicate-looking Miss Yan shook hands with the grizzled veteran, extending her thin ivory arm from the fashionably boxy fur draped over her shoulders. Beneath, Hilda wore an ankle-length *qipao* that broadly announced her Far Eastern origins, but her high-heeled shoes asserted just as loudly that she was also a modern woman, comfortable in the West.

The aircraft presented to her was a Porterfield 35-W, a two-passenger high-wing cabin monoplane.[3] Roscoe Turner was vice-president of the Porterfield aircraft company, a fresh appointment he had just received, and it is possible that this aeroplane, although of a model that was three years old, embodied some custom design elements that were introduced by him.[4] The publicity engendered by the presentation of this gift plane by the flashy aviator was as valuable to Turner's business as it was to the successful kick-off of Hilda's goodwill mission. Painted blood red, the Porterfield monoplane bore the same name as Miss Li's aircraft—*Spirit of New China*—and in an identical manner, this was printed on the cockpit doors and sprawled in bold lettering across the plane's under wings. As well, the nose of the Porterfield bore the crossed flags of the United States of America and the Republic of China.[5] However, there the similarities ended. Hilda's aircraft could not compete with Miss Li's Stinson, a larger and more powerful machine that enjoyed a much longer range and was able to fly almost twice as far without having to refuel. More than once on her ill-fated tour, Hilda would have cause to envy this valuable attribute.

At the outset, however, she was delighted with the aircraft, and when the first day of her expedition dawned brilliantly sunny and warm, it seemed that even the weather was blessing the enterprise. Dressed in the classic uniform of the aviatrix—goggles, white coveralls and leather helmet—Hilda posed for photographs before climbing into the cockpit and lifting off into the blue. The next several weeks were a blur of distance flying and public engagements: Richmond, Raleigh, Columbia, Savannah, Jacksonville… 'China's Amelia Earhart' touched down confidently at her destination cities and delivered eloquent speeches in precise English, but the genteel aviatrix would grow noticeably belligerent when proudly describing the activities of the Chinese guerrillas who were snapping at the heels of the invader.

With one eye always cocked on the weather, and the other on her speech, Hilda spent anywhere from two to three days in each city until it was time to move on to the next. Safety was always uppermost, and it was important she be rested before flying off to another engagement, but when required to make several public speeches during the day, and another one at the requisite evening banquet, adequate relaxation was sometimes a luxury. She was also plagued by anxiety regarding the performance of her aircraft. Its tank held eighteen gallons of fuel, sufficient to carry her over a distance of three hundred miles, but due to some glitch in the engine—perhaps an incorrectly adjusted carburetor—she had to be extra vigilant about the distances she was flying. As she stated in one of her regular reports to the Bishop's office, mechanical problems had already caused her to make several forced landings, a nerve-wracking expediency that steadily gnawed at her confidence in the aircraft.

Hilda had gradually worked her way southward and was making a tour of Alabama when the accident occurred. She had made an uneventful touchdown in Mobile on Thursday afternoon, April 27, where, as usual, the arrival of the winsome aviatrix was well received. After continuous travel, Hilda was finally going to be in one place for a few days, and was staying, not in an impersonal hotel, but at the comfortable home of Tom and Rose Chin, a couple prominent in the local Chinese community.

Hilda applied herself to the crowd of Mobile citizens who gathered to hear her address, and by all accounts, made quite an impression. Tailoring her speech to the interests of her listeners, Hilda cautioned that, in its drive for self-sufficiency, Japan was plotting nothing less than the downfall of Alabama's cotton empire. Having captured the undivided attention of her audience, she went on to explain that Japanese cotton mills, hitherto dependent upon American and Brazilian cotton, would soon be receiving their raw materials from high-yielding cotton fields planted in China by the Japanese usurpers.

7. MAY DAY

With mission accomplished in Mobile, Hilda set her sights toward Birmingham, Alabama, her next port of call. On Monday morning, May 1, 1939, the weather was clear, the winds were light, and the day promised to be sunny and warm. In short, flying conditions were ideal. She took off from Mobile's Bates Field and headed in a northeasterly direction toward Birmingham where she was slated to speak at a banquet that very afternoon. She never kept that engagement.

Although she followed the rail tracks that led from Mobile to her destination, Hilda somehow lost her bearings, and grew anxious when she realized she was running low on fuel.[1] Knowing that few sophisticated service facilities existed in rural areas, she also feared having to make another forced landing. This added to her disquiet. Rather than attempt to reach Birmingham at one go, she decided it would be wiser to touch down and refuel at the state capital of Montgomery, a city that lay mid-way between her points of departure and arrival. In an effort to conserve fuel, she flew at low altitude, but this tactic backfired when she apparently flew too low to spot Montgomery. She overshot it by some ten miles before she realized her error. Sighting a large farmhouse in the countryside below, she decided to cut her losses by landing and asking for directions to the capital city. The house was bordered by a long green field running from east to west, hedged by windbreaks of soaring mock orange shrubs. She reckoned that the field was about a thousand feet long, a potential runway that was of adequate length for a safe landing and takeoff.

The farm she had spotted was the residence of the Joe Chambliss family, and their property was located a mile south of Prattville, Alabama, a farming community of some twenty-five hundred souls just northwest of Montgomery. A black woman farm worker spotted Hilda's descent to earth, and, as she had never before seen an aircraft at close quarters, she ran off in terror to fetch Mrs. Chambliss. The lady of the house seemed slightly less taken aback by Hilda's unusual arrival, and when the aviatrix hopped out of the plane, the two women chatted briefly before Mrs. Chambliss pointed her striking visitor in the direction of the Montgomery Municipal Airport.

Being low on fuel, Hilda had kept the motor running during this exchange, and she wasted no time in jumping back into the aircraft and taxiing to the top of the field. Then she revved up and sped off down her runway. The oats growing at the field's edge were only a foot high, but as Hilda raced along, she was unpleasantly shocked to discover that the grain growing luxuriantly in the middle was fully three times that height. It wrapped around the wheels of her aircraft and dragged at its underbelly. When it became apparent she could not pick up sufficient speed to clear the windbreak at the end of the field, Hilda aborted the takeoff and taxied slowly back to her starting point.

Hilda was suddenly alive to the realization that, if she could not achieve adequate groundspeed, she could well be trapped. The gnawing anxiety that had been her almost constant companion since the tour began kicked in with a vengeance.

With time and fuel running out, she decided on a risky maneuver for her next takeoff attempt. She gazed into the distance at the high windbreak of mature mock orange trees at the end of the field. There was a ten- to fifteen-foot gap in the middle of the ragged hedge, and this represented a possible route of escape to the trapped aviatrix. If she were able to achieve sufficient groundspeed—enough to let her become airborne—she could bank her wings slightly just after takeoff, dip one wing into this gap, and raise the other over the taller section of the shrubbery. With a bit of skill and a great deal of luck, she could just clear the fragrant barrier and be on her way. She decided to put her plan into effect. On this, her second attempt, she applied more throttle at the outset, and raced at maximum speed down the field. When it seemed she had sufficient momentum to clear the hedge, she pulled back on the stick and lifted off into the blue.

It was all over in a second.

Unable to climb steeply enough or swiftly enough, one of the wings just clipped the flowering hedge, and in the next instant, the *Spirit of New China* was sent plummeting earthward. With a sickening thud, the aircraft crashed perpendicularly near a clump of trees, its propeller drilling a passage into the Alabama soil. The tremendous force of the impact sent Hilda crashing forward onto the control panel, a helpless victim of gravity, and the baggage stowed in the rear of the plane came tumbling down on her back. In the breathless silence that followed the collision, the only sound was the hiss of escaping fuel. Its reek roused Hilda to semi-consciousness, and she slowly became aware that she had survived, but was trapped.

By purest chance, two young local men, Joe Andrews and Taxi Nosworthy, were driving along the edge of the field in a pick-up truck when they spotted the downed aircraft, weirdly vertical with its tail pointing skyward. They raced to the scene.

"I didn't see the crash," Andrews later told reporters, "but we must have gotten there minutes after it happened. Gasoline was spewing out of the plane and I thought it might explode at any time."

The youths were not intimidated by the obvious danger. Andrews continued:

"I got to the plane and could see Miss [Yan] struggling with her hand across her face to open the door. Heavy bags pinned her right arm behind her. I opened the door, and, working fast, removed the bags and tried to take her out. I had to get her parachute off before I could manage it."

The two boys lifted Hilda as gently and expediently as possible out of the Porterfield, and, still mindful that it might explode, led her away from the disabled aircraft to their vehicle. They were relieved to note that their crash victim did not seem to be seriously injured.

"Taxi and I put her in the car," Andrews recalled. "She was dazed but rational, and asked us to get her pocketbook and something else. We did. As we drove her to the hospital, she kept adjusting the mirror and trying to look at her face."[2]

Small wonder. The terrific force of the impact had sent Hilda's lovely countenance, the pride of Shanghai, smashing into the control panel with sufficient force to splinter the glass dials and spatter them with her blood. The young men rushed the injured aviatrix to the Prattville General Hospital, by which time she had lapsed into unconsciousness. The town's physician, Dr. George Taylor, made an initial examination, but aside from diagnosing shock and facial lacerations, and the possibility that her nose might be broken, he could not know if she were suffering more serious internal injuries until x-rays could be taken.

News of the Chinese aviatrix and her strange accident traveled rapidly in the small town, and a crowd of locals rushed to the crash site to witness the up-ended aircraft for themselves. The press was also quick on the scene to interview the principals involved. Meanwhile, Dr. Taylor notified the appropriate authorities in Washington of Miss Yan's mishap, and the Chinese Embassy staff immediately relayed this shocking news to their consular colleagues throughout America and abroad.

Soon the tiny Prattville hospital became the unlikely focus of international attention, and within hours, was bombarded with over fifty telegrams and phone calls from New York, San Francisco, Washington, D.C. and other large centers. It was impossible for Dr. Taylor to respond to the concerns of all these worried well-wishers, however, he did take time to send a wire to Hilda's colleague, Li Xiaqing, who was on tour in Sacramento, CA and had both a personal and professional interest in the incident.

"Face badly lacerated," he telegraphed, "Has regained consciousness impossible to determine seriousness of injury for 18 hours yet."

Remarkably, even Hilda's father in China learned of the accident only a few hours after it occurred, and, because initial reports suggested her condition was grave, the anxious parent made a frantic telephone call to Prattville. This technological feat was made possible, in the days before the laying of oceanic cables, by overseas radiotelephone, the circuitry of which had been established only a few years before. Over the crackling line, Dr. Yan spoke personally to Dr. Taylor, and the latter calmed the parent's fears as best he could, assuring him that his daughter's injuries did not appear to be life threatening.

In fact, Hilda was apparently nonplussed by the event, so much so that when she regained consciousness that afternoon (and in a move that surprised even the reporters), she allowed representatives of the press into her hospital room for what the *Montgomery Advertiser* described as "an ordeal of picture taking." The aviatrix allowed this intrusion on her privacy, the paper surmised, "because she realized the possible aid to her cause." It seems more likely, however, that Hilda was concussed and still in shock, and had little notion of what she was doing.

During the terrible seconds when she plunged to earth, she must have thought that the end had come, but apparently, even the horror of these last moments had been erased from her mind:

"Crash? Crash?" asked the dazed aviatrix lying prone on her hospital cot, a huge bandage covering her nose and mouth. "How stupid of me. My poor people. I must work for them. Did I crash? I must work for my people. I don't want to stop."

As photographers scrambled to capture images of the pale flyer languishing in bed, her raven curls and red-varnished fingernails providing a startling counterpoint to the starched whiteness of the sheets, Hilda grew more calm when she was reassured that neither the damage to her aircraft, nor to her person, was serious. Then she seemed to shrug off her injuries, and pointedly laid blame for the incident where she felt it belonged.

"If the Japanese had not invaded China," she declared with some vehemence, "it would not have happened."[3]

The next day, the story of Miss Yan's accident was front page news from coast to coast. The *San Francisco Chronicle* dramatically reported, "Severely injured as her plane, 'Spirit of New China,' crashed, Hilda [Yan], pretty Chinese girl flyer, regained consciousness tonight, turned in her hospital bed and said, 'I would gladly die for the cause.'" A portrait of the downed pilot taken in happier times appeared above the fold on the front page of the *Washington Post*, and a photo of the upended aircraft, its nose stuck the ground, even ended up in a Canadian paper. "End of Goodwill Tour," morosely announced the *Victoria Daily Colonist*.[4]

After initial worries over her condition had subsided, representatives of the War Refugees Relief Committee must have paused to marvel over the ironic turn of events. Hilda's crash had brought better publicity to their cause than they ever dreamed possible. Their aviatrix was accomplishing more for China lying flat on her back in the Prattville infirmary than she had when she was airborne.

Although their initial concerns had been allayed, Hilda's family in the Far East was still anxious. Exercising his clout as a senior member of the diplomatic corps, Hilda's uncle Yan Huiqing fired off a telegram to Washington and received an almost immediate response from the Chinese Embassy describing his niece's crash landing and its consequences. Hilda's ex-husband, P.T., who was working with the evacuated Nationalist Government in Chongqing, was also kept apprised of her condition, and he telegraphed whatever scraps of news he was able to receive to the rest of the family. They learned that the day after the accident, an ambulance had conveyed her to St. Margaret's Hospital in nearby Montgomery, a larger institution where x-ray facilities were available.[5]

No sooner was Hilda admitted to a hospital ward in the Alabama capital than the state's Governor, Frank M. Dixon, hurried over to comfort the downed celebrity. A decorated air veteran of World War I who had lost a leg in combat, the Governor regarded Hilda as a kindred spirit, a courageous flying casualty of war. He was the first in a steady stream of distinguished Alabamans to beat a path to her hospital bed, all of whom, it is safe to say, pledged healthy donations to the Relief fund as tangible demonstrations of their esteem and goodwill. On behalf of the Embassy, the Chinese military attaché in America, the urbane aviator, Colonel Kuo Teh-chuan, lost no time in flying in from Washington, D.C. to see for himself that Hilda was comfortable. He was delighted to find her relaxed and amiable.[6]

Sidney Li, Bishop Yubin's secretary, also arrived in Montgomery to visit the patient and he even made arrangements to take a reconnaissance flight over the Chambliss farm where the accident occurred. On his return to the hospital, he agreed with Hilda that, from the air, the benign-looking field she had chosen as her runway certainly looked like the best possible site in the vicinity to make an emergency landing. He brought her greetings from Dr. H.H. Kong, P.T.'s employer, who sent warm words of praise for the fine work that Hilda and Miss Li were accomplishing in America.

Meanwhile, Hilda's injuries had been x-rayed and authorities discovered she had suffered no serious internal damage. One of the hospital staff confirmed to the press that, despite the terrifying accident and the head injuries their patient had sustained, Miss Yan was psychologically intact and maintaining a stoic outlook. He confided that Hilda was "displaying a fine sense of humor and is standing the ordeal of an invalid well."

So astonishing was the appearance of this cultured Chinese woman in the relatively insular community of the Deep South, and so startling the mode of her arrival, Hilda understandably became a hot topic in the local papers. Hitherto, the Far Eastern conflict had seemed remote and unreal; now Alabamans found it had literally fallen into their backyards.

The *Birmingham News* pragmatically remarked that Hilda's "unfortunate crash should inspire among Americans a more determined effort to aid the cause she represents." An editorial in the *Birmingham Age-Herald* waxed more lyrical, and mused on the extraordinary circumstances that had led to a "Chinese girl flying and falling for peace in Alabama," her accident having been caused by nothing more sinister than Alabama oats and a mock orange tree. This relatively small incident was seen as a metaphor for the larger calamity. "Great armies and a lone girl flier for peace measure the chasm," reflected the editor, "terror and sacrifice contend for the earth."[7]

Cartoonists even got into the act, depicting China as a mighty soldier, roused to defend its homeland, and menaced by a tiny, ranting Japanese officer. Another showed Miss Hilda zooming low in her aircraft over an Alabama highway which (in the cartoon, at least) was now thoughtfully painted with prominent, arrowed directions to Montgomery so the aviatrix could not possibly lose her way again.

Amidst all the hoopla, Hilda lay quietly in her hospital bed and pondered over her miraculous escape from serious injury or death. She remained hospitalized for ten days, one of the longest periods of forced inactivity she had experienced in recent years, and had ample opportunity to review her life and its purpose. Had she been spared for a reason, she wondered, and had the crash been an instrument to goad her into deeper consideration of the meaning of her existence? Over the next several years, these thoughts were never far from the surface.

St. Margaret's discharged Hilda on May 11, 1939. Charmed hospital officials were sorry to see her go, but she was eager to be off and departed the next day for Washington, D.C., advising her new Southern friends that she could be reached through Father O'Toole. She left in her wake the usual gaggle of admirers and well-wishers. It appears that she still had no fixed plans, and, as her doctor had ordered rest and repose for another two weeks, she went to spend the remainder of her convalescence at Twin Oaks, the Chinese Embassy. Witty family friend and one of China's foremost intellectuals, Hu Shi, was now in residence as Ambassador, and the well-stocked library was as alluring as ever.[8]

While Hilda mended in Washington, mechanics at the Montgomery airfield patched up her aircraft. She had promised that she would return, possibly after completion of repairs, to reclaim the *Spirit of New China*, and at the end of May, she made good on that pledge, once more arriving in the Alabama capital. Before she did anything else, she checked in at the hospital where the doctors pronounced her healthy and fit, and gave her the green light to embark on a fresh round of speaking engagements.

After the wide publicity her accident had attracted, Montgomerians were keen to see and hear Hilda for themselves, and she was only too willing to give them that opportunity. One of the sponsors of her tour was Alabama-born Helen Keller, and, having secured the backing of the state's most respected daughter, she was assured of a warm welcome wherever she went. Hilda's agenda was packed. On Monday, May 23, she arrived at Montgomery City Hall where she showed a movie depicting the desperate situation in China. On Tuesday, she addressed a Rotary Club luncheon on 'What is Happening in the Far East,' and that same evening, gave a lecture at City Auditorium. On Wednesday, she was back at it, running the movie for an appreciative audience at the Exchange Club.

Honoring her work on the board of the Shanghai Y, the Montgomery

YWCA held a special tea party for Hilda at its Women's Residence. In a hall brightened with spring flowers and crammed with hundreds of women guests, Hilda described the horrors her countrymen were facing. As ever, she took pains to stress that Japan's leadership, and not the Japanese people, were to blame for the present conflict. China was fighting against an idea, not a nation, and she expressed her yearning for the day when her homeland and its invader could normalize relations once more.

In her spare time, Hilda answered her fan mail. The Montgomery Hospital handed over a stack of correspondence that had piled up while she had been in Washington, letters from people all across America who had been impressed by her courage and resolve, and had written to tell her so. Many requested her autograph, and she was happy to oblige... for a price. She charged a dollar for her signature in English, and another dollar for writing it in Chinese as well, with all proceeds going toward the thirty million of her fellow countrymen who were now refugees. The fee might seem steep, she admitted, but it was actually a humanitarian bargain; two dollars would save a life for two months.[9]

Hilda was back, capitalizing on the publicity surrounding her accident, and as effective and efficient as ever. However, she continued her tour of the South, not by air, but by automobile. Had she been so unsettled by the accident that she lost her nerve and feared to take to the skies again, or did her family—grateful that she had been spared—prevail upon her to forsake this dangerous activity, arguing that she could work for China just as effectively in some less hazardous capacity? Or perhaps she had made a rational and considered decision to abandon what she once thought had been her calling as an aviatrix and heed what she came to regard as a wake-up call, an intimation that her life's true vocation might be less circumscribed than she imagined, and that her efforts to secure peace and justice might become more spiritual than political.

After her tour of the South, Hilda returned to New York City. She had a plane to meet. On June 15, 1939, Li Xiaqing flew triumphant into that city after successful completion of her goodwill aerial tour of America, and Hilda was on hand to cheer her friend's arrival and to celebrate Li's 10,000-mile achievement. It was a bittersweet moment. While Hilda regretted not having completed her own tour of duty by air, yet she was relieved that Xiaqing had been delivered safely home, and that, together, their efforts had shone a brilliant spotlight on

China's desperate need for aid.

By mid-August, Hilda had escaped the noise and heat of New York to enjoy a well-earned vacation at Maine's charming seaside resort, Northeast Harbor, when she received an invitation from Governor Lewis O. Barrows to appear as a special guest at one of America's most popular air meets, the Maine Aero Rendezvous. The event was planning to focus on prominent women flyers, and the governor argued it would not be complete without the participation of Miss Hilda Yan. Her aero accident had earned huge headlines from coast to coast, and the organizers reckoned that the heroic Chinese aviatrix would attract large and interested crowds. Unwilling to pass up this first-rate opportunity to draw attention to the plight of her homeland, Hilda acquiesced and flew to Augusta, Maine where the event was held from August 26-27, 1939. As anticipated, the meet enjoyed good attendance, and the featured aviatrix, 'China's Amelia Earhart,' missed no opportunities to exploit her popularity. She was photographed participating in the festivities and shaking hands with high-profile American pilot, Laura Ingalls, and she granted interviews to the press. She explained the nature of her motivation to work on China's behalf.

"I am not employed by anyone," she revealed, "but I have been deeply moved by the crisis my country is facing, and when the spirit moves in that fashion, I must do all I can to help."[10]

This was Hilda's mission statement and it explained everything about her driving force. She was an activist, ruled by the heart, and impelled to obey the dictates of God and her conscience.

A couple of days later, she was off again, flying to Cleveland, Ohio, in the company of Li Xiaqing and Colonel Kuo Teh-chuan. Together, China's three representatives participated on their nation's behalf at America's most prestigious air show, the National Air Races, and then, duty done, they parted, and Hilda returned to the peace of Northeast Harbor to relax and complete her seaside vacation.

8. AMERCIAN BUREAU FOR MEDICAL AID TO CHINA

In the years before the eruption of World War II, there were relatively few international humanitarian causes competing for the hearts—and wallets—of

Westerners, and China's pleas for help in her war of resistance against the Japanese fell on fertile ground. A variety of 'Aid to China' funds sprouted up across North America. The cause for which Hilda had flown, the War Refugees Relief Committee, eventually merged into the China Emergency Relief Committee, a voluntary group formed and chaired by eminent author, Pearl S. Buck. Miss Buck's committee gradually joined hands with the American Bureau for Medical Aid to China (ABMAC), one of the most reputable of the many fundraising organizations. The Bureau was founded by Dr. Frank W. Xu Zhaodui (Dr. Frank Co Tui), a highly esteemed scientist and researcher who was head of the experimental surgery lab at New York University's School of Medicine.[1]

Dr. Xu took his philanthropic responsibilities seriously, and devoted about half of his time to the Bureau. A variety of eminent physicians and volunteers lent him their assistance, as did his wife, who had served with Hilda on the board of the Chinese Women's Relief Association. The eminent Colonel Theodore Roosevelt, Jr., who was one of those who had sponsored Hilda's flight, had taken on the presidency of the ABMAC. In the early days, the Colonel raised the bulk of the Bureau's relief money through so-called Rice Bowl parties—gala social evenings that enjoyed good attendance across Canada and the United States—and also through the activities of Pearl Buck's China Emergency Relief Committee. Miss Buck forwarded the funds raised by her committee to the ABMAC where they were used for the purchase of medical supplies that were sent from Rangoon into China's interior via the Burma Road.[2] A plethora of distinguished Americans and Chinese sat on the ABMAC's board, and these included many of Hilda's friends—Bishop Yubin, Anna May Wong, and Mrs. Edward H. Hume, wife of Yale-in-China's president whose life Hilda had saved in Changsha some ten years before.[3]

The ABMAC had no shortage of horrifying wartime statistics to convince the American public of the need for aid. Hilda's father, who, as China's National Minister of Health, was dug in at Chongqing with the rest of the government, regularly provided the world's wire services with figures so colossal that they were difficult to comprehend. To date, he reported in May 1939, there had been one million army casualties, six million children orphaned, and more than fifty million citizens rendered homeless refugees. Fully sixteen million of these were destitute and had to be supported by a government whose regular sources of income were laid waste by the war. Even worse, only six thousand doctors catered to the needs of China's total population of over four hundred million souls; this woefully inadequate number of health care professionals represented approximately half of the medical doctors practicing in New York City alone. Dr. Yan sent out an appeal to physicians around the world to come to China and tend to the lives and bodies shattered by Japanese air raids.[4]

Hilda became involved in promoting the ABMAC's agenda through public speaking. As a daughter of the Minister of Health, she was a credible speaker and was swamped with invitations to articulate her nation's needs. In July, she was interviewed on New York radio station WJZ as one of the 'Women of To-morrow,' and later that month, was invited to address a dinner held by the AB-MAC to honor Ambassador Hu Shi. As ever, she described the determination of the Chinese people to fight on despite the hardships they had endured. In October, the New York radio station WMCA delivered a live broadcast of her speech, "The Spirit of Young China," delivered at a Lion's Club luncheon. The next month, she was guest speaker at the annual general meeting of the World Center for Women's Archives.

However, any inroads she and her colleagues might have been making into the hearts and minds of the American people received a temporary set-back in early September 1939 when Adolf Hitler's military might rolled over Poland. Britain, the latter's ally, declared war on Germany, and for the next several months, all eyes focused on Europe and the growing emergency while America reluctantly debated the wisdom of entering the conflict. China now occupied second place, but its ongoing needs made some impact on New York's collective consciousness when October 10 (or 'Double Ten' to commemorate the anniversary of China's Republican revolution) was declared 'China Day' at that year's World's Fair. There were more than three weeks of events, includ-ing a new series of 'Rice Bowl' and other festivities to be held in more than six hundred cities throughout America.

In the lead-up to events, the Civilian Relief public relations machine moved into high gear. Famous musician, Artie Shaw, was commissioned to compose a special orchestration of the Chinese national anthem, *San Min Zhu Yi*, and school children were offered cash prizes for writing essays on the impor-tance of lending aid to China. New York's Chinatown festooned itself with lanterns and colorful banners while dragon dancers undulated through the streets, dodging exploding strings of sizzling red firecrackers. However, these special festivities were scarcely sufficient to put to flight the gloom that descended on Chinese nationals that fall. The war was going badly for China, and she was seriously short of committed allies.

For Hilda, however, these dark clouds were temporarily dispelled when, on October 28, she welcomed her beloved uncle, Yan Huiqing, to New York. He arrived in America aboard the *s.s. President Harrison*, and he was traveling in the company of his daughter, Nansheng and his niece, Lillian Shu, both of whom were about to begin their studies in American colleges. Yan himself had arrived to head up the Chinese delegation at an important meeting of the Institute of Pacific Relations, slated to be held that year at Virginia Beach, Virginia. The family reunion was a joyous one, and for their part, the newcomers were relieved to see for themselves that Hilda had suffered no long-term ill effects from her airplane crash six months before. The scar that ran downwards from the middle of her lower lip was still slightly apparent, but it tended, if anything, to enhance her unusual beauty. Hilda's family excitedly took turns to tell her about their voyage, unexpectedly extended when the war broke out in Europe and their British-registered boat had suddenly been pressed into military service. They found themselves stranded in Bombay. Yan Huiqing put this enforced leisure time to good use by meeting with Indian Congress leaders and Mr. Nehru, by whom, he informed Hilda, he had been deeply impressed. Three weeks later, they were able to catch the ship that finally carried them to New York.

The next day, Hilda treated her cousins to a tour of the World's Fair (it was in its closing days), and then on Halloween, she invited them to a rehearsal for a fashion show in which she was participating. The show, headlined as 'Chinese Dress, Old and New,' was scheduled to be part of New York City's upcoming Rice Bowl Ball. Hosted by the United Council for Civilian Relief in China, it promised to be a gala event attended by the cream of New York society.[5] Both Hilda and Li Xiaqing were active members of the Council's executive committee, chaired by Hollywood actress, Tallulah Bankhead. Sultry Miss Bankhead, 'the Wham from Alabam,' had spent much of her childhood in Montgomery where her father had served as congressman and her grandfather as senator, so she and Hilda were able to exchange fond reminiscences of people and places in the Old South. Both women were also fiercely opposed to America's isolationist policy that avoided committing the U.S. military to any of the serious conflicts that were then raging in the world.

However, Hilda and Tallulah had little time to talk politics; they were too busy planning the fashion show. 'Oriental' style had been in vogue since the war in the East had begun, and the planners anticipated a good turnout, but just to make sure, the names of the two, now famous, Chinese aviatrixes were used to promote the event.

Several of the antique gowns that Hilda and Xiaqing were asked to model were almost personalities in themselves (culled from Madame Sun Yat-sen's private collection, they included garments from the Imperial Palace and the Imperial Theater), but the modern Chinese outfits that were also part of the show were just as eye-catching. They were designed by none other than Zhang Qianying, known to the fashion world as Hélène Tsang, or 'Shanghai's Schiaparelli.' Miss Zhang had arrived in America in 1938, and, phoenix-like, re-established her business in New York where she used precious scraps of antique fabrics to create her lavish designs and raise support for her homeland. One of the slim hostess gowns she designed was fashioned out of soft velvet slashed with bright diagonal strips of Chinese satin, and Hilda's graceful modeling of this lovely garment and other outfits was captured on film by newsreel movie cameras.

It seemed as if all of New York was eager to ensure the event was a success. Saks Fifth Avenue loaned the models' shoes, Jacqueline Cochran donated a debutante's jewel case for the raffle, and Katharine Hepburn contributed two tickets from her successful Broadway play, *Philadelphia Story*. In the end, the Rice Bowl event, whose patrons included the Archduke and Archduchess Leopold of Austria and Princess Farid-es-Sultaneh of Persia, was a triumph, and the participation of the two famous aviatrixes was held to be at least partially responsible for its success.[6]

At the end of November, Hilda's private pilot's license expired, but she may have been too busy to notice. While her work for China occupied much of her time, she also had a new man in her life, known to history only as 'George,' and she appeared to be seriously involved with him. At the same time, P.T. Chen turned up in America. He had flown from China to San Francisco on the *Honolulu Clipper*, and he had recently arrived in New York *en route* to the Pan-

Pacific Relations Conference at Virginia Beach. He planned to attend the meeting with his fellow-delegate and former uncle-in-law, Yan Huiqing. The recent outbreak of war in Europe made travel difficult, and the usual roster of Chinese delegates were unable to arrange passage to the United States, but those who did manage to arrive decided to recruit additional members from the ranks of their colleagues in America. Hilda was one of those asked to attend the meeting.[7] Items on the conference agenda included social questions, and these certainly fell within Hilda's area of expertise. One of the most important issues that was due to be discussed was the appalling influence of the Japanese invasion on the trade and consumption of narcotics in China, the noxious use of which was reaching record levels.[8] The Institute was also interested in liaising with the Chinese relief agencies in America with which Hilda was affiliated.

Virginia Beach was located near the first permanent English settlement on American soil and as such was regarded as the 'Nation's Cradle.' Huiqing especially was looking forward to doing a little sightseeing.[9] It was like old times as Hilda and her uncle once more traveled together to the conference. They took rooms in the elegant Cavalier Hotel, the venue for the meeting where they discovered that, as the number of delegates was relatively low, the facility was far from crowded. The Japanese had refused to attend, and, due to the European war, official representatives from the United Kingdom, France, the Netherlands, Italy, and the Soviet Union all sent their regrets. It was also the tourist off-season. The delegates who did manage to convene rattled about in the near-empty hotel and they had the run of the place. Inevitably, P.T. and Hilda were thrown together, and with their uncle acting as buffer, their meetings were amiable, so much so that when the conference closed in early December, they made plans to drive together back to New York City. Huiqing closely scrutinized the interactions of the estranged couple, hoping to observe signs that they were not entirely indifferent to each other, but he confided to his diary that, although they seemed friendly enough, there appeared to be no possibility of reconciliation. He also idly wondered if his niece would marry George.[10] After a sightseeing excursion in the country, Huiqing diplomatically asked to be let off at Richmond. Hilda and P.T. drove on to New York without him, but thereafter, they continued to go their separate emotional ways.

9. RETURN TO THE FAR EAST

Despite the dangers of traversing the Pacific in wartime, traffic through-out the region did not cease. In fact, it increased. Several highly placed Chinese, anxious to engage American support for their nation, routinely crossed and re-crossed the treacherous ocean by sea and air during the war years. Many, when they arrived back in China, opted to stay in the war-weary country, voluntarily choosing to forsake the material comforts and safety of the West for the deprivations and horrors associated with living in a war zone.

One of the teen-aged daughters of author Lin Yutang tried to articulate why she and her family were so anxious to return home to their fellow country-men. "They suffered, they fought, while we were leisurely enjoying ourselves and traveling around in foreign lands… I must go back no matter what or how."[1]

It was also a glorious relief to be amongst one's own people again. "Chinese faces, Chinese figures, Chinese eyes, and Chinese hair!" she wrote, "I could look and look and make up for all the foreigners I had seen in the past years."[2]

On March 10, 1940, Hilda's uncle Huiqing and her ex-husband P.T. also returned to the Far East.[3] Initially, the two men had stayed on in America after the Pan-Pacific Conference had adjourned, but they, too, were now anxious to return home. For his part, P.T. had an additional motivation. He was embarking on a new life. While in the U.S., he had married Miss Lilian Liang. The second Mrs. Chen had been a fashionable pre-war resident of Shanghai and a prominent socialite who was well acquainted with Hilda (they were both active members of the Shanghai Chinese Women's Club), and it is likely that Hilda wished the newly-weds *shuangxi*—double happiness—in their new life together. Ultimately, however, P.T. was destined to be once more unlucky in love. Several months after they arrived in Chongqing, his wife, pregnant with their child, died of childbed, or puerperal, fever.[4]

When he first arrived in America in October 1939, Yan Huiqing had had a long talk with Hilda, trying to persuade her to return with him to her family. She had finally agreed. Hilda packed up and left America for the Orient, flying by Pan-Am Clipper from San Francisco to Manila, and then on to Hong Kong.

She found an apartment at 3/F 42 Wood Road. Several members of her family were now living in the Crown Colony, including her sister Dorothy and her father who had resigned from his post as Minister of Health in Chongqing.[5] Despite their comforting presence, Hilda seems to have been deeply troubled by the war and the course her life had taken. On March 19, her uncle reported in his diary that he had discussed 'the Hilda matter' with her father, but he gave no clue as to what the problem might be.

It is unlikely that Hilda's mental state would have been improved by the general atmosphere of Hong Kong which could not have been entirely to her liking. The population of the Colony had swollen to one and a half million souls, many of them refugees, and with them came a bloated, cosmopolitan lifestyle that included rowdy all-night cabarets, an over-abundance of sing-song girls, and other extravagant entertainments. Yet, in tandem with the social laxness, there was not the same free mixing of races that had been the norm in Shanghai, and with her internationalist outlook, this was particularly vexing to Hilda. Her uncle mused that the strict separation of the races was likely due to the influence of the British.

"Perhaps one must excuse the British on this count," he observed, "as they are by nature and upbringing cold and stiff and difficult to get acquainted with, but no doubt those in the colonies seemed particularly imbued with a superiority complex, so that social intercourse between them and the 'natives' could not be maintained on a natural footing."[6]

Hilda and her uncle were also deeply disappointed that Hong Kong refused to allow China to establish a consulate-general in the Colony even though all the other great powers were represented. This proud attitude was to seem particularly short-sighted—and insulting—when, in December 1941, Japan was to invade Hong Kong and the British would suddenly turn to China for aid.

Hilda was at loose ends and unhappy, and without gainful employment. She was also trying to care for her children who had been evacuated to Hong Kong. At the beginning of the New Year 1941, her father and uncle met yet again to discuss the thorny question of how she would be able to manage on her own. The next month, Hilda told her uncle she had resolved to take a job as a teacher at Custom School, and he hoped for the best, but by May, Huiqing learned through a relative that she was consulting a psychiatrist.[7]

However, there was a bit of welcome excitement that summer when a newsreel appeared in Hong Kong theaters entitled, *The American Overseas Chinese Bowl of Rice Movement.*[8] This documentary about refugee aide workers in America included footage of Hilda and her uncle participating in a ceremony at the famous stainless steel statue of Dr. Sun Yat-sen in San Francisco's Chinatown. The engaging Dr. Yan, a keen movie buff, was likely tickled to see his own larger-than-life image flickering before him on the big screen.

At the end of November 1941, Hilda announced that she had decided to leave Hong Kong, but in the meantime, she went up into the hills to tour the city's air raid shelter just in case the city fell under attack before she and her family were able to get away. As this was just a few days before the Japanese invasion of the Colony, it might seem that she enjoyed a remarkable prescience, but there were many like her in Hong Kong who felt that rumors of a potential peace in the Pacific were unfounded, and they grew increasingly restless as tensions in the area heated up. With the threat of invasion hanging over the Colony like the sword of Damocles, many had already vacated the city for the relative safety of Macao or Shanghai; those who remained took some comfort in the reassurances of the British military. The arrival of the Canadian forces was met with glad cries, and their presence was doubly appreciated when, on December 6, a mighty Japanese armada was observed steaming southward off the coast of Indo-China. That same evening, Hilda gave a rendition of songs at a Royal Air Force fund-raiser held in the Peninsula Hotel.

And then, abruptly, it all began. On December 7, the Japanese Imperial Air Force bombed Pearl Harbor and forced the United States into the war. For their part, the Chinese were relieved that they now had a strong ally in their struggle against the enemy, but there was little time for celebration in Hong Kong. The very next day, the Colony also fell under attack.

Hilda saw them coming,—dive bombing planes—row upon row of them, one after another, and then suddenly the earth shook with their bombs and the air around her was concussed with the shock of explosions. The shelling was incessant. Hilda's first thoughts were for the welfare of others, and she somehow made her way to a first aid station to render whatever assistance she could. It was there that she spent her first twenty-four hours of hell under constant bombing and shelling. She had an idea that displaying the flag of the

Red Cross would help protect the wounded from enemy fire, so she and others risked their lives to make their way to the roof of the station and set it flying. It was only then she realized that the banner of this organization, representative of mercy, was serving to make them a target. Hilda was suddenly staggered by the dastardly injustice of the situation. The strike on Pearl Harbor had been made against a military objective, but the wounded women and children under her care in the Hong Kong infirmary were unarmed and defenseless victims, non-combatants on the killing fields of battle.

Like everyone else over the next two weeks of the siege, she existed as best she could. As each of her successive shelters was destroyed, she moved house a total of five times until, ultimately, she was obliged to take cover in the corner of a porch owned by a French family. She was grateful to have a roof, however inadequate, over her head.

By Christmas, it was all over. Despite meeting with heavy resistance from the Colony's defenses, Japan finally got the upper hand.

"After we surrendered," Hilda grimly recalled, "we had our 'March of Death' just as the heroes of Bataan, and the Japs had their victory march."[9]

The occupying power formally took many prominent Chinese, including Hilda's uncle, into custody. Yan Huiqing was put into detention at the Hong Kong Hotel (renamed the Greater East Asia Club by the new regime) where he lived under house arrest.[10]

Hilda cursed herself for failing to act on her plans to leave Hong Kong, and like her neighbors, she was now was forced into an ignominious and dreary existence under the Occupation. The pettiness of the conquering officialdom enraged her. Japanese bombs had damaged the Colony's water system and caused the pipes to leak, but when the invaders took over the utilities, they charged the people of Hong Kong for the lost water. More injustices followed. As a hedge against poverty, and to protect herself and her family, Hilda had secreted two thousand dollars on her person, but this small fortune was soon nullified when the canny occupying powers decreed that all paper money larger than a ten-dollar bill was officially rendered void. Then they took over the money exchange and gave back half the value for notes exchanged.

The incessant rains and the strain of living under the thumb of the occupation plunged Hilda into a black mood, but matters grew even worse. She was consigned to an internment camp. In America, she had been an effective and outspoken foe of Japanese aggression, and she realized that, if her overseers realized who she was, she could expect no mercy. Hilda resolved to 'lose' her identity. This proud member of the distinguished Yan family resorted to shielding herself behind a mask of anonymity. Formerly renowned for the beauty of her wardrobe, she now owned only the ragged clothes she wore upon her back. Soon, food was hard to come by, and she experienced the gnawing misery of hunger, as she put it, three times a day. Rice, when it was made available to the inmates, was wormy. She heard reports that some were eating human flesh.

When, after eight numbing months of this existence, an opportunity came to escape, she seized it with both hands. The once elegant Miss Hilda Yaqing Yan, darling of Shanghai, Washington and New York society—now starving and desperate—donned coolie clothing and slipped over the border into occupied China. She commenced her long and dangerous northward march to freedom in her nation's capital, the besieged city of Chongqing.

"When we crossed the bridge into Free China, we had lost all sense of possession, but," she proudly recalled, "we had our integrity, our love for freedom and our principles."[11]

Hilda had always cherished these essential human ideals, but now their price was above rubies, and even though she was exposed to the regular bombing of Chongqing, her newfound liberty was sweet and overrode all other considerations. She was finally free, and able to live and work at the nerve center of her nation's war effort. P.T. was there as well. He was a director of the Central Bank of China, and volunteered his spare time to the Social Rehabilitation Committee. Hilda needed rehabilitation herself—she had lost forty-three pounds during her internment and flight to freedom—but she entertained no thoughts of scaling back her war efforts. She began to work with Song Meiling and became one of the official aides of her nation's first lady.

Set aflame by the injustices inflicted on her people, Hilda burned like never before to win the aid for her country that would help to redress the balance. She knew her value to China would treble if she were located overseas. In November, Song Meiling departed Chongqing for New York City to seek attention for an old medical problem before making her landmark tour of the United States. Hilda left for America, too. She found space aboard a cargo plane flying out of Chongqing, and soon she found herself leaving China over the 'Hump' of the Himalayas *en route* to Calcutta. From India, she was able to make her way steadily westward, catching successive flights that took her over Africa and then across the Atlantic to South America. From the southern hemisphere, she found another plane heading north to the United States.

On this amazing journey that took her half way around the world, Hilda had plenty of time to consider the events that led to the hateful war now engulfing the planet. She shuddered over the inadequacies of the old League of Nations, an organization she had once supposed would save the world.

"The League was a place to play power politics," she scornfully recalled. "The British and the French used it as a smoke screen. Action was decided in the closed hotel suites while the open meetings of the League were staged to meet the approval of the public."[12]

Now she was counting on one nation—the United States of America—to lead the way. During her previous sojourns in the U.S., she had closely studied its systems of political administration and had come to the opinion that it enjoyed the best possible form of government. A newly created global federation, built on the ashes of the old League, could do worse than to model itself on the American pattern, and if she were granted the privilege of working towards the inception of a 'new world order,' Hilda vowed she would do all in her power to ensure that its government ran along similar lines.

At the conclusion of this excursion that took her across four continents, she finally arrived back on American soil, her fourth visit to the country that she would soon come to recognize as the greatest nation in the world. Since her last visit, Hilda had witnessed the reversal of many fortunes and the destruction of much she held dear. Deeply affected by the deprivations she had undergone in the East (and stunned by the plenty she now encountered in the West), she rejoined the Chinese delegation working to counter Washington's 'Europe First' policy that consigned China's military and economic needs to the back burner. Changed forever by the horror of her experiences, she was more than ever deeply committed to the elimination of tyranny and the establishment of everlasting world peace. She longed to make these heart-felt ideals a reality.

The foreign minister, Song Ziwen (T.V. Soong), was at the forefront of the China lobby deputed to change the hearts and minds of the American people and to win more aid for the homeland. He lived in Washington, D.C. from mid-1940 to 1943, and shuttled back and forth from the capital to New York City. It may have been during this time that Hilda and T.V. became romantically involved. Song was the brother of Madame Chiang Kai-shek, but despite this important connection, his considerable power derived largely from his own efforts. He was also reputed to be the richest man in the world. It is difficult to know how serious his affair with Hilda became, or how long it lasted, nor is it possible to know what drew them together. Eleven years her senior, Song was married to dimpled beauty, Zhang Yueqia (Laura Chang), another of Hilda's wealthy friends who had served with her on the executive of the Shanghai Chinese Women's Club.[13] Song was regarded as an intellectual, and this would have been a powerful attraction for Hilda. Then, too, they were thrown together by their work on China's behalf, efforts which would have been given additional zest by the intensity of the times. Like Hilda, Song was deeply interested in the possibilities of the new order that would emerge from the peace, and also like Hilda, he actively lobbied for the formation of a workable, postwar United Nations.

In December 1942, Hilda made her way to Canada to attend the Eighth Conference of the Institute of Pacific Relations at Mont Tremblant, Québec. At this meeting, China's affairs were high on the agenda. Looking ahead to the postwar environment, the conference focused on the status of settlements and extraterritorial rights, foreign concessions, the postwar position on Manchuria, and China's aims for peace. No fan of colonialism and its mechanisms of exploitation, Hilda looked forward to the meeting with especial zeal. Still gaunt from her ordeal, she was a walking advertisement for the tragedy of modern warfare and hostile occupations visited on a civilian population.

In early January 1943, she arrived back in Washington, D.C. to lend support to a musical performance by contralto, Marian Anderson. The concert, which took place in Constitution Hall, was a landmark recital. The black artist was finally being allowed to appear at this 'white performers only' venue some four years after her original attempt to sing there had been rebuffed by the Hall's owners, the Daughters of the American Revolution.[14] Miss Anderson now made her triumphant maiden concert in this auditorium before First Lady

Eleanor Roosevelt and a sold-out crowd of thirty-eight hundred fans, and she directed that the proceeds of her performance be channeled to the coffers of the United China Relief. Hilda, always quick to bristle at any form of injustice, was immensely gratified by the happy resolution of this inequity, and delighted by the singer's impressive generosity to her favorite cause.

While Hilda was in Washington, and a guest staying at the stately Roger Smith Hotel, her interest in aviation apparently flared up again. She made a phone call to the local offices of the Civil Aeronautics Administration to inquire about reactivating her private pilot's certificate. She explained that it had been four years since her registration had expired, and she wondered how she might reinstate it. An official of the CAA forwarded a formidable list of requirements she would have to fulfill before she could once more go aloft, and these included sitting again for the same batch of exams she had passed in 1938, as well as the submission of her logbook and a recent medical certificate. Of course, she would have to take yet another flight test, and her Consulate would need to verify that she was a loyal Chinese citizen in sympathy with the objectives of the United States Government.

In the end, nothing came of her inquiry. By the time the letter from the CAA arrived at the hotel, Hilda had moved on, leaving no forwarding address. She continued to lobby on China's behalf, but apparently never again sought recertification to fly in the United States. Thereafter, she continued her public speaking, but she appears to have kept her feet firmly on the ground.[15]

By this time, Song Meiling had recovered her health and was scheduled to begin her celebrated tour of North America, kicking it off with a speech to the U.S. Congress on February 19, 1943. Song's high profile expedition throughout America helped to launch 'Aid to China' benefits in major centers across the United States and Canada, and the public's love affair with China's First Lady redoubled the West's appreciation of 'Things Chinese.' Far Eastern-inspired fashions and hair-dos became even more popular, and almost overnight, China's plight became topical.

10. "COMING OF AGE OF THE ENTIRE HUMAN RACE"

The year 1944 would be a seminal one for Hilda, and would prove to be most satisfying, both professionally and spiritually.

In February, she made a mini-tour of Western America. She spoke at colleges in California and Missouri where she recounted her recent escape from enemy-occupied territory, but the focus of her presentations dealt with China's proposal for world government. Now consumed by the concept of global unity, she addressed the urgent need for a federation of all peoples. This was the only form of government, she insisted, that could ensure world peace. Sensitive to all who shared her vision, Hilda gradually became attuned to a religious community, the Bahá'í, who were preaching a similar gospel.

Her grandfather had been a pastor of the Episcopalian church, and she had been raised as an Episcopal Christian, but after her airplane crash in Prattville, Hilda had become ever more aware of a spiritual vacuum in her soul. The senselessness of the suffering she had witnessed in China only compounded matters. Her maternal uncle, Cao Yuxiang, had long ago told her about the Bahá'í faith and the peace it had brought him. Hilda loved her uncle, but she also respected and admired him. His credentials were impeccable. A brilliant overseas scholar at Yale and Harvard universities, he served not only as China's Consul-General at London, but also as president of Tsing Hua University in Beijing. In 1923, he and his Swedish-born wife became devout followers of the Bahá'í faith. As a tangible representation of his zeal, he translated the faith's important holy books, notably the *Bahá'u'lláh* and *New Era,* into Chinese for the benefit of his fellow countrymen. Excited about the Bahá'í vision of the world, Cao had hoped to interest Hilda in his adopted faith, but as a young woman, she remained unreceptive.

As time passed, however, the knowledge that her dear uncle was an enthusiastic follower of Bahá'u'lláh began to carry considerable weight, and after the trauma of her plane crash, she became increasingly curious about the faith. Her experience of living under the siege of Hong Kong, when persons of every social strata had been reduced to poverty and starvation, had impressed upon her the realization that all humanity was one, and she was pleased to note that this precept was a basic tenet of the Bahá'í. Some members of the faith were among her acquaintance (notably Mildred Mottahedeh, renowned Chinese porcelain expert and importer), and they persuaded her to attend the Thirty-Sixth Convention of the Bahá'ís of the United States and Canada at Wilmette,

Illinois, on May 23, 1944. No ordinary conference, the Convention was held on the centennial of the founding of the faith, and this milestone was celebrated in a vast and impressive new temple constructed in honor of the anniversary.

The Bahá'í teaching that the human race was one was Hilda's most deeply felt ideal, and it had long informed her own efforts with the League of Nations. She also applauded the Bahá'í goal to found a global government in the spirit of a world religion that would be an addition to, not a substitute for, all the other religions of history. When she witnessed black and white members embracing at the convention with no signs of racial prejudice, she took this gesture as demonstrable proof that these adherents actually practiced what they preached. Of especial importance to Hilda, the faith also promised to be a guide toward living a better life. She enrolled as a Bahá'í.

Thereafter, Hilda was no idle adherent. Postwar, she would become an active spokeswoman for the Bahá'í, and would lobby to have her new religion recognized by the United Nations. In March 1948, she would be instrumental in having her bureau, the United Nations Office of Public Information, arrange to have the name of the Bahá'í International Community placed on the list of non-governmental organizations. In this capacity, the Bahá'í were granted observer status at the U.N. Historically, her efforts in this regard have won for her the international recognition of the Bahá'í, and have served to join her name with that of her uncle, Cao Yunxiang, as one of the most prominent Chinese pioneers of the faith to help advance its cause within the global community.[1]

Invigorated by the tenets of her new faith and inspired by the possibilities of a new world order, Hilda now tackled her mission with a fresh enthusiasm, and resolved to make her own personal contributions to universal peace. By mid-1944, international events seemed to be running in tandem with her personal goals. As the end of the war seemed almost in reach, representatives from the Allied nations attended a series of three momentous meetings that would one day be recognized for their extraordinary significance. Hilda was present at each of them.

During the first three weeks of July 1944, she attended the monetary conference, known to history as 'Bretton Woods,' that convened to make postwar economic plans for the inevitable peacetime. Held at the sprawling Mount

Washington Hotel in Bretton Woods, New Hampshire (a splendid resort that was now reduced to operating with a wartime skeleton staff), this economics-based meeting was attended by representatives of forty-four nations, and it prefaced the eventual development of corporate capitalism on a global scale. Leading the Chinese delegation, Dr. H.H. Kong joined other prominent economists, including Henry Morgenthau, Jr. and John Maynard Keynes, to prepare the groundwork for the establishment of the International Monetary Fund.

Another important milestone of 1944 was the decisive meeting organized at Dumbarton Oaks that laid the foundations for the establishment of the United Nations. The League of Nations had failed miserably in its mission to keep the peace, and would have to be scrapped, but the premise of a global organization existing for the good of humankind was still a sound one. Four major world powers, the United States, Britain, the Soviet Union and China, were invited to Dumbarton Oaks to hammer out the initial framework of the postwar U.N. Acting in the capacity of technical advisor, Hilda was honored to be one of those chosen to accompany the official Chinese delegation to the autumn meeting.

The formation of the new organization got off to a shaky start. The Soviet Union put the lie to the notion of a 'united' body of nations when it refused to deal directly with the Chinese. The Soviets argued that, as they were not at war with Japan, they had no wish to give offence to that nation by meeting with China. As a result, the conference had to be divided into two parts, with the Americans and British meeting first with Russia (August 1 – September 28, 1944), and then with China (September 29 – October 7). Hilda's long-time colleague and friend, Dr. Wellington Koo, led the Chinese delegation, but as most of the details had already been agreed upon in the first round of meetings, China was not destined to be a major player in the process.

Building on the resolutions of the Big Four at Dumbarton Oaks, a two-month international conference was then convened on the West Coast of America to deal with procedural matters and to sort out the myriad details that would prefigure the creation of United Nations Charter. Delegates of forty-six nations were summoned to attend the meeting, known to history as the San Francisco Conference (April 25 – June 26, 1945), and on the last day, they appended their signatures to the completed charter. T.V. Song led the official Chinese delegation, and Hilda, with her abiding interest in world government, once more played an important role as technical advisor. Several of the delegates, many of whom went on to dominate the postwar political arena, recalled in their memoirs the excitement sparked by the international gathering, and the exhilarated optimism they felt for the future of world peace, but when the meeting finally adjourned, Hilda found she could not share the general enthusiasm.

"They have solved many things at this conference, but they have left God out," she sadly observed. "We cannot have a lasting peace without first turning to God."[2]

In addition to the spiritual sterility of the proposed charter, she pointed to the many loopholes that would hamper the effectiveness of this vaunted new global government. She had spent the whole of her confinement in occupied Hong Kong dreaming of the day when she could once more work toward the establishment of a world united, and she obsessed about the need to get it right.

Embarking on a speaking tour to criticize the problematic charter before it was ratified, Hilda enumerated her four major concerns. These included the formal recognition of the principle of sovereignty ('an international bugaboo,' she termed it) which would hamstring close cooperation between nations; the emasculation of the General Assembly that was empowered to act only in an advisory capacity and with no powers to legislate; the retention of trustee practices; and the overreaching powers granted to large member nations who alone reserved the right to veto amendment processes.

Once Hilda got going, she would warm to her subject. She declared that, while these procedural snafus would constrain the efficacy of the U.N., there was another large problem—its apparent support of colonialism—that gave the lie to the body's purported backing of universal democracy. This obsolete form of governance, she argued, had no place in the new world order, and she scored the U.S. for knuckling under and siding with imperialist European nations who had promised to grant their colonies self-government, but not the national independence they so earnestly craved. Why, she asked, if America were such a champion of colonialism, had it vowed to give independence to its own protectorate, the Philippines? Hilda also ridiculed the proposed establishment of military bases in the Pacific region, arguing that they were no deterrent to future hostile acts. She envisioned a time when robotic bombs would possess the capability of speeding across the span of continents to achieve their objectives. The notion that a military base could prevent a calamity of this caliber was laughable.[3] Hilda's speeches had always had an edge—now they were rapier-sharp.

Despite her many disappointments with the new organization, Hilda still saw an opportunity to make changes from within, and after the ratification of the charter, she became involved with the United Nations as a point person for the Chinese delegation. Her effectiveness and convivial personality attracted notice, and she was selected to serve as public liaison officer at the U.N. Office of Public Information, later renamed the U.N. Department of Public Information. Her new job entailed her having to travel, much as she did during the war, to promote the United Nations and to explain its function, and to this end, she spoke to clubs and organizations throughout America. She had the advantage of having worked within the League of Nations and could explain how the new organization differed from, and was superior to, the old. Her presence at the seminal conferences that led to the formation of the U.N. lent her public reputation an additional *gravitas*, and she made her speeches with the voice of authority. There were few on the lecture circuit who could match Hilda's expertise, and as a tribute to her proficiency, she was nominated to train other potential lecturers, a task she carried out for two years as head of the U.N. speakers' bureau.

In her spare time, she promoted the Bahá'í peace program. Peace was a highly topical subject, and her addresses attracted many curious spectators. Just days after the atomic bombs dropped on Hiroshima and Nagasaki finally brought a long-desired end to the war, Hilda declared to a Bahá'í gathering in Grosse Pointe, Michigan, that this was less an occasion for celebration than an opportunity for sober reflection.

"We should be ashamed," she admonished her listeners, "to think that it takes so tiny a thing as an atom in the form of an atomic bomb to make us realize that we must live together in harmony on this planet or we shall destroy ourselves."[4]

She pointed out that, while the U.N. Charter hoped to provide political unity throughout the world, lasting peace could not be assured unless social, cultural and religious unity became a global reality. Happily, she declared, this universal harmony was attainable through application of the teachings of the Bahá'u'lláh.

In February 1947, Hilda was delighted to welcome her father who had come to America on a medical-related visit. She was proud to inform him of the significant work of international importance with which she had recently become involved. Eleanor Roosevelt, widow of former U.S. President Franklin D. Roosevelt, had been elected chair of the United Nations Committee on Human, Social and Cultural Concerns. As the world's foremost spokesperson for Human Rights, Mrs. Roosevelt had been directed to develop a permanent U.N. Commission on Human Rights. She began the great task of drafting a Declaration of Human Rights, and Hilda was honored to be one of those who were assisting her in this vital endeavor. In many ways, her efforts in this regard were an extension of the important work she had first undertaken at the League of Nations.

For the remainder of the year, she traveled the country, lecturing in public on the organization of the United Nations, and in private, addressing those interested in the tenets of the Bahá'í. To both audiences, she issued a plea for the unification of humanity. In a world still reeling from the effects of the Second World War and the omnipresent threat of a future nuclear holocaust, she encountered many like-minded individuals who shared her global vision and were inspired to conduct replica 'U.N. Assemblies' in their own communities. Hilda was always pleased to participate in these grass roots learning sessions, and in many cases was invited to be the keynote speaker.

11. JOHN GIFFORD MALE

While its new headquarters were being constructed in Manhattan, the offices of the United Nations, including Hilda's department, were temporarily located in the Sperry Gyroscope Company building in Lake Success, New York. In 1948, Hilda sat for a working photographic portrait as she sat at her desk. In her mid-forties, she is shown opening a letter addressed to her in her capacity as liaison officer of the U.N.'s Department of Public Information. Soignée and impeccably groomed, she is sitting at her desk clad in a *qipao*. She is wearing little makeup, and there is just the suggestion of a scar on her lower lip, a souvenir of her plane crash almost a decade before. She has regained the weight that she lost in Hong Kong.

It was around this time that she fell in love with John Gifford Male, a man of letters who hailed from Wellington, New Zealand. John Male had joined the U.N. in Montréal in about 1946, and he was serving as Social Affairs Officer of the United Nations' Division of Human Rights. He would ultimately rise to become Chief of the U.N.'s Advisory Services. Some eight years younger than Hilda (he was born on January 16, 1913), with an irreverent wit as keen as her own and a happy propensity for telling fascinating stories, he was a captivating man who shared just as deeply her vision of a united world. John was also a veteran of the Second World War. During his distinguished service in the Italian and North African campaigns, he had been mentioned in dispatches and was awarded the African Star.[1] On May 15, 1948, John and Hilda were wed by a justice of the peace in New Canaan, Connecticut. It was the second marriage for each.[2]

Shortly afterward, Hilda lost her position at the Secretariat (women were required to give up their jobs when they married), and she became a dependent of her husband. John took advantage of Hilda's enforced inactivity by taking her abroad and introducing her to his homeland.

Wherever they traveled in New Zealand, John's many acquaintances warmly greeted the newlyweds, and the new bride invariably made a positive and lasting impression on those to whom she was introduced. One of John's closest friends was the renowned New Zealand poet and Renaissance man, A.R.D. Fairburn, known to his friends as Rex.[3] Rex Fairburn and his family welcomed the Males with open arms, and decades later, his children still retained vivid memories of the happy impact Hilda made upon their household. They recalled her gentle charm and the ease with which she blended in with the family's activities. Hilda further endeared herself to one and all by preparing several delicious Chinese meals for the large family—a gesture much appreciated by Fairburn's busy wife—and her delectable recipes for Chinese pork and cabbage and marinated grilled spare ribs were carefully collected and became perennial favorites of the Fairburn household.[4]

In New York, John and Hilda took an apartment at Parkway Village in Queens, a newly built housing development that was created expressly for U.N. employees whose offices were temporarily located at the Lake Success site. Living in this microcosm of the global community epitomized all that they cherished, and it suited them both. Now that they were settled, Hilda sent to China for her son, William, and in the grand tradition of the Yan family, the 20-year-old arrived to take his overseas schooling in America. Initially, he lived in residence at the YMCA while he attended the Polytechnic Institute of Brooklyn (later known as the Polytechnic University of New York), but he spent his weekends at the Parkway Village apartment. For legal purposes, John Male officially regarded William as his stepson, and the young man arrived in the United States in that capacity.

Meanwhile, China was in the throes of another revolution, the second in less than forty years. By 1948, Chiang Kai-shek's Nationalist military regime was steadily losing ground to Mao Zedong's People's Liberation Army, and soon the north of China was solidly in the hands of the Communists, whose forces brusquely began pushing southward. The volatility of the situation alarmed Hilda. When gainfully employed by the U.N., she had received children's allowances for both of her offspring and used these monies to augment the support that P.T. was affording them, but after she lost her job, these allowances evaporated. Then suddenly, P.T. was no longer in a position to support their children either; in December 1948, political instability caused the new Chinese currency to collapse, reducing P.T. to near penury. He was unable to continue paying William's tuition. Even more worrying, Hilda was anxious about her sixteen-year-old daughter, Doreen, still living in China and subject to the chaotic forces that were buffeting her homeland. With John's emotional and financial support, Hilda decided to do all in her power to bring her daughter to America. Just before Christmas 1948, she wrangled a plane ticket and arranged for Doreen to fly from Shanghai to New York on a coveted U.N. passport, a *laissez passé* that guaranteed the young woman safe passage during those troubled times. She was listed on the passport as John's dependent stepdaughter.

Doreen arrived on Christmas Eve, 1948. Within weeks, the Communists took Beijing without a struggle, and over the next few months, the remainder of China's great cities 'fell like ripe melons' to the PLA. John Male took seriously his role as stepfather, and undertook to support his suddenly burgeoning family by applying to the U.N. for dependents' allowances. These were granted. Through her new husband, Hilda finally took personal responsibility for the raising of her children. William carried on with his education in engineering, and Doreen enrolled at Jamaica High School in Queens.

In May 1949, Hilda was back in the news once more, but not for the usual reasons. She made headlines when she appeared in a Washington District courtroom to launch a lawsuit against Norman Seldenberg, a D.C. jeweler.[5] In 1945, Hilda testified, she had left three gemstones in the care of Mr. Seldenberg on the understanding that he would undertake to have them remounted. The items in question were a piece of Chinese jade worth $6,000, a star sapphire valued at $1,125, and another sapphire pegged at $495. After the gems had been remounted and were still in the shop, they had somehow vanished. The jeweler recognized his culpability, but he argued that Hilda had grossly overvalued her trinkets. The craftsman who had done the remounting supported Seldenburg, and he took the stand to testify that they were worth, at most, $300. Hilda countered by asking another jeweler to study photos of the gems and provide an appraisal. In the plaintiff's defense, the expert agreed that Miss Yan's evaluation was the more accurate. Members of the jury deliberated for an hour and a half, and in the end they awarded Hilda a judgment of $4,870, plus six per cent interest.

As a sharp counterpoint to this rather bourgeois news item, other headlines screamed that the situation in the Far East was reaching a boiling point, and Communism, the people's choice, was on the verge of total victory in China.

By late 1949, the Nationalist party finally lost its running battle with the mighty forces of Mao Zedong. Fleeing the Communist menace, Generalissimo Chiang Kai-shek and his clique were forced to retreat to the island of Taiwan, and others who were identified with the fallen government ran for their lives to Hong Kong or further afield. However, the Liberation that brought the Communists to power was not as cataclysmic an event to the Yan family of China as it had been for many others. After the People's Republic was established, those who were recognized as members or sympathizers of the Nationalist Party, or Guomindang, were arrested or shot outright, but the non-partisan Yans had always risen above party politics. Widely respected for having dedicated themselves to the benefit of China and her people in general, they escaped general vilification.

Many years before, in an act that now redounded to his credit, Hilda's father had treated Yang Kaihui, the first wife of Mao Zedong, for malaria. After he came to power, Chairman Mao invited Dr. Yan to dinner, and referred to this incident with gratitude. He commended the elderly medical man for not having dismissed his wife out of hand as a poor peasant woman unworthy of consideration. Mao declared that he himself was also in the doctor's debt, recalling that he, too, had once sought and received medical treatment from Dr. Yan. Initially at a loss to remember the occasion, the doctor later recalled the arrival at his Henan clinic of an unusually tall and imposing young man. This could only have been Mao Zedong. For his manifold services to the Chinese people, Yan was warmly received many times both by Mao and by China's Premier, Zhou Enlai.

China's new government also recognized Hilda's uncle, Yan Huiqing, for his lifetime of dedication to China, and he, too, remained unmolested. Immediately after Liberation, despite his obvious fragility and failing health, the elderly statesman became a voluntary member of the delegation that flew from Shanghai to Beijing to meet with Mao and other leaders to discuss the possibility of a peace between the Communists and the old regime. He also sought amnesty for the Guomindang officials who were suffering from wholesale labeling as war criminals by the People's Republic. Traveling to his meeting with Mao, the globe-trotting diplomat made his first flight in an aircraft, and it is likely that he was nervously reminded of his niece's plane crash a decade earlier.

Despite Yan's efforts, this was one of the few occasions in his long and stellar career that he was unsuccessful in his negotiations. Mao remained obdurate and refused to consider a *rapprochement*. The elder statesman flew back to Shanghai a disappointed man. A little over a year later, on May 25, 1950, he passed away at his home on Chungcheng Road. Yan Huiqing was seventy-four years old. He died full of honors, and diplomatic circles around the world mourned his passing. The People's Republic officially expressed its regret, and his family received a personal message of condolence from Mao Zedong himself. But few would have been as saddened by his death as Hilda, who remembered with gratitude the heady days of her newly won independence when she traveled to Russia and the capitals of Europe in the company of her loving and engaging uncle, who taught her so wisely and cared so deeply always about her happiness.

With time on her hands, Hilda began to worry about the health and safety of her remaining family in China. Since the Revolution, communications with the Mainland were fraught, and she no longer received regular correspondence from her aging father. She learned that he had participated in the Korean War by organizing surgical and anti-germ warfare teams, and had even made a personal visit to the northeast front to ensure that Chinese troops were receiving adequate medical care.

When his letters finally managed to get through, Yan Fuqing reassured his daughter that, although he was not able to work the long hours that had once been his *forte*, he was otherwise in good health. He admitted that his memory was no longer as sharp as it had been, but that was to be expected, and although his eyesight was failing, he kept handy a magnifying glass to aid with his reading. This news was little comfort to Hilda, but rather than obsess about circumstances beyond her control, she set about to find some form of meaningful employment to occupy her time. She remembered the exciting days of her young womanhood when she first graduated from Yali and went to work in her father's hospital as an amateur social worker. Resolving to recapture this happy time, she decided to re-enter the vocation on a professional basis. In 1951, she applied for admission to the fall semester of the New York School of Social Work, but her hopes were dashed when this request was rejected on the grounds that she was over thirty-five years of age.

Hilda's children had both embarked on advanced studies, and she and John were now empty nesters. William was taking engineering at the Massachusetts Institute of Technology, and Doreen had returned to China to study medicine.[6] Hilda was not entirely at loose ends; she was still involved with the United Nations (she also was an accredited observer for the Bahá'í U.N. Committee), and, in August 1951, she and John were among the U.N. delegates who took part in New Haven's three hundredth anniversary celebrations. Coincidently, the master of ceremonies at these festivities was Hoyt Caitlin, the justice of the peace who had wed them almost three years before.

Politically, John and Hilda both leaned to the left of center, so much so that during the era of the House Un-American Activities Committee, the liberal lifestyle they maintained, and the irreverent friends they cultivated, caused them to fall under the dreaded scrutiny of the Federal Bureau of Investigation. John Male was unaware he was under suspicion until he was tipped off by one of his U.N. co-workers who had been grilled by the FBI about their friendship. The federal agents had asked this colleague if he thought that John was a communist, or if he had ever noticed any inappropriate Marxist literature lying about in the Male household. Initially, John chuckled to learn that he was under investigation as an irregular character, and, knowing it would amuse Rex Fairburn, he proudly announced this latest development in a letter to his anti-establishment friend. But he was also somewhat unsettled. Fully aware of the broad powers enjoyed by the Communist witch-hunters, he asked Rex to keep the news under his hat.[7]

John loved the sea, and not long after he and Hilda were married, he bought a derelict, twenty-three-foot ship's lifeboat for $25. He refurbished it and converted it to sail. Increasingly overwhelmed by the fierce rush of life in New York and the pressures of work at the U.N., John regarded the battered vessel as an indispensable symbol of the possibility of escape. In 1954, he and Hilda built a home in South Norwalk, Connecticut, a venerable seaside community located on the broad estuary of the Norwalk River that dated its founding to the seventeenth century. Located some forty miles northeast of New York City, 'Sono' was an easy train commute to the bustling metropolis, and it afforded a peaceful contrast to the hurly-burly of big city life. The Male's secluded property overlooked Long Island Sound, and Hilda enhanced the lovely view from their contemporary-style home by cultivating a splendid perennial garden. Gardening soon became a cherished hobby.

South Norwalk was the birthplace of the revolutionary Colonel Thomas Fitch, the iconic figure known as 'Yankee Doodle,' and, entering into the spirit of their historic environment, the China and New Zealand expatriates quickly became proud 'Connecticut Yankees.' Their new lifestyle in this peaceful seaside town was probably John's attempt to reproduce the cherished days of his youth in his New Zealand homeland (the entire population of which was one fifth that of Shanghai). It bore little resemblance to any way of life that his cosmopolitan wife had ever known, but Hilda entered into the bargain with love and enthusiasm. The couple spent their spare time yachting and exploring the ever-varied coastline of Long Island Sound.

In the autumn of 1954, they experienced an unforgettable sea adventure when they were caught out on a sailboat during a hurricane. On September 30, they were aboard the *Luau* with their friends, Anita and Henry Willcox (who were also under FBI investigation for their 'un-American' activities), and they weighed anchor near Point Judith, Rhode Island, to spend the night.[8] They were north of the relative safety afforded by the Sound and this became problematic when, early next morning, strong winds began to whip up the sea. John carefully recorded the deteriorating weather conditions.

At 6:30 a.m., when the barometer read 29.70 inches and falling, an announcement barked out over the onshore loud speaker, "No Fishing Today!" Shortly thereafter, as the northeast wind began to rise and the barometric pressure continued to fall, they took the precautionary measure of dropping the boat's heavy storm anchor. After breakfast, Hilda brought out her box of watercolors and tried to paint nearby Tenants Harbor in the unusual light, but she quickly abandoned this bucolic project when terrific rains moved in and reduced the visibility to zero. The slashing winds became intense. By 10:30 a.m., they were suddenly obliged to apply full throttle to the engine and full right to the rudder in order to dodge a house that had dislodged from the land and came bobbing towards them in the foaming surf. At the same time, terrific waves swamped and flipped their dingy. By 11:30, the barometer had plunged to its lowest level—28.70 inches—and although the sun had come out, its garish light only served to highlight the wreckage of boats and houses all around them. Wind velocity still ranged from ninety to one hundred five miles per hour, and at 12:45 p.m., they were sufficiently alarmed to dismast the boat. Abandoning their stiff upper lips altogether, they finally helped each other into lifejackets. An hour later, however, with the barometer rapidly on the rise and the sun shining brilliantly over the yardarm, their prospects had improved to such an extent that Anita went below and made a hot lunch for the hungry sailors. John was finally at leisure to document the events surrounding their remarkable experience.[9]

In addition to participating in hair-raising leisure activities, Hilda also pursued less frivolous pastimes. She was still deeply interested in psychology and volunteered twice a week as an amateur occupational therapist at nearby Fairfield State Hospital in Newtown. The red brick colonial-style institution where she served was a sprawling psychiatric facility that encouraged self-sufficiency in its inmates. Working with the patients and observing their progress gave Hilda so much satisfaction that she decided to take professional training in occupational therapy. She was nearing fifty years of age, but she crossed her fingers and applied to the College of Surgeons and Physicians of Columbia University, requesting that she be considered as a candidate for an advanced course beginning in the fall of 1955. Again, her application for admission was rejected on the grounds that she was too old; the age limit for graduate therapists was capped at thirty-five. Disappointed but undaunted, she continued with her volunteer work at the hospital.

In the meantime, she also kept a close eye on the health of the United Nations. Hilda was unimpressed by its performance. Events were unfolding just as she had predicted when she had gone on her speaking tour prior to the ratification of the U.N. Charter. She was frustrated to note that the effectiveness of the organization was continually being hamstrung by various member nations who attempted to dictate policy by threatening withdrawal. She felt that only a strong revision of the charter would halt this ongoing 'blackmail' and allow the organization to fulfill its mandate. In an effort to help sway general opinion, she gave at least one public address on the subject.

John continued to look ahead to his retirement. In the mid 'Fifties, he wrote to Rex Fairburn in New Zealand, asking his friend to look for a "few acres by the sea" where he and Hilda could relax and enjoy a contemplative life in a natural setting. Rex obliged and discovered a former holiday camp for orphans near the northernmost tip of the North Island. The site was located on the western shore of the middle peninsula of the Mahurangi Harbor, and it was for sale. John leaped at the chance to possess this scenic toehold on his home country and snatched up the property for £2,500. The rickety main house, fitted out, as Rex described it, with "an old rafferty harmonium, 30 bunks, 20 mattresses, double oven stove, big safe and a nine-foot dinghy," had little to commend itself, nevertheless his friend hastened to add that there was no need to tear down the structure and begin anew. All it needed were some judicious renovations.[10] John took his advice and left the property as it was, making only necessary improvements. The view of the island-dotted bay from the nearby height of land was breathtaking.

While John continued to dream of escape, Hilda was still making plans to re-enter the workforce. She was anxious to find a profession that would provide her not only with personal satisfaction, but also with an opportunity to be of service to others. To her delight, she learned that Columbia's School of Library Service placed no age limit on the students it was willing to accept, but its school catalog did advise persons over thirty-five not to apply unless they had been continuously engaged in library work or intellectual pursuits. Having spent her life in intellectual pursuits, Hilda decided to take a chance. Accordingly, she asked George D. Vaill, Executive Secretary of the Yale-in-China Association, to write a letter of reference to the school on her behalf. He had already vouched for Hilda's scholastic excellence when she had applied to enter the occupational therapy program, and he was happy to oblige once more. This time, in an effort to give her application an additional boost, he paid her a handsome tribute.

"It might be instructive," he pointed out to the School's board of admission, "to note that Mrs. Male completed the degree requirements of the full four year course in three years and was graduated in June of 1925, five months short of her twentieth birthday. This is a record which is equaled by few in academic circles."[11]

The combination of a distinguished international career, coupled with first-rate grades and a cracking good reference, finally did the trick. In the fall of 1956, Hilda's application was accepted and she began her studies in library science. Upon graduation, she was pleased to accept a position in the New York Public Library system in Brooklyn. There could have been few reference librarians to match her talent for languages and science, or her knowledge of world events, in many of which she herself had been an active participant.

12. ENDINGS

During the course of their married lives, John and Hilda maintained a wide circle of freethinking and remarkable friends and acquaintances, world figures many of them, who were, for the most part, enthusiastic exponents of liberty and the fraternity of all peoples. However, a decade after they had wed and despite the many similarities in outlook that had drawn them together, the couple grew unhappy in their marriage, and Hilda's old restlessness returned. She left her husband for another man. Ultimately, she and John made the unhappy decision to divorce, and their marriage was dissolved on December 18, 1959. John had already begun to look elsewhere for companionship, and three days after the divorce was finalized, he married Martha Catherine Winstone, a widely read and intelligent woman who had formerly served on the staff of the *Monthly Review*. Five years later, John ceded to his yearning to return to the land of his birth, and he and Cathy retired to New Zealand.

Hilda's new relationship, and the others that followed, turned out to be not as long lasting as John's third marriage. However, despite—or perhaps because of—the distances between them, Hilda and her first husband, P.T. Chen, continued to cherish an affectionate regard for each other, and they nourished this fondness for the rest of their lives. In the 1960s, P.T. wrote to his ex-wife and asked for her portrait, noting that she still held a special place in his heart. Their grandson also recalls that the family managed a long-distance phone call to P.T. in Communist China (as difficult a feat then as it had been when Yan Fuqing had phoned the Prattville hospital more than twenty years before), and he remembered his grandparents enjoying a very convivial chat. Wondering at the reasons for the breakdown of their marriage, he asked his mother why the union had failed. In her reply, she reckoned that P.T. had been unable to keep up with his peripatetic and precocious wife. In the end, Hilda had simply worn him out.[1]

In the last years of her life, Hilda finally grew more settled as the passions that once drove her in her younger years abated. Her association with the Bahá'í was no longer as strong as it had been, and, returning to her Chinese roots, she took to studying the ancient Daoist philosophy of the *Yi Jing* (I Ching). However, her health was far from robust. In the 1960s, she underwent a mastectomy for breast cancer. Although her physicians predicted she would die within the year, Hilda triumphantly overcame this dire prognosis, but she had other concerns. She was beset by nagging worries for her aging father. For no particular reason, Yan Fuqing had run afoul of the 'Gang of Four' and, in spite of his incalculable services to China, the distinguished doctor had fallen into disgrace, was stripped of his honors, and marginalized. The persecution of her elderly parent lay heavily on Hilda's heart.

Verging on her senior years, she continued to work as a librarian in Brooklyn, but on March 18, 1970, she collapsed in her bath and died. Hilda Yaqing Yan expired eight months shy of her sixty-fifth birthday. The coroner ruled that the cause of death was occlusive coronary arteriosclerosis. She was survived by her two children, William and Doreen, her brothers, Victor and William, and her sister, Dorothy Lieu. Sadly, Hilda's father (who was still out of favor with the Chinese authorities in Shanghai) also knew the bitter sorrow of having to outlive a beloved daughter.

A memorial service for Hilda was held at Riverside Church in the City of New York. A wide-embracing, ecumenical facility whose soaring architecture approximated Chartres in France, Riverside was a venue that appropriately reflected Hilda's respect for the dignity of all peoples and religions. Her remains were interred at Ferncliff Cemetery in Ardsley, New York, the final resting place of many notables, from Joan Crawford to Nelson Rockefeller. More importantly to Hilda, the cemetery was also the final resting place of many of her companions and colleagues; an expatriate far from home, she had always voiced her desire to be buried in the company of friends.[2]

A plain bronze marker designates Hilda's grave. Throughout the eleven years that followed her second divorce, she had continued to refer to herself as 'Mrs. Male," but her son decided that the marker should read neither 'Chen' nor 'Male,' but simply, 'Hilda Ya-tsing Yen.' Her name is inscribed in both English and Chinese, a fitting tribute to a woman of the world who was equally at home in the East and West, and one whose idealism and courage required the support of no man.

During the span of her lifetime, Hilda lived through remarkable upheavals in political and social history. Born a subject of the Dragon Throne, raised in revolutionary Republican China, a heroic participant of World War II, and resident in America during the angst of the Vietnam conflict, Hilda witnessed cultural rituals and styles that ranged from foot-binding and ancestor worship to the mini skirt and psychedelia.[3] Her own spiritual journey was just as immense a voyage, and was informed by her wide travels, the people she encountered, and the mentors she found within the ranks of her own formidable family.

Throughout the course of her life, while she often seemed to flounder in her search for personal fulfillment, Hilda never strayed from her belief in the rightness of the community of nations and the fraternity of humankind. Injustice, an intolerable sin, was not to be borne, and rendering compassion and aid to suffering humanity was a cause for which one might gladly choose to die. These lodestars caused Hilda Yaqing Yan, in her most tangible demonstration of idealism, to take to the skies as a winged champion of her people in their darkest hour, and win for them the support they so desperately required.

13. EPILOGUE

In 1973, at the age of seventy-four, Hilda's first husband, P.T. Chen, died in China.

Hilda's second spouse, John Male, who had moved with his third wife to Warkworth on New Zealand's North Island, reveled in his new life (which closely approximated the one he had established with Hilda in South Norwalk), living off the produce of his own garden and the fruits of the sea. Even in retirement, he carried on with those activities that had made him so attractive to Hilda, continuing to lobby for peace and human rights issues. He became co-founder and president of the New Zealand Foundation for Peace Studies. A sensitive poet, in 1989 he published in limited edition an account of his World War II experiences entitled, *Poems from a War*. He also continued to maintain a friendly correspondence with Hilda's family. For his conspicuous services to the peace and human rights movements, in 2002, he was named a Member of the New Zealand Order of Merit. The next year, John Gifford Male died at the age of ninety.

Yan Fuqing survived his daughter by a few months. After a lifetime of dedication to China, Dr. Yan died unheralded and in disgrace on November 29, 1970. He was eighty-eight years old. A decade later, after the smashing of the odious Gang of Four, Dr. Yan's memory was 'rehabilitated.' For his immense contributions to medical research and education in China, as well as his steadfast devotion to the common people, a grand memorial service was held in his honor, and his ashes were re-interred in the Revolutionaries' Crypt at the imposing Martyrs' Cemetery at Longhua.   The Shanghai Medical College, renamed Fudan University, also celebrated its founder by erecting a huge statue of his likeness in its courtyard and naming the library for him, an honor Hilda surely would have relished. Today he is remembered as a great hero of China whose efforts, like those of his cherished daughter, were unswervingly directed toward the greater good of humanity.

fig. 1

fig. 2

From a portrait by Miss Doris Montagu Bell

MRS. F. T. CHEN

A prominent member of Sino-foreign circles, in Shanghai, Mrs. Chen, who is the daughter of Dr. and Mrs. F. C. Yen, left for Moscow in February with her uncle Dr. W. W. Yen, Chinese Ambassador to Moscow. Mrs. Chen is acting as official hostess to the Legation there.

fig. 3

fig. 4

fig. 5

fig. 6

fig. 7

fig. 8

fig. 9

fig. 10

fig. 11

fig. 12

Itnerary of Miss Hilda Yen

April:

    15, Richmond
    18, Raleigh, N. C.
    20, Colombia, Lancester, S. C.
    22, Savannah
    23, Jacksonville
    24, New Orleans

May:

    1, Birmingham
    3, Atlanta

    5, Chattanooga,
    7, Nashville,
    13, Oklahoma City,

    16, Tulsa Okla.
    18, Kansa City,
    21, Omaha,
    23, Des Moines,
    24, Minneapolis,
        St. Paul ?
    27, Miwaukee,
    28, Chicago.

June:

    6, St. Louis,
    9, Louisville,
    11 Cincinnati,
    14, Indianapolis
    16, Toledo,
    18, Detroit,
    22 Cleveland
    25, Colombus,
    28 Charleston, W. Va.

July:

    1 Pittsburgh
    6 Buffalo
    9 Rochester

    11 Albany,

    14 Manchester, N. H.
    16 Boston,
    21 Providence,
    24 New Port,
    29, New Haven
    31 New York.

fig. 13

fig. 14

POST CARD

PLACE STAMP HERE

Girl Pilot on Mercy Flight Over U. S. A.
To Seek Funds for Chinese Civilian Refugees.

SPIRIT OF NEW CHINA

Miss Hilda Yen 顏雅清

fig. 16

fig. 15

fig. 17

fig. 18

108

It Must Be Very Disappointing

fig. 19

fig. 20

fig. 21

fig. 22

fig. 23

fig. 24

UNITED COUNCIL FOR CIVILIAN RELIEF IN CHINA

NATIONAL COMMITTEE

COLONEL THEODORE ROOSEVELT, JR., *National Chairman*

DR. JOSEPH D. McGOLDRICK, *National Treasurer*

DR. DONALD D. VAN SLYKE, *Secretary*

DR. MAURICE WILLIAM, *Chairman Fund Committee*

DR. FRANK CO TUI

DR. FRANK L. MELENEY

MR. BRUNO SCHWARTZ, *National Campaign Manager*

NEW YORK CITY BOWL OF RICE BALL

MISS GWEN DEW, *Director of Ball*

PATRONS

MRS. MYRON TAYLOR, *Honorary Chairman*

Archduke and Archduchess
Leopold of Austria
Princess Farid-es-Sultaneh
Dr. Tsune-chi Yu, *Consul General*
Dr. and Mrs. Frank Co Tui
Madame Alma Claybergh
Mr. and Mrs. James S. Cushman
Mrs. William H. Harkness, Jr.

Mr. and Mrs. Roy W. Howard
Mr. and Mrs. Robert Lehman
Mr. and Mrs. K. C. Li
Mr. and Mrs. Henry R. Luce
Mr. and Mrs. Clark Minor
Col. and Mrs. Theodore Roosevelt, Jr.
Mr. and Mrs. Bruno Schwartz
Dr. and Mrs. Lin Yutang

EXECUTIVE COMMITTEE

MISS TALLULAH BANKHEAD, *Chairman*

Mrs. F. H. Anspacher
Miss Louise Franklin Bache
Miss Anne Batchelder
Mrs. Richard Boardman
Miss Louise Branch
Miss Si-Lan Chen
Dr. and Mrs. Farn Chu
Miss Alice Fitzgerald
Miss Gretchen Green
Mr. William Griffin
Miss Malvina Hoffman
Mrs. Francis S. Howard
Countess La Salle
Miss Ya-Ching Lee
Dr. and Mrs. Frank L. Meleney

Mr. Harold C. Murray
Mr. and Mrs. Marsden J. Perry
Mrs. Edgerton Parsons
Miss Marjorie Riordan
Miss Liza Sergio
Mr. Guy E. Snavely
Mrs. Oscar Stevens
Mrs. William Johnston Taylor
Dr. and Mrs. Donald D. Van Slyke
Miss Florance Waterbury
Miss Gladys Weatherley
Dr. and Mrs. Maurice William
Mrs. Cecelia Wyckoff
Miss Hilda Yen

fig. 25

fig. 26

fig. 27

fig. 28

fig. 29

fig. 30

BAHA'I WORLD FAITH

"The well-being of mankind, its peace and security are unattainable unless and until its unity is firmly established . . . Soon will the present day Order be rolled up, and a new one spread out in its stead."—(Baha'u'llah.)

• free public lecture •

"PEACE PLANS COMPARED" AND
"THE PRICE OF WORLD PEACE IS WORLD RELIGION"

Speakers: HILDA YEN, student of international peace plans; attended League of Nations, Dumbarton Oaks, Bretton Woods and San Francisco Conferences. Flew for China, 1939; escaped to America, 1941—brilliant Baha'i speaker.

CARL SCHEFFLER, nationally known Baha'i lecturer with an outstanding record in the field of education . . . Director of The Evanston (Ill.) Academy of Fine Arts—recognized for training professional artists—eloquent and forceful speaker.

Date: Monday, March 25th, 8:15 P. M. Brooklyn Academy of Music
30 Lafayette Avenue

————EVERYONE CORDIALLY INVITED————

fig. 31

113

PART II

LI XIAQING 李霞卿: PROFILE OF A LEGEND

He who wishes to secure the good of others has already secured his own.

—Confucius

14. INTRODUCTION

From the time she was a little girl, Li Xiaqing knew she was not like anyone else. According to the Western calendar, she had been born on the sixteenth day of the fourth moon in the year that coincided with 1912, but more auspiciously, she had come into the world in Year 1 of the *zhonghua min guo*, the calendar that charted the life of the recently established Republic of China. When she learned that the new state had been born of a Revolution, a bloody uprising in which her family had been intimately involved, she knew in her heart that the propitious year of her birth and the heroism of her family cast her as a distinctive individual with solemn responsibilities to China. More than anything, she wanted to make her own singular contribution to her homeland.

Ever alert to opportunities for service, she found inspiration at an early age while cuddling in the arms of her great-grandmother. She loved to hear the age-old fairy tales recounted by the old woman, and would listen intently as her grandma recalled the noble deeds of *apsaras* who lived on sacred Mount Emei and flew magically through the air to avenge the oppressed. It was through these stories that Xiaqing saw her destiny unfold. She, too, would become a winged avenger and take to the skies, punishing the tyrants and caring for the weak and vulnerable. Still wrapped in the spell of these enchanted fables, she ran out into the courtyard and climbed the boulders that ringed the garden. Then she leapt out into space, willing herself to become airborne. To her surprise, she came thudding down to earth. She climbed and jumped again, but to no avail. Immensely disappointed, she told herself that this was merely a temporary setback. She would not be vanquished by gravity. Someday, somehow, she would succeed.

Time passed, but this shining dream never left her. The notion of duty to China stuck fast and she matured to become a highly principled young patriot, a deep conservative who cogitated on her responsibilities. As a teenager, she managed to find some release of passion through her temporary occupation as, of all things, a movie actress, but this career was never truly satisfying and provided her with no opportunity for the commission of noble deeds on China's behalf. It was not until her homeland was threatened by foreign invasion that she saw her chance. Xiaqing's love of country burned like a brand as she remembered her old vow to become a winged avenger—a childish notion that was now fired by new meaning—and she resolved to follow her young heart's desire. No less a personage than Dr. Sun Yat-sen, the founder of modern China, had declared "Aviation Will Save the Nation," and with calm determination, she embarked upon the study of aeronautics.

It was a happy inspiration, uniting ardent patriotism with personal fulfillment. Through the miracle of flight, Xiaqing knew she could make a tangible contribution to her nation's sovereignty, but she was also elated to discover that her new avocation brought her the most delicious contentment. Only when she was alone in the sky, it seemed, could she relax and let go. In the rough and tumble of aerobatics—rolling, looping, diving, taking the aircraft to the outer limits of its design—she finally found release. Plummeting nose-down, a thousand feet above the ground with the world spinning madly in her windshield, was the nearest thing to heaven she had ever found, and the hair-raising off chance that this time the plane might not recover was that for which she lived.

15. REVOLUTIONARY TO THE CORE

The people of China have never forgotten the deep involvement of Li Xiaqing's family in the uprising that overthrew the Manchu dynasty, and today, waxworks figures of her grandmother, Xu Mulan, and great aunt, Xu Zonghan, are on display in the Zhuhai museum that celebrates the heroes of the Revolution. The name of her uncle, Li Peiji, is etched on the list of martyrs who lost their lives in the Wuchang Uprising of October 1911.

Biographer Victoria Glendinning observes, "Family history is hard to absorb, but it is important..." The story of Xiaqing's family members and their participation in the Revolution bears close examination because of the inevitable impact their fabled lives would have on the young girl's upbringing, and the place she would be expected to occupy in the new China that, in large part, had been created by her family.

Xiaqing's famed paternal grandmother, Xu Mulan, and paternal great aunt, Xu Zonghan, were daughters of a successful tea broker, but they were also nieces to Xu Run, one of the greatest industrial tycoons in modern Chinese history. The sisters' exalted social status gave them the leverage to marry well, and the sons of Li Qingchun, a rich government official, were chosen for them.[1]

Xu Mulan was selected to wed Li's number one son, Li Zishi, and her sister Xu Zonghan was joined to his brother, Li Jinyi. Unfortunately the young women's brilliant marriages did not insulate them from misfortune. Zonghan was widowed fairly early in her marriage, and her sister Mulan also suffered when her handsome husband, Li Zishi, turned out to be something of a playboy. Li Zishi also confounded his family by following his dream of becoming a counter tenor in the theater. This was an honorable profession, and his career was notable (it was said he had a 'poetry voice' that rose up and wrapped around the rafters), but his occupation did not accord him the same respect he would normally expect to receive as scion to an ancient family of high social standing.

When the sisters' father-in-law was widowed, it fell to eldest daughter-in-law, Xu Mulan, to take over management of the Li household and its large extended family. She quickly won a favorable reputation as an excellent housekeeper and mother (she gave birth to at least three children), and as a philanthropic and strong-minded woman. However, it was little known that she also led a secret life. With the encouragement of her two sons, Li Yingsheng and Li Peiji, Xu Mulan became a keen revolutionary and an early member of the Tongmenghui, a group of radicals that was dedicated to the overthrow of the Manchu dynasty and eventually evolved into the political party known as the Guomindang. With missionary zeal, and camouflaged by the vaunted social standing of the Li family, she encouraged her siblings to join the organization. She even roped in the family retainers.[2] Despite her deeply committed participation in the rebel organization, her clandestine activities were never exposed, and the distinguished clan patriarch, Li Qingchun, never learned of his family's involvement in the Revolution that worked to undermine the same Dragon Throne that he had served so many years with such devoted zeal.

As Xiaqing later told the story, her grandmother Xu Mulan operated an embroidery shop in Guangzhou. Stocking it with foreign sewing machines, Mulan publicly claimed she was providing training and employment opportunities for disadvantaged young women in the community—and this was true—but the apparently respectable establishment also served as a front for a backroom bomb-making operation. The whirr of the sewing machines disguised the metallic sounds of the bomb manufactory located in the cellar. The small munitions operation was run by Mulan's own sons, Li Yingsheng (the future father of Li Xiaqing) and Li Peiji. The family preyed together, becoming actively involved in the production and transportation of deadly explosives for the Republican cause.[3]

One of the most charismatic and ardent leaders of the Tongmenghui was the legendary Huang Xing. His importance to the prosecution of the Revolution is considered to have been secondary only to that of Dr. Sun Yat-sen himself. Huang Xing became romantically involved with Xu Mulan's widowed sister, Xu Zonghan. In the spring of 1911, Huang led his army of revolutionists in a disastrous assault on Guangzhou's government forces, and his lover, Zonghan, was among the combatants. So were Mulan's fearless sons, Li Yingsheng and Li Peiji. They were all lucky to survive the grisly encounter. The battle, known to history as the Huanghuagang Uprising, was a rout, and imperial troops slaughtered over one hundred of Huang's followers. The remains of seventy-two dead martyrs were retrieved by the survivors of the debacle and interred in the Hill of the Yellow Chrysanthemum where they are venerated to this day.

However, although he managed to escape death under fire, Li Yingsheng (whose daughter, Xiaqing, would be born one year later) immediately fell under suspicion of the authorities, and he was among the unlucky participants who were arrested the day after the massacre and dragged before a judge for sentencing. In the courtroom, Li Yingsheng listened as, one by one, his comrades were sentenced to death for their treachery. Finally, it was his turn to approach the bench. Steeling himself to bear the weight of his own sentence, he was stunned to hear the judge declare that he was pardoning the young man because it was beyond belief that the grandson of the illustrious Li Qingchun could possibly engage in traitorous activities.

Li's pale young wife was in the courtroom to bear witness to the verdict delivered against her husband, and she was staggered by the merciful pronouncement. Unbeknownst to all, she had managed to smuggle one of Li Yingsheng's percussion bombs into the courtroom and was clutching it beneath her garments, ready to fling it at the judge when the awful sentence of death was pronounced against her husband. Together, the young couple tottered from the courtroom into the sunshine, keenly alive to the strange machinations of fate that had spared them both that day.

In the end, the ghastly defeat suffered by the revolutionists who led the Huanghuagang Uprising actually became a victory of sorts. The outrage occasioned by the massacre sparked a general uprising amongst the populace, and this revolt culminated in the overthrow of the Manchu administration on October 10, 1911.

During the tumultuous period that followed the abdication of the existing government, the revolutionaries realized that their goal was far from being a *fait accompli*. For one thing, Guangdong province still had not yet won its independence; for another, Huang Xing burned to avenge his dead comrades whose lifeless bodies now reposed in the Hill of the Yellow Chrysanthemum. He resolved that General Feng Shan, the commander in charge of the torture and elimination of the revolutionists, must die. Learning that the General would be passing through Guangzhou on his way to Shanghai, Huang devised a plot to kill him, and his nephews, Li Yingsheng and Li Peiji, volunteered to carry out the deadly deed. On the morning of October 25, 1911, the brothers took up a rooftop position on the route along which Fengshan would pass, and as the hapless general and his procession paraded beneath them, the young men lobbed their mighty bomb into the street.

The tremendous force of the explosion killed not only the General, but also some twenty armed escorts in his entourage and caused half a dozen nearby shops to collapse. Huang Xing had finally won his revenge—but not without cost. Also killed in the collateral damage caused by the spectacular explosion was Li Peiji, the seventeen-year-old son of Xu Mulan.

The repercussions of this single bombing spread far and wide, and it was said thereafter that government officials trembled with fear because of it. On November 9, 1911, Guangdong finally announced its independence from the Qing government, and the terrible bomb that killed Li Peiji was considered to be instrumental in this positive development.

On January 1, 1912, the Republic of China was born. Some four months later, so was Li Xiaqing. The birth of the child must have helped to fill the vacuum caused by the untimely and violent death of her young uncle, but even in these post-dynastic times, there were daily reminders of her family's earlier revolutionary activities. Her mother named her Xiaqing, or 'sunset glow,' but informally, the family called her 'Dandan,' a homonym for *zha dan* or 'bomb,' because her parents had used her baby carriage to transport explosives.[4]

The efforts of the Li family on behalf of China did not end when the Republic for which they had fought was securely won. Their revolutionary zeal simply morphed into concern for the welfare of those whose lives were irretrievably altered by the imposition of the new order. Xiaqing's grandmother, Xu Mulan, became president of the Institute of Women's Education, a facility that offered a fresh start to former prostitutes, concubines and homeless women. When the Institute was forced to close, she continued to aid these indigents, as well as orphans of the Revolution, by going into debt and selling her own jewelry to ensure they received adequate care. Before her premature death in 1922, she was considered to be the first disseminator of socialist ideology in South China.

Her sisters, Xu Zonghan and Xu Peiyao, became closely involved with the education of children in the new Republic. Xu Zonghan, who had earned widespread respect for her fearless role in transporting explosives for the Revolutionaries pre-1912, continued to be lauded in Republican China, this time for her work with refugee children.

After the death of her lover, the celebrated Huang Xing, in 1916, she redoubled her efforts in this regard until, like her sister Mulan, she learned that her charitable work had won the coveted approval of Dr. Sun Yat-sen. She, too, was soon impoverished by her good deeds—Xu Zonghan fell into debt as she funded opportunities for young people to take their education overseas in France—but this did not put a damper on her benevolence. In 1931, Xu Zonghan went abroad to solicit money for children's education and traveled to the United States, Mexico, Brazil, Cuba, and Peru where she addressed overseas Chinese communities to win their support for the education of China's young people.[5] Xu Zonghan also organized the Shanghai Women's Federation, and when the Japanese overran the city in 1937, she led the Shanghai woman's patriotic movement against the invaders, overseeing the evacuation of children to Thailand and the raising of funds for the use of the troops. On International Women's Day, 1944, she died at the age of 68 without knowing whether or not her beloved China would manage to shake off the yoke of the oppressor.

Although her family members were central figures in the successful prosecution of the Revolution, young Li Xiaqing, known to her family as Dandan, never heard the stories of their lofty deeds from their own lips. It was as if the details of those tumultuous years were too traumatic to recall, and it was only by talking to others that she was later able to piece together the fragmented history of their involvement. But while they were reluctant to speak about their own participation in the history of the new China, they were always happy to recite the more ancient tales of their personal forebears.

Long, long ago, Dandan was told, members of the mighty Li clan had been important members of the Dragon court. One of their more distinguished ancestors had served as personal physician to the emperor himself, and after the good doctor had restored his desperately ailing sovereign to good health, he was awarded a token of the emperor's gratitude, a large round medallion of black jade. Carved with stylized serpents and bats, symbols of the most potent healing agents in the traditional physician's pharmacopoeia, this treasure had been passed down to succeeding generations of the Li family. Young Dandan was allowed to hold this compelling reminder of her ancestor's potency in her small hands, and so reflect on the early days of her family's glory. She also learned that at some point the Li clan had suffered a disastrous falling out with the emperor. They quit the court, packed up their belongings, and set off to make a fresh beginning in faraway Guangdong province. Accompanying them on their long journey south were the bones of their ancestors that had been disinterred, and, with filial piety, laid out on ox carts for transport to their new home. The resulting dolorous procession of living and dead stretched as far as the eye could see, and as the creaking cortege slowly wound its way through the countryside, it was the source of much amazement to those who witnessed its passing.[6]

A lavish family compound was built in Guangdong to house the hundreds of family members, concubines, servants and slaves who had made this journey southward, and this ancient palace was the home of Dandan's childhood. No one knew how many people lived there—a self-sufficient village, it simply grew organically—and the child found it a place of delight. Like the scene on a blue and white porcelain teacup, its large courtyards boasted lovely gardens of landscapes in miniature, accented by mimosa-bordered pools where tame fish sought shade under floating lotus leaves. Visitors arriving through the gilded lacquer gates were ushered into airy reception rooms decorated with painted vases and furniture of dark polished wood. Amidst the potted plants, one could refresh oneself by reading wall hangings on which were inscribed famous poems, regularly rotated to reflect the changing seasons. The Hall of the Ancestors, illuminated by a lantern that was never extinguished, was dedicated to the deceased, and the names of those departed spirits were etched on panels that ringed the room. This Hall was one of Dandan's favorite chambers in the compound. To her way of thinking, it was never gloomy; on the contrary, contemplation of the lives of her ancestors engendered within her a calm sense of the rightness of her place in the world, and was a reminder of her duty to those who had gone before.

Although she lived in surroundings redolent of Old China, Dandan made significant connections with the modern West almost from her birth. In the first year of her life, her parents took her with them to France where Li Yingsheng had enrolled at the Sorbonne to study chemistry and engineering. As a student, he carried out original research in the science of electroplating. Never one to let a business opportunity pass, in his spare time, Dandan's enterprising father also sold Oriental antiques to the European market, satisfying a craze for *chinoiserie* that was currently in vogue.

After the family returned to the Far East, it was discovered that Li Yingsheng's wife had contracted tuberculosis. The ailing woman withdrew from society, and thenceforth, even her young daughter was rarely granted an audience. For the rest of her life, Dandan cherished recollections of those all too few and precious moments when she was allowed to enter the Lotus Chamber where her wasting mother languished on a divan, surrounded by flowers and flanked by a statue of the Goddess of Mercy, Guan Yin. Dandan worshipped her mother and was just four and a half years old when the doomed woman finally succumbed to her disease. Forever seared into the child's memory was the horrifying sight of her mother's alabaster-still body lying in a coffin banked with white roses.[7]

Shortly thereafter, her grandfather also became mortally ill. The old man's physician advised that the evil which had invaded the patriarch's ailing body could be expelled only if joy entered the house. Accordingly, grandfather ordered his recently bereaved son to remarry at once. The bride (probably a concubine) who was chosen for Li Yingsheng was neither of his choosing nor to his taste, but the mourning young widower dared not refuse the edict of his stricken father. The marriage went forward as ordered. Despite this drastic expediency, the old man died, and young Dandan was now saddled with an incompatible stepmother with whom she was never able to feel at ease. Still grieving for her birth mother, she clung obsessively to her father and resented anyone who came between them. Of necessity, he became her primary care-giver, and, having little experience in these matters, Li Yingsheng reared his daughter as a tomboy, placing much emphasis on the importance of sports and self-reliance.[8]

Dandan was also raised in the company of her grandfather's concubines, and spent considerable time among them. These women were among her first mentors, and she unwittingly acquired from them the alluring, flirtatious charm of the brothel that she would use one day to great advantage when working in public relations. More significantly, the concubines also taught her another early lesson that was to leave an even deeper imprint upon her psyche. It was vital, they advised, that a woman never show her emotions. This old chestnut was an essential truism in a world where women had long been required to share their men with other women. Wives and concubines had survived for centuries by clinging to this coping mechanism, hiding their vulnerability and jealousies behind an agreeable mask of acquiescence and cordiality. Dandan absorbed this recommendation with gravity.

"A Chinese woman is taught not to reveal her feelings," she conceded years later. "Through a long period of discipline, she learns to be pleasant and gracious under all circumstances."

Although she had inherited quite a different world from that of the con-cubines, and would be in the vanguard of modern Chinese women who had shaken off the shackles of the past, nevertheless young Dandan took this semi-nal lesson to heart. Throughout her life, although she became ardently involved in all those projects that claimed her loyalty, she was rarely visibly passionate in her dealings with others, and seldom displayed more than practiced good manners in social settings. This apparent disengagement from her feelings often rendered her unable to demonstrate true affection, even to her first-born children from whom she was to become unavoidably estranged, and to whom, in later life, she sometimes seemed more of an automaton than a loving mother.

Shortly after her father's remarriage, Li Dandan was sent to Hong Kong to be taken under the wing of her paternal grandmother, Xu Mulan, the renowned revolutionary. Exotic Mulan, her beautiful face carefully painted and her tiny lotus feet crammed into brightly embroidered slippers, fascinated the child, and Dandan would always claim that her grandma was the most interesting woman she ever knew.

"Between us existed a bond of congeniality that easily spanned the years between us," Xiaqing fondly recalled. "I can still see her in her neat black coat and trousers, instructing us in Buddhist doctrine and punctuating her lecture with great puffs from her water pipe."[9]

Dandan was sent to St. Stephen's mission school in Hong Kong to receive her initial education, but although the facility was renowned for the quality of its instruction, her school days there were deeply unhappy. She was the object of racial bullying by her British and American classmates, and the unkindness she received at their hands engendered in her a lifelong defensiveness of her race. As she later admitted, they almost gave her 'a permanent complex' against foreigners. When she was ten years old, she left the school and moved from the Colony to Shanghai where her father had re-settled and begun his operation of a jewelry and silver electroplating business. Li Dandan was then enrolled at the city's prestigious and fashionable McTyeire School for Girls, an American-Chinese mission school regarded as one of the finest institutions of education in China.

Disciplined learning came easily to Dandan. After four years of instruction at McTyeire, she could claim familiarity with the three hundred Tang poems (the mark of an educated Chinese gentlewoman), and could converse in French and English. The institution acclaimed her as one of its most outstanding students. However, when she was but fourteen years old, the days of her formal education at McTyeire abruptly came to an end. With her father's blessing, she withdrew from the school to take her first job of work. She became a movie actress.

16. STAR OF THE SILVER SCREEN

So it was that Dandan entered the first phase of her very public life wherein she would become a cinematic personality beloved by film audiences throughout China. In company with six other supernovas of the silver screen, Li Dandan would one day be regarded as one of the outstanding stars in the 'Seven Sisters Constellation,' and grouped with such popular luminaries as Butterfly Wu, Wang Renmei, Zhou Xuan, Wang Ying, Gao Qianping, and the immortal Ruan Lingyu. Her soon-to-be-familiar and charming face would be used to sell everything from movie magazines to hasty notes.[1] Sadly, modern day audiences have little opportunity to discover for themselves the magic she brought to the screen. Only one of Dandan's movies, *Romance of the Western Chamber*, also known as *Way Down West*, survives today, a copy of which (with French subtitles) was unearthed in the film archives of the Netherlands.

In a round about way, her entrance into the film world was due to her father's participation in the Revolution. As a member of the elite group of radicals who helped to overthrow the Qing dynasty, Li Yingsheng was acquainted with revolutionary filmmaker, Li Minwei. Li Minwei, who today is considered the father of the Hong Kong cinema, had early on allied himself with Dr. Sun Yat-sen's world-shattering ideals. In 1911, he lugged his movie-making paraphernalia to the front to record on film the great battles that were the birth pangs of the new Republic of China. In 1925, Li Minwei moved his base of operations from Hong Kong to Shanghai where he founded Minxin Film Company, an art house dedicated to excellence in cinematic production. Recognizing the company as a good investment opportunity, Li Yingsheng joined Minxin as its major shareholder and general manager, and he soon began a hands-on relationship with the company, even taking his turn behind the camera as a movie producer. Through his good relations with the Guomindang, he was in an ideal position to ensure that the new company received the active support of China's governing party. His involvement in the Minxin venture marks him as one of the founders of the motion picture industry of China.

Li Yingsheng's effectiveness in the film business was particularly enhanced by his close acquaintance with Du Yuesheng, better known as 'Big Eared' Du, king of the triads and a notorious opium dealer. Ruling with an iron fist, Du was godfather of a dreaded mob of hooligans known as the Green Gang, and was said to be so powerful that he even counted Generalissimo Chiang Kai-shek as one of his puppets. Virtually no lucrative business could be conducted in Shanghai without his personal involvement. When Du needed a man of integrity to act as his translator in the French Concession, the heart of the city's opium trade, he engaged Li Yingsheng, a fluent francophone from his days at the Sorbonne. Li became a trusted confidant, and ultimately, it was whispered, even rose to become Du Yuesheng's second lieutenant.[2] The jewelry store that Li operated in the French Concession was said to be a front for the Green Gang's opium operations.[3] Certainly, the first Minxin film studio in Shanghai was located in a building owned by 'Big Eared Du' (No. 38 Dumei, now Donghu, Road), and the company's first movies were produced there. Acting on Minxin's behalf, Li Yingsheng negotiated the acquisition of this building from Du Yuesheng, and then he and his daughter moved in to live, as it were, over the shop.

The story of Dandan's involvement in film is a simple one. As legend has it, one day in the spring of 1926, the young teenager wandered onto a Minxin movie set and was spotted by director Bu Mocang. The girl made a fetching sight. In the fashion of the time, her black hair was parted in the middle and tightly woven into a long braid that fell down her back. Wispy bangs just grazed her eyelashes, and her genuine smile was shy and warm. Bu asked the girl if she wished to participate in a movie they were filming. Entitled *Why Not Her*, it featured Li Minwei's number two wife, Lin Chuchu, and another leading actor, Ou Yang.[4] Li Dandan boldly declared that she was indeed interested in appearing in the film, and she was hired on the spot. Although her role was a small one, she applied herself to the task at hand with the single-minded dedication she was accustomed to devoting to those enterprises that claimed her allegiance. Almost at once, it seemed, she knew what was required of her. For a girl who had been trained not to show her emotions, it must have been a pleasant relief to lose herself in a character that could give rein to her passions.

A star was born. Audiences were enchanted with the artless, charming girl and immediately fell in love with her. Even top actress, Butterfly Wu, was reported to have been so impressed with the fledgling's maiden performance that she prophesized Li Dandan would soon replace Lin Chuchu in the audiences' affections.

It was the beginning of a stellar, if brief, career in film. That same year, Dandan played an important supporting role with Lin Chuchu in *God of Peace*. This movie was a scant half hour long, and there was little opportunity for her to stretch her wings, but this was remedied by her next movie, *A Poet by the Sea*, in which Li Dandan was given her first leading part. Her performance caused a sensation, both with the public and the cinematic community. Playing the daughter of a poor fisherman who is loved both by a besotted student poet and a dangerous hoodlum, she falls from a rocky prominence into the sea to escape the unwanted advances of the latter. The ardent scholar rushes to her rescue, and the young lovers are saved by a lighthouse keeper.

With the alacrity of youth, Dandan quickly became a convincing actress, well able to embrace whatever mood was required of her. In the grand tradition of silent film, where facial expressions needed to communicate what words could not, her features had to be broadly emphasized, and she became an adept at applying her own stage makeup. As a child, she had watched with fascination as her grandmother, Xu Mulan, had sat at the ritual of her *toilette*, whitening her delicate complexion with rice flour and tinting her lips and cheeks with moistened red silk. Now, kneeling on the ground in the open air movie sets, Dandan painted her own face from a modern traveling cosmetics box fitted with a mirror. The aesthetic tricks she learned in these early days of film would be of enormous help to her a dozen years later when she would reprise her 'acting' role and need to look her best at the countless stage appearances she would make throughout the Western hemisphere as China's ambassador of goodwill.

The success of *A Poet by the Sea* was followed by a string of movies in which she was assigned important roles: *Wandering Songstress, Romance of the Western Chamber, Five Vengeful Girls, Hua Mulan Joins the Army* and *Reviving Romance*. *Romance of the Western Chamber*, the only one of her early movies still extant, is based on the classic Chinese drama wherein a highborn wealthy woman (Lin Chuchu) has a chance meeting with a poor scholar (Ge Cijiang). Li Dandan played a supporting role as Hong Niang, the serving girl who works to bring the lovers together. Today the movie is a favorite at international film festivals where it has won renown for its imaginative special effects and guileless charm.

Of all the movies in which she performed, *Hua Mulan Joins the Army* was the mightiest undertaking, and probably had the greatest impact on her life. In this film, Li Dandan played the eponymous and daring heroine of the traditional tale wherein a young girl disguises herself as a man and goes to battle in her father's stead. Entering into the rough and tumble of combat, she becomes the ideal warrior, fighting valiantly for a noble cause. The film's producer, Li Minwei, was the David Lean of Chinese cinema, and he poured all of his resources and imagination into the rendering of this beloved classic. Taking almost two years to complete, the movie was filmed in seven different provinces. Produced during the white heat of summer and amidst the deep snows of winter, it included sequences shot on location in barren deserts, at the Great Wall, and within the parapets of ancient fortresses. It is likely that Dandan first acquired a keen taste for travel and swashbuckling adventure while making this film. She got plenty of both on the sets of *Hua Mulan*.

Partway through production, in January 1928, the acting company quit the studio and the familiar urban bustle of Shanghai for a two-month winter shoot in the remote interior of central China. The excursion would leave its indelible mark on Li Dandan. Visiting unusual locations and meeting people with whom she would otherwise never have come in contact was an exciting experience for the fifteen-year-old, and she reveled in its novelty. The actors and crew boarded a ship at the Shanghai docks and proceeded up the Chang Jiang, steaming past unstable regions where dangerous warlords held sway, and then on to Hubei province where they went ashore and traveled rough by freight train into the interior. At one location, they were obliged to take quarters in an ancestral hall piled high with coffins.

Moving northward into Honan by truck, they encountered army general, Fang Zhenwu, who was part of the Northern Expedition taking up arms against the rebel warlords. Li Minwei persuaded the great military leader to lend them his troops to serve as extras in the movie's army sequences. This 'cast of thousands' was realistically kitted out in accurate period costumes and enthusiastically entered into the spirit of the production. As the cameras rolled, the soldiers fought mock battles hand-to-hand. To add even more realism to the production, Li Minwei shot footage of Fang's men as they arrived back at camp, injured and bloody, from the frontlines of the actual fighting.

Although the costs of production were colossal, there was no money squandered on comforts for the cast and crew. Life in the field was rudimentary in the extreme, but Dandan, for one, was not dismayed by the harsh conditions. On the contrary, she was exhilarated by the austere beauty of the experience. Hunched over a blazing bonfire and eating steaming noodles in the snow, making a night shoot by the light of a wood fire, hunkering down to sleep with the crew in the back of an army truck while the white swirling weather closed in—this rustic living struck a romantic chord in Dandan's soul and she fell in love forever with unfamiliar places and situations. Just as the character Mulan sported warrior's garments, so Dandan took to wearing men's clothing, and her audaciously androgynous appearance in jodhpurs and high boots matched her cavalier spirit as she strode among General Fang's troops for all as if she were one of them.[5]

Li Dandan received special training to enable her to play the part of Mulan. In order to ensure the authenticity of her performance, she was taught archery (and on one occasion, almost put out the eye of the director with a misplaced arrow), and was assigned a martial arts expert to teach her all the skills that would have been required by a warrior of the period.[6] These included boxing, fencing, horseback riding, and the deadly use of knives, spears and sabers. In a classic example of life imitating art, a curious incident is said to have taken place on the set near the outskirts of Shanghai, and one that adds special luster to the legend of Miss Li as a courageous and independent woman.

Late one night, as the story goes, a pair of thieves crept onto the set and carried off the strongbox containing the money that bankrolled the production. To add insult to injury, the scoundrels made their getaway in the accountant's automobile. When the alarm was sounded, Dandan instinctively leapt into action. Jumping onto a horse, she took off in hot pursuit of the miscreants. Knowing that they would need to cross a bridge over the Huangpo to make their escape, she raced ahead and arrived in advance of thieves, blocking their passage across the bridge deck. The burglars assumed that the petite girl who barred the way could not possibly pose a genuine threat to their escape, so they blithely got out of the car to deal with her. They could not have known that she possessed the heart of a tigress, nor did they realize she had received personal training from one of finest martial arts masters in the land. To their surprise, she confronted them boldly and tossed them off the bridge and into the river below.

The thieves were thwarted and the money was saved. Li Dandan's father was so proud of his daughter—and so unwilling to pass up a brilliant marketing opportunity—that he appended a short trailer to the *Mulan* movie entitled, *Pursuing the Enemy on Horseback,* wherein this exciting episode was recreated.[7]

Despite all these heroic efforts, *Hua Mulan Joins the Army* did poorly at the box office. In advance of its release, a rival production company shot its own fast and snappy version of *Mulan* in just two weeks... and without ever having left the studio. This 'bargain basement' adaptation opened in theaters before Li Minwei's epic treatment of the subject was due to be aired, and it poached the latter film's potential audience. However, those who did bother to take in the Minxin production were full of praise for its lyric beauty and obsessive attention to detail. More than this, they were deeply impressed by the performance delivered by the lead actress. A fulsome and illustrated review in *Le Journal de Shanghai* declared that, despite her tender years, sixteen-year-old Li Dandan was a prodigious talent—the very heart and soul of the film—and possessed of a radiant beauty. "Si vous la rencontrez, vous la prendre pour une petite fille. Mais sur l'ecran, elle deviant la grace, l'ardour, l'énergie mêmes..." [8]

For those film-goers who were lucky enough to catch the movie's premiere at the Central Theater in the Yunnan Road, they were also treated to a special on-stage performance by Li Dandan herself who made an appearance during the interlude and sang the moving words of the ancient *Mulan* poem.[9]

Li Dandan was now a successful professional film actress, and she had won the respect of her co-workers and the devotion of Chinese moviegoers. But what of her personal life? It is difficult to imagine she would have had much in common with other girls of her age, many of whom were closeted and raised in the traditional manner, and she probably presented an intimidating prospect to most young men of her acquaintance. Like many of her generation, she was keen on sports, especially swimming and tennis, and was an experienced dancer, but unlike others, she was a cinematic superstar whose face routinely appeared on the covers of movie magazines. Accustomed to making public appearances to promote her films, and granting interviews to representatives of the press, her very grown-up lifestyle likely served to drive a wedge between her and her peers. It also meant that she was maturing quickly, but almost exclusively, in the company of adults. Even her ability to drive a car when few Chinese women could operate a bicycle, not to mention her disturbing tendency to wear trousers, served to set her apart, and it is easy to imagine that her unique status, for all its glamour, isolated her from those who might have been her friends.

Li Yingsheng was proud of Dandan's acting ability and all her other accomplishments, but he had been unsettled by the robbery incident. While he was pleased by the heroic part his daughter had played in confounding the thieves, he knew that she might easily have been injured—or worse—and he worried that her growing fame made her vulnerable to kidnappings and other attacks. Perhaps he regretted having exploited her courage in the *Pursuing the Enemy* trailer, or maybe he had received intimations of threats to her safety and wellbeing. He also felt her education had been neglected and she needed to receive proper schooling among young women of her own age. Perhaps most telling, he had recently 'married' his latest concubine, Minxin actress Xu Yingying (she and Dandan had appeared together in *God of Peace*), but this did not ensure harmony within the Li household. Dandan did not get on with Miss Xu, either.[10] Li Yingsheng resolved to act. Muddying his daughter's trail by discarding her childhood nickname in favor of her proper name, Li Xiaqing, he withdrew her from filmmaking. After some consultation with others, he decided to send her to Europe so that she might be enrolled in a private girls' school in England.

As regards his business partnership with the Minxin Film Company, Li Yingsheng was at loggerheads with Li Minwei. Their philosophical differences regarding the purpose of the cinema seemed to be irreconcilable. As a businessman, Li Yingsheng was concerned with profit and loss, and alarmed by the enormous cost overruns incurred by the filming of *Romance* and *Mulan*. For his part, Li Minwei was unmoved by the balance sheets that demonstrated the woefully low returns on his lavish productions. As an artist, he had dedicated his life to the notion that attitudes in China could be changed through the medium of film, and money was irrelevant in his efforts to achieve this objective. Li Yingsheng felt that, in the face of what he believed to be an unreasonable attitude, he had little choice but to dissolve the partnership.[11]

The split appears to have been somewhat amicable (Li Yingsheng was, after all, godfather to one of Li Minwei's son; he also held the mortgage on the producer's home), and Miss Li, in particular, was not estranged from her colleagues. In addition to her expectations of receiving a conventional education in Europe, she left China with the firm intention of studying the art of movie-making in the West so that she might be able to improve and develop the motion picture industry of her homeland.[12] This notion of looking abroad for solutions to help her country came to be characteristic of Xiaqing's patriotic sense of duty, and echoed the attitudes of her forebears.

On September 2, 1928, Li Minwei wistfully noted in his diary that his star performer had departed Shanghai for England via France, taking the sea passage in a French vessel.[13] It was the beginning of a new phase in Xiaqing's life that increasingly would be spent abroad. Her father soon followed her to Europe, and, as an astute man of business, Li Yingsheng appears to have taken the precaution of loading his steamer trunk with Minxin movies for promotion and distribution in Europe where their potential popularity might serve to offset cost overruns. Less than a year later, *Romance of the Western Chamber*, now bearing the title *The Rose of Pu-chui,* was shown in London at a Shaftsbury Avenue motion picture theater. It ran for three weeks and even received a positive review in the *Times*: "...we can only marvel at the fact that so innocent a film can still be found and that it leaves behind such pleasant memories."[14]

Xiaqing and her father made a Grand Tour of Europe by automobile. Some of the Minxin movies traveled with them (the Li family members all had a stake in their success), and the films, now bearing French titles, were shown in the countries they visited. In 1928, *La Rose de Pushui*, as well as *La Rose qui Meurt* and *Le Poème de La Mer* (or *Poet by the Sea*, Li Dandan's first starring picture), were screened in Paris at Studio 28.[15] The films' French subtitles were likely composed and appended by Li Yingsheng himself. They also received a showing in Geneva, Berlin and other European capitals.[16]

Xiaqing claimed to have studied at a private school in England for almost two years during this period. She continued to maintain a tenuous connection with the movie industry, befriending mainstream Western movie stars (including Charlie Chaplin), and appearing in occasional newsreels that documented her life abroad for audiences back home who were always hungry for news of their favorite performer. However, it was the end of her career as a popular star of the Chinese silver screen. It seems that she herself had come to be less than enamored by her singular life as a child actor. Years later, when she returned to China as a professional pilot, she was asked by a journalist if she might reprise her filmmaking days by appearing in movies that would promote aviation. Xiaqing is reported to have flushed and looked uncomfortable. "Please do not even mention the idea," she declared with some embarrassment, as if she were deeply insulted by the notion.[17]

It is possible that Li Yingsheng was growing weary of the responsibilities of parenthood (particularly as Xiaqing and his concubines were incompatible), and was becoming increasingly powerless to deflect the admiration that his beautiful daughter was receiving. If she were married, this burden could be offloaded onto her husband. Li Yingsheng was well acquainted with the feminist politician and activist, Dr. Zheng Yuxiu, a fellow revolutionary and China's first woman lawyer and judge. In addition to her many remarkable achievements, Dr. Zheng was also a dedicated matchmaker, and she was able to recommend a potential spouse for Li Xiaqing—her own nephew, Zheng Baifeng.[18] Despite the fact that upper-class Chinese women were becoming increasingly westernized at this time, the ancient custom of arranged marriages still endured.

Zheng Yuxiu was responsible for brokering many prominent marriages, several of which ended in tears, but it is not known if this young couple felt any sense of foreboding.[19] The Zheng family could scarcely fail to be impressed by the many positive attributes of the prospective bride. Her lineage and intelligence were irreproachable, her beauty and dignity obvious to the beholder, and her reputation as an acclaimed actress was nothing short of dazzling. She was also rich. However, from the standpoint of the Li family, the potential groom was a good catch, too. Like many other members of his illustrious clan, Zheng Baifeng was a keen patriot and a member of China's Foreign Service where he enjoyed a promising future. A graduate of the Sorbonne in Paris, he was also charming, handsome, and witty.[20] The match was accepted by both families. Through his business connections with 'Big Eared' Du, Li Yingsheng was in a position to offer his new son-in-law a most handsome dowry consisting of three percent of the municipal bond of the City of Shanghai. To his credit, Zheng Baifeng refused this munificent, but specious, offer, fearing that the acceptance of such a gift from one of the Green Gang's most highly placed henchmen would taint his diplomatic status and slow his advancement within the Waijiaobu.[21]

The couple was married in 1929 when the bride was seventeen years old and her husband her senior by some eleven years or more. By traditional Chinese standards, the difference in their ages was ideal, and besides, Xiaqing was mature beyond her years. Well-accustomed to meeting strangers, she possessed excellent public relations skills that would make her the perfect partner for a budding diplomat. As well, her proficiency as an actress would enable her to survive with aplomb the interminable dinner parties and often stultifying social events that marked the days and nights of those in the diplomatic service. Together, the newlyweds set off to Geneva to begin their married life. Zheng Baifeng quit his old quarters at the Pension Favorite and moved with his bride into their new home at 22 avenue William-Favre, a central location in the city's *quartier chic* that overlooked leafy Parc la Grange. A short stroll down the avenue led to a small beach with a splendid view of the famous giant water fountain that threw its spray into Lac Léman. After they settled, Zheng Baifeng resumed his work with the Secretariat of the League of Nations World Court while Xiaqing went back home to China for several months, then returning to Europe via the Soviet Union (where she traveled by the Trans-Siberian Express), Germany, France and Italy before arriving back in Geneva.

Suddenly, in quick succession, two children, a boy and a girl, were born to the young couple. Their son, who arrived on September 1, 1931, was named Zheng Baishi, or Pax. Baishi was the Chinese phonetic for '*pax*,' the Latin word for 'peace,' and he was so named as a tribute to a treaty his father had been helping to negotiate at the time of his birth. A daughter, Mary Mulan, was born a year later on September 7, 1932, also in Geneva.

After her very unconventional youth, Li Xiaqing, or Madame Zheng as she was known to her husband's colleagues, appeared to be settling into a contented and predictable life as a respectable matron, wife to a distinguished diplomat and mother of two lovely children. In reality, aside from their offspring, Li and Zheng had few other interests in common, and worse still, Xiaqing was rapidly becoming bored with her new life. While her husband was busy at the bureau, she had relatively little to do. Her children were safe in the care of a nanny and their flat was meticulously maintained by housekeeping staff. With no stimulating occupation to fill her hours, she spent frivolous and insubstantial days in the company of other young residents of Geneva who were nearer her own age.

However, there was one area in which she and her husband were solidly as one. They both loved China with an abiding passion and shared an unequivocal concern for the welfare of their homeland. They were deeply shaken when, less than three weeks after Pax was born, the Japanese army invaded Manchuria. Suddenly, their nation was vulnerable to attack, and the danger posed to China was never far from their thoughts.

17. "ISN'T FLYING THE TOP OF EVERYTHING?"

In 1933, Xiaqing happened to attend an air show in Paris and was stirred beyond imagining when she witnessed the aerobatic performances of the pilots who confidently soared overhead. At once, she lost her heart to aviation, and when she returned to Geneva, she signed up for a test flight at l'Aéroport de Genève-Cointrin. Her first time aloft, when she ascended for her *baptême de l'air* in a 'shaky' war surplus biplane (likely a Caudron owned by local pilot François Durafour), she was unsure of the wisdom of her decision. Nevertheless, she was irresistibly intrigued and went up again, this time in a Moth biplane that was distinctly less rickety.[1] The scene below her was stunning. Mont-Blanc, '*La Dame Blanche*' as she was known, and the rest of the Alps were plastered with snow. Geneva's lake sparkled like a rare sapphire. As they soared ever higher, she could see the whole of Switzerland and the borders of France and Italy, as well.

The experience was an epiphany. Xiaqing suddenly felt she had found her true life's vocation. She would become an aviatrix, return to China, and promote the importance of flight to her countrymen. The more she considered the notion, the more everything fell into place; aviation seemed to be the answer on so many levels. It would not only satisfy the restless craving for danger and excitement that possessed her and so many of her kinfolk, but it could even become a tool to speed up the modernization of her homeland. Considering the recent incursions of the Japanese into Manchuria, it could be argued that a strong air defense was the only curb that China could offer to the overreaching ambitions of its restless neighbor. If Xiaqing could somehow convince her fellow countrymen of the importance of aviation, she would be doing her homeland as valuable a service as her family had done during the Revolution. As she later exclaimed to a reporter, "Isn't flying the top of everything?"[2]

On a trip home to China, she consulted her father who enthusiastically backed the idea. With his blessing, she returned to Switzerland and began to spend more time in aeronautical circles, and in October 1933, she enrolled for flying lessons at Geneva's Cointrin-Ecole d'Aviation. The small airfield with its three hangars was located on the edge of the city, just a half hour's drive from her home.[3]

In the spring of 1934, 'la charmante chinoise,' as she was known to her flying colleagues, made her first solo flight. Thereafter, her passion for aviation grew steadily, and it was genuine. Even on the days when poor weather kept her on the ground, she was supremely content simply to be at the aerodrome in the midst of the aircraft she loved. When the skies cleared and she was finally able to go aloft, she felt an unmatched, almost spiritual, contentment.

"The mountain of clouds underneath you forms an ocean of snow-white fleece," she explained, and "… you say to yourself, nature is Beauty."

She also appreciated the sense of omnipotence that flight bestowed upon her. "You are now sitting on top of the world," she exalted, "sailing by a magic craft that has mastered the mystic powers of wind and rain, and surpassed the dreams of the Arabian Nights."[4]

She loved to fly at night, especially over Paris as it sparkled, diamond-like, against a night-black backdrop of velvet, the glowing Arc de Triomphe shooting starry points of light into the darkness.

"Those were the most wonderful months," she later recalled, "flying, and dreaming and feeling so free… everything looks so beautiful and you feel so detached from earth – you are so much closer to heaven."

Xiaqing's allusions to feelings of freedom and detachment were telling;

her marriage had started to unravel.

Her dedication to aviation was somewhat baffling to others. A flight examination officer is said to have questioned her decision to become an aviatrix.

"But you're so beautiful," he exclaimed. "Why have you decided to learn to fly?"

"Because," Xiaqing answered, "as far as the average person is concerned, flying is a man's business—as if women should be excluded—but I want to do something women usually don't have an opportunity of doing."

"But isn't it a fact," he insisted, "that the feet of your countrywomen are bound?"

"I come here," she replied firmly, "to let the world know that, not only can a Chinese woman walk on the ground, she can even fly through the air."[5]

Winning her wings was more than a personal goal. The reputation of China's womanhood was at stake. Accordingly, Xiaqing worked diligently toward completion of the course until success attended her efforts. On 6 August 1934, Madame Zheng Xiaqing passed the requisite practical and theoretical exams and received her private pilot's license from the Aéro-Club de Suisse, 'Brevet I de pilote d'avion de tourisme No. 0586.' She was the first woman of any race or nationality to receive a flight brevet in Geneva and was probably among the first ten women in Switzerland to be so certified.[6] Thereafter, Europe was her oyster. Clad in natty white flying togs and high heels, she routinely hopped off to various capitals, making herself conspicuous at the aerodromes of Vienna, London or Paris by her knack of descending from the cockpit as soignée and elegant to her fingertips as if she were emerging from a beauty salon.

However, while others may have been impressed by her glamour and derring-do, Xiaqing was aware of the limitations of her knowledge. If she wanted to aid her country in a tangible manner, she would need to hone her credentials and augment her knowledge of flight and aircraft maintenance. The finest aviation school in the world was reckoned to be the Boeing School of Aeronautics in Oakland, California, and, after she received permission from her father, it was to this academy that she applied to receive advanced flight education. The school took some persuading—it had never before admitted a female student—

but she persevered, and to her delight, she was finally accepted for the new term starting in January 1935.

On January 9, just before she set sail for America, the Aéro-Club de Suisse awarded Li Xiaqing with Brevet II. There was some initial confusion when the next day she received a terse letter from the Swiss Department of Post and Transport advising her that, as she had not taken the requisite medical exams, she was therefore ineligible for the Brevet. Some days later, however, after she and her family had set sail for America and had arrived at the Chinese legation in Washington, D.C., she received a cordial note from the secretary of the Aéro-Club announcing that all was well. She had been granted Brevet II after all. With her impressive credentials intact, she was ready to commence instruction at the Boeing School in California.

The Boeing School of Aeronautics was a division of United Airlines and catered to serious, full-time, transport aviation students only. Its eighteen flight instructors were veteran military, airmail and commercial pilots who were considered the best in their field. The training aircraft at the students' disposal were among the most up-to-date in the world of flight, and these included a variety of models, such as Boeing, Stinson and Stearman trainers.[7] One of the jewels of the fleet was a Ford tri-motor powered by three Wasp engines, a rugged transport plane designed to carry passengers in the budding commercial aviation business. It was quite a thrill for Xiaqing when, barely four months into the course, she and her fellow classmates were allowed to fly the big Ford from Oakland to Chicago, taking turns operating the controls.

Ground school training also accounted for a large part of the curriculum and included lessons in celestial navigation, motor mechanics, metallurgy, instruments, radio, aircraft assembly and repairs. With such comprehensive instruction under their belts, the school's graduates could expect to find ready employment in the airline industry, and for many years after having received her training, Xiaqing was rarely able to board a commercial transcontinental aircraft without recognizing the flying crew, usually Boeing alumni like herself.

But what of her husband and small children? They had accompanied her to San Francisco and they saw her installed at her new school, but at that point, they left America and steamed off to China. Xiaqing took a room at the San

Francisco Young Women's Christian Association, a residence traditionally considered a safe haven for women who were living alone and away from home.[8] *Miss* Li Xiaqing, as she was known to her two hundred fellow students—all of them men—was a lovely young woman with no apparent ties.

The asperity of the school's training regimen came as a brutal shock. Unlike the gentle instruction of treasured memory she had received as a sort of pampered pet in Geneva, her American teachers were merciless. She was so petite that she needed to sit on a fat cushion to see out the window of the training aircraft, and blocks had to be attached to the foot pedals so she could reach them, but despite her sex and seeming fragility—or because of these apparent drawbacks—she was ruthlessly grilled by her instructors. Her every decision in the air was questioned. She redoubled her concentration and intensified her dedication to her studies, but despite unceasing efforts, her work seemed to please no one.

After a month of unrelentingly harsh instruction, a discouraged Xiaqing finally broke down in front of her flying teacher and wept tears of exasperation, quite a departure for a woman who had been taught since childhood to mask her emotions. Her instructor was so taken aback by this uncharacteristic outburst that he hastened to comfort her by conceding that, while it was true she had been the recipient of unusually martial training, her teachers had acted with the best of intentions. From the outset, they feared they would spoil her, and to counteract their natural feelings, they decided to mete out the gruff treatment that had so confounded her. Upon hearing this confession, Xiaqing took heart, and thereafter, her training proceeded more smoothly. She also had the satisfaction of knowing that she was not being patronized because of her sex.

Soon she learned to dismantle and reassemble an airplane engine with aplomb. She became conversant with the mysteries of aerodynamics, meteorology, aircraft design and radiotelephony. One of the thrills of her training included a successful blind flight from Oakland to Reno, a distance of 181 miles; the cockpit of her aircraft was completely hooded and she was required to navigate entirely by instruments.

For all her satisfaction with the essentials of the course, Xiaqing was disappointed to discover that aerobatic training was not part of the core syllabus. Her cherished goal was to return to China and draw attention to the importance of aviation through exhibitions of stunt flying, so it was absolutely vital that she acquire this precious skill. She made a formal request that the school provide her with private lessons in stunt flying, and, to her delight, she was granted this privilege. Seasoned pilot, LeRoy B. Gregg, was assigned as her personal instructor.[9] Shortly after she began this specialized training, however, she received some extra instruction that was definitely not on the curriculum.

On May 15, 1935, Xiaqing was slated to go aloft with Gregg to learn aerobatic maneuvers over San Francisco Bay. As usual, she wore her bulky leather flying suit, and, before take-off, carefully inspected her safety belt. When it came to stunt flying, nothing could be left to chance. Then the two aviators clambered into the open cockpit trainer, with Gregg taking a position in the front seat and Xiaqing in the rear. They took off and were flying over the Bay at about 2,200 feet when Gregg signaled to his student that he was about to begin a barrel roll. Then he flipped the aircraft over onto its back. At this moment, Gregg happened to glance in the rear view mirror and was shocked by what he saw. His student was half out of her seat, and desperately clawing at the fuselage. Then to his horror, he watched as she suddenly shot completely out of the aircraft. Her safety belt had snapped! Gregg just caught the flash of Xiaqing's shiny overshoes as she was hurled into the void. For a moment, he continued to fly upside down, fearing he might strike her with the wings if he flipped the plane too abruptly, and then he rolled upright and peered fearfully over the side, terrified by what he might see.

"All the time I was praying that she would know what to do," he recalled. "She had never made a parachute jump in her life. I didn't know what she would do. Even the coolest lose their nerve on the first jump."[10]

He saw her tumbling head over heels below him, hurtling at a terrific speed toward the ocean. Fearing the worst, yet he hoped for the best, and at the last minute his prayers were answered.

"I wanted to cheer," he exclaimed with relief, "when I saw her jerk the ring about 800 or 1,000 feet down and the parachute bloomed out..."

Overcoming her initial shock, Xiaqing had had the presence of mind to pull the rip cord, remembering with grim humor the parachute company's disclaimer that, "If it doesn't open, you can always get your money back." But as she floated earthward, buoyed by the 'chute, she realized with a start that she was dropping, not over land, but over water, and this would complicate her landing considerably. Even if she survived the plunge into the bay, she might well become entangled in the parachute's rigging or be dragged below the waves by the weight of her clothing. There was also the very real possibility that she might succumb to hypothermia in the cold waters.

Her instructor was likewise aware of the deadly dangers. He banked and sent his aircraft into a screaming dive back to the airport to sound the alarm. He made a hurried tailwind landing, called for a couple of life preservers and roared off again, returning to where Xiaqing had splashed down just moments before and was now a small thrashing speck in the sea. Fortunately, the billowing swell of her descending parachute had been spotted on shore by airmen at the nearby U.S. Naval Reserve Base in Alameda. Two of the reserve pilots had already climbed into their rescue aircraft and were readying it for takeoff. The plane was a Loening OL-8 amphibian, and it was ideal for ocean rescues.

Meanwhile Xiaqing was doing her best to cope with her predicament. When she had plunged into the sea, the parachute that could have smothered her was blown aside by the wind. She released it so it would not pull her down, but she found that her all-leather flying suit had become incredibly cumbersome. With its five zippers, it was impossible to shed while she was busy treading water. Xiaqing had never been cowed by danger—on the contrary, she embraced it—so she saw no reason to give in to panic, but she realized that the icy coldness of the water was rapidly becoming her worst enemy. Although she was an expert swimmer, the shore was more than half a mile away and the drag of her suit meant that swimming to safety was out of the question. She found she could not even maneuver to reach the preservers.

"I didn't dare go after the life preservers that Gregg dropped," she explained. "I couldn't swim."[11]

There was nothing for it—she would have to keep afloat to the best of her ability. Propping her feet on the parachute's cushion to keep them as high as possible, she lay on her back with her head up and paddled with studied calm in the numbing water while praying for help to arrive.

She did not have long to wait. Over the sound of her chattering teeth, she suddenly heard the approach of the Naval Reserve's amphibian, and soon saw it circling overhead, making ready to land. But her joy turned to dismay when she realized that the excited pilot had inadvertently jammed the landing gear and was unable to release the aircraft's pontoons. Growing increasingly desperate, she watched in disbelief as her rescue plane retreated and flew back to base.

Unable to move her limbs properly, and irritated by the cold water that lapped continuously into her nose, eyes and ears, Xiaqing's spirits started to sag. She finally began to admit the unthinkable—she was losing ground in her efforts to keep afloat—but she was not yet ready to consider defeat. After what seemed an eternity, she saw that a second Loening had left the reserve and was winging its way to her rescue. Fortunately, the pilot was able to deploy the pontoons successfully and he made a splashdown on the water nearby.[12] Over twenty minutes had elapsed since Xiaqing had plummeted into the sea, and she was glacially cold, but when the aircraft motored alongside, she had sufficient strength to grab the aircraft's floats. She held on until the reservists could pull her in. When they had gotten over their surprise that the downed pilot was a lovely woman, and a Chinese one at that, they were further astonished when their waterlogged survivor announced that she had only two complaints. She was a trifle chilled, she declared, and she had lost one of her shiny overshoes in the briny deep.

Xiaqing was flown back to the Naval Reserve. Swaddled in blankets but smiling broadly, she was swiftly carried by her rescuers into the base hospital. The doctor who examined her judged that, although Miss Li was suffering from mild shock and exposure, she was otherwise in good condition. Just for form's sake, he admitted her to hospital for observation.

It seems that half the Bay Area had witnessed Xiaqing's descent from the sky, and in no time, press reporters converged on the infirmary to interview the lovely Venus who had miraculously emerged unscathed from the sea. A photograph of the young woman appeared in the next day's *San Francisco Examiner*. It showed her tucked warmly in bed, wearing her usual thousand-kilowatt smile. Her makeup was perfect, and she bore no trace of her recent ordeal. Certainly, Xiaqing would have been forgiven if the fall had caused her to renounce aviation forever, and this possibility was likely on the minds of the reporters who gently asked if she had been terrified by the potentially fatal incident.

"No," she airily replied. "I wasn't scared. Just thrilled."

Nevertheless, to ensure she did not lose her nerve, the next day the young aviatrix went up again over the Bay in the same stunt plane.[13] Was it truth or bravado that later caused her to declare she had actually delayed pulling the rip cord because she so much enjoyed the free fall in space? The courageous spirit of the fast-thinking girl who had foiled the plans of the movie set burglars on the outskirts of Shanghai was alive and well in the young woman who fed off the exhilaration of her dangerous skydive into San Francisco Bay.

This incident entitled Xiaqing to join the exclusive ranks of the Caterpillar Club, membership in which was limited to those whose lives were spared through an emergency parachute jump from an aircraft. On June 12, 1935, the Irving Air Chute Co. Ltd. presented her with the small gold caterpillar pin that signified her entry into the elite fraternity. The ruby-eyed caterpillar represented the tiny silkworm of her homeland which had spun the parachute silk that had saved her life. She became the first Chinese woman member of the club.[14] It was a seminal moment in her career, and one of the exploits that added luster to her growing reputation as a female flying phenomenon.

On November 5, 1935, Li Xiaqing acquired another 'first' to add to her growing list of achievements. With straight 'A's' (and a 'B' in Engine Shop) she became the first woman to graduate from the vaunted Boeing School of Aeronautics.[15] When she received her diploma, she was also granted a U.S. private pilot's license, certificate number 33654.[16] A fully-fledged aviator whose intelligence and courage had been thoroughly tested and established, she was primed to return home and save her nation through aviation. Trailing clouds of glory, in December of that year, she boarded the luxury liner *s.s. President Coolidge* and steamed off to China. In retrospect, it was just as well that she had been toughened by her training at Boeing boot camp. Her initial reception in Chinese aviation circles was going to be distinctly chilly.

18. RETURN TO CHINA

Xiaqing's first port of call was Hong Kong where she visited her father who, among his many business endeavors, owned and operated the Keen Sang Brickworks. Then she sailed on to Shanghai to meet with the rest of her family. By this time, her life as a married woman had become distasteful to her, and she saw her husband as a liability. Her meeting with Zheng Baifeng was doubtless painful and acrimonious.

Before the Chinese New Year of 1936, she established a permanent residence in Shanghai. At that time, the city had gained a reputation as the center of aviation activity in China, and it was the logical place in which to base herself if she wished to promote air-mindedness among her fellow countrymen. Some of the groundwork had already been laid.

The China Aviation League had been founded in September 1932. A handful of enthusiasts supported the League, but it was slow in getting off the ground, hampered by the fact that China prohibited private flying. Designed to put a crimp in the ambitions of self-aggrandizing warlords, the prohibition served to protect the government from possible air attacks, but it also quashed legitimate flying interests. Generalissimo Chiang Kai-shek weighed the perceived dangers of personal flight against the need to promote aviation, and in the spring of 1934, he ruled that civilians would finally be allowed to operate private aircraft. Buoyed by this pronouncement, a group of aviation enthusiasts inaugurated the Shanghai Flying Club, the first of its kind in China. As an official arm of the Aviation League, its members persuaded local merchants to donate two aircraft to the club, a Junkers Junior A50 (a two-seat monoplane clad in Junkers' trademark corrugated skin) and an Avro Avian biplane. With two fine airplanes in its hangar, the club ramped up its activities and soon declared its intention of providing trial flights and lessons to all who were interested.

The League decided to create an impressive building for its headquarters and made plans for its construction. On October 9, 1935, Shanghai mayor, Wu Tiecheng, laid the foundation stone and enthusiastically applauded the lofty aims of the League. Aviation having come of age at last, the League's building was destined to become part of the city's vast and sprawling plans for a new civic center complex to be built over several acres in the Jiangwan district. The sincere enthusiasm of the association's members for the romance of flight may be gauged by the whimsical appearance they chose for the exterior of their new headquarters. Designed by renowned architect, Dong Daqiu, the building was shaped like a biplane, and, appropriately, this feature was most obvious when seen from the air. Completed early in 1936, it was put into official use in May of that year. (Curiously, when Japanese bombers attacked Shanghai in September

1937, they flattened the new civic center located next door, as well as everything else in the vicinity, but left the aviation structure more or less intact. The enemy birdmen were likely so enchanted by this fanciful structure's homage to flight that they chose to spare it.)

For all the hoopla, however, the average citizen was still unconvinced about the value and safety of flight. Li Xiaqing was keen to change this prevailing attitude, and from the moment of her arrival in Shanghai, she allied herself with the League which hailed her as China's first aviatrix.[1]

Frustratingly, she was surprised to discover that, at the official level at least, her ambitions would be met by a great deal of resistance. The government of China was not disposed to grant a license to a woman—an upper crust beauty at that—and did everything in its power to disabuse her of her objective. However, she had not gone to all the trouble of honing her craft on China's behalf to be rebuffed. Her rigorous training at Boeing lent her all the backbone she needed to lay siege to her opposition. Finally, after much lobbying, she was told her licensing request would be considered… but only upon successful completion of a test flight with a professional examiner of the Chinese Air Force at Nanjing.

Government officials either assumed Miss Li would be cowed by the request, or would be unable to fulfill the exacting requirements of the military, but they were mistaken on both counts. Xiaqing was more than willing to acquiesce to this condition, and, in the end, she expertly passed all tests with flying colors. As there was no longer any excuse to keep her grounded, remaining official opposition crumbled at once. Not only did she become the first of her sex to be granted a rare government pilot's license, the Generalissimo himself issued it to her. Like a precious jade pass, this document gave her leave to fly anywhere in the country, and she was able to take immediate advantage of it.

Once she became established, other honors followed. Xiaqing was granted the use of a government plane, and was given a special assignment. She was asked to fly throughout China to inspect all civil and military airfields in the country to determine their states of readiness. While eager to oblige, she soon discovered that the defective aircraft put at her disposal, whose engine needed constant maintenance, mirrored the woeful state of China's aero infrastructure, and she noted the need for light years' worth of improvement in airfield upkeep and repair. In addition, she discovered that maps were inaccurate, weather reports were largely unreliable, and there were virtually no guidance systems, such as radio beam facilities, in use at any station. She described some of the challenges:

"In one instance, I had to follow a very sharp winding river in order not to get lost because the instruments in my plane were not working. It was foggy and mountains arose [on] each side of the river. It seemed as though the river hardly gave me elbow room and that my wingtips just missed touching the mountains. I couldn't fly any higher because of the fog and couldn't go lower because it was too narrow."[2]

Laid against the flying hazards she faced, and the distressing state of the aeronautical network of her homeland, was the ever-varying beauty of China itself that she encountered on her tour of duty. She had a bird's eye view of its majestic splendor—camel caravans padding across rolling sand dunes, the watery sheen of rice paddies contoured to the relief of the land, crumbling mounds of long-forgotten temples that pushed up from the earth in the most forsaken landscapes—and she had occasion to pass over many of the areas where she had filmed *Mulan* a little more than a decade before. During this tour of inspection, Xiaqing came to know China as few of her fellow countrymen ever would. She flew its length and breadth, from Shanghai in the east, to Chengdu in the west, and from northern Beijing to the southern colony of Kwangchowwan, today's Leizhou Bandao. She was staunchly proud of her 30,000-mile long-distance achievement.

Once back in Shanghai, she quickly moved to help organize the Aviation League's new flying school—the government partially subsidized its operation—and became its only female flight instructor. On March 1, 1936, she was present at the inauguration of the China Flying Club (open to Chinese members only) at Longhua Aerodrome. Two hundred aviation enthusiasts showed up that first day to launch the club... and to take advantage of the free flights over Shanghai offered to whet the public's interest.[3] The results of the membership drive were so encouraging that the club made immediate plans to purchase two more training planes.

However, with the probability of war looming on the horizon, yet more needed to be done to impress on the public the vital importance of aviation to the nation. Xiaqing managed to do just that when she dropped a 'bombshell' in late March. A sensational announcement appeared in the local press:

"Miss [Li Xiaqing], a prominent Chinese aviatrix who recently returned from the United States, is reported by Chinese newspapers to have been unconditionally divorced from her husband, [Zheng Baifeng], in order that she may devote her life to development of aviation in China."[4]

While there was undoubtedly more involved in the collapse of the marriage than Xiaqing's ardent desire to serve her country, this public declaration that she would become a sort of vestal virgin for flight shone a spotlight on the imperative of aviation as little else could have done. Privately, she also hoped that the patriotic nature of her announcement would help to dilute the criticism she could expect to endure as the mother of two small children leaving her husband at a time when divorce was considered highly irregular. By turning this traumatic event into a promotional tool, Xiaqing demonstrated just how much business savvy she had absorbed from the successful marketing techniques of her father.

The aunt of her estranged husband, feminist lawyer and lawmaker, Zheng Yuxiu, who had arranged the marriage in the first place, now became the one who sadly drew up the divorce papers. The rights for women she had personally helped to enshrine in the newly minted constitution of China became the tools by which Li Xiaqing was able to shed her husband. Miss Li became one of the first women in China to divorce her spouse under the new laws.[5]

This drastic action, and the intense publicity it received, caused her ex-husband to suffer a severe loss of face. Zheng Baifeng knew full well that the very public split would have an embarrassing impact on his upwardly-mobile aspirations in the heavily competitive diplomatic arena, and he could not forgive and forget this highly personal slight. In those days, it was still customary for estranged spouses to adhere to the ancient custom of disowning the once-beloved by giving her a 'funeral' replete with an empty coffin paraded through the main street followed by monks, musicians and professional mourners. It is not known if Zheng resorted to this drastic expediency, but thereafter, and for the rest of his life, whenever mention was made of Li Xiaqing, he would reply, "She is dead," and his friends and acquaintances took their cue from his behavior.

A stubborn and judgmental man, he also took steps to deny his ex-wife access to their offspring, Pax and Mulan, and over the next decade, Xiaqing was only able to see her children during the rare and fleeting intervals when she bribed her husband's servants to look the other way and let her pass. The sense of guilt that she must have felt at her inability to participate in the raising of her family can only be imagined; the natural yearnings of motherhood had to be squelched entirely. After her children were grown and she was able to see them without restraint, her interactions with them were not as free and easy as the children would have wished. The distance that had physically separated them for so many years remained like a ghost between them, and Xiaqing seemed unable to lavish her children with the motherly love and affection they so earnestly craved. Even though she, too, had been denied maternal love, and always lamented that she had enjoyed very little intimacy (and only four years) with the mother she worshipped, she was hamstrung by her inability to display her emotions to the offspring of her now-despised former spouse.

The same day that the news of her divorce appeared in the English language press, Li Xiaqing attended a high profile annual benefit of the Chinese Women's Club at the luxurious Paramount Hotel. Unescorted, and with head held high, she sat at dinner with the cream of Shanghai society, the elegant Madame Wellington Koo, the Countess de Courseulles and her sisters Itala and 'Mats' Chieri, the Yang Guanshengs, and other prominent diplomatic representatives. They were her friends, but they were also associated with her husband and his colleagues. Thereafter, the 'socialite aviatrix,' as she was now labeled, was a glamorous and valued guest at the city's most glittering galas, and her name cropped up regularly in the social pages of the newspapers. As a result, however, the enmity between her and Zheng Baifeng grew even more bitter.

Xiaqing was never without admirers, but one suitor was particularly persistent. While she had been at flying school in Oakland, she received a letter from a young man who had met her in Europe and could not forget the lively young woman who enjoyed the active life as much as he did. Noting her crumbling marriage, Peter Doo tentatively made his move, writing to Xiaqing in May 1935 from London where he was on business.

"I am sure you and I can get along fine," he pointed out, "as we both almost have the same taste in everything."[6]

A couple of weeks later, when he learned of her emergency parachute jump into San Francisco Bay, he sent her a telegram voicing his concern for her safety, but also tendering his enthusiastic congratulations on the success of her jump. Rather than try to discourage her from continuing with the adventurous life she loved, he chose to applaud her efforts. Xiaqing likely appreciated his unqualified support.

After her divorce from Zheng Baifeng, she and Peter became romantically involved, and their relationship continued for some eight years, mostly over long distances. In an effort to endear himself to his beloved, Peter even went into business with her workaholic father, and together the two men spent long, dusty days trudging through the hinterland, prospecting for potential mineral deposits (Li Yingsheng already owned two silver mines), or investigating profitable business deals that would line their pockets and, later, aid their nation's war effort.[7] Through his devotion and business acumen, the young man seems to have won the approval of Xiaqing's daunting father.

"Some day," Peter wrote to his darling after an all night, heart-to-heart session with Li Yingsheng, "your papa said [he] will build a nice hut in the mining district for you and us to stay. We can enjoy fresh air, horse riding, hunting, etc. That will be heaven for you and I. Do you think we need this kind of environment for a change instead of the glooming Nanking Road of Shanghai?"[8]

While the picture Peter painted certainly seemed idyllic, their simple life together in a little hut in the wilderness would have required an adequate supply of servants. While Xiaqing could take apart and reassemble an aero engine with ease, she was no domestic diva, and could scarcely boil water.

Meanwhile, Xiaqing applied herself to her chosen profession, and she was all business. When she was not taking students aloft for their training at Longhua airfield, she was teaching ground school to some of the thirty-six students (two of them women) who had enrolled for lessons during the Shanghai Flying Club's membership drive.[9] To cope with the unexpectedly large numbers, the flying school divided the students, sending half of them to take instruction at Longhua airfield five miles south of Shanghai proper, and the others to Hungqiao airfield, an alternate aerodrome some six miles to the southwest of the city. Xiaqing taught at Longhua.

In September, the China Aviation League was formally amalgamated into the newly created China National Aviation Reconstruction Association. By way of demonstrating the importance of this budding organization, Generalissimo Chiang Kai-shek agreed to be named as its first president, and Shanghai Mayor, Wu Tiecheng, its chairman. Work began at once to publicize the association's agenda and the importance of flight. This was most attractively accomplished that same month when a smiling photo of Li Xiaqing appeared on the cover of the popular monthly illustrated magazine, *Zhong Hua*. Impeccably groomed and wearing a form-fitting plaid-print *qipao* (bias tartans were all the rage in 1936), she is shown standing in front of one of the school's aircraft, her manicured hand confidently cupping the blade of its propeller. She was also photographed with her sole female student, Yang Jinxun, a young woman who fervently hoped to follow in her flying mentor's mighty footsteps.

As the probability of war with Japan continued to mount, the obvious need to bolster aviation for China's defense finally began to win hearts and minds. The Generalissimo was celebrating the fiftieth year of his birth in October 1936, and the nation proposed that this milestone be marked by presenting its leader with fifty new aircraft.[10] A national fund-raising campaign was launched, and various organizations—even whole cities—vied with one another to see who could donate the most planes to the cause. Shanghai movie stars held benefits, boy scouts solicited funds door-to-door, and merchants dug deep into their profits to see who could make the biggest contribution. All citizens were asked to donate one day's pay to the Aviation Fund, and in recognition of the growing need for adequate national defense, this request was met with singular enthusiasm. On October 24, 1936, one week before Chiang Kai-shek's birthday, a special aircraft dedication ceremony was held at Longhua aerodrome. It was estimated that one hundred and fifty thousand souls made their way to the celebration, and when traffic became hopelessly snarled *en route*, they abandoned their cars on the highway and made the rest of their way to the airfield on foot. The Generalissimo, pleading modesty, was not in attendance, but this did not dampen the enthusiasm of those who gathered to enjoy the day's events. At the center of attention were the ten khaki-colored gift aircraft whose fuselages all bore the eighteen-pointed white sun-star of China.

The most prominent citizens of Shanghai (including the future aviatrix, Miss Hilda Yan) were seated on a bunting-draped podium erected directly adjacent to the airfield, and it was from this stage that the speeches of the civic leaders were made. Their lofty words were soon lost in the roar of the planes taking off and soaring overhead, accompanied by the wholehearted cheers of the crowds who were thrilled beyond measure by the magnificence of the aircraft that they themselves had helped to fund.

But the most exciting moment of the day came when Xiaqing took to the skies alone to perform aerobatic stunts for the audience below. It was the largest moment in her aviation career thus far. Xiaqing had the undivided attention of that massive crowd, and she had to deliver a perfect, and perfectly thrilling, performance. She did. Drawing on all the maneuvers and tricks she had learned at the Boeing school, Xiaqing flawlessly executed a brilliant series of breathtaking aero exercises—the first ever performed by a Chinese woman over her native soil—and then ended her program with a hair-raising finale. Soaring to a great height, and then plunging downwards, Xiaqing made a power dive directly towards the central podium. When she was within inches of the dignitaries' heads, she pulled up at the last minute and thundered past into the blue. The audience went wild.

The effect of the daring flyover (which, at one fell swoop, might have wiped out the cream of Shanghai's leadership mere months before the outbreak of war) was electrifying, and likely did more to inculcate air-mindedness than the exhibition of any number of birthday planes.

When she touched down, the triumphant aviatrix was escorted, queen-like, through the cheering crowd. Stylishly kitted out in white leather flying helmet and polka dotted ascot, her hands shoved in the pockets of her spotless boiler suit, Xiaqing grinned self-consciously at the maelstrom of rowdy enthusiasm her performance had unleashed. It was a supreme moment for the young woman who had sacrificed so much to realize her dream, and had struggled with government red tape at every turn. It was also deeply satisfying to know that her ex-husband could not help but learn what an enormous success she had become. Henceforth, he would have trouble continuing to insist that she was dead. Certainly no one could have felt more vitally alive on that day than Li Xiaqing, and she savored every morsel of the crowd's adulation.

Her performance was lauded on the editorial pages of the *North-China Herald*: "Miss [Li Xiaqing's] part in the day's ceremonies was, of course, greatly to the taste of the crowd," reported the paper. "Women have played so admirable a role in developing aviation in other countries that China is right in welcoming this young lady's vindication of her sex's ability in the air."[11]

It was shortly after this stirring event that Xiaqing met with Yan Yaqing, a young woman of the Foreign Service popularly known as Hilda Yan, and together they made their plans to put women at the core of their country's aviation endeavors. Hilda had recently returned from the Soviet Union where she had been chatelaine at the Chinese Embassy in Moscow. The two women shared much in common. In connection with her work with the League of Nations, Miss Yan was as familiar with the city of Geneva as Li Xiaqing, and she, too, was the mother of a son and daughter. Like the famous aviatrix, she had also recently divorced her husband. The rebellious, independent streaks that ran through both women tended in some ways to marginalize them from mainstream Shanghai society, and through their friendship, they took comfort in their shared nonconformity. They also both cherished a passionate love of homeland and had the vision to realize that aviation was the key to China's defense.

Together, the two women made plans to endorse the need for air power amongst others of their sex. Xiaqing elaborated on their plans in an interview. "Recently," she reported, "Miss Yan Yaqing and I, as well as others, have initiated the creation of a women's group, the purpose of which is to encourage women to promote aviation." She hastened to add that the club was not at all exclusive. "All women who wish to become aviatrixes, but who cannot yet fly, are welcome to join..."

Despite her enthusiasm, however, she had to concede that flying was not an appropriate activity for every woman. "Actually, learning to fly is not easy," she admitted. "It requires a strong physique, and, even more important, a lot of money, otherwise one has no hope of flying."[12]

With the dawn of the fateful New Year of 1937, a year that would mark the beginning of the disastrous eight-year war of resistance against the Japanese military might, Xiaqing ratcheted up her plans to raise awareness of flight's potential. She resolved to write a two hundred thousand-character book on aviation, and publish it in both English and Chinese. Entitled *The Romance of Airways in China*, it was projected that the manuscript would be completed in the fall of that year. In an effort to make the work as comprehensive and up-to-the-minute as possible, she embarked on a series of aerial tours to research China's civil air routes.[13]

The topic was an ambitious one, and it demonstrated how serious she was about her intention to drag China's transportation industry into the twentieth century. When interviewed, she stated that the book would be "designed to further the growth of airmindedness in China. It will describe in popular form the development of civil aviation in China in connection with the great international routes, with special emphasis on its future, and on problems that concern every citizen, such as its commercial possibilities, sporting aviation and gliding, and airport development."[14]

Xiaqing made the first leg of her national fact-finding tour aboard a Junkers tri-motor operated by the Eurasia Aviation Corporation.[15] More than just another passenger, Xiaqing was given coveted permission to join Captain Walther Lutz, one of Eurasia's most experienced and glamorous pilots, in the cockpit.[16] As she had already logged some time on a tri-motor aircraft at the Boeing School in Oakland, Captain Lutz allowed her to take the controls of the big 16-seater Junkers JU/52. It was equipped with state-of-the-art technology, including precious radio direction finders, and over the next several days, Xiaqing logged twenty hours' worth of flying time with Eurasia: Beijing—Taiyuan—Zhengzhou—Wuhan—Nanjing—Shanghai; and Shanghai—Nanjing—Zhengzhou—Xi'an—Chengdu—Kunming.[17] Upon completion of these junkets, Xiaqing was the undisputed record-holder for long-distance flying by a Chinese woman.

Near the end of February, she was back in Shanghai organizing her notes for her book when she was contacted by pioneer pilot and representative for Southwestern Aviation Corporation (SWAC), Liu Peiquan. Liu persuaded Xiaqing that her investigations would not be complete until she came home to Guangdong for a stint of flying with the SWAC, a government-owned airline that connected China with Europe via Air France. The only airline that employed Chinese personnel exclusively, it was a small company and it had only four five-place Stinson aircraft to carry the mail and passengers on each of its four routes in the south-west area of China, but it was serving a real need and entertained ambitious plans for the future. However, the airline had been experiencing a run of bad luck. One of its aircraft had crashed in March 1936, and had been repaired, but in February 1937, it crashed again, this time with fatal results. It was likely with an eye to restoring public confidence that Liu invited the celebrity aviatrix, Li Xiaqing, to fly his aircraft.[18]

Xiaqing accepted Liu's offer, and spent six weeks with the SWAC as a volunteer transport pilot.[19] At the beginning of May, she returned to her temporary lodgings at Shanghai's Bailemen Hotel to much acclaim. As she intended, her flights in the south had drawn the attention of the media, and she was invited to describe her tour of duty to the subscribers of *Ling Long* women's magazine. The reporter dispatched to conduct the interview, plainly enraptured by her subject, was almost more interested in Xiaqing's stylishness than in her story, and painstakingly described the appearance of the flyer for the benefit of her readers:

"Her hair was rolled up in a half curve," she raptly noted, "the newest style of 1937. She wore a set of evening clothes, and her upper garment and long trousers were of a grey-green color covered with light red flowers. She wore a becoming outer cape of pale, green-figured satin. Her finger and toenails were varnished purplish-red. Her skin was very delicate, with just a few freckles. She looked extraordinarily beautiful. She is graceful, has an oval face, lips like a cherry or a water chestnut, and eyebrows slightly crooked, and you can tell, just by looking at her, that she is a typical Cantonese girl."[20]

It was difficult for the journalist to reconcile Xiaqing's alluring appearance with the very real dangers the woman aviator had faced during her sojourn as a volunteer SWAC transport pilot.

"When I flew the lines," Xiaqing recalled, "the weather was poor, with heavy fog almost obscuring the roofs of the houses below. There are also many mountains in the southwest, an area very hard to fly."

In the SWAC's short history, poor weather had caused so many accidents and disruption of services that they had almost become routine, and yet Xiaqing had safely flown all the unfamiliar routes without incident. She went on to confess her heart's desire.

"I hope I can fly from China to Europe," she confided. "This experience would develop the skills I have already acquired, and it would be a dream come true, while also promoting aviation in China." She acknowledged the hold that flight had taken upon her. "I want to serve Chinese aviation all my life," she declared with conviction. "In addition, I hope all Chinese will gain some knowledge of aviation and this will help to strengthen national defense."[21]

For the remainder of that final spring and summer of peace, Xiaqing continued to promote aviation by day, and to party by night. In late May, she managed to slip away to Hangzhou's West Lake for a brief holiday, but this excursion would be her last vacation for some time. On July 7, 1937, a seemingly insignificant skirmish at the Lugouqiao bridge near Beijing signaled the beginning of China's long-anticipated war of resistance against the Japanese, a conflict that would last for eight long years.

Initially, Shanghai was uninvolved. Its citizens remained on edge, but tried to carry on as usual. A couple of days after *dashu*, the 'Day of Great Heat,' Xiaqing and Peter Doo attended a dinner party thrown at Ciro's nightclub in honor of former mayor, and now governor of Guangdong, Wu Tiecheng. However, this celebration was the exception; the enervating high temperatures and nerve-wracking political climate inevitably led to cancellations of the usual social activities. For the next few weeks, Shanghai watched and waited until August 13 when the war finally erupted on its doorsteps and the city fell under Japanese attack. Citizens of all nationalities immediately rallied to support the Nationalist troops who struggled to keep the enemy at bay, and one of the first who came to forefront at this desperate juncture in the city's history was Li Xiaqing. She immediately approached the government to offer her services to her country.

Once more, Xiaqing thought, she would have an opportunity to play the role of the noble warrior woman, Hua Mulan, but this time, it would be for real. Armed with an impressive record of safe flight, and the grudging admiration of aviation officials nationwide, she marched to the offices of the aviation commission and made a special request—that she be put in command of a combat squadron and be allowed to engage in operational flying. If necessary, she was prepared to die for her country. To her shock and dismay, her request was peremptorily refused and she was told it would not even be considered. Regardless of her superb qualifications, and despite the fact that China desperately needed airmen, the notion of a woman flying for her nation was out of the question. Scaling back her request, she asked permission to fly on the periphery of the war, either as a ferry pilot or as a courier, but she met with the same crushing response. Worse, she learned that she was grounded for the duration.[22]

Bitterly disappointed, she swallowed this edict with difficulty, but immediately turned her attention to fighting the war on the ground. Three days after the attack on Shanghai had begun, she held an urgent meeting for fifty acquaintances at her Tifeng Road apartment, and the fruit of this gathering was the creation the First Citizens' Emergency Auxiliary. Her good friend, Percy Chen (son of Eugene Chen, one of China's most prominent political figures), was elected president of the auxiliary, and she herself was named its vice-president.

She became deeply involved in hospital work. With her friends and fellow-members of the Chinese Women's Club War Relief program, she took charge of Red Cross Emergency Hospital No. 24, located near her home on the Jessfield Road.[23] Formerly a hotel, the building's owner converted it to an infirmary after Xiaqing persuaded him to do so. Her own sacrifice was just as impressive; in the grand tradition of her forebears, she used her own money to help finance its operation. She also played a part in its management. No job was too menial. She cared for the wounded, did administrative work, helped to coordinate nursing classes, and assisted with surgical procedures in the operating room, refusing to stand down whenever the hospital was bombed. As much as possible, she and her colleagues were determined to coddle the injured soldiers in their care, and went so far as to prepare rice in three different consistencies (soft, hard and soupy) to accommodate their preferences.[24]

Xiaqing was deeply moved by the stoicism of these hospitalized men. Every evening, after she dimmed the lights and passed through the wards, she was overwhelmed by the courage of these grievously injured soldiers who, despite their pain, uttered no moans and expressed only gratitude for the care being offered them. Inspired by the lofty example of her patients, she allowed herself no idle moments. In addition to her hospital work, she also helped organize a refugee camp and an orphanage. Recognizing the morale-boosting value of positive propaganda, she ran a radio station dedicated to the dispersal of propaganda aimed at unsettling the enemy.[25]

Despite these heroic efforts, by the autumn, much of Shanghai was under Japanese control, but the city's International Settlement and French Concession continued to maintain their sovereignties, and these foreign zones in the center of town provided havens for Chinese who chose not to flee the area. Xiaqing was one of those who opted to stay on until the last minute. She was already in the initial stages of formulating an impressive scheme to help save China. It was one that would require her to leave the land she loved, but if she were able exploit her impressive flying skills abroad, she knew she could win support for her suffering people.

In the meantime, she continued her work at the Red Cross hospital until finally she learned that her name had been added to the Japanese blacklist. Although taking some grim satisfaction from this obvious tribute to the effectiveness of her efforts, she also knew her days were numbered if she did not take evasive action. When she could no longer delay her departure, she quit Shanghai, literally fleeing for her life, and caught one of the last steamers leaving the city.

Xiaqing arrived in Hong Kong via the motor vessel *Victoria*, weary from her labors, but not too tired to give a statement to the press. Although she was proud of all she had accomplished in Shanghai, she was still smarting from the strictures that had been placed on her flying freedom and she took a swipe at the aviation authorities, declaring that, if given leave, women pilots could make an especially solid contribution to the war effort. She insisted that, by acting as couriers, especially in the Interior, they could fly medical supplies to areas where they were most needed, thereby freeing male aviators for operational flights.

Xiaqing took up residence at the family home in Kowloon at No. 1 Ho Man Tin Hill. After re-marshalling her strength and spirit, she recommenced her relief work. The Crown Colony was still untrammeled by the war that raged around it, but Xiaqing continued to court danger by traveling regularly via commuter train to Guangzhou. The railway routinely came under enemy aerial attack, and she and her fellow passengers were often forced to 'duck and cover' in the ditches running alongside the tracks, but she continued to make the trip regardless. With Percy Chen, who had also evacuated to Hong Kong, Xiaqing drove into the Guangdong countryside to search for appropriate areas of re-settlement for the refugees who were fleeing south ahead of the enemy's reach. Building on the experience she had gained while working for the Red Cross in Shanghai, she liaised with Guangdong authorities to deliver her findings and to help expedite the transport of medical services throughout the province.

Despite the intensity of her efforts, Xiaqing was still frustrated by her inability to do more to save her country, and she fretted that her unique skills were going to waste. Over the spring and summer, she hammered out a vision-ary plan that would exploit her extraordinary assets—aviation expertise, smiling personality and shining beauty—to the full, while working enormously to the benefit of China. By visiting dozens of American cities and stumping hard to raise support for her people, she could make a truly substantial contribution to her country in its war of resistance against the Japanese, but she knew that, to be effective, a plan of this magnitude would require official support.

As ever, her lover, Peter Doo, was staunchly in her corner, and he lob-bied the government to win official backing for her endeavor. In this regard, he received some help from mutual friends, and on March 15, 1938, he wrote to Xiaqing to give her the results of the inquiries that he had been making on her behalf.

"As to your proposition of going abroad," he reported, "Mr. [A.L. 'Pat'] Patterson has talked to Madame Chiang to sanction your trip abroad so you will have a government name behind you which will make your work much more effective and efficient."[26]

If she could be persuaded to act as Xiaqing's sponsor, the name of Ma-dame Chiang Kai-shek carried sufficient clout overseas to assure the aviatrix of a warm reception wherever she traveled, so the plan was a sound one, but initially, the First Lady was reluctant to cooperate. Believing that the proposal needed to proceed through proper channels, she hesitated to lend her personal support until the expedition had received appropriate scrutiny. She had also recently resigned her seat as chairman of the National Aeronautics Commis-sion in favor of her brother, T.V. Song, and believed that she no longer wielded adequate power in the realm of aviation.

"Unfortunately," Peter continued, "Madame Chiang says the whole thing had better [be] referred to the Minister of Foreign Affairs, C.W. Wong. I told Patterson, better not try the foreign minister, I am sure [there is] not much chance on this guy."[27]

He was probably mistaken in his assessment of Wong's commitment to Xiaqing's plan. Although she had several champions lobbying government officials on her behalf, old family friend, C.W. Wong, was a highly placed linchpin, and the one most likely to promote her scheme to the utmost.

At last, their combined efforts finally won Madame Chiang's full support. Xiaqing now had the backing she needed, as well as the authority that went with it, and she took immediate steps to secure several appointments as the official delegate of a plethora of national relief organizations. Buoyed by the support she was receiving, she announced her plans to the press and revealed that, upon completion of her tour of the United States, she would carry her message even further afield. She intended to fly throughout Europe and the Soviet Union on behalf of national relief. Of course, she had an ancillary agenda. Not only would this ambitious program work to China's advantage, but it would also give Xiaqing an opportunity to fulfill her cherished dream of flying from Europe to China. Unfortunately, with the outbreak of the European war a year later, this latter plan would have to be shelved.[28]

She had laid the groundwork, but several large unanswered questions still loomed over the endeavor. Could a lovely young aviatrix descending from the heavens on American towns and cities actually become a magnet for financial and political support, or would the ploy simply be dismissed as a clever gimmick? Was it feasible to expect 'China's First Lady of the Air,' no matter how experienced a pilot, to fly several thousand miles in unfamiliar skies, persuasively address crowds of strangers on China's plight, and then jump into her plane and fly off tirelessly and safely to the next port of call? Could any gains, no matter how robust, possibly offset the huge risks? Xiaqing's proposed expedition was Herculean in scope and filled with any number of unseen hazards. She could hardly wait to get started.

19.   RETURN TO THE NEW WORLD

In advance of her tour, and near the end of August, Li Yingsheng invited his daughter to Hawaii for a brief holiday. Xiaqing needed a break, and it gave her an opportunity to spend some time with her father before wishing him farewell for the duration. She flew by Clipper ship to Honolulu, and a few days later, returned refreshed to Hong Kong to make the final preparations for her excursion. On October14, 1938, the great day arrived and she proceeded to Kai Tak airport to embark on the first stage of her journey. As she climbed aboard Pan American Airways' flying boat, the *China Clipper,* bound for the United States of America, the press was on hand to record this historic occasion.

Did she have any doubts or reservations about her upcoming American odyssey? None whatever. She had made a recent pilgrimage to view the wreckage of the *Kweilin,* an experience that left her deeply shaken. This DC-2 aircraft, a passenger liner of the CNAC, had been downed by Japanese fighter pilots the previous month, and its battered carcass was towed to Kai Tak where Xiaqing was allowed to examine the remains. Fourteen out of sixteen persons aboard, including women and children, had been killed in the attack, thereby earning for the *Kweilin* the lamentable distinction of being the first commercial airliner in history to be lost to hostile aerial action.[1] Viewing the crumpled body of the death plane, its skin honeycombed with eighty bullet holes, only reinforced Xiaqing's resolve, and as she took her seat aboard the Clipper, she knew her plan to seduce America was entirely just and appropriate.[2]

The Clipper's trans-Pacific passenger route to San Francisco, a distance of over eight thousand miles, had been inaugurated two years before, and, barring typhoons, the flight routinely took about a week to complete, with overnight stops at Guam, Wake Island, Midway, and Honolulu, before the final splash down in San Francisco Bay. Xiaqing had sufficient leisure time to review her preparations.[3]

As far as she could determine, nothing had been left to chance and all the necessary groundwork for her tour had been completed. As a 'hands on' person who preferred to control her own circumstances, she herself had been responsible for tending to the details that would ensure its success. Having secured letters of introduction from prominent Americans stationed in China—men who were leaders in the worlds of banking and aviation—she could produce them Stateside wherever necessary to establish her credentials.[4] She had also written formal letters to her friends in California, notably the Chinese-American film actress, Anna May Wong, and the wealthy socialite, Mrs. Bernadine Fritz, to enlist their aid in introducing her to people and organizations that might be able to render some assistance. She entertained a hope that the two women could help her secure an aircraft for the tour.

"I shall be most happy," she wrote to the well-connected Anna May, "if you can succeed in obtaining or borrowing a plane for me, as I intend to tour the various cities by plane which I will pilot myself."[5] She made a similar request of Mrs. Fritz.

The sincerity of Xiaqing's intentions can be gauged by the extent to which she was prepared to shore up her own expedition. In the jewelry bag that traveled with her, she was carrying more than US$7,000 worth of jewelry, sufficient collateral to enable her to borrow a private plane, or, in the absence of willing sponsors, to bankroll its outright acquisition. Her collection included rings, bracelets, necklaces and brooches of jade, pearls, diamonds and rubies, many of them uniquely Chinese in design. While she enjoyed adorning herself with these sparkling bibelots, they held little sentimental value. To Xiaqing, their true worth lay in their purchasing power.[6]

On October 20, 1938, the Clipper ship splashed down in San Francisco Bay, the same waters into which Xiaqing had parachuted some three and a half years before, but the elegantly suited and gloved young woman who stepped forth from the plane and onto U.S. soil in her fashionable spectator shoes was a different person. She had been toughened by her unpleasant divorce and tempered by her wartime experiences. She was also determined not to forget, even for a moment, her responsibilities to her fellow citizens who were sacrificing their lives to defend their nation. Her arrival in America received national press coverage, and it was announced that she would fly throughout the U.S. on behalf of the Red Cross. The Chinese of San Francisco were elated to have in their midst such a distinguished fellow countrywoman, and immediately put at her disposal all the help they could muster. A couple of days later, they were inspired to redouble their efforts when they received the disturbing news that Guangzhou, the ancestral home of so many Chinese Americans, had fallen to the enemy. Xiaqing's work was given additional impetus.

She arranged for her jewelry to be appraised and, on the strength of its assessment, hoped to secure the temporary loan of a small aircraft. She applied for, and was granted, a private pilot's certificate. With a mix of sentimentalism and superstition, she requested that her original U.S. certificate number, 33654, be reinstated, and this wish was granted. She was not yet ready to begin her landmark flight of America, but she tested the waters by making an initial flight to Los Angeles to win support for China.

The papers back home proudly covered this event: "Miss [Li Xiaqing], Chinese aviatrix, well known in Shanghai and Chinese nationalist circles, recently landed at Los Angeles in her own plane. She was met by members of the China Aid Council which is engaged in raising funds for civil relief in China."[7]

It was a good rehearsal for the big cross-country flight to come, and her arrival received prominent coverage in the Los Angeles dailies. She spent a week or two in the area, staying at the luxurious home of Mrs. Bernadine Fritz, a friend whom she had met years before in China. Mrs. Fritz, whose husband, Chester, was a founding partner of the Shanghai-based brokerage firm, Swan, Culbertson and Fritz, laid careful plans to ensure that Xiaqing would make a big splash in local high society, and thanks to her support, the aviatrix began to move in exalted circles almost at once. At the end of November, and in the company of her friend, she attended a party at the sprawling Santa Monica residence of movie actress, Dolores Del Rio. Other notable Hollywood guests included Basil Rathbone, Edward G. Robinson, Claudette Colbert, Darryl Zanuck, Norma Shearer, Merle Oberon, Cesar Romero, Ginger Rogers, and Errol Flynn. Xiaqing was always in her element at a party, and her bubbly and exotic presence made such a compelling impact that the Edward G. Robinsons invited her to a soirée at their home the following weekend. Many of the same film stars attended the Robinson's gathering, and their numbers were augmented by the presence of yet more legendary celebrities. Joseph von Sternberg, Frank Capra, William Powell, Aldous Huxley, and Constance Collier all put in an appearance, but according to the gossip columns, it was Miss Li, attired in a stunning lamé Chinese gown, who stood out in the luminous crowd.[8]

A couple of days later, Xiaqing was back in the news when the Mexican citizens of Olvera Street in the heart of old Los Angeles invited her to be their special guest of honor at festivities celebrating Catarina, the sainted Chinese princess of Mexico.[9] As in Beverly Hills, Xiaqing was once more the center of attention, a modern-day Chinese princess who was treated to tea and sweets and conveyed with respectful ceremony through the streets of the Mexican district, but despite her burgeoning star status, her thoughts rarely strayed from the ambitious project she had carved out for herself—her upcoming mega-tour of America.

She knew that her friend from Shanghai, Hilda Yan, had settled in New York and was enrolled at a flying school, and she learned that Hilda was coming to the end of her flight training. While their plan to start an aviation club for Chinese women was no longer feasible, they still shared a dream to bring world attention to China's plight and succor to her refugees, and they made a special pact to work together. As soon as Hilda earned her U.S. flying certificate, the two women resolved to make a joint mercy flight across America.

In the meantime, Xiaqing toured up and down the California coast making a variety of public appearances, and finally met up with legendary aviator, Jacqueline Cochran. Miss Cochran was one of the finest pilots, male or female, that America had ever produced, and she was fresh from having won the Bendix Transcontinental Air Race in a Seversky pursuit plane. The U.S. State Department, no doubt reassured by Madame Chiang's backing of the project, had asked Miss Cochran to assist Xiaqing to secure an aircraft for her tour, and the American aviatrix had obliged by winning the cooperation of the Beech Corporation. The two women flew together to the East coast in Cochran's high-speed Seversky to lay the groundwork for the tour.[10] Cochran graciously agreed to act as one of Xiaqing's sponsors, and her formidable name was added to the growing list of notables who had already been encouraged to support the endeavor. All the threads were finally coming together. Hilda Yan had successfully won her flying certificate, and when she and Xiaqing met again in New York, they began to finalize their plans. With the assistance of various China aid organizations across America, they were optimistic that their joint appeal could not fail.

The women found an appropriate single banner under which they would fly—the China Civilian Relief Committee. This agency was headquartered in Washington, D.C., and was chaired by the highly respected Bishop of Nanjing,

His Excellency, Paul Yubin, a newly named bishop who was destined one day to wear the red biretta of a cardinal of Rome.[11] At the request of Generalissimo Chiang Kai-shek, and with the blessing of Pope Pius XI, the bishop was in America to raise funds for the millions of Chinese rendered homeless by the conflict, and this cause immediately appealed to Xiaqing. Seared into her memory was the recollection of a long line of small children she had witnessed standing against the wall of an overflowing Shanghai orphanage too crowded to admit them all. The waifs held up pitiful signs begging passers-by to adopt them.

In late February 1939, the Chinese community celebrated the Year of the Rabbit. Traditionally, the rabbit favored diplomacy and international relations. The outbreak of hostilities in Europe would crush that year's expectations, but until September, when the war would divert America's attention from the conflict in the Orient, the two women pilots had a clear field in which to win the hearts and minds of the people of the United States.

Xiaqing made a few public appearances in advance of the tour, tentatively scheduled to commence on March 23, 1939, and in order to win some additional last minute publicity, she flew to Pittsburgh in the aircraft Miss Cochran had secured for her, a Stinson Reliant SR-9B that had been painted an eye-catching red and trimmed with deep yellow. It was christened *Spirit of New China*.[12] She arrived in Pittsburgh in time to participate in that city's annual air show, and, as anticipated, her flight to the steel town turned out to be an excellent opportunity to raise China's profile. Unexpectedly, however, her return trip to New York almost ended in disaster.

On March 17, she left the air meet, anxious to reach New York to begin preparations for her upcoming tour. Xiaqing intended to return via Newark, New Jersey, a little over three hundred miles to the east of Pittsburgh, but *en route*, she encountered a thick bank of fog that blanketed the sky down to the ground. Xiaqing quickly lost her bearings. Huddled in her fur coat against the damp cold, and keenly aware that her gas tanks were emptying, she flew gamely onwards, descending from time to time in a fruitless effort to find some break in the mist. When she was three hours overdue at Newark, a global alarm was broadcast to alert all airmen that she was missing.

Just when the situation began to look very grim indeed, Xiaqing had a timely break. She found a gap in the fog and made her way through it, finally emerging into blue sky. Her relief, however, turned to apprehension when she discovered she was out over the open Atlantic. Fortunately, she was just within sight of land, and, spotting a coastal air field, she made for it. Flying on fumes, she descended at Groton aerodrome in Connecticut, halfway between New York and Boston, and, after refueling, took off at once for Brooklyn's Floyd Bennett Field, one hundred miles away, where she safely landed a short time later.

This dangerous misadventure that could have ended in disaster turned to China's advantage when Xiaqing was met at the airport by bouquet-bearing supporters and a sympathetic press who had been notified she was missing. Her narrow escape received maximum media coverage, even in China, and drew positive attention to her country's plight. It was a simple process for the American public to extrapolate the courage of the unflappable solo aviatrix, who stoutly announced that she was never afraid, to the bravery of the Chinese people who were fighting the invader alone and ill-equipped. She was quick to make a pitch for her upcoming flight.

"I hope to make a goodwill tour of thirty-five cities," she told the *New York Herald-Tribune*. "There is much to do. For one thing, we need money for trucks. Medical supplies cannot reach the vital places behind the war fronts because of lack of transportation."

She was also optimistic about the war's outcome.

"We're going to win," she declared with assurance, "but it will take a long, long time."[13]

Xiaqing had recognized her potentially deadly flying incident as a brilliant marketing opportunity and used it to China's advantage. It was an auspicious beginning to her American odyssey.

On the morning of Thursday, March 23, 1939, Li Xiaqing and her colleague, Hilda Yan, arrived at the airfield to commence their great tour. Philadelphia was slated to be their first port of call, and Xiaqing graciously allowed Miss Yan to occupy the left-hand seat. Xiaqing was modeling a whimsical new swagger coat, its front boldly appliquéd with a sporty aircraft spiraling dangerously downward at the end of a ribbon contrail.

The women took off for Camden airfield, located just across the river from Philadelphia, where they were met by enthusiastic supporters and air maintenance personnel. The next day they flew on to Washington, D.C. where they were welcomed by the relief committee and Bishop Yubin himself. They had decided to use the capital city as their home base for the next few days; until Hilda's own aircraft arrived and they could carry out their solo engagements, the two women were content to make several trips together to nearby centers to speak on China's behalf. As a neophyte public speaker, Xiaqing was happy to play a lesser role and learn lessons in speechcraft from her distinguished friend. Finally, on April 3, Hilda's plane was due to be delivered. Xiaqing accompanied her colleague to the Washington airport to witness the aircraft's arrival (it was also named *Spirit of New China*) and to meet the legendary aviator, Colonel Roscoe Turner, who flew it into town. With just a touch of condescension, the flamboyant Turner presented Xiaqing with an autographed glossy photo of himself. "To [Xiaqing Li]," he scrawled above his signature, "a great little flyer."

Henceforth, the two aviatrixes would be going their separate ways and Xiaqing would be flying solo, but this was certainly no hardship. Independent by nature, she preferred to control as many aspects of her flights as possible (she equated self-reliance with safety), and despite the many headaches that were likely to crop up on a tour of this magnitude, she relished having the opportunity of making another long-distance junket. However, flying was expensive and the cost of traveling across America promised to be steep. Although the Friends of China association had promised to donate the costs of gasoline, Xiaqing would be responsible for her own personal expenses. Fortunately, she was soon to discover that she would rarely need to buy meals (she was invited to speak at countless teas and banquets and was able to take advantage of the spread that was laid on in her honor), and as for lodgings, some hoteliers were even willing to support Chinese relief by hosting her stay at their establishments at no cost to herself.

The great adventure had begun at last, and after months of meticulous preparation on two continents, Xiaqing was finally able to carry her scheme forward, putting into action those plans that, up to now, had only been committed to paper. To her delight, she discovered that, from the outset, the tour was even more successful than she had imagined. She rapidly became America's darling.

Those who gathered at the nation's airports to greet her arrivals were invariably taken aback by her diminutive appearance. A journalist observed, "...one would imagine a buxom and powerful looking girl taking on the job," but the reality was far different. A Boise, Idaho, newswoman reported that, when Xiaqing descended from the cockpit of her aircraft, "Everyone got the surprise of their lives." The famed aviatrix with the larger-than-life reputation was petite, stem slender, and patrician-looking.[14] This scarcely accorded with anyone's preconceived notions of what a burly barnstormer ought to look like.

The next bombshell was the shock of her beauty. Declaring she was pretty enough to be a movie actress or a beauty queen, news reporters paid tribute to her beautiful smile, gleaming white teeth and honey-colored skin.[15]

For those who were expecting Miss Li to emerge from her aircraft in greasy overalls, they were also favorably impressed by her casual chic. She looked as fresh and invigorating as a sprig of mint. A women's reporter for the *Idaho Statesman* told her inquiring readers what they wanted to know: "The spirit of New China was wearing immaculate white sharkskin slacks. No hose. Natural leather sandals and a flashing smile, handsome black eyes, skin as creamy as a rose petal..." In short, she was perfectly groomed from head to toe. "Miss [Li] keeps her fingernails modishly long," she continued, "and modishly tinted to match her toenails and her lipstick...she carried a huge black patent leather envelope bag that was not a whit shinier than her long gleaming hair. She stuck a white carnation behind her ear, and primped in odd moments like a high school girl."[16]

Wearing a flower tucked behind an ear was a favorite device of Chinese beauties of the day, and in America, it became a recognizable Xiaqing trademark; she was rarely seen without a fresh white blossom of some kind adorning her coiffeur. (There was no shortage of available posies; she simply plucked a flower from the previous day's welcoming bouquet.) This was especially true in the evening when she wore the ankle-length *qipao* of her native land. She made a striking entrance at one banquet arrayed in a delicate gown of rose-colored silk figured with silver threads, her appearance set off to perfection, it was reported, by the fragrant lily of the valley that garnished her dark locks.

However, she also made concessions to her country's status as a nation at war. In Vancouver, she appeared on the arm of the city's mayor at a May Day celebration attired in an alluring Chinese gown… and cotton stockings. It was a sweltering hot day, and she would have been forgiven had she gone bare-legged altogether, but Xiaqing was making an important statement. Silk hosiery was a primary Japanese export, and it was partly through worldwide demand for this commodity that Japan could afford to wage war on China. Xiaqing was more than willing to renounce silk stockings for the duration if this minor sacrifice would bring a speedy and successful conclusion to the war.

Nor was she averse to a little 'cheesecake' if it would help the cause. At Miami Beach, she fetchingly posed for publicity shots on the city's seaside boardwalk. The resulting photos showed her lovely legs (this time without any stockings at all) to great advantage. She wore only an abbreviated swimsuit cover-up and skyhigh heels.

Naturally, there was considerable curiosity about the personal life of this pretty, and pretty sensational, young woman. Everyone wanted to know if she were married. Xiaqing just laughed outright and declared she was single.

"Aviation has been my whole life ever since I began to fly at the Cointrin-Ecole d'Aviation in Switzerland. I have no hobbies," she assured them, "but my career."[17] To another reporter, she provocatively admitted that she liked "all men—but just to look at."[18]

She was so fresh and young looking that no one could have guessed she was a divorcée and the mother of two young children. Reinforcing the illusion of innocent youthfulness were the two stuffed toy mascots that always flew with her, a pig fashioned out of pink cotton and, in a nod to the Year of the Rabbit, a white, pert-eared bunny sporting a jaunty plaid suit.

As she smiled and posed for photos with these naïve talismans of youth, she could not have known that her ex-husband, serving in the foreign service as the Chongqing government's European affairs manager, had left their children in the care of servants in war-wracked Shanghai. Young Pax and Mary Mulan were now on the run, hiding from Japanese soldiers who had occupied the city and were acting on orders to execute the offspring of Chinese high officials. Xiaqing was flying on behalf of war refugees; ironically, her own terrified and hungry children were among their numbers.

Meanwhile, Xiaqing carried on with her tour, all unawares. Gaggles of welcoming aircraft sometimes met her arrivals at the various cities on her itinerary. In Vancouver, a government airplane and several private planes flew out to greet her, and on her approach to Salt Lake City, some fifteen aviators were slated to escort her into town.

The people who met her on the ground were generally a distinguished mix of government and consular officials, executives of various organizations, local Chinese dignitaries, and just plain folks, and the welcoming crowds were large in size and excited in demeanor. Descending from the skies in her highly visible red and yellow *Spirit of New China*, she never failed to impress those who had made the effort to be at the airport to witness her arrival. And when they spotted the crossed flags of China and the United States painted on the fuselage of her aircraft, they burst into spontaneous and thunderous applause.

Sometimes, she muffed her landings, and this rankled her. In San Diego, she blushed and confessed to the welcoming committee, "I made a bad landing. I apologize!" And when she arrived in Canada, she did it again. Bouncing a couple of times in a cross wind at the Vancouver airport, her aircraft bobbled dangerously, and the waiting crowd of three hundred anxiously held its collective breath. Was the famed aviatrix in trouble? But no, she waved to indicate all was well and redeemed herself by taking off again, circling the airfield, and making a perfect three-point landing smack in the middle of the runway.

Although she was invariably buried in bouquets of flowers presented to her by the inevitable official welcoming committees in each of the cities she visited, she never gave the impression of being jaded by the attention that was so lovingly lavished upon her. She was representing China, and as such, it was her responsibility to be the epitome of charm and diplomacy. She treated each city as if it were the very first on her itinerary. When introduced to the mayor of Boise, Idaho, she pulled out all the stops.

"You're the youngest Mayor I have ever met," she gushed. "I am so proud."

And while being conducted into town by a motorcycle escort of the city's finest, she quipped, "I am so glad to ride *behind* a policeman, and not in front of him!"[19]

Soon she acquired an impressive collection of 'keys to the city' presented to her by mayors of the biggest metropolises in North America. In the surviving commemorative photos of these ceremonial presentations, the veteran public officials have the bug-eyed, deer-caught-in-the-headlamps look of the willing victim as they gift the lovely Miss Li with the freedom of their cities.

Xiaqing always kept one eye on the weather, and the other on her itinerary. She had a great number of cities to visit, and she hated to disappoint the crowds who stood patiently waiting on the tarmac, scanning the skies for her arrival, but safety concerns needed to remain uppermost in her consideration. Bishop Yubin, who likewise knew the tyranny of a fully-loaded date book, probably had the best intimation of the pressures she felt to fulfill her engagements. Accordingly, he asked his secretary to instruct Miss Li not to risk flying in bad weather simply for the sake of her schedule, advising that any delay in her arrivals would not matter so long as the welcoming committees were telegrammed with news of any possible postponements.

He also offered soothing words of praise and encouragement. The cleric's secretary wrote a caring letter on his behalf, "The bishop has been very much pleased [by] your courage and discipline in offering your service to the country and also for the people, and he appreciated the fighting spirit you possessed in going through all the hardships and difficulties. It is to his knowledge that you certainly will work hard for the noble cause which we are fighting for, but also it is his sincere wish that you will take care of yourself."[20]

Indisputably, her arrivals made the greatest impact on the overseas Chinese of the cities she visited. Her fellow countrymen regarded her as a heroic and inspiring mentor, and no matter how small or humble their population, they turned out to do her proud.[21] In the various Chinatowns of the nation, she was welcomed like a goddess descended from the clouds, but even so, these rapturous receptions received little or no coverage in the English press. In the absence of surviving Chinese media of the day, it is difficult to appreciate the splash she made among her own people, but Vancouver's *Chinese Times,* one of the only dailies extant from this period, gives an impression of the impact of her eleven-day visit to the city. One can assume that the fuss made by Vancouver's Chinese population was likewise accorded her by all the other Chinatowns across North America.

For instance, on May 12, 1939, the day after she arrived in Vancouver, Xiaqing was invited by the local branch of the China National Aviation Reconstruction Association to attend a banquet at the Overseas Chinese Restaurant. It was packed with representatives from all the organizations and tongs of Chinatown. Those present reverently rose when the aviatrix was led into the restaurant, and many flowery speeches of welcome and elaborate ceremonies preceded the meal. Afterwards, she was conducted in state to the assembly hall of the local Guomindang building where she delivered an address on one of Dr. Sun Yat-sen's pet subjects, 'Saving the Nation by Aviation.' Three or four hundred persons packed into the hall to hear this, her first Chinese speech in the city, and those who were unable to squeeze inside listened on loudspeakers positioned on the front of the building. Four thousand inhabitants of Chinatown, over half of the population of the community, filled the streets outside.

This became the pattern of her visit to Vancouver. When she was not invited to speak to the white community, she was fondly welcomed into the bosom of Chinatown where various organizations vied with one another to fête her with endless toasts and glowing speeches. On the third day of her visit, with her popularity snowballing, one thousand folks defied the fire marshal and shoe-horned into the Far East Theater to listen to her address to the 'Save China General Society.' More than six thousand gathered outside to hear the proceedings, once again via loudspeakers.

"I oftentimes say the same words several times a day," she admitted, "But that is because there is only one big thought in my head. And that is 'China will win.'"[22]

Her positive message was of vital importance to the morale of the overseas Chinese whose homeland was taking such a beating from the enemy, and they gratefully lapped up the healing balm of her words. Just as significant to them were her good looks and perfect grooming, and they burst with pride to think that these attributes made such a positive impression on her white audiences.

Certainly, her beauty was not wasted on Hollywood. While on tour in California, photos of her million-dollar smile and lovely figure graced the front pages of local newspapers and eventually grabbed the attention of the major motion picture company, Metro-Goldwyn-Mayer. Just as she had been 'discovered' on the Minxin movie set more than a decade ago, MGM representatives approached her and asked if she would be willing to appear in *Lady of the*

Tropics, an upcoming film slated to star Hollywood beauty, Hedy Lamarr. They told Xiaqing that she would be assigned to play the part of companion to Miss Lamarr's character. In the end, negotiations fell through, but Paramount Studios was waiting in the wings to snap her up. Its management felt that Xiaqing would be perfect for their latest movie, *Disputed Passage*, whose cast included Akim Tamiroff, John Howard, and the sarong girl herself, Dorothy Lamour. Xiaqing agreed. The filming dates fit in with her flight schedule, and press coverage of her celluloid appearance would give yet another boost to the tour, especially after she declared that all her earnings would go to the war refugee fund.

None of the syndicated press reports flashing this story across America ever hinted that Xiaqing was no stranger to the acting world and that she had once been one of the most beloved stars of the Chinese cinema. Like many other aspects of her private life, she preferred to keep the activities of her early years strictly confidential, boxed off from the present. She claimed to reporters that she had no anxiety or misgivings about appearing before the movie cameras (hardly surprising since she was already a seasoned professional), but she hastened to add that she would not be considering a future career in film. In the end, the bit part Xiaqing was called upon to play certainly required no great stretch of her talents. She was cast as a Chinese aviatrix.[23]

After filming her rushes, Xiaqing was back on tour throughout California, where low ceiling weather conditions regularly obliged her to do some blind flying, but the even rhythm of her efforts were suddenly interrupted by some shocking news. On May 1, she was staying at Sacramento's Senator Hotel when she learned that her flying colleague, Hilda Yan, had crashed her aircraft outside the town of Prattville, Alabama. Frustratingly, initial reports were sketchy. Anxious to learn the fate of her friend, she made a telephone call to the Prattville hospital and left a message, asking the attending physician to send a wire, collect, to her hotel with information on Miss Yan's condition. Shortly thereafter, she received a telegram from the doctor who, less than six hours after the accident, was not yet in a position to declare whether or not his patient had sustained any serious internal injuries.

The next day, Xiaqing's worries were somewhat allayed when she learned that Hilda would suffer no permanent physical damage, but this incident struck a nerve and continued to haunt her. One month later, when Miss Yan had recovered and was back on the talk circuit (this time via automobile), Xiaqing was still fretting about the root causes of the crash, and closely grilled Bishop Yubin's secretary to find out all she could about his understanding of the accident.[24] Acutely aware that she herself was not immune to possible disaster, she hoped to learn from Hilda's mistakes and forestall the same sort of calamity in her own flying, but she must have been unsettled to discover that, through some mix-up, most of Hong Kong's popular newspapers mistakenly reported that it was *she*, and not Hilda, who had crashed and sustained serious injuries.

By the time Xiaqing reached Chicago, she was nearing the last laps of her tour when her aircraft ran into mechanical difficulties. She acquired a new one from Walter Beech, trading her Stinson Reliant SR-9B for a Stinson Racer SR-5E, and she arranged for the new aircraft to be painted in the same colors and given the same name—*Spirit of New China*.[25] As before, she used her own jewels as collateral to secure the plane, and she also picked up the tab for $115-worth of insurance. The Racer was an older, less powerful aircraft with a shorter range, but as her tour was entering its Eastern phase, the distances she needed to travel between major centers would be far less. She received a corresponding adjustment in her itinerary from the Bishop's office.

Then suddenly, Xiaqing was nearly home. On June 15, she was in Pittsburgh and scheduled to arrive back at New York that same day, but she ran into bad weather. It looked as though her triumphal return might have to be delayed. She touched down in Philadelphia to await better conditions, but to her delight, the skies suddenly cleared and the weather improved. Xiaqing leapt into her aircraft to complete the final miles of her tour. She flew to Newark where she was honored at a special reception convened by a delegation of American and Chinese women members of the New York's Women's International Association of Aeronautics, and then she took off for Flushing Airport, just twenty miles to the west, her final destination. Touching down lightly on the tarmac, she taxied to where Yu Junji (Yu Tsune-chi), the consul general of New York, was waiting to congratulate her on the successful completion of her remarkable odyssey. Xiaqing had been on tour for three months. She had safely flown nearly 10,000 miles, and raised US $10,000 currency for civilian refugees, and double that amount in Chinese dollars.

Clad in her trademark white sharkskin flying outfit, and with two white flowers tucked into her hair, she grinned with joy and posed for photos as the consul extended his hand to help her down from the cockpit. Prominent among the members of New York's 'Welcome Home' committee were Bishop Yubin and Hilda Yan, the two individuals who, more than anyone, were in a position to recognize the scope of her achievement.

Upon her arrival in New York, Xiaqing immediately sought to tie up loose ends. She paid a visit to the World's Fair to present the exhibition's president with a scroll of friendship from China to the United States. The scroll was an impressive symbol of her achievement. Decorated with the flags of the two nations, it was crowded with the signatures of all the senators, mayors and official representatives that Xiaqing had met on her flights throughout America and Canada. In recognition of her landmark tour, and in thanks for the presentation of the scroll, she was made an honor guest of the World's Fair.

In a private capacity, Xiaqing returned to the fairgrounds a couple of days later in the company of an old friend, Dr. Xu Zhaodui (Frank W. Co Tui). Dr. Xu was chairman of the American Bureau of Medical Aid to China (ABMAC), and he ran the organization in New York City out of its Broadway offices. China was officially mourning the invasion of its country and had no pavilion at the fair, but it was sponsoring a Lama Temple for the edification of the fairgoers, and Xiaqing and Dr. Xu toured the spectacular green and gold structure whose tip-tilted roofs were supported by a forest of red pillars.

The eminent physician confessed he had not invited his friend to the fair for recreational purposes only. He had a proposition to make. He asked Xiaqing if she would be interested in mounting yet another aerial tour on behalf of her fellow countrymen, this time in aid of ABMAC. Pumped with self-confidence after the enormous success of her recent expedition, Xiaqing was intrigued by the proposal. Dr. Xu's organization had become increasingly more efficient and effective (it now liaised with the Chinese Red Cross, one of Xiaqing's favorite agencies, for whom she had organized the hospital on Shanghai's Jessfield Road), but she pointed out that she had just barnstormed almost every major city in the United States. 'Donor fatigue' would likely have a negative impact on the amount of funds she could attract to the cause. Nevertheless, Dr. Xu had planted the seed, and soon, Xiaqing could think of nothing else.

In the meantime, she continued to maintain a high profile and, eager to trade on the positive publicity accrued by her flight, she responded to all requests for public appearances and speechmaking. In September, she attended the Annual National Air Races at Cleveland's Municipal Airport with the military attaché of the Chinese Embassy, Colonel T.C. Kuo, and her flying colleague, Hilda Yan, and it was there that she met legendary aviatrix, Louise Thaden, whose opinion it was that women were "innately better pilots than men." Upon her return to New York, Xiaqing was honored for her recent flying tour of America with a dance and reception hosted by the Women's International Association of Aeronautics (of which she was a member), held at the rooftop ballroom of Brooklyn's Hotel Bossert. At the end of the month, and in company with Hilda Yan and other New York socialites, she helped convene a Rice Bowl fundraiser on behalf of China's refugees and was one of those who modeled Chinese garments on the catwalk. Among these fashions was a modish flying suit created especially for her by Zhang Qianying (Hélène Tsang), a designer friend from her Shanghai days. Wearing one of Zhang's evening gowns, she also posed for a publicity portrait while standing beside a statue of Guan Yin, her beloved mother's favorite goddess.[26]

By November, *Disputed Passage* began to make the rounds of movie theaters across America, and in advance of this, publicity pictures of Xiaqing began to appear in the media. These varied a great deal from her usual descending-from-the-cockpit professional photos. In *Film Fun,* a 'girly' movie magazine that specialized in pinups of film stars wearing as little apparel as possible, she was shown sporting Dorothy Lamour's skimpy sarong, a demure smile, and little else.

In December, she reflected on the year's achievements. On behalf of her country, Xiaqing had flown to forty-two American states and raised thousands of dollars, and she celebrated that year's Christmas by remembering those who had helped to make the year such an outstanding success. She was particularly grateful for the assistance of Jackie Cochran, and she sent the American aviatrix a gift of Chinese jewelry to thank her for securing the *Spirit of New China* aircraft, and for lending the considerable weight of her reputation to the sponsorship of the national tour.

As the New Year approached, there were few women in America—or men, for that matter—who could lay claim to Xiaqing's long distance flying feat, but if there were those who thought she could not possibly trump this achievement, they were quite wrong.

20. FLYING DOWN TO RIO

In February 1940, Xiaqing celebrated the Year of the Dragon, one of the most potent and lucky years in the Chinese calendar, by developing a power-house plan to kick off the year in grand style. With the approval of Madame Chiang Kai-shek, she announced that she would embark on yet another cross-country tour, one that was to be even more ambitious than the last. Under the auspices of the American Bureau for Medical Aid to China, chaired by her friend Dr. Xu Zhaodui, she intended to fly almost the entire length and breadth of the world's fourth largest continent, South America. Her tour would involve visits to some sixteen South American cities, and would include touchdowns at centers in Mexico, Central America and the Caribbean.[1]

Madame Chiang was the honorary chairman of the ABMAC, and her involvement in this undertaking was paramount. Tens of thousands of orphaned refugees were living in camps under her direct protection, and the persuasive power of her name had the potential to bring immediate attention and masses of aid to any appeal. Her highly respected sister, Song Qingling, the widow of Dr. Sun Yat-sen, was also intimately involved in the care for 'warfans,' as the sisters dubbed the homeless waifs, and between them, these women were able provide the ABMAC with the up-to-the-minute information it required to make an impact on the sensibilities of the overseas public. The Bureau needed money, and lots of it. Madame Chiang sent a terse cable to the ABMAC's New York office underlining China's desperate need: "Children undernourished, causing night blindness, rickets, anemia, etc. etc."[2]

Xiaqing knew that the costs of conducting such a mammoth expedition would be enormous—she would need room and board, not to mention fuel, over a three-month period—but South America was a vast, as yet untapped, area, and she was convinced she could make the tour pay. It had been nine years since her maternal great aunt, Xu Zonghan, had made a similar, albeit less extensive, trip to the southern continent on behalf of Chinese refugee children. Her aunt's success at that time was partly due to the fact that South America was physically and intellectually detached from newsworthy events that affected the northern half of the hemisphere, and chaffed at its isolation. Xu Zonghan had known that, by making personal contact with those to whom she made her appeal, her pleas for help could not possibly go unheeded. Xiaqing was convinced she could duplicate her aunt's success.

She persuaded philanthropist, Cornelius Vanderbilt 'Sonny' Whitney, to lend her the use of his Beechcraft Staggerwing C17R biplane (NC-15833) for the tour. The speedy five-place aircraft that he placed at her disposal boasted a 450-horsepower Wright engine, and was equipped with oxygen for flying at high altitudes over the Andes Mountains. Painted glossy black with red trim, she christened her craft *Estrella China,* Spanish for 'Star of China,' and as usual, Xiaqing summoned the press to publicize her tour. To an interviewer who declared her surprise that a Chinese woman could be an air pilot, the aviatrix explained,

"There are only a few Chinese girl fliers, but after all, our own First Lady, Mme. Chiang Kai-shek, was head of the air force at the beginning of the war… Though she is not herself a pilot," Xiaqing continued, "she put the feminine stamp on aviation in China."

When the interviewer expressed astonishment that her family had not thought to restrict this sort of dangerous activity, Xiaqing explained.

"…my father is very liberal. And it was he, in fact, who encouraged me. He is an aviation enthusiast and since he had no sons, he had to let me become the family flier. My father is the kind who considers girls quite as intelligent as boys."[3]

Again, Xiaqing posed for the ever-important publicity shots to advertise her mission. An unlikely-looking candidate for such a weighty endeavor, the aviatrix seemed keen to emphasize the fact. Sitting on the lower wing of her Beechcraft bi-plane, her legs demurely crossed and her slender body wrapped in a luxurious fur coat, she daintily waved to the news cameramen, petite, feminine and seemingly unconcerned by the huge challenge she had carved out for

herself. One of the resulting photographs that featured in the press was cap-
tioned in pidgin English, "Confucius Say: Fewer Die Because Lady Fly," but this
clumsy phraseology struck a rather jarring note considering the sophistication
and courage of the subject.

And courageous she was. Never reckless—she always ensured her trips
were painstakingly well organized—Xiaqing tended to embrace projects that
would have daunted even the most stout of heart. Although the route she
chose would keep her well away from the trackless jungles of the Amazon (for
the most part, she would skirt the shorelines of the continent), Xiaqing would
be flying through territory completely unknown to her, and where the pre-
dominant languages would be either Spanish or Portuguese. She also had little
knowledge of the integrity (and scope) of South America's aeronautical facilities and if they would be on a par with those to which she was accustomed in
the United States. In addition, the pace of the tour would be exceedingly brisk,
allowing for very little leisure or mechanical down time. Although she would be
traveling during the autumn, those areas near the equator knew only one season,
and the heat and humidity would be enervating.

Yet, as ever, Xiaqing was prepared to take things as they came. She recalled that, on her first solo inspection tour of China, an adventure undertaken
exactly four years before, she had encountered so-called air strips that were little
more than cow pastures lacking even the most rudimentary aeronautical equipment, but her ability to deal with these limitations reinforced her already healthy
streak of independence and boosted her 'can do' attitude. As well, the excellent
mechanical training she received at the Boeing school gave her confidence that
she could tackle all but the most complicated mechanical difficulties that might
arise (which was just as well—she was to experience some dissatisfaction with
the operation of her borrowed Beechcraft).[4]

Xiaqing acquired a clutch of high scale navigational charts of the areas
over which she intended to fly and carefully pored over them to ready herself
for the expedition. Today, these relics are the only charts that still exist among
her private papers, and they exhale something of the heady and colorful adventure she enjoyed in those southern climes.

On March 12, 1940, Xiaqing took off from New York's Roosevelt Field *en route* to Havana where she would begin her tour.[5] Four days later, she departed Cuba for Miami and then made for Brownsville, Texas. From there, her tentative itinerary called for her to proceed south to Mexico City, through Central America and the Canal Zone, and thence down the western coastline of South America. She would visit smaller centers *en route*, as well as the capital cities of Lima and Santiago, fly eastward over the Andes to Buenos Aires and Rio de Janeiro, and then swing back to the west coast, retracing her flight path up the Pacific coastline and over the top of South America. From Caracas, she would fly up through the West Indies back to Miami. In all, the expedition would take a little over three months to complete.

To say her tour caused a sensation among the people of the South would be an understatement. Some indication of its impact can be gauged by the effect of Xiaqing's one-hour demonstration of a military aircraft in the skies over Peru. Her brilliant aerobatic performance garnered so much positive attention that this single exhibition raised $40,000 in relief aid. To commemorate the event, the Peruvian Air Ministry awarded her a gold medal.[6]

Sadly, no records have been saved of the monies she collected during her hundred days' sweep of the southern half of the Western hemisphere. Judging by that one day's take in Lima, these sums must have been considerable.[7] The ABMAC's motto, 'Humanity Above All,' apparently struck a philanthropic chord in the hearts of generous South Americans, but so did the undoubted appeal of the impressive Chinese aviatrix who was all business by day, and all charm and glamour by night. Xiaqing routinely arrived for her evening public relations appearances attired in silken *qipao*, draped in furs and sparkling with jewels. She remained, for the most part, undaunted by the high dignitaries who were so clearly dazzled to meet her. As usual, she accepted no donations of money herself; these were to be forwarded to the ABMAC offices in New York City.

As on her previous year's tour of America, she was cosseted by the various China Aid organizations she encountered—agencies that had sprung up to meet the demands of the Far Eastern emergency—but she was also surprised to find many small and enthusiastically welcoming Chinese communities in even the most unlikely places. This was particularly so in the Caribbean where some of the Chinese she met were descendents of sugar cane slaves who had been forcibly brought to the area almost one hundred years before, as well as the offspring of those who had voluntarily arrived more recently to seek a better way of life.[8]

After her whirlwind tour, Xiaqing returned to New York in July 1940. During the course of her trip, she had logged at least 18,000 miles and safely visited nine out of South America's fourteen countries, not to mention most of Central America and three Caribbean islands. However, while her tour represented a tremendous achievement, and the mileage she logged was almost double that of her American tour, Xiaqing was somewhat dissatisfied. The cities she did not have an opportunity of visiting, particularly those on the northeast coast of South America, were like 'the ones that got away' and the perfectionist in her was niggled by an uneasy sense that she still had unfinished business in the south. Some four years later, she would take steps to remedy these omissions by returning to the continent to barnstorm those areas she had missed the first time. Her eventual return speaks to the economic success of this, her first tour of the region.

What drove Xiaqing's almost manic need to take on these perilous projects? Was she merely determined to alert as many people as possible to China's plight? Certainly this was her acknowledged goal, but perhaps there was an additional motivation at play. It appears that her urgent desire to aid her country was equally mixed with a love of dangerous exploits, and these voyages happily enabled her to indulge both passions. In advance of her trip to South America, she was asked by a reporter why she was taking unnecessary risks in flying solo to unknown parts of the world. Xiaqing replied,

"Faced with foreign invasion, we must endure bitter trials as we work to save China. That is a kind of adventure."[9]

'Adventure' was the operative word; these journeys were enormously exciting to one who courted danger. However, aside from her feelings of genuine patriotism and love of exciting escapades, she may have had another undeclared motive. The psychological trauma she suffered when she severed her marriage and lost her children may have triggered in Xiaqing a subconscious need to prove her worthiness to the world... and to her ex-husband, Zheng Baifeng.

While she had been in South America, *Disputed Passage* had finally opened in Hong Kong, and although Xiaqing's name lurked at the bottom of the list of cast members, ads for the movie played up the role of the local girl who was appearing so briefly on screen as a Chinese aviatrix. At the end of September, the movie opened at Shanghai's Rialto Theater. Those of her friends and acquaintances who yet remained in the city were tickled to watch Xiaqing alive and well on the silver screen, rubbing shoulders with American movie stars.

On October 6, 1940, the aviatrix and her actress friend, Anna May Wong, were both in Hollywood to help promote a party being held for China Relief. Convened by generous-hearted actress, Rosalind Russell, it was held at Pickfair, the sprawling estate of movie legend, Mary Pickford, who graciously offered to host the extravaganza. All of Beverly Hills was invited, and a string of beauteous actresses, including Anna May and Dorothy Lamour, dressed up in Chinese costumes and modeled them for the attendees. The guests were all encouraged to bring gifts and curios, and these were raffled off for the benefit of war orphans. The stars also signed a book of support and encouragement that Xiaqing promised would be delivered to Madame Chiang Kai-shek.

A month after the Pickfair event, Xiaqing and Anna May again joined forces for additional fundraising, this time for the ABMAC, when they traveled to the East coast to participate in New York's annual Rice Bowl celebrations at the Waldorf Astoria Hotel. They appeared together in a Chinese pageant. Then on December 2, 1940, Xiaqing attended an ABMAC fundraiser in Hartford, Connecticut, where she introduced British novelist and social critic, H.G. Wells, to an excited audience that was keen to see and hear the celebrated author of *The Time Machine* and *War of the Worlds*. Much of the crowd's excited curiosity was also directed toward the famous aviatrix who had recently flown throughout so much of the Western Hemisphere.

Xiaqing decided the time had come to write her autobiography. Although only twenty-seven years of age, she had already experienced a lifetime of unusual adventures and reckoned the American public might be interested to read about them. Any publicity stimulated by the book would also draw attention to her people's struggles, and it is likely that she intended the profits to go to China relief. She engaged foreign correspondent and former resident of Shanghai, Elsie McCormick Dunn, to ghost the account.[10] Xiaqing was a veritable pack rat when it came to collecting items related to her personal appearances, and she had managed to accumulate an impressive assortment of memorabilia over the course of her tours that would be of value to her biographer. She had saved boxes of *cartes de visite*, photos, letters, magazine interviews, airline tickets, and even the little cards that come with bouquets of flowers. She had also hired a clipping agency to save all and any news articles relating to her mercy flights. After a couple of interviews with her subject, Mrs. McCormick Dunn got to work and hammered out a draft of the story.

21. RELIEF WINGS & UNITED CHINA RELIEF

At the end of 1940, Xiaqing was able to give a boost to the long-cherished dream of another prominent aviatrix, Ruth Nichols. Miss Nichols was a pioneering pilot who held an impressively long list of aviation records, but she was also a practicing Quaker who took seriously the Christian dictum to have compassion for the suffering and unfortunate. At one point in her career, she had sustained serious injuries in a plane crash, and, having to endure nightmarish pain during the course of a long commercial flight to hospital, she resolved to supply and equip a fleet of air ambulances for the benefit of those who needed rapid aero transit to medical facilities. In May 1940, she organized Relief Wings, a civilian air ambulance service, and developed a fund-raising organization to outfit the fleet. Her project garnered a great deal of interest, especially as it was likely to be of vital importance if America happened to be drawn into the European war. There were even plans to send Relief Wings units to China.

Nichols persuaded noted philanthropist, Cornelius Vanderbilt Whitney, to lend his Beech aircraft to the cause (the same plane he had recently put at the disposal of Li Xiaqing for her South American tour), but despite his and others' support, by the winter of 1940, the Relief Wings campaign had run out of steam. On one cold and dismal day in December, Nichols and her two colleagues sat shivering in their chilly aircraft hanger wondering how best to jump-start the scheme when suddenly "in walked an exotically beautiful Chinese girl, trim, alert and smiling."[1] It was Li Xiaqing. She had come with an offer of help, and she was full of novel ideas to revive the Relief Wings campaign. Nichols was delighted to welcome this new recruit who, as she noted, "seemed to bring with her a brisk air of youthful energy and confidence," and was so obviously "a confederate worth having!"[2]

At once, Xiaqing breathed fresh life into the enterprise. A strong believer in the usefulness of air shows, she recommended that they give the aircraft a medicinal-looking coat of white paint and then fly it down to the upcoming Miami All-American Air Maneuvers. This would drum up some much-needed free publicity. For every objection Nichols broached—What would they eat? Where would they stay?—Xiaqing had a solution: she knew the proprietors of all the Chinese restaurants in Miami, as well as the owner of the city's finest hotel. They would have food and shelter at no cost to themselves.

In the end, Ruth Nichols and her two colleagues followed Xiaqing's advice and were eternally grateful that they had. On January 8, 1941, the four women climbed into the Beechcraft at Floyd Bennett Field and took off for the Miami air show. As Xiaqing had predicted, their arrival in the spanking-new white aircraft before a crowd of twenty-five thousand avid spectators was well received, and they were even granted an audience with the show's official guest of honor, the Duke of Windsor. They made many other friends that day, the most important of whom was Daniel Mahoney, managing editor of the *Miami Daily News*. Mahoney was so charmed by Xiaqing that he was inspired to suggest they hold a 'Wings of Mercy Ball' to be hosted by the cream of Miami society. The newspaper would handle all the publicity, he assured them, and he could virtually guarantee that the Ball would receive the enthusiastic support of the vaunted millionaire philanthropists of Florida.

Held on February 7 just outside Miami at Hallandale's Colonial Inn (owned by crime syndicate kingpin, Meyer Lansky), the Mercy Ball was indeed a potent money raiser. The patroness of the gala was Mrs. Dorothy Lee Ward of Washington, D.C., supreme doyenne of the Miami Beach set, and she persuaded famous entertainers, Joe E. Lewis and Sophie Tucker, to forego their usual fees and entertain the crowds *pro bono*. The final verdict? The event was "one of the most brilliant charity affairs of the season."[3]

But although she was running with a rich crowd, Xiaqing had no stomach for conspicuous consumerism.

"I really do not enjoy going out and spending money," she admitted. "Everything I see wasted here reminds me of the bowls of rice it would buy for my people at home." Given a choice, she confessed, she would have preferred to be back in China.

"I long to be with them all," she sighed, "and share in their fate. But my father, who is a great liberal and a friend of the revolution from the beginning, brought me up to think first of how I could serve my people, rather than of my own wishes."[4]

Filial piety and duty to country were Xiaqing's prime motivators, and she had long ago resolved to sacrifice her personal freedom and do whatever it took to help her people win their liberty.

Having advanced the Relief Wings agenda, Xiaqing was free to return to New York City where, on the same day the Mercy Ball was launched in Florida, the United China Relief (UCR) organization was officially founded. President Roosevelt had issued a memorandum to the more than three hundred charities of various stripes that were then functioning in America, requesting that they consolidate their efforts. There were eight established Chinese relief organizations operating independently throughout the United States, and these responded to the president's edict by uniting their forces. The merger was intended to be temporary in nature, but when the joint campaign managed to raise five million dollars, its very success ensured that the UCR would become a permanent entity.[5] Under the UCR umbrella, Xiaqing was hired as a staff member and was to remain an employee of the charity until the end of the war. In the course of her trips throughout the United States, Xiaqing had met thousands of people, and she developed the theory that all Americans automatically loved China, but they did not always know why. She felt it was her special responsibility to build on that pre-existing goodwill and convert it into tangible support for her homeland. She was delighted to be able to do this under the auspices of the United China Relief.

Through her association with the UCR, Xiaqing was released from the necessity of personally having to see to every detail of her publicity appearances. She now enjoyed the incomparable benefit of having Marian Cadwallader, Director of the UCR's Speakers and Entertainment Department, plan her days and nights. Miss Cadwallader possessed no-nonsense organizational abilities, and she kept everyone in her department on a short leash. Her typed memos to Xiaqing, meticulously outlining her itineraries on a daily basis, covered every possible contingency and allowed the aviatrix to devote herself to charming her public rather than worrying over travel connections and wondering who would be greeting her when and where. Settling into her new job, Xiaqing took a suite in a desirable new building at 25 East 83rd Street. Located on Manhattan's Upper East Side, it was one of the first air-conditioned apartment blocks in the city, and was located just a couple of miles away from the UCR's Broadway offices. It was also within easy walking distance of Central Park, as well as Fifth, Park and Madison Avenues.

Meanwhile, author Elsie McCormick had completed her second draft of Xiaqing's biography, and in March 1941, she announced that it had been forwarded to the publisher. However, the project appears to have foundered, and there is no evidence to show that the book was ever printed. Perhaps publication was delayed to include Xiaqing's ongoing activities, which seemed to be never-ending.[6] At the beginning of May, she flew with Ruth Nichols and her colleagues to Albuquerque, New Mexico, to promote Relief Wings. A week later, she helped First Lady Mrs. Eleanor Roosevelt, who was serving as honorary chairman of the China Emergency Relief Committee, to choose a Chinese *qipao* as a gift for Madame Chiang Kai-shek, and she modeled the gown for press photographers. High profile activities of this nature certainly would have merited inclusion in the book, and, as Xiaqing was exceedingly busy through to the end of the year, her biography would have required continuous amendments.

In June, she made headlines again when she scornfully announced,

"We don't think much of the Japanese pilot."

She went on to analyze why.

"Of course, in formation and precision flying, he is good," she admitted, giving him his due, "but once we get him in a position where he is unable to operate directly on orders, his weakness becomes evident."[7]

She went on to describe how, although normally outnumbered five to one, the Chinese aviator would almost always manage to inflict the heavier losses in any aerial engagement. Xiaqing had long appreciated that she could inflict heavy losses herself simply through the spread of propaganda, and she used words as formidable weapons at every opportunity.

On September 9, 1941, she made a whirlwind, morale-boosting trip to Canada, flying via American Airlines to Toronto where she received a warm welcome from the Chinese Patriotic League. She had come at the invitation of the Canadian Red Cross, and upon arrival, she immediately plunged into benefit work that showcased her piloting skills. Accompanied by Jack Gibson of the Piper Cub aircraft company, she departed Toronto's Malton airport for Hamilton, Ontario in one of the corporation's monoplanes. The bright red Cub was destined to be raffled off by the Red Cross for the relief of Chinese civilian war victims, and Xiaqing was delighted to win publicity for the lottery by taking the lead position in an impressive V-formation of forty aircraft flying in the annual Canadian Air Cruise to Algonquin Park.

The following morning, Hamilton organizers invited her to undertake a strenuous round of public appearances on behalf of the Red Cross. Her day was packed. She gave an early radio interview, dropped by a local sanatorium to visit with its inmates, addressed a meeting of the Chinese Patriotic League, and gave a speech to the convening delegates of the Canadian Congress of Labor. Later that evening, she was conveyed to the city's Palace Theater to address filmgoers who had gathered to watch *They Met in Bombay,* a movie starring two of Xiaqing's Hollywood acquaintances, Clark Gable and Rosalind Russell. Then she was whisked away to a Friends of China reception where she was invited to give a speech. It had been a long day, but she showed no evidence of fatigue. She informed her audience that she had already recorded some five hundred and fifty hours of flying time in her logbook, and hoped to return to her homeland at year's end to accumulate yet more hours by flying hospital planes or transports for her country's war effort. However, although the notion of returning to China was a heart-felt dream, she did not have an opportunity to fulfill it. She was to remain at her post in North America until the end of the war.

The next day, she flew back to Toronto via domestic carrier, arriving just in time to participate in the Red Cross parade where she officially kicked off the campaign to raise $100,000 for the Chinese Relief Fund. Her popularity had soared to such an extent that Ontario Premier, Mitchell Hepburn, invited her to address the Ontario Legislature. However, her day was not yet over. In the evening, she was asked to reprise her early career as an actress by taking part in a Peking Opera performance in Chinatown. It had been years since she had acted on stage, but she agreed. As she went through the age-old motions of her character, Xiaqing probably spared a thought for her rebel grandmother, whose love of the opera was legendary.

"The old lady adored the theater," she once recalled, fondly remembering Xu Mulan's predilection for taut suspense. "Though dramas often continued until four o'clock in the morning, she was strongly opposed to going home until the last villain had been foiled."

Xiaqing looked out over the footlights and wondered if the thoughts of the audience were wandering, just as her grandmother's had done.

"She picked up and put down the thread of the play at will," Xiaqing chuckled in remembrance, "giving her attention in the interlude to eating candied water chestnuts and shouting gossip to friends seated several rows away. In the incredible hurly-burly of a Chinese playhouse, with candy sellers shrieking their wares, towel vendors hurling hot towels toward the upstretched hands of their customers, and cymbals clashing as the military hero strutted across the stage, my grandmother was able to snatch peaceful half hours of sleep."[8]

But no one napped during Xiaqing's performance. Toronto's Chinatown was enthralled.[9]

A couple of days later, on the last lap of her tour, Xiaqing visited the city's military air base at Manning Depot to watch sporting activities, sample air force rations and just generally fly the flag for China. During her five-day raid on Canada, she had willingly fulfilled all her obligations, and then some, and returned to America with the satisfying sense of a job well done. The weary 'ambassador of goodwill' flew back to New York via Canadian Pacific Airlines, but after her heroic tour of duty for the Allied cause, it must have been galling to be required, as she passed through La Guardia's customs, to pay the eight dollar head tax levied on all Chinese nationals entering the country.[10]

Xiaqing returned to her suite on the Upper East Side, relieved to have an opportunity to put up her feet for a well-deserved rest, but just four days later, she was back on the relief trail. The unrelenting Miss Cadwallader presented her with an itinerary for a fastidiously planned, intensive junket through Eastern America on behalf of the UCR. Like a war horse responding to the call of the bugle, Xiaqing roused herself and energetically obliged, covering three states in as many days, touching down in Cincinnati, Cleveland, Buffalo, Rochester, Syracuse, Albany, and Bendix. From Bendix, she flew by domestic carrier to La Guardia airfield where she was met by a starry host of Friends of China VIPs, including Governor Herbert H. Lehman, actress Helen Hayes and philanthropist John D. Rockefeller III. Standing in the midst of this constellation of well-known personalities, she attracted the hoped-for attention of the media and once again obligingly flashed her stunning smile for photographers.

Although most of Xiaqing's air miles that year had been logged as a passenger of various commercial airlines, she was soon destined take to the skies again as a pilot in her own right. The Aeronca aircraft company donated a straw and red-colored Super Chief to the United China Relief and arranged for the airplane to be delivered to Flushing airfield for the exclusive use of China's star pilot in her work for the UCR.[11] Aeronca was presenting the plane with no strings attached. It was to be the sole property of the UCR and could be disposed of as the agency wished. This munificent gift was an obvious tribute to the effective publicity that Xiaqing had attracted to the relief agency, and its board of directors was delighted. In an effort to gain maximum exposure for its new campaign, targeted to raise a quarter of a million dollars, the UCR put the plane on eye-catching display in the middle of New York City's Columbus Circle where it was exhibited, along with appearances by popular entertainers, for three weeks, from September 30 until October 20, 1941. Then it was sent back to Flushing where Xiaqing took possession and went aloft for a test flight.[12] She was preparing for a flying tour of Ohio, a courtesy flight designed to pay tribute to the Aeronca company whose head offices were located in that state. On November 4, she set off for Toledo.

In contrast to the days when she made mercy flights under her own recognizance, all arrangements for her upcoming tours in the new aircraft, including the acquisition of gas and oil credit cards, insurance for every contingency, pilot licensing, newspaper releases, publicity photos and their captions, were now handled by the UCR. While it was a relief to leave these planning details to others, nevertheless Xiaqing insisted that she have control over the most important aspect of these flights—the final inspection check of the aircraft itself—and she was adamant that these inspections be carried out by her alone. As ever, Xiaqing equated aviation safety with full control of her flights. No less a personage than Douglas Auchincloss, Director of the UCR, took the time to write an open letter to all the airports she intended to visit, requesting that she be accorded this vital privilege.

Although she arrived in Toledo one day late due to bad weather, she received a royal welcome. The usual officials met her at the airport, but they were accompanied by a delegation representing the city's entire Chinese population of one hundred and forty souls. Two young Chinese sisters, Mary and Nancy Lewis, aged seven and ten, presented the aviatrix with a bouquet, and a photo of the awed youngsters offering their floral tribute to Miss Li appeared on the front page of the *Toledo Blade*. One wonders if Xiaqing was reminded, as she tenderly accepted the flowers from the girls, of her own children, Pax and Mulan, who were much the same age, and stranded, she knew not where, in China. But there was little time for reflection. Whisked off by an escort of motorcycle police, sirens wailing, and a dozen fast autos, she arrived at the city's finest hotel, the Commodore Perry, and freshened herself for the usual grind of speaking engagements. She addressed the Kiwanis Club, the Toledo Club, and the Chinese community at a restaurant gala before flying off to Philadelphia and Boston for more of the same.

The UCR had taken out flight insurance in her name sufficient to last until the end of the year, so Xiaqing just kept on flying for China until it ran out. She made a small, four-day trip to New England at the end of November, departing New York for New Hampshire (Nashua and Manchester) and Massachusetts (Lowell, Holyoke, and Springfield). She also visited Maine, and as she flew over the State Capitol, she dipped her wings, and dropped 'greetings of flowers.'

Xiaqing had now flown some 45,000 miles throughout America and was such a national celebrity that the UCR could rely upon her to attract noteworthy donations.

"Miss Lee has a particularly strong appeal to large contributors," wrote one of her organizers, "and it is our belief that her approach should be directed primarily to Special Gifts."[13]

'Special Gifts' were, of course, significant amounts that the UCR hoped to receive from its most well-heeled supporters. Again, no records exist that tally the totals she was able to raise, but as she hobnobbed with the most prominent individuals resident on the Eastern seaboard, it is likely that she won many of these anticipated special contributions to China.

By the end of a hectic 1941, Xiaqing may have been relieved to note that the aircraft's insurance policy had finally expired, and her pilot's license was no longer in effect until renewal. Henceforth, she would confine her traveling activities for the UCR to trips she could make by train and commercial air carrier. Her solo American air tours for China would become more or less a thing of the past.[14]

On December 7, 1941, the Japanese Imperial air force bombed Pearl Harbor in Hawaii, and this cataclysm finally drew the United States into the war, both in the Pacific and in Europe. China and America were now solidly linked in their resolve to defeat Japan, and it was a heady time for Chinese nationals working in the United States on behalf of their fellow countrymen. Opportunities for publicizing China's plight simply fell into Xiaqing's lap. In January 1942, flash bulbs popped while she presented legendary radio newsman, Walter Winchell, with a special certificate declaring he was an honorary 'Esteemed Grandparent' for his impressive donation to Chinese orphans. That same month, she was invited to New Orleans to appear with her friend, Anna May Wong, at a Red Cross fundraiser.

In mid-March, she flew down to Palm Beach, Florida, and was conducted from the airfield by motorcycle escort to attend a Chinese relief play. She then rushed back to New York to begin a dizzying tour of the New England States and New Jersey. This latter expedition had been slated to take place the year before but had been out of the question due to her many commitments. Again, the UCR asked her to focus on the acquisition of 'Special Gifts,' but she was careful not to neglect mainstream donors. She addressed labor groups, faculty clubs, war services committees and war bond rallies in the states of Connecticut, Massachusetts, New Jersey and New York. She maximized her listening audience by giving interviews on radio stations WTTM of Trenton, WOR of New Rochelle, WHN of Jersey City, and WABC and WMCA of New York City. She also moved into the realm of television broadcasting, a medium that was a scant three years old, by appearing on NBC-TV at the corporation's Rockefeller Center studios. The Chinese Consulate-General had its offices in the same building.

As ever, her coordinator, Marian Cadwallader, was invaluable when it came to planning her invitation-packed days and nights. Miss Cadwallader's memos to Xiaqing routinely ran to several pages and included a mountain of detailed information regarding proposed junkets to other cities and states. A number of these memos for the year 1942 still exist, the briefest schedule of which is dated April 27, 1942:

"Tomorrow you will leave Grand Central Station on the New York, New Haven and Hartford train (per previous memo) at 10:00 a.m., arriving in New Haven, Connecticut at 11:30 a.m. Mr. G. Harold Welch, New Haven Bank, New Haven, will meet you at the train and take you to the luncheon at the Faculty Club, attended by various New Haven people and chairmen of outlying towns.

"You will leave New Haven on the New York, New Haven, and Hartford train at 2:25 p.m., arriving at Grand Central Station at 3:55. Mr. Wiley Kinney will meet you at this train and take care of you from then on. You will go with him to Ardsley, New York, to speak at the dinner at 7:00 p.m. at the Ardsley Country Club, together with Mr. H.R. Ekins and showing of the film 'Western Front.'

"On Wednesday, April 29th, you will go to Stamford, Connecticut, to speak at the Kiwanis Club luncheon at the Hotel Davenport at 12:15 noon. You will leave from Pennsylvania Station on the New York, New Haven and Hartford train at 11:00 a.m., arriving at Stamford at 11:49. The contact there is Dr. Thaddeus Hyatt, Windover, Davenport Ridge, Stamford, Connecticut (Telephone: Stamford 3-6185). We are writing him to meet you at the station. Trains leave Stamford for New York very frequently and you can take the one that suits you best.

"On May 1st you will go to Manhasset, Long Island. All arrangements on this will be between you and Mrs. Chamberlain..."[15]

Xiaqing spent the simmering summer of 1942 largely in New York City, and although her public appearances were scaled back during the vacation season, she showed up in Times Square for a July rally sponsored by Twentieth Century Fox. A week later, she returned to Times Square once more, and, flanked by a variety of Hollywood actors, including Lili Damita, Nanette Fabray, and Max Showalter, she spoke on behalf of the United China Relief to the passers-by who thronged the streets. In August, she was still at work, but the pace grew more leisurely when she took her message to Maine and managed to work in a brief holiday while she was there.

When she returned to the UCR offices, she found waiting for her one of the usual memos from the inestimable Miss Cadwallader:

"I hope you have had a wonderful time on this last trip to Maine, and that you will be fully rested and ready for very hard work."[16]

This was nothing less than the truth. Throughout September and October, the pace rarely slackened as Xiaqing concentrated her efforts and made personal appearances in the heavily populated, moneyed areas of Connecticut, New Jersey, Massachusetts and New York. On September 2, she attended a Southampton, Long Island, festival in aid of China relief where she read out to the audience a telegram sent to the UCR by Lieutenant-General Joseph Stillwell who was serving in China. Then prominent society figures paid tribute to bombed-out Chongqing by dressing up in Chinese costumes and performing in the appropriately entitled ancient drama, *The Sorrows of Man*. Two days later, Xiaqing was back in New York to present a ceremonial Chinese gown to Hollywood actress, Irene Dunn, at a rally in Times Square. This was just a foretaste of the busy days that lay ahead. Again, Miss Cadwallader provided her with carefully detailed instructions:

"September 18 – New York City. You will speak at the Civilian Defense Volunteer Office at Pershing Square. This is the booth just east of the Airlines Terminal Building, on 42nd Street under the ramp. They would like a talk of about 20 minutes, bringing in the question of civilian defense in China, and there may be some questions from the audience after your talk if you have no objections. The audience will no doubt be a good-sized one (today they had about 500 people at the meeting). The meeting is to begin at 12:30 noon, but they would like you to arrive a few minutes ahead of time to have a little discussion about the meeting. The purpose of these meetings, of course, is to increase the number of people – women in particular – who are active in civilian defense. When you get there, ask for Miss Nadine Sachs, who is in charge of the speakers for these meetings. The person with whom we had contact in arranging this is Countess L.I. Zamoyska, of the Inter-Allied Information Center.

"September 21 – Philadelphia, Pennsylvania. You and Mrs. Chu are to be honor guests at the Snellenburgh Auditorium, Snellenburgh Store, on Market and 11th to 12th Streets, at their tea and meeting. Word just came in that they have scheduled you to be broadcast at 1:30 p.m. on Station KYW. This is an informal interview – no script. Also, they would like to have a Mr. Peter Fingesten model your head during the tea.[17] They claim that Mr. Fingesten has been asked to exhibit two of his figures at the Metropolitan Museum this year, and he can make an amazing likeness in half an hour. This came in to Mr. Ekins and he thinks you might be interested. With these additional plans for you, I believe it might be best for you to get to Philadelphia around 11:30 in the morning…

"September 22 – You are to be an honor guest at Rockefeller Plaza in New York City at 5:00. You have the details on that…"[18]

And so it went to the end of the year. Xiaqing always enjoyed a good party, and New York's brilliant nightlife was vital to her survival during this hectic year. Although she was never known to touch alcohol, she loved to dance (especially the rhumba and the tango), and she went out to the clubs as often as she could. New York gossip columnist, Leonard Lyons, reported catching a glimpse of Chinese aviatrix, 'Mei Lee,' out on the town in one of his articles, but he could only have been referring to Li Xiaqing. Mr. Lyons recounted that she was spotted sitting at a table at the popular 21 Club in the company of voluble drama critic, George Jean Nathan, when a parade of other men began to drop by for a visit, the most notable of whom were movie stars, Burgess Meredith and Orson Welles. At midnight, Xiaqing reportedly left with Welles who escorted the aviatrix first to the Stork Club and then to Fefe's Monte Carlo. When reminded that her date had been with someone else, Xiaqing just shrugged and offered an excuse: "It's a strange thing," she mused, "but to me, all Americans look alike. I can't tell them apart."[19]

Xiaqing quietly spent the Christmas of 1942 with American pilot, Jacqueline Cochran, who invited the Chinese flyer to spend the holiday at her home in Indio, California, but immediately thereafter, Xiaqing joined the West coast party scene. She was observed at the Beverly Hills Hotel expertly dancing the rhumba in the arms of a handsome lieutenant.

A measure of the fame and recognition Xiaqing had achieved can be gauged by the appearance that same year of her cartoon likeness on that quintessential American collectable, the bubble gum card.[20] Tickled to find herself a pop icon, Xiaqing acquired a few dozen of these cards to distribute to the folks back home, but that oft hoped-for dream to return to China was to elude her yet again. Her exhilarating and relatively carefree days in Shanghai seemed very far away, and there had been oceans of suffering since then. So many friends had perished. Most recently, she had received the shocking news that Yang Guansheng (Kuangson Young), a distinguished Princeton graduate in international law, and a good friend, had been executed by the Japanese. Although he was serving as consul-general in Manila, his diplomatic status had not spared him death by firing squad.

As 1943 opened, Xiaqing continued with her fast-paced program and maintained a high profile in the media. On January 25, NBC's radio program *Cavalcade of America* devoted one of its shows to the Flying Tigers, and Xiaqing was invited to appear as a special guest. She was billed as 'China's first woman pilot.' A week later, she addressed the American Jewish Women's Congress and received a favorable mention in *Time* magazine. On February 17, she spoke in Washington, D.C., and four days later, shuffled off to Buffalo to speak at a war plant rally.

In early March, Xiaqing invited syndicated columnist, Inga Arvad (who was then dating future American president, John F. Kennedy), to her 83rd Street apartment where she granted the journalist a personal interview. Arvad, in common with other reporters, was plainly struck by her subject's glamour.

"When she sits down on a huge pastel-blue couch," wrote the captivated Arvad, "and leans her head with the large intelligent eyes, the arched eyebrows and the crowning glory of blue black hair against a pillow, it is hard to believe that those eyes have, for hours at a stretch, been glued to an instrument board.

Or that the tiny hands with the lacquered nails have been grimy with the dirt of a mechanic."

Xiaqing confided to Arvad that it was difficult for her to be cut off from news of her family in occupied Hong Kong, but she had an abiding faith that all was well with them. She also tried to express the strongly emotional nature of her mission in America.

"I want to be worth while to my people and to my family because they are so idealistic and because I love them so deeply."[21]

That same year, she was also the subject of a true-life adventure comic book story. In the fine tradition of action heroines, Xiaqing was depicted as a noble, self-sacrificing superwoman suffering innumerable trials in her efforts to aid the downtrodden. And it was all true. Shown running from the murderous enemy in Shanghai, Xiaqing and a confederate take cover in a foxhole.

"If only we had more money," laments her male companion, "we could cause the Japanese more trouble!"

"There's my chance," comes the stout reply from China's No. 1 Aviatrix. "I can go to America to raise funds. You carry on the hospitals."[22]

However, aside from these flattering publications and the usual publicity appearances, the year 1943 would mark a distinct slowdown for Xiaqing, especially when compared to the punishing pace she had maintained since the war had begun. She apparently had decided to take a well-deserved breather.

Since her arrival in America in late 1938, she had driven herself relentlessly and done a lifetime's worth of charity work. It was an adventure, yes, and she gained a deep sense of well-being through her ability to relieve the suffering of her people, but she had deprived herself of essential personal time. Madame Chiang Kai-shek was due to make her landmark tour of America, and now the spotlight was about to be focused on this vigorous woman who had already won the respect of the Western world. Xiaqing was more than willing to step out of the spotlight in favor of her esteemed leader.

Madame Chiang was received in the United States as a conquering heroine, and even before she arrived, the nation was at her feet. By the time she laid siege to New York City, she enjoyed unprecedented public adulation. On March 3, 1943, 'Missimo' gave a speech at Carnegie Hall to the various Chinese groups in the city. Like the rest of her community, Xiaqing was in attendance, and while she was working her way through the milling crowds, she was pleasantly surprised to run into an old acquaintance, Chen Wenkuan (Moon Chin), who was passing through New York.

Chen was a native of Baltimore who had gone to China in 1933 to fly commercial aircraft with the CNAC, and he had been stationed in the Far East ever since. During the previous year, he had been involved with a couple of high profile flights, the most prominent of which involved his flying Lieutenant Colonel Jimmy Doolittle out of China following the latter's April raid on Tokyo. He had also won headlines when he flew President Roosevelt's personal representative, Wendell Wilkie, into China in October 1942. Both these flights, like so many others Chen had undertaken, involved evasion of hostile enemy action, and he was now in America to enjoy some time off and to take four-engine training in Washington, D.C.[23]

Li Xiaqing and Chen Wenkuan had met years before at the Longhua airfield in Shanghai, and they were delighted to see one another. The next day, they met again at a massive reception thrown in Song Meiling's honor at the Waldorf-Astoria's Starlight Roof. Thereafter, and in the company of mutual friends—other pilots for the most part—they went out on the town. Although Xiaqing was still passionate about aviation and talked about little else, Chen could not help but notice that she seemed lonely and at loose ends. She was not working, and this unaccustomed leisure time lay heavily on her hands.[24]

Three weeks later, Xiaqing attended a united nations rally in Chicago where she revealed she now had six hundred flying hours to her credit.[25] However, aside from making a smattering of personal appearances throughout the year, there is no evidence that she undertook any large traveling engagements until late September when she made a month-long flying tour for the United War Fund through the states of Pennsylvania, Ohio and New York. In November, her U.S. private pilot's license, granted five years before, finally expired.

22. SOUTH AMERICA REPRISED

By 1944, Xiaqing was refreshed and ready to re-enter the fray on behalf of her beloved China, but in the meantime, the relief landscape had changed. Americans were now besieged by a wide variety of wartime appeals for a number of worthy causes. Xiaqing knew her petition for aid might well fall on deaf ears unless she had a fresh audience. South America still held considerable allure, and because it had proved to be such a money-earner for Chinese relief in 1940, she now made plans to return. On this extended trip that would, in the end, take up the better part of a year, she intended to touch down in those regions she had left unvisited on her earlier expedition. Principally, these would include several islands of the Caribbean, as well as the northeastern coast of the South American continent.

The United China Relief furnished her with letters of introduction and a list of Latin-American connections—persons on whom she could rely in the various countries she would be visiting—and these included southern representatives of the UCR, various American relief agencies, and attachés of Chinese consulates. The UCR also provided her with an itinerary of airline connections. On this occasion, she would fly, not in her own aircraft, but via domestic carrier. The airfare alone would amount to over one thousand dollars, an immense outlay for a non-profit organization, but Xiaqing now held the status of a national treasure, and the Chinese Government and the UCR were growing increasingly wary of putting her life at risk as a solo pilot. They also anticipated that her efforts in the south would more than offset the costs of travel. This time, however, she would be speaking, not only on behalf of the UCR, but also in her own right. Some of her appearances would be managed by an agency, the National Concert and Artists' Corporation of New York City, to which she would submit invoices for the speeches she made.

She was now thirty-two years old. Replacing the wide-eyed look of the innocent ingénue that had so charmed the hearts of America on her first mercy flight was the chic polish of the elegant sophisticate. In preparation for the trip, she commissioned a series of portraits that could be affixed to official documents and visas *en route*, but these images were far removed from the typical passport photo. They showed a stylish woman, hair piled high, fixing the camera with a beguiling look. Pride in her ancestry was simply declared by the stand-up collar of her Chinese dress, and her avocation as an aviatrix by the splendid, diamond-encrusted airplane brooch pinned above her breast.[1] After five years in the public eye, she had much in common with the Hollywood movie stars who were her friends—she knew how best to face the lens so that light and shadow would caress her features in the most becoming manner.

The pace of this great expedition south was to be much less hectic than it had been four years earlier; now that the Allies had come to its aid, China was no longer in immediate danger of extinction. Xiaqing began her trip in late March, departing Miami via Pan-American Airways for La Guaira airport in Caracas, Venezuela.[2] Using that city as a base for three weeks, she took side trips to the Venezuelan cities of Maracaibo and Barcelona before departing for Port-of-Spain and then Belém, Recife and Rio de Janeiro. At last she had an opportunity to visit the tropical northeastern areas of Brazil she had missed on her previous trip. Returning to the Caribbean, her ports of call included Curaçao and Aruba, but, unable to resist taking a turn at the controls, she flew herself to these islands in a speedy Lockheed 12A twin-engine aircraft (PJ-AKC) made available to her by the Royal Dutch Airlines, KLM. She also visited Cuba and Jamaica, and made side jaunts to Mexico City, Lima, Peru and Potrerillos, Chile.

Although initial plans called for her to return to the United States at the end of June, the momentum of Xiaqing's work began to build, and her appeals become so effective that she decided to stay on and travel further south. She made arrangements to fly from Caracas to Rio de Janeiro and was delighted when José Bento Ribeiro Dantas, president of Serviços Aéreos Cruzeiro do Sul airlines, generously provided her with a complimentary flight via an exciting new air route that cut over the heart of Brazil and made pit stops at Manáus and Corumbá.[3] Upon her arrival in Rio, China's ambassadress of goodwill granted an interview to the press from her room at the luxurious Copacabana Palace-Hotel where she described her impressions of the pioneering 3,000-mile flight, much of it over the impenetrable jungle of the Amazon River basin.

"I was very moved when flying, for hours and hours, over the gigantic forests of Brazil, so dense and green. It gave me a vivid sense of the largeness of this magnificent country."

Lest it be thought that she did not properly appreciate the urban delights that Brazil had to offer, Xiaqing declared herself just as fascinated by the allurements of Rio de Janeiro.

"There was never a city like this," she exclaimed, "so clear, so washed by sun, so much in tempo with the sea and mountains..."[4]

Her trip to the southern regions was a great success. It was just like old times—her days were fully booked. She granted radio interviews, attended silver teas convened by the Chinese communities, made speeches in movie theaters, and took in tours of petroleum refineries, aircraft factories and industrial sites throughout Brazil and Venezuela. Although she was still representing Chinese refugees, there was a subtle shift in her focus; increasingly she was also acting as her nation's unofficial ambassador of trade and commerce, and with an eye to future postwar business deals between China and South America, she spoke knowledgably and confidently about industry and finance. Having been raised by the entrepreneurial Li Yingsheng, this came naturally to her. In Rio de Janeiro, where the press described her as having "an extreme intellectual vivacity, paired with physical enchantments," she was affectionately dubbed Luz de Crepúsculo, the Portuguese translation of 'Xiaqing' or 'sunset glow.'[5]

On the first of August, she flew to Buenos Aires and, giving her profession as 'aviadora,' made an application to Argentina's board of immigration, requesting a three-month tourist certificate so that she could stay on and continue to promote her nation's needs. A month later, she received the extension and established herself in Buenos Aires, making the seductive colonial port city her home base for that period.

Her visa finally expired in the last month of the year, and she returned to America on December 3, 1944, flying via Pan-Am to Brownsville, Texas. She had been away for eight months. When she arrived back in New York via Eastern Air Lines, the UCR officials accorded her a hearty welcome. As usual, her personal appearances had netted substantial contributions. Included among them were several large donations. Alex Curiel of Maduro & Curiel's Bank of Curaçao personally wrote a check to the UCR for one hundred pounds sterling, along with a tribute recognizing Xiaqing's "splendid work on behalf of our common cause [which] deserves real appreciation by us all belonging to the Allied Nations."[6]

Again, while no record exists of the amount of funds Xiaqing collected for the UCR, there is little doubt that the total would have been substantial. Sadly, however, China's currency had begun to spiral completely out of control, and the lion's worth of these contributions would have been gobbled up by inflation. As well, there was reason to believe that many gifts to China were ending up in the pockets of unscrupulous officials.

A notable and tragic accident occurred while Xiaqing was in South America, and this misfortune may be the source of persistent rumors that have endured for decades—rumors insisting that 'China's First Woman of the Air' died prematurely in a wartime flying accident. This accident resulted in the death of a Chinese American woman pilot, Hazel Yueying Li. In 1932, Hazel Li had taken flying lessons in her hometown of Portland, Oregon, and she won her wings a year later. After the Manchurian Incident, Hazel sailed to Shanghai where she was allowed to fly for a time with the Chinese army. When the war began, her request to join the Chinese Air Force was rebuffed and she was reassigned to the aeronautical library. She returned to America, enrolled with the U.S. Women Air Force Service Pilots (WASPs), and was assigned the task of ferrying airplanes across America for the military. On November 23, 1944, while making a landing at Great Falls, Montana, her plane was struck by another aircraft, resulting in a horrific fiery crash. Hazel Li clung to life for two days, but eventually succumbed to her appalling injuries.

News of Hazel's death reached China, and it is possible that her name became confused with that of Li Xiaqing. Thereafter, reports began to circulate claiming that Xiaqing had died. The fact that both women pilots shared the same surname, and were both flying in America in the service of their countries, likely contributed to the unfortunate mix-up. As a result, and for decades thereafter, Xiaqing was mistakenly believed to have died a wartime martyr's death while working for the benefit of her countrymen. Perhaps her ex-husband's continued insistence that she was dead also added credence to the myth. In truth, she was to live for more than fifty years after her supposed demise.

23. BLUE SKIES

Xiaqing had prolonged her stay in South America to such an extent that, when she returned to America, the U.S. Customs would only admit her on a temporary basis for a four-month period. In March 1945, using New York consul, Dr. Yu Junji, as a reference, she applied for a one-year extension, noting on her application that, as she was kept by her family in China, and as her financial condition could be described as 'Excellent,' she could scarcely be considered at risk of becoming a refugee or a burden to the state. For those in the know, even her Kowloon address at No. 1 Ho Man Tin Hill proclaimed her healthy monetary status. Her request for an extension was granted.

In the neighborhood of her old Manhattan apartment, Xiaqing found a suite at 114 East 84th Street and continued to work for the UCR, but there was a general realization that the war was winding down. She found time for romance and fell in love with a captivating Chinese national, however, he was married with children. Xiaqing later claimed to be blissfully unaware of his domestic attachments.

In August 1945, with the American atomic bomb attacks on Hiroshima and Nagasaki, the war finally came to a close. With this longed-for resolution to the conflict, Xiaqing yearned to return home. For seven years, she had worked for China with all her heart, and now she felt a need to aid in its reconstruction. But she knew her homeland had been altered almost beyond recognition. While the United States had endured less than four years of conflict, China had been either occupied or under siege for double that amount of time; its infrastructure was in ruins.

Of especial concern to Xiaqing was the condition of China's aviation services. Before the war, the aviatrix had energetically put herself at the forefront of those who tried to urge a skeptical public that the integrity of their homeland's borders could not be maintained without a strong air presence. This prediction soon became self-evident, and now that the peace had come, Xiaqing was eager to change the focus and trumpet the advantages of a strong commercial air industry. Through the joint U.S.A. Air Force Air Transport Command and U.S. Air Naval Transport Service, she requested coveted priority clearance to fly immediately to the Orient.

"Miss [Li] is one of China's leading aviatresses," declared the official who filled out her special pass, "and requests transportation by air to Shanghai where she will be engaged in rehabilitation of aviation."

In the busy postwar environment, official air passage from America to the East required considerable justification and was granted to a very few individuals, but the certificate went on to defend the nature of her trip. It stated that her immediate presence in China "was deemed to be in the national interest of the

United States to the resumption of economic and other activities disrupted by the war that are necessary for the prompt re-establishment of peacetime conditions."[1] She was granted permission to fly to the Far East.

At the beginning of May 1946, Li Xiaqing set out for China "in the national interest of the United States," flying via commercial carrier from San Francisco to Shanghai. She anticipated that she would find China in a state of turmoil; nevertheless, the social disarray that confronted her in Shanghai was a shock. Of all the changes that had taken place in China since the war, perhaps the most appalling was the manner in which corruption had wormed its way into every stratum of society. A subtle constant of life in pre-war days, it was now audaciously rampant. Black marketeering and acute shortages plagued the lives of those who had once lived in plenty. In one respect, at least, Xiaqing was able to inject some joy and color into the lives of her female friends. Before departing New York, she had paid a visit to Elizabeth Arden's Fifth Avenue beauty headquarters and purchased over two hundred dollars worth of cosmetics—perfumes, makeup, toothpaste—for distribution in China. Emergency postwar economic decrees banned the importation of cosmetics, and lipstick fetched such exorbitant prices in the interior that it was being smuggled, along with gold bars, on commercial airliners. The number of lipsticks she brought to China (over one hundred and fifty) indicates that, in addition to passing them out among her friends, she planned to retail them.

From Shanghai, Xiaqing flew to Hong Kong for a reunion with her father, and she once again took up residence at the family mansion in Kowloon, but her good intentions to help reconstruct China's aeronautic infrastructure apparently ran out of steam. The industry she had done so much to promote in pre-war China had now gathered impetus and was operating under the aegis of the mighty American government. It certainly needed no prodding from private citizens. This realization came as a relief to Xiaqing, and after eight closely packed years of intensive activity on her nation's behalf, she allowed her life as a semi-professional pilot to come to a skidding halt. Essentially, she 'retired.'

The Communist Liberation of China, when it came in 1949, did not impact Xiaqing's life in Hong Kong as it did so many others of her rank who remained on the mainland. She was able to maintain her lifestyle and her flight status (she re-applied for a Hong Kong private pilot's license throughout the 1950s), but by this time, she flew mostly for pleasure, darting off to Singapore or Bangkok at the drop of a hat. When Jacqueline Cochran paid her a visit in 1953, Xiaqing confessed over dinner that she no longer flew as much as she once had. She was certainly not in the same category as Miss Cochran, a smasher of speed records who had just become the first woman pilot to break the sound barrier, but by anyone else's standards, Xiaqing was still a flying phenomenon, regularly winging throughout Southeast Asia seemingly on a whim.

In the late summer of 1958, Hong Kong's spectacular new Kai Tak runway was completed. Built on a reclaimed promontory stretching out into Kowloon Bay, the re-born airport was now able to accept arrivals of the world's largest planes, and the authorities invited Xiaqing to give a flying demonstration at the opening ceremonies on September 12. The Chinese press hailed her as an aviation pioneer and a mentor to other women pilots.[2]

She met a successful international businessman, George Yixiang Li. Younger than she, in Hong Kong he was known as the 'Prince of Sham Shui Po.' They had much in common, including a love of travel, golf and horse racing (they were both regulars at the Happy Valley Race Track), but George was married. Estranged from his spouse, he earnestly sought to regularize his relationship with Xiaqing, however, his wife initially refused to grant him a divorce.

When Hong Kong experienced an economic downturn in the mid-1960s, Xiaqing and George began spending time in the United States where the financial climate was more robust. They settled in the San Francisco Bay area, taking an apartment in Oakland, near the University of California Berkeley campus, and lived just up the road from International House where Xiaqing had boarded some thirty years before while she attended the Boeing School. Their suite's proximity to Oakland airfield was not coincidental. One of Xiaqing's first priorities was to obtain a flying certificate. In 1963, she had been granted a Hong Kong Special Purpose Pilot's License, and she submitted this permit when applying for an American license. However, while the Colony's certificate might have been readily transferable to other countries within the British Commonwealth, it held no currency whatsoever with the U.S. Federal Aviation Administration. The FAA informed her that, if she wished to fly in the United States, she would have to begin flight training anew.

On June 30, 1966, this veteran aviator, who had flown hundreds of thousands of miles and had landed at nearly every airfield on four continents, was duly issued with Student Pilot Certificate S-347502, and was obliged to adhere to those requirements issued to fledgling flyers. She commenced flight instruction at Oakland airfield. Now fifty-four years of age, she was still youthful-looking and had maintained her trim shape. She gave her height as five feet four inches, and her weight as one hundred twenty pounds.

Having taken into consideration her vast experience, the course of study she was required to fulfill was relatively brief and easy to manage. By September 27, 1966, she had passed her written and flying exams, and had successfully completed a solo cross-country flight. She was eligible for a U.S. pilot's license. With more than a touch of nostalgia, she applied for the same license number she had received after her graduation from the Boeing school. Her examiner obligingly wrote on the license application, "Applicant respectfully requests that her original Private Pilot Certificate number be issued to her. Her original certificate number was 33654 and was issued to her on November 5, 1935. Same was reinstated November 16, 1938, which was kept active until 1943."

However, by this time, the numbering system had moved on; the FAA refused Xiaqing's request and issued her with Temporary Airman Certificate number 1714300.

No longer needing to live so near to the Oakland airfield, she and George decided to relocate, and they found an apartment on the other side of the bay in San Mateo, just ten minutes from San Francisco International Airport. By 1971, they were married and had settled permanently in the United States, at which time they moved back to Oakland, taking a home in the hills some six miles from the airfield.

In middle age, Xiaqing's lust for excitement endured unabated. One day while touring the California countryside, she spotted a crop duster sitting in a farmer's field and asked permission to take it aloft. She proceeded to put the old plane through its paces, performing a series of spins and complicated aerobatic maneuvers until its wires were screaming and its wings were shaking. And then, having taken the machine to the outer limits of its endurance, she calmly landed and politely thanked the astonished owners for their indulgence.[3]

'No fixed address' would almost characterize the couple's life over the next few years. She and George became enthusiastic jetsetters, traveling in style to countries around the world that took their fancy. Xiaqing purchased a condominium at Cannes, France, the playground of the rich and famous, and this became the couple's base whenever they were in Europe. When back in the United States, Xiaqing maintained an active social life, meeting regularly with friends to gossip and play bridge or *mahjong*.

Pax, her son by her first marriage, also lived in the San Francisco area, and mother and child were able, to some extent, to pick up the threads of their lives together, but their rapport lacked closeness. Typical of Xiaqing's tendency to box off various portions of her life and her refusal to concede many events that had occurred in her past, she apparently did not even wish her friends to know that she had borne two children during an unsuccessful marriage to a man with whom she had been estranged for decades. As much as possible, she kept the existence of her firstborn offspring under wraps.[4]

As the years passed, she aged gracefully, and never thought of herself as being elderly. Indeed, she scarcely looked the part. A keen exponent of modern fashions, she maintained her bandbox appearance with carefully applied cosmetics, expensive shoes and handbags, and designer fashions that set off to perfection her lithe shape. As a product of her generation, she was a very much a 'lady,' conservative and proper in all respects. She was never heard to utter a loud word or refer to past triumphs. She did not smoke or drink. Her concern for those less fortunate never abated, and she was a generous benefactor to a multitude of charities.

Xiaqing had always been close to her father, and when he died in Hong Kong in 1971 at the age of 84, she deeply mourned his passing. In his extraordinary lifetime, Li Yingsheng had been a bomb-throwing revolutionary, pioneering scientist, movie mogul, prospector, jeweler, mobster, opium eater, factory owner, renowned philanthropist and wartime fire commissioner of Hong Kong. A man of upright integrity, he nevertheless enjoyed the affectionate confidence of China's most notorious gangster, "Big Eared" Du.[5] As an anti-monarchist who was willing to die to establish China's republican system, he was nevertheless elated to be decorated by the world's ultimate monarch, Queen Elizabeth II, for his wartime services to Hong Kong.[6] During his salad years, he maintained many concubines, and by the time of his death, he still retained five or six. In a typical act of lavish generosity, he bequeathed them the homes in which he had installed them when their love was young.

In February 1993, Xiaqing's ex-husband, Zheng Baifeng, died, but this was no occasion for nostalgia or sad regret. Both parties to the disastrous marriage had continued to nourish a lifelong hatred for each other that, nearly sixty years after their divorce, had never abated. After World War II, Zheng had served as China's ambassador to Cuba, but in the midst of the confusion that surrounded Mao's rise to power, he quit the diplomatic field and permanently relocated to the United States. Thereafter, he pursued a series of stimulating careers that included working for the United Nations, Chinese news agencies, and, finally, Northwest Airlines, this last occupation rather ironic considering Xiaqing's passion for aeronautics. He remarried and fathered two more children, but he never veered from the position that his first wife was "dead."

In 1997, Xiaqing traveled to Hong Kong to be present for the historic handover of the Crown Colony from Great Britain to China. She was determined to be in attendance at the actual ceremonies themselves, and used all the arrows remaining in her quiver to ensure she was one of the four thousand persons lucky enough to be present in the Hong Kong Convention and Exhibition Centre when history was made. At the very moment of the handover when, after one hundred and fifty-six years, Hong Kong was finally returned to the bosom of China, 85-year-old Li Xiaqing let out a rebel yell to make the welkin ring. All her life, her closest friends had been Westerners and she had chosen America as her final home, but at her heart's core, she was a Chinese chauvinist, and this supreme moment was deeply satisfying to her. As China's President Jiang Zemin observed: "July 1, 1997 will go down in the annals of history as a day that merits eternal memory." Xiaqing could not have agreed more.

Later that same year, she went on a riverboat tour of the Yangtze Gorges, whose winding channels she had once navigated by air, flying low beneath the treacherous fogbank with her wingtips almost grazing the rocky cliffs. However, this was not destined to be the pleasure cruise she had hoped it would be. Many of her fellow travelers had persistent coughs, and by the time Xiaqing returned home to Oakland, she was coughing, too. Her lungs had always been weak, and she was susceptible to respiratory problems, but she was not prepared to knuckle under to her present condition. Over the protests of her worried family, she carried out standing plans to visit Europe in the New Year.

She had cause to regret this decision. While abroad, her illness got the upper hand, forcing her to return home ahead of schedule. Finally giving herself over to the care of her children, she consented to be admitted to Oakland's Kaiser Medical Center. A couple of days later, it was over. On January 24, 1998, Li Xiaqing died in hospital of respiratory disease. She did not seem to suffer, but simply slipped away.

Xiaqing's intrepid spirit was laid to rest at a service in the Gothic Chapel at Oakland's Mountain View Cemetery. The lovely old burial ground, last home to some of San Francisco's first families, was just awakening to the initial whispers of spring when her mortal remains were conveyed to a high slope in the Chinese section of the graveyard. Prior to her demise, Xiaqing had acquired for her final resting place a block of four adjacent plots and directed that she be buried in their precise geographical center. This supremely reticent woman, who, in many ways, remained throughout her lifetime a mystery to her family, refused to have any close neighbors—even in death—and chose to pass eternity in splendid isolation.

From the height of land where she is interred, one can just glimpse in the far off distance the gleam of San Francisco Bay where, so many years before, a determined young aviatrix tumbled from the sky like a goddess of old, and plunged feet first into its frigid waters.

fig. 1

fig. 2

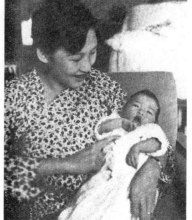

fig. 3

fig. 4

fig. 5

fig. 6

AERO-CLUB DER SCHWEIZ · AÉRO-CLUB DE SUISSE
ZENTRALVORSTAND   COMITÉ CENTRAL

L'Aéro-Club de Suisse atteste par la présente que

Madame Yaching Tscheng,

né à Schanghai le 16 avril 1912

a subi avec succès les épreuves pratiques et théo-
riques pour l'obtention du

Brevet II de pilote d'avion de tourisme

et que ce Brevet lui a été délivré sous le No.II 586
à la date du 9 janvier 1935.

Le Président de la
Commission Sportive de l'Aé.C.S.:

Le Secrétaire général de
l'Aé.C.S.:

Clerc

Signature du titulaire:

Copie de ce document va à l'école de pilotes de la section
de Genève de l'Aé.C.S.

fig. 7

212

fig. 8

fig. 9

fig. 10

fig. 11

fig. 12

fig. 14

fig. 13

fig. 15

214

fig. 16

fig. 17

fig. 18

fig. 19

Tour of the UNITED STATES by
Miss LEE YA CHING.

March	23	New York
"	23	Philadelphia – Charles Morrison – Public Ledger
"	24	Washington – John O'Rourke – The News
"	26	Boston
"	28–29	Richmond
"	29	Charleston
"	30	Jacksonville
"	30	Miami – Jack Knight, Publisher or managing editor – Herald
April	7	Jacksonville
"	8–9	New Orleans
"	10	Houston – A.C. Bartlett, editor, Bud Myers – The Press
"	11	Austin
"	11	Fort Worth – Dallas – Don Weaver – The Press
"	12	Oklahoma – Walter Harrison – Oklahoman
"	15	El Paso – Ed Pooley, editor
"	16	Phoenix
"	16	San Diego – Richard Chase, editor
		Coronado – Jack Joung
"	19	Los Angeles
"	23	San Francisco – Wm. Burkhardt, editor, or Chris Lykke (News)
"	30	Sacramento – Charles Lilley – The Union
May	3	Portland, Oregon
"	7	Seattle
"	11	Vancouver, B. C.
"	14	Spokane
"	15	Boise
"	16	Salt Lake City
"	18	Denver – Lee Casey, Rocky Mountain News (editor)
"	?	Cheyenne
"	20	Omaha
"	22	St. Paul
"	24	Des Moines – Henry L. Martin, Chas. Lounsbury (Register & Tribune)
"	?	Kansas City
"	?	St. Louis – Frank Taylor, editor, Star-Times
"	28	Chicago
June	4	Detroit
"	6	Cleveland – LB Seltzer, editor or Chas. Schneider – The Press
"	8	Buffalo – George Lyon – The Times
"	9	Pittsburgh – Bruce Horton or Wally Forster – The Press
"	11	New York

fig. 20

216

fig. 21

fig. 22

Girl Pilot on Mercy Flight over U. S. A. to
Seek Funds for Chinese Civilian Refugees

fig. 23

fig. 24

廣都大戲院
RIALTO THEATRE

Commencing Sunday September 29th, 1940.

映起日期星九十二月九年九廿國民

PROGRAMME
— Subject to alteration at the discretion of the Management —

I OVERTURE
II FEMALES IS FICKLE *(Cartoon)*
III BLUE DANUBE WALTZ *(Musical)*
IV PARAMOUNT PRESENTS
"DISPUTED PASSAGE"
THE CAST

Audrey Hilton	DOROTHY LAMOUR
Dr."Tubby" Forster	AKIM TAMIROFF
John Wesley Beaven	JOHN HOWARD
(Bill) Anderson	GORDON JONES
Winifred Bane	JUDITH BARRETT
Dr. (Wm.) Cunningham	WILLIAM COLLIER, SR.
Mrs. Cunningham	ELISABETH RISDON
Mr. Merkle	WILLIAM PAWLEY
J. Merkle	BILLY COOK
Abbott	KEYE LUKE
Aviatrix	LEE YA-CHING

映開(三·二期星)日二至日一
OCTOBER 1—2
錢文半偵不命性中之獄地間人
瑪格蘭姍反六位小大亨
片巨情熱感哀會社的性露暴制我張緊

HELL'S KITCHEN

小大亨素
邪歸正
老大亨重
長輕肘

| 獄地黑似賽間刑冰
| 王闖活番不長院老

With The "Dead End" Kids

雄 英 獄 地

映開(六·五·四期星)日五至三
OCTOBER 3—5
偷要又了摸··手隻三裏陣魂迷
士爵勇變忽兇能低　　于帽方偶滑皮蕉香

剃衣克僕
歐暗精來賓

扮女人當場

With STAN Laurel & Oliver Hady
"A CHUMP AT OX ORD"

津到牛
去半
哈台
令再
作度
萊勞
環獨
以出
清道夫留學記

學做罪活　出夜套讚　返志虫糊　行路官垣
生大難受　現鬼半園　洋嚮立達　遷交馬坂

fig. 25

fig. 26

fig. 28

fig. 27

fig. 29

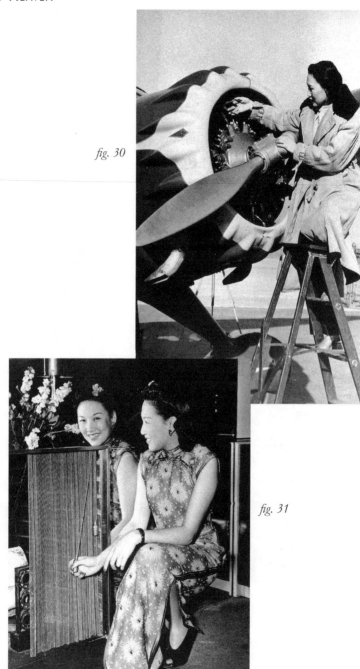

fig. 30

fig. 31

fig. 32

fig. 33

fig. 34

fig. 35

fig. 36

fig. 37

fig. 38

223

fig. 39

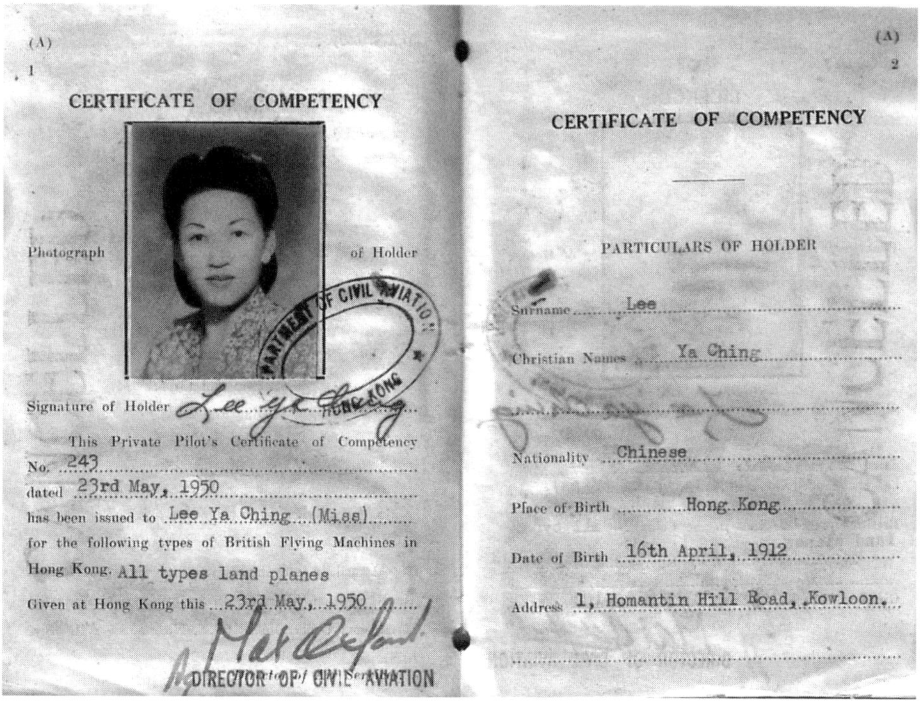
(A)
1

CERTIFICATE OF COMPETENCY

Photograph of Holder

Signature of Holder Lee Ya Ching

This Private Pilot's Certificate of Competency No. 243 dated 23rd May, 1950 has been issued to Lee Ya Ching (Miss) for the following types of British Flying Machines in Hong Kong. All types land planes

Given at Hong Kong this 23rd May, 1950

DIRECTOR OF CIVIL AVIATION

(A)
2

CERTIFICATE OF COMPETENCY

PARTICULARS OF HOLDER

Surname Lee

Christian Names Ya Ching

Nationality Chinese

Place of Birth Hong Kong

Date of Birth 16th April, 1912

Address 1, Homantin Hill Road, Kowloon.

fig. 40

PART III

ZHENG HANYING 郑汉英: UNEASY SPIRIT

床前明月光，疑是地上霜。— 举头望明月，低头思故乡。

So bright a gleam on the foot of my bed –
Could there have been a frost already?
Lifting myself to look, I found that it was moonlight.
Sinking back again, I thought suddenly of home.

—李白 : 夜思

—Li Bai, *In the Quiet Night* (Tr. Witter Bynner)

24. INTRODUCTION

In the spring of 1941, 26-year-old Miss Jessie Hanying Zheng arrived in Vancouver, Canada, to serve as attaché with the Chinese Consulate, and in very short time, everyone in the city knew her by sight and by reputation. This slight, pensive woman automatically turned heads whenever she clipped briskly to and from the Hastings Street Consular offices in her Western high-heeled shoes. For one thing, she was young and pretty, but her physical attributes were only part of her charm. Striding energetically amidst the wartime swirl of khaki uniforms that filled the streets, her forehead puckered in thought, petite Miss Zheng caused a sensation by her exotic appearance in the resplendent costume of the Chinese Air Force—a dark slit skirt, cut in the Chinese fashion, topped by a bright scarlet tunic emblazoned with golden wings. She was an aviatrix, one of a tiny handful of women fliers in China, and the only woman officer in the Chinese Air Force.

The remarkable Miss Jessie Zheng had a string of other 'firsts' to her credit: first Chinese woman to learn to fly in Hong Kong; first Chinese woman sent to Canada in any official capacity; and first woman in Canada to possess an International Flying License issued by the Royal Aero Club of London. One of the few women diplomats in the world, she was also a linguist, proficient in five languages, a graduate in law, and an authority on flood relief and Red Cross work.

As one of the brightest stars in her nation's firmament (she was a personal friend of Madame Chiang Kai-Shek, and niece of China's ambassador to the United States), Jessie seemed truly blessed, and one who was destined to blast into oblivion the West's image of China as a medieval kingdom of bound-footed women. Remarkably, for one who had so much of which to be proud, she was surprisingly modest, and her shy humility caused people to warm to her. Hard-nosed veteran journalists went limp when they interviewed her, comparing her 'creamy' skin to the petals of the lotus blossom, and her voice to the sound of muted silver bells. One spellbound reporter apparently lost all grip on reality by describing her as an "ivory princess that had stepped from her carved pedestal..."[1]

Reading between the lines, it appears that Miss Zheng was possessed of a charismatic personality, that, when combined with her accomplishments, turned much of Vancouver on its ear. Which was why her premature death at the age of twenty-eight occasioned so much shock and grief and caused her coffin to be carried through the streets of Vancouver by a Royal Canadian Air Force honor guard, a singular distinction usually reserved for victorious generals or long-serving prime ministers. How did she become such a paragon of her sex? What was a Chinese Air Force aviatrix doing in Vancouver in the first place? How was she struck down in the flower of her young womanhood?

25. ORIGINS

There are several gaps in Jessie's story, and many important details remain unknown. Her life and career, as short-lived and brilliant as a meteor, left few traces and fewer still who survive to have any memory of her existence. An intensely private person, she went to great lengths to obscure details about her personal life; indeed, she was even successful in blocking the particulars of her out-of-wedlock pregnancy at the height of her career. Of her early years, nothing can be reconstructed, and all that can be definitely stated is that she was born Zheng Hanying in the dying days of the Year of the Tiger in China's Guangdong province on January 17, 1915. Her friends knew her by the English name of Jessie.

At the time of her birth, Guangdong enjoyed a well-deserved reputation for independent and revolutionary thought. The Father of Modern China, Dr. Sun Yat-sen, was its most celebrated native son, and the Revolution he set alight had its origins in this southern province. It was also China's cradle of aviation. Feng Ru, the first Chinese aviator, hailed from the region, and the first indigenous aircraft built on Chinese soil was constructed here.

Jessie was born just a handful of years after Dr. Sun's revolution overthrew the Qing dynasty, and this seminal event inevitably colored her childhood. Other children may have been raised on fairy tales, but Jessie was nurtured on legends of the martyrs who had freed China from the yoke of the Manchus. While girls her age might be trained in the virtues of compliance and gentleness—traits that were the hallmark of the traditional Chinese woman—Jessie was reared on the deeds of Mulan, the sixteenth century warring female who, disguised as a man, won glory on the field of battle.

Little is known about her immediate family. Jessie had an older brother named Zheng Yun. He was three years her senior, and one report suggests that the siblings were the only two children born to their parents, but it is likely that the family was much larger. Jessie claimed to have four brothers, one who was in the Chinese Air Force (likely Zheng Yun), two who worked for the Chinese government, and one who served as a Chinese consul in the United States. There is also some evidence that she had a sister.[1]

The Zheng family's ancestral village was Lequn Cun, located in Guangdong province, Xiang township, Baoan county. By her own account, Jessie was born to an old and aristocratic family of mandarins who had long served the emperors of China. Her legendary aunt, the revolutionary Dr. Zheng Yuxiu, also shored up this notion, and was at pains to establish the long and patrician pedigree of the family's forebears. However, it seems more likely that the Zheng acquisition of wealth and power dated only to the late nineteenth century, and had its origins in Jessie's dynamic great-grandfather, Zheng Yao.

In 1840, Zheng Yao was born the son of an impoverished carpenter in Lequn Cun. His mother died while he was yet an infant, and his bereft father was left with no means of nourishing the newborn. The desperate widower Zheng wrapped the hungry toddler in swaddling clothes, hooked the tiny bundle onto the end of a pole, and padded up and down the streets of the town, begging the village women to spare some milk for his son. Responding to the widower's sad appeal, they took turns suckling the child, and thereafter it was said that Zheng Yao was raised on the milk of a hundred women.[2]

When he grew to manhood, Zheng Yao did not allow his disadvantaged start in life to slow him down. Entering the carpentry trade as his father had done, he became known as 'Wooden Yao,' both for his skill as a cabinet maker and for his appreciation of fine wood, but he soon discovered that this profession did not satisfy his energies or his dreams. Possessed of ambition beyond his lowly station in life, as well as the high-strung energy that would mark certain of his descendants, he beat all the odds to become a wealthy developer and speculator of real estate in Hong Kong. A wily and hard-nosed man of business, he is credited with having built up whole sections of the city. As a consequence, he amassed (and eventually lost) a large fortune in his lifetime, but his ruthlessness was tempered by his great heart, and he was renowned for his philanthropy. Among his good works, he hosted banquets twice a year for the poor of his village, thereby repaying the kindness of those who were responsible for his survival as a child. For his manifold charities, he received a commendation from the Emperor who personally inscribed a panel in his own hand: "Zheng Yao, a philanthropist who loves to give."

In about 1885, Zheng built a lavish palace in Lequn Cun that was vast enough to accommodate his extended family of some sixty relatives, forty servants and their families. Visitors gaining entrance to the walled compound might be forgiven for imagining they had entered a small city. Its multiple dwellings and labyrinthine interiors boasted grand courtyards, grottos, sylvan pleasure-gardens, and separate apartments for men and women. The main reception room, the Zheng Ancestral Hall, was at the very heart of the compound. Paved with marble flagstones, its green-lacquered, upward-sweeping roof was supported by soaring columns of costly hongmu wood, and its cross beams were richly carved with classical Chinese motifs. Nearby was located the Zheng Shrine, on the walls of which were inscribed the names of the Zheng ancestors, and these spirit-tablets looked down upon the large altar where religious festivals and family milestones were celebrated.

The patriarch Zheng Yao was wealthy enough to support a great nuclear family, and he is said to have had seven wives, seven sons and seven daughters. It was his third son, Zheng Wenzhi, who would become Jessie's grandfather.

Zheng Wenzhi was a mandarin official in China's Ministry of Finance, and a staunch royalist. He wed the daughter of General Liu Changhua, but the union was unhappy, and Zheng Wenzhi spent most of his middle years living in Beijing with his concubine. Before their estrangement, however, the married couple produced four offspring—two sons and two daughters—all of whom were to rebel and embrace the movement that sought to rid China of their father's employer, the Manchu usurpers. The names of the two sons, one of whom became Jessie's father, are unknown. The names of the two daughters were Zheng Xuean and Zheng Yuxiu. Zheng Yuxiu, a larger-than-life character, was destined to have an enormous influence on young Jessie's formative years, and, indeed, was to leave her indelible imprint on the ancient land of China itself, so much so that one day she would be considered one of the most significant women in Chinese history.

When grown to young womanhood, Jessie would claim that, ever since she could remember, she had always nourished an intense concern for the welfare of her nation. This was an unusual passion for a young girl, but even her name, Hanying or 'Heroine of China,' seemed to mark her for the service of her nation and obliged her to perform noble deeds on behalf of the motherland. The remarkable strength of her love for China derived largely from the atmosphere of revolutionary zeal that animated her immediate household.

Her father had been one of those committed to the overthrow of the Qing dynasty, and he was an active participant in the Revolution of 1911. Her aunt, Zheng Xuean, was not a bomb-throwing revolutionary, but she was closely involved with the radical movement—and in love with a young republican suicide bomber. Weeping, she watched him go to his death in order that democracy might be more speedily achieved.[3] However, Jessie's most formidable aunt, Zheng Yuxiu, made the deepest impact on the young girl's sensibilities and charted the course that her life would follow. At the height of her authority, Zheng Yuxiu not only wielded considerable influence over her own family, but she was also one of the most powerful women in Republican China, superseded only by Madame Chiang Kai-shek. A warlord in her own right, she buttressed her authority with the personal army of crack soldiers she maintained below stairs in her household. Small, gregarious, loud and adventurous, Zheng Yuxiu was a standout in any crowd.

In her two biographies, Zheng Yuxiu proudly acknowledged that she was a born rebel, and unlike her older sister, who took delight in learning the womanly arts of painting, embroidery and music, she cared little for the traditional refinements that defined the ladies of her day. Some indication of the strength of her character can be gauged by her adamant refusal, as a child, to allow her feet to be bound. Perhaps more surprising was the reaction of her family who acquiesced, and, bending to the iron will of this extraordinary youngster, removed the despised bandages. When she was thirteen, Zheng Yuxiu once more bucked authority and risked disgracing her family by refusing to marry the high-born man chosen for her, the son of the Governor of Guangdong province. In the year 1906, when she was just fifteen years old, she joined Dr. Sun Yat-sen's secret revolutionary society, the Tongmenghui, and finally found a cause worthy of her mettle. From that time forward, she was unequivocally dedicated to the fulfillment of the party's ideals, the chief of which was the overthrow of the Manchu dynasty and the union of China under a single republican banner.

By exploiting the diplomatic immunity she enjoyed as the daughter of a senior official of the Manchu regime, Zheng Yuxiu repeatedly imported bomb-making materials from Tianjin to Beijing by train. The secret society assembled and employed these materials to assassinate important officials attached to the Dragon Throne. Their terrorist tactics finally got results. In 1912, the 268-year-old Qing dynasty finally fell, largely due to the extreme measures employed by Zheng Yuxiu and her ilk. Even so, the revolutionaries felt their work could not be considered completed until Yuan Shikai, the first president of the budding Republic of China, was exterminated. Yuan was, ironically, an anti-Republican and he was said to entertain dreams of becoming an emperor himself. The rebels resolved that he, too, would have to be eliminated. Zheng Yuxiu volunteered to become his assassin. The assignment would surely have cost the young woman her life, and she was fully conscious of this inevitability, but she was willing to make the supreme sacrifice for the sake of the Republic. At the last minute, however, her superiors dropped these plans when authorities discovered the murderous plot and Zheng's part in it. She was ordered to stand down.

In the year before Jessie's birth, the precocious Zheng Yuxiu began to set the tone for other Chinese of her class and generation by sailing to France and entering into studies in the Sorbonne at the University of Paris. While abroad, she became known by the French version of her name, Tcheng Soumay (Soumé), and, indeed, she embraced the French language and culture with alacrity. Upon completion of her studies, she would receive the Doctor of Laws degree from the Sorbonne (1925) and return home to become China's first woman lawyer and first woman judge.

Among her many accomplishments, she was a member of the Chinese delegation to the post-World War I Paris Peace Conference, and, with Song Meiling, became the first woman to serve on China's legislative Yuan at Nanjing. In 1928, she was appointed to a five-man Civil Codification Commission whose assignment was nothing less than the drafting of the civil laws of China. Taking maximum advantage of this opportunity, Zheng Yuxiu ensured that women's rights were enshrined in law, with the result that China's legal system was considered one of the most equitable and enlightened in the world. Yet for all her overseas training and appreciation of western culture, she remained a committed Chinese nationalist.

Zheng Yuxiu married one of her Sorbonne classmates and the man with whom she shared her legal practice, Dr. Wei Daoming. It was an ideal match. The contemplative and steady Dr. Wei managed to temper the more excessive characteristics of his wife's explosively spontaneous personality, and for her part, Zheng Yuxiu valued her husband's calm and reasoned approach to any dilemma. In turn, she had a positive effect on his career, propelling him to excel and carve out ambitious roles for himself that otherwise he might not have considered. Dr. Wei ultimately rose to acquire one of the plum positions in the diplomatic arena when he was tipped to serve as China's wartime Ambassador to the United States from 1942 to 1946. It was widely whispered, however, that the job would not have been his but for the influence of his astonishingly capable wife.

During the era of budding emancipation in post-Revolutionary China, Jessie was born into the remarkable Zheng family. She fell within the orbit of her powerful aunt, Zheng Yuxiu, supreme embodiment of China's new womanhood, who aggressively encouraged her niece to become aware of her responsibilities to China.[4]

It is not surprising then, that upon graduation from a Hong Kong high school in the early 1930s, Jessie chose to follow the example of her aunt and other Zheng family members by sailing to France and entering the Sorbonne. France was one of the preferred destinations of overseas students because, like China, it had overthrown its monarchy in a revolution. Following in her aunt's footsteps, Jessie also chose to study law. With devotion to country uppermost, her ultimate goal was to enter China's foreign service just as many of her relatives had done before her, and earning a degree in law would be a stepping stone to that ambition. Since the Mukden Incident of 1931, Japan had left no doubt of its imperialistic ambitions towards China, and Jessie seriously believed that it was the responsibility of every Chinese woman to improve herself so as to be better equipped to serve her nation in its hour of need.

The Sorbonne suited her well. Founded in the thirteenth century, the university's venerable antiquity was a feature that Jessie, from the ancient land of China, instinctively appreciated, but apart from her academic studies, she quickly discovered that as much could be learned outside the walls of the Sorbonne as within. Paris of the 1930s was a mecca for the *avant-garde*, and freethinking intellectuals congregated and fed each other's energies in the Latin Quarter.

The liberality that Jessie encountered in *la Ville Lumière* contrasted sharply with the immoderate intolerance that overshadowed the politics of France's immediate neighbors. In Germany, Adolf Hitler had come to power in 1933 and almost immediately presided over the confiscation of Jewish property. In Italy, Dictator Benito Mussolini had impulsively acted on his overarching ambitions by invading Ethiopia in December 1934.

By a curious chain of events, Mussolini's imperialism was indirectly responsible for a number of riots that erupted at the Sorbonne's law school during Jessie's final year. One of the school's most distinguished professors, Dr. Gaston Jèze, had denounced the Italian dictator, both in the Court of the Hague and at the League of Nations, for his invasion of Ethiopia. Dr. Jèze declared his support for the African country's autonomy, but his vigorous anti-Mussolini attacks were deprecated by right-wing students who believed the university was acting against the interests of France. For several months, the professor's law lectures at the Sorbonne were disrupted by stink bombs, loud calls for his resignation and general hooliganism. He was even burned in effigy.

It is probable that Jessie took this rumpus in stride. Growing up in the company of ardent revolutionaries, the volatile mix of passion and politics was as mother's milk to her, but she would have sided with Professor Jèze. The Italian occupation of Ethiopia was disturbing, especially as it echoed troubles in her own homeland and reminded her all too well of Japan's occupation of Manchuria where the Imperial government had recently established the puppet state of Manchukuo, placing on its 'throne' none other than China's last Manchu emperor, Puyi. This act underscored the ever-present threat to China's sovereignty posed by the imperialism of her hostile neighbor. At the same time, China was also threatened from within. The escape of rebel, Mao Zedong, from the clutches of the Nationalist Government, and the dogged endurance he and his followers showed on their celebrated Long March, demonstrated the strength and unmistakable allure of communist idealism in China. Its threat to the supremacy of Generalissimo Chiang Kai-shek's power base was ongoing and palpable.

While she kept a nervous eye on political events back home, Jessie made the most of her time in Paris, a city of enchantment she had come to love. The beauty of its architecture, the panache of its fashionable women, and the omnipresent pride of its people in their revolutionary history resonated in her soul. She thrilled to the stirring words of *La Marseillaise*, the martial hymn of France, "*Aux armes, citoyens! Formez vos bataillons!*" The splendid slogan of the Revolution—*Liberté, Egalité, Fraternité*—was the lodestar that guided her aspirations for China. She came to speak French as easily as her native tongue, and quickly adopted the mantle of stylish chic that was the hallmark of the Parisian woman. She also rounded out her education by learning Italian and German, and she slipped over to Britain to buff up her English. By the time Jessie received her degree in law in 1936, she was polished, traveled, well educated and more than ever imbued with the idealism that had motivated the prime movers of the Revolution.[5] Thanks to her aunt, she also held decided views on the important place of women in modern society. She returned to China a mature and motivated citizen.

26. WINGS FOR CHINA

While she was in Paris, Jessie's parents had moved to Shanghai, and when she returned to China, she traveled there to be with them. Aunt Zheng Yuxiu also lived in Shanghai and had already made her mark on the city by co-founding Shanghai's first school of law and initiating the Women's Commercial and Savings Bank on the Nanjing Road. As the so-called 'Paris of the East,' Shanghai was in its heyday, and Zheng Yuxiu very near its epicenter. Jessie discovered that, through her gregarious and famous aunt, she had an entrée to the city's most exalted social circles.

Zheng Yuxiu loved to entertain at the luxurious Avenue Haig residence she shared with her husband and son, and as she could not bear to sit down to less than three tables of guests, most of her 'evenings in' were riotously convivial. Jessie's attendance at these soirées in her aunt's lavish, *chinoiserie*-decorated household brought her into contact with the most prominent figures of the Far East. Although she was still in her early twenties, by her wit and intelligence she was able to hold her own among the wealthy, renowned and notorious of Shanghai.

Jessie's keen sense of style, honed in Paris, also held her in good stead. It is recounted that she and her aunt attended a tea party celebrating the opening of an atelier operated by up-and-coming fashion designer, Zhang Qianying (Miss Hélène Tsang). The wealthiest and most beautiful women in Shanghai, arrayed in their finest, attended this event, but it was Jessie's quietly elegant appearance in a rich black gown, piped with scarlet and black satin, that grabbed everyone's attention and made her a standout among the silk and diamond-draped socialites.[1] Coincidently, a friend of her aunt, Miss Hilda Yan, was also a guest at the party, and she, too, would have plans to become an aviator for China.

Jessie's striking cousin-by-marriage, the well-known society aviatrix, Li Xiaqing, also lived in Shanghai.̓ The famous woman pilot had recently returned to China following the completion of her aviation studies in California. Jessie and Xiaqing were related through the latter's marriage to Jessie's cousin, Zheng Baifeng, but the union, arranged by Zheng Yuxiu, had recently collapsed. Li Xiaqing divorced her husband in March 1936, ostensibly so that she might 'devote her life to the development of aviation in China' without encumbrance.

Miss Li's commitment to her country and love of flight struck a corresponding chord in Jessie Zheng. Like so many other young females of her generation, she was alive to the intrepid verve of women who had chosen to take to the skies. While she was in Paris, all of Europe had been electrified by the daring-do of France's cherished aviatrix, Maryse Hilsz, who, in 1930, had become the only woman to fly from Paris to Saigon and back, and in 1933, she repeated this feat, but trumped it by flying on to Tokyo and setting a speed record in the process. Almost every town in France celebrated this accomplishment by naming a street in honor of Miss Hilsz. Jessie was entranced by the romance of flight, but, ever the patriot, was also intrigued by the possibilities that aviation held for the defense and unification of her own country. She even

237

had some first-hand flight experience. Her elder brother, Zheng Yun, who had long been enthralled by aviation (his flying lessons were subsidized by Zheng Yuxiu), had already taken her aloft once or twice.

"He talked about [aviation] a good deal," she explained some years later, "and occasionally took me up with him. Then I knew I wanted to be a flyer, too."[2]

It is also tempting to suppose that she met with her cousin-by-marriage, Li Xiaqing, and went flying with the famed aviatrix in one of the aircraft belonging to the newly established Shanghai Aviation Club. Miss Li was a flight instructor at the Club, and, in an effort to promote airmindedness, she regularly took interested individuals for exhilarating flights along the Huangpo River shoreline and up over the city skyscrapers that lined the Bund.

It is also more than likely that, along with everyone else in Shanghai, Jessie was present at the October 1936 air show, held in honor of Generalissimo Chiang Kai-shek's fiftieth birthday, and had an opportunity to witness Li Xiaqing's heart-stopping aerobatic performance. Shortly after this triumph, Li Xiaqing, Hilda Yan, and a handful of others organized a special group, the purpose of which was to promote aviation among young women, and it is altogether probable that Jessie also aligned herself with this movement at that time.

What is known for certain is that shortly after Miss Li's aerobatic performance, Jessie decided to embark on a career in aviation in the service of the Government of China.

In the New Year of 1937, Jessie said goodbye to her friends and family in Shanghai and returned to Hong Kong where she enrolled at the Far East Flying Training School (FEFTS).[3] There were several reasons why she opted to leave Shanghai in favor of the Colony. In the first place, Hong Kong was home, but more importantly, her dashing older brother, Zheng Yun, was already a second year student at the FEFTS, having enrolled at the school in March 1936. He would be available to give her encouragement on difficult days, and to provide the fraternal support and protection often required by a young woman invading an all-male preserve. In addition—and perhaps the most important consideration—the Hong Kong school was arguably the finest flying academy in Asia.

Located at Kai Tak airport in Kowloon, the facility had recently enlarged its premises to create flying and engineering sections. The school boasted that, since its formal inception in 1934, its aircraft had flown half a million miles, and yet no student had ever been involved in a serious accident. The fleet of training airplanes consisted of two Avro 626 Trainers and two Avro 631 Cadets. There were also two other planes in the fleet, one of which—a Fairey Fox—was used for ground instruction. Later that year, a Hornet Moth was also acquired for the students' use. Unlike the Avros, whose open cockpits made the wearing of goggles and helmet a necessity, the Moth was a cabin monoplane, and both teacher and student could sit side-by-side in comfort—and within earshot—inside the aircraft and out of the elements.

The teaching staff was second to none, and included Lord Malcolm Douglas-Hamilton, son of the thirteenth Duke of Hamilton, who was late of the Royal Air Force and also held a commercial flying license.[4] Additional worthies on staff were the British RAF-trained pilots, Flight-Lieutenant P.H. Smith and Flying Officer G.P. Longfield, and Chinese instructors, not to mention a special officer, Mr. Hong Jiaming, whose function it was to liaise between the English-speaking staff and the Chinese students.

As a result of the high standards maintained by the FEFTS, the institution was granted the right to train the pilots of the Hong Kong Volunteer Defense Corps, and, more significantly, it also won coveted approval as an official Royal Air Force Training School. As such, it was the only academy of its kind operating outside of England. At the time, the RAF enjoyed a reputation as the world's finest air force, and learning under its tutelage meant that Jessie would be training with the best. The same year that she enrolled, six officers of the Reserve were also registered at the school to carry out their annual training, and to accommodate their requirements, one of the Avros was kitted out with advanced training gear that allowed Jessie and her fellow students to learn bombing, gunnery, aerial photography, and blind flying.[5]

Kai Tak aerodrome itself was a bustling facility. It had come of age the year before when it won approval as an international airport. As well as welcoming the aircraft of the Eurasia Aviation Corporation, the China National Aviation Corporation (CNAC), and Britain's Imperial Airways, Hong Kong had won coveted rights to become a Pan-American Airways terminus, and its specially enhanced marine docking facility regularly received the celebrated trans-oceanic Clipper flights from San Francisco. As a result, the effectiveness of the airport was enhanced by the most up-to-date lighting and safety systems, and these were augmented by a fully equipped ambulance and fire engine vehicles that could be deployed immediately in the event of an emergency.

Located on the edge of the airfield at the junction of Sam Tak and Sai Kung roads, the flying school's main building sat close to the Kowloon City bus stop. It included a mess where students could eat and reside, and it even boasted a women's dressing room. At the orientation session, Jessie learned that the school's usual working hours were from 8 a.m. to 5 p.m. on weekdays, and from 8 to 2:30 on Saturdays. Training was full-time; a leave of absence would be granted only under exceptional circumstances. Jessie's attention was also directed to the forced landing ground located at some remove from the regular runways. Aviation mishaps were a fact of life, and she would be required to learn how to make emergency landings, just in case.

On February 2, 1937, just two weeks after her twenty-second birthday, Jessie began instruction at the Far East Flying Training School, one of eighty flight and engineering pupils. Although she was not the first female student to enroll (that distinction belonged to FEFTS graduate, Miss Jean Mackie, who won her wings three years before), she was the first Chinese woman to sign up for flying lessons at the school.[6]

She knew Hong Kong well—her great-grandfather, after all, had been responsible for the construction of much of it—but the first time Jessie went aloft was a revelation. The scene was somewhat familiar to anyone who had climbed Victoria Peak to see the city jumbled below like the hoard of a jewel thief, but the aerial view was even more spectacular. On her first low flight along the crowded harbor, she saw structures piled crookedly upon structures like rock formations, with barely an inch of space between. Narrow streets cut through their midst like dark fissures. Fragile-looking jetties poked out into the misty blue harbor that streamed with junks and ships from many lands. She had taken up aviation to serve her country; its vulnerable beauty from the air caught at her heart and strengthened her resolve.

Her unique status as sole Chinese woman student at the school immediately attracted the attention of the media, and on the second day of her training, a reporter from the *South China Morning Post* arrived to interview her for the paper. Intensely shy, Jessie was mortified, and refused to cooperate. This intrusion was not only an invasion of her privacy, but also a glaring spotlight shone on her activities, and she wanted no attention drawn to her flying attempts.

"What if I should fail?" she cried, hedging her bets.

The reporter, however, was not to be dissuaded from his objective, and even without his subject's collaboration, managed to pen a flattering article about the polished and pretty 23-year-old flyer. He also appears to have gained access to Jessie's logbook, and revealed her weight (104 pounds) and her height (under five feet, four inches). At the time, the inclusion of physical details was *de rigueur* in any article whose subject was a comely young female, but Jessie was too self-conscious about her size (her tiny waist, it was said, could be encircled by two hands) to appreciate these very public revelations. Her embarrassment was such that, thereafter, she steadfastly refused to provide personal information to any of her subsequent interviewers. This, however, did not stop them from 'guess-timating' these statistics anyway and providing them for the entertainment of their readers.

Jessie's goal was to obtain her 'A,' or private, license in a few months' time. This would entail her having accrued several hours' worth of solo flight time, as well as having passed two flying tests involving a demonstration of various skills, such as completing figure eights, and landing within a circle from a height. She would also be required to sit for an oral exam on air law and navigation. The entire testing process promised to be rigorous and would take anywhere from eight to ten hours to complete. Her brother was already working toward his 'B,' or commercial, license. Considered one of the most capable of the FEFTS flying students, his confidence and success served as a goad to her own ambitions. She threw herself into her studies.

Each morning, she experienced the same thrill when the school's planes were wheeled out of the hangar and onto the tarmac in the brilliant sunshine. The school's parent company, the Far East Aviation Company, was in the business of importing a wide variety of British aircraft to Kai Tak where they were assembled and tested before being delivered to customers in China. As a result, she enjoyed the additional benefit of being able to acquaint herself with a number of different flying machines, the most exotic of which was a Cierva autogyro that arrived in May 1937. Jessie quickly became a 'hangar rat,' spending all her free time at the airport and at Kai Tak's Hong Kong Flying Club, into which she was enrolled as an active member. Her entire world revolved around aviation.

Two months after Jessie's training commenced, Li Xiaqing flew into Kai Tak to apply for a Hong Kong 'B' license. The celebrated aviatrix was then in the middle of a six-week stint of flying as a volunteer transport pilot with Guangdong's Southwestern Aviation Corporation (SWAC). She had embarked on a one-woman crusade to bolster airmindedness in China, hence her high-profile involvement with SWAC, and her appealing presence and 'can-do' attitude provided Jessie with a valuable psychological boost during these early days of her training.

For Jessie, however, the most noteworthy incident of the year involved her brother. On June 7, 1937, Zheng Yun and He Desheng, an 'A' license student in Jessie's class, took off in separate aircraft and went on what was subsequently described as a 'joy ride.' Several hours passed, but the pair did not return to Kai Tak. The school publicly expressed confidence in the boys' flying ability, but Jessie was frantic with worry. To her intense relief, the next day the errant pair was found to be alive and well in the neighboring province of Guangdong.

As Zheng Yun later told the story, he went aloft to find his friend who had inexplicably flown off in the direction of Guangdong province, but was unable to locate him. In fact, He Desheng had grown hopelessly lost when he was about two hundred miles from Hong Kong and had brought down his aircraft on the mud bank of a river. When the tidal waters rose, his plane became partially submerged and he was unable to take off again. Meanwhile, Zheng flew on and got lost in a cloud bank only to re-emerge over the Guangzhou airfield where he landed without difficulty, but with an almost-empty tank. The boys had no authorization to fly into Chinese territory and they had come away without even the most elementary documentation, such as their logbooks and the aircrafts' certificates of registration and airworthiness. These oversights represented serious breaches of air law and, in those troubled times, left them open to charges of espionage. They were detained, and their aircraft impounded.

The local papers—both English and Chinese—had a field day. Zheng Yun, described as the nephew of Zheng Yuxiu, was allotted the bulk of the headlines. One of the FEFTS instructors traveled by train to Guangzhou to plea for the young men's freedom, and it was only the timely mediation of Guangdong's governor, General Wu Tiecheng, that ultimately greased the skids and led to their release. General Wu, the former mayor of Shanghai, was an old friend of Zheng Yuxiu, and it is probable that she persuaded him to intercede on behalf of the family. This was neither the first, nor the last, time that well-placed friends would assist the Zhengs in their hour of need.

In Guangzhou, and in the presence of the provincial government and police department, the shamefaced pair were brought before a military tribunal of the Fourth Route Army. Released on bond, they were required to return to Hong Kong and appear before the Kowloon Magistracy. The abashed young men were fined and charged with a variety of aviation offences. Their so-called 'foolish escapade' and its fallout must have seemed especially imprudent falling so close to the outbreak of hostilities exactly one month later.

At first, the skirmish at the Marco Polo Bridge on July 7, 1937, that would mark the beginning of the eight-year Sino-Japanese conflict, had little effect on the Colony. Soon, however, there was no escaping the gravity of the situation, especially when refugees of all stripes and social classes began to flood into south China and Hong Kong, fleeing from the hostilities in the north. Jessie saw first-hand the problems caused by the abnormal and rapid swelling of a city's population in wartime.

Although Japanese operations extended to the very verges of Hong Kong, its citizens fervently hoped that the Colony itself would continue to remain un-molested. If an attack did come, Jessie had some confidence that the British Commonwealth forces stationed in Hong Kong would emerge victorious in any struggle. This belief was bolstered by the remarks of Sir Robert Brooke-Popham, the British Commander-in-Chief of the Far East forces, who stoutly declared that any notion the area could be captured in a few days or weeks was entirely without merit.[7]

Throughout this uncertain period, Jessie steadfastly continued to study aviation. Each new stricture on her life, and every hostile act perpetrated against the Chinese people, only reinforced her zeal to learn her craft and fly for her country. Now subjected to wartime regulations, she and her fellow students received orders not to fly at less than ten thousand feet over designated anti-aircraft firing ranges. They were also obliged to keep strictly within the boundaries of the Colony, and not to stray beyond a three-mile radius of the aerodrome. Hong Kong was a tranquil island in the midst of Japanese depredations, but once an aircraft left its boundaries, it was vulnerable to attack.[8]

Amidst the chaos that gripped her world, Jessie focused on the task at hand and took advantage of all that the school had to offer. In the summer of 1937, she sat for her final flying test. Requiring proficiency in both aerobatics and blind flying, the exam was not for the faint of heart, and it was a proud moment when she won her wings. Keeping in mind her intention to join the foreign service, she augmented her qualifications by earning, through the Royal Aero Club of London, an International Flying License from the Fédération Aéronautique Internationale (FAI). The FAI license would allow her to fly anywhere in the world, an important consideration for a young diplomat-in-training.

On August 13, 1937, Shanghai fell under Japanese attack, and less than a week later, even neutral Hong Kong felt the repercussions of this event. Boats laden with women and children escaping the beleaguered city began to arrive in the Crown Colony. The first ocean liner, the *Rajputana*, steamed into harbor overflowing with one thousand passengers, and she was closely followed by the *Empress of Asia* and other great ships bearing yet more refugees. Jessie scanned the lengthy passenger lists printed in the papers and found the names of many Shanghai acquaintances, both foreign and Chinese, who were seeking shelter in the Colony. Hong Kong scrambled to house the newcomers, and impromptu refugee centers sprang up at the Jockey Club, the Happy Valley racecourse, and anywhere else the newcomers could be accommodated. Then suddenly, another wave of terror-stricken refugees arrived, this time aboard packed trains from Guangzhou fleeing Japanese depredations in Guangdong province. An air of urgency and panic gripped the Colony as local citizens rushed to provide aid to those who needed it, and to make plans for their own protection in the event that the conflict eventually involved Hong Kong.

Jessie was deeply disturbed by these developments, and almost desperate in her need to do something of value for her country, but she sought to do more than fold bandages or knit socks. In her capacity as an aviatrix, she had offered her services to her country when the conflict first began, yet several weeks had passed and she still had received no reply. She was on tenterhooks waiting for an answer. It was not until the third week of August that the telegram arrived, and, ripping it open, Jessie realized with delight that it was the answer to her prayers. The wire was from the National Government, and it invited her to journey north to help fight the enemy.[9] Jessie was ecstatic. She had been granted an appointment to the National Commission on Aeronautical Affairs, the body that regulated all aviation matters in the country. Even the Chinese Air Force fell under the Commission's broad control. The board was chaired by Song Meiling and was composed of several departments and committees that oversaw a variety of aeronautical activities, including aviation training, personnel, air bases, aircraft manufacture, and air defense.

Madame Chiang was a long-time friend of the Zheng family (she and Zheng Yuxiu had served together as the Republic's first women legislators), so it is probable that nepotism played some part in Jessie's appointment, but it is difficult to imagine anyone more admirably suited for the job. With a family background of service to country, her overseas degree in law, and her superb flying qualifications, Jessie had earned a place on the Commission. It is altogether likely that her sex also had something to do with her placement. Madame Chiang encouraged women's participation in aviation and she would have been delighted to have on board someone who represented all the stellar qualities that she hoped to encourage in China's young womanhood.

Jessie's main interest in aviation lay in the development of innovative flying techniques (and it is said that she herself carried out considerable personal research in this regard), but she learned that one of her most important duties on the Commission would involve public relations. She would be required to publicize the benefits of aviation to a public still unsure about its safety or usefulness, and become a booster of the 'Saving the Nation Through Aviation' program.[10] This vital movement had grown out of Dr. Sun Yat-sen's National Defense Plan of 1921 that called for improvements in the area of aviation, and ultimately resulted in the creation of overseas flight training facilities for young Chinese living and studying abroad. Jessie was already a strong supporter of this strategy; she deeply believed that only through aviation could China become a progressive and united country, well able to defend itself, and one of her jobs on the Commission became the national promulgation of airmindness through the contribution of articles on flight to major journals. She also flew many thousands of miles on China's behalf to make public appearances throughout the nation.

Jessie's passion for aviation and her outstanding flying abilities—not to mention her advanced training with the Royal Air Force—inevitably caught the eye of Chiang Kai-shek himself. In 1938, the dazzled Generalissimo personally granted the aviatrix a commission in the Chinese Air Force. Flight-Lieutenant Zheng Hanying became the only woman in the CAF. She was issued a specially-designed dress uniform fashioned in the colors of China's flag: a bright red tunic with a stand-up collar edged in gold and blue braid, accompanied by a navy-colored slit skirt that fell just below the knee, the hem and sides of which were finished with red piping.[11] Jessie was petite in stature and modest in demeanor, but when arrayed in her uniform, she possessed all the dignity of an Air Marshal.

Again the specter of nepotism rears its head. Did Jessie receive this remarkable appointment because of her well-placed family connections? Other aviatrixes could only dream of receiving such a commission. At the outbreak of war, China's so-called 'First Woman of the Air,' Li Xiaqing, requested, and was refused, an air force commission, and in many respects her flying experience surpassed that of Flight-Lieutenant Zheng. Another aviatrix who had studied under Miss Li in Shanghai, Yang Jinxun, also made an impassioned, but unsuccessful, plea to be allowed to fly for China. They were not the only hopefuls. A Chinese-American pilot from Oregon, Hazel Yuying Li, entertained ambitions of joining the Chinese Air Force and she arrived in Shanghai with flying qualifications equal to those of the Chinese American men of her graduating class who had already been accepted into the CAF. To Hazel Li's intense disappointment, the drafting board refused her entreaties, even though, a few years later, the elite U.S. Women's Air Force Service Pilots, the WASPs, offered her a position as ferry pilot.

How then did Jessie manage to succeed where others had failed? Admittedly, her aunt Zheng Yuxiu, as one of China's most powerful women, had the ear of the Generalissimo and his wife, and it is altogether likely that she exerted herself on her niece's behalf. However, Jessie came to the CAF equipped, not only with a first-class university degree, but also with highly coveted RAF instruction in operational flying. She had even trained for the foreign service. These credentials, not possessed by any other women who tried to enlist, made her a uniquely suitable candidate for her nation's air force. In truth, she was more qualified for a commission than most of her male colleagues.

The Sino-Japanese conflict provided an opportunity for the women of China to demonstrate both their dedication to country, and the might of their collective will. From the very outset of hostilities, girls and women of all ages flung themselves into the war effort, organizing hospitals and disaster relief. Some even joined the suicidal 'Do or Die' guerrilla fighters. The potential power of their exertions was immense, but without synchronization on a national level, much of this power was dissipated and not as effective as it might have been.

Early in 1938, Song Meiling recognized the need for a coordinated war effort and sent word to her fellow countrywomen to gather in the centrally-located city of Kuling (Lushan) for a special conference. The object of the five-day symposium, slated to begin on May 20, 1938, was to organize and consolidate women's efforts, and to discuss social problems, including the status of women's work in China, war relief and child welfare. Always supportive of the empowerment of her sex, Jessie departed in high spirits for the conference with her aunt, Zheng Yuxiu.

Western missionaries had developed Kuling as a retreat, but it had become a popular getaway for Chinese government officials, and during the malignant heat of summer, their offices and departments were temporarily relocated to this cool and tranquil hill station. The Generalissimo and his wife both had a great affection for Kuling, and they built a holiday residence in its mountains, high above the cloud line.[12]

The abundant rains that washed over Kuling each spring were responsible for the waterfalls, rushing streams and lavishly blossoming azaleas that combined to make the area a picturesque and relaxing haven. Built high among the peaks of Jiangxi, the resort was inaccessible to motor vehicles, and coolies conveyed the delegates up the steep contours of the mountainside in sedan chairs. The hike took almost five hours, but once they finally arrived, the women realized the wisdom of convening the meeting in such a remote, but soothing, setting. Kuling seemed designed to foster serenity and clear thinking, and indeed, the event was destined to be a great success.

Jessie never forgot the excitement that charged the gathering, or the energizing qualities of the delegates themselves who gathered on China's behalf. They came from all walks of life—students, teachers, writers, clubwomen, professionals—and when they met in the great auditorium of the Kuling library, they listened in silence as Song Meiling opened the Conference.

"One of the first tasks," she told her audience, "lies within each one of us. We must realize that it is essential for us to strive and work for unity and cooperation; now, China in war must prepare for peace; and in war or peace, the women of China must lead the way."[13]

Thus it was thereafter that the delegates focused, not solely on the conflict itself, but on the positive ending of that conflict, and on the continuous process of Resistance and Reconstruction that must precede and pave the way toward the successful resolution of the war. Their duty was to rebuild, and, as much as possible, not to mourn over loss.

For Jessie's aunt, the meeting was the most exhilarating event she had ever attended, and the farsightedness of her fellow delegates stimulated her to such an extent that she was unable to sleep at night. Zheng Yuxiu tried to put her feelings into words.

"Having been an ardent feminist ever since I had started working for the Revolution in those early days in Peking when I was hardly more than a child," she wrote, "I realized now that my dream of the day when women would have a vital part in the destiny of the country was coming true at last, right before my eyes. Listening to them, I realized how much China had changed. They were well informed, poised and mature; at the same time, they were humane and courageous. It was as if two centuries of social development had been covered in two decades."[14]

For the rest of her short life, Jessie, too, would continue to be electrified by the spirit that animated Kuling. She took seriously her commissioning at the Conference to go forth and serve her country. Some three years later, when she finally realized her dream, she was a foreign diplomat addressing audiences across Canada on China's behalf. She would recall for her listeners the birth of the National Women's Advisory Committee at that meeting (a committee of which she was a proud member), and the mechanisms that were set in place by Song Meiling to bring relief to the nation's refugees, orphans, the sick and wounded. She would also describe the initiation of a variety of programs that trained young women like herself in health, social service, agriculture, teaching or political organization before being dispersed throughout the land in service of their nation.

Just a few days after the Conference adjourned, the vast library where the women had met was bombed to bits by Japanese flyers, but Jessie and the other delegates had already departed. Refreshed and renewed, they were homeward bound, bursting with energy and enthusiasm, and optimistically planning for the future peace. Soon they would need all the confidence they could muster. The road to peace would be strewn with many disasters.

One of the constants of Chinese history has been the ubiquitous flooding of its mighty rivers. The Yangtze, Chang Jiang, China's main artery, has always held the potential to affect millions of lives. In 1931, the same year the Japanese invaded Manchuria, this swollen river surged over its banks as it had done for millennia, but this time it killed over three and a half million people. The tragedy came to be regarded as one of the worst natural disasters in recorded history. The scale of the calamity prompted the establishment of the National Flood Relief Commission whose international team of workers provided relief for survivors.

Jessie worked for this Commission in 1938 when, on June 12, the Yellow River rose inexorably and inundated an enormous area. Although the flooding of the Yellow River was a perennial problem, this particular disaster was deliberately man-made. Japanese soldiers had begun their thrust into the heart of China, and as they made their way inland via the river valley, Chiang Kai-shek ordered the destruction of its levees, reckoning that the rush of floodwaters would halt the enemy's progress. Many of the Chinese who lived on its banks were not notified, and the resulting wall of water that surged through the valley killed almost one million peasants. More than twelve million were rendered homeless. The Flood Relief Commission moved into high gear, its humanitarian efforts complicated by the ravages of the relentless Japanese, whose progress was not halted by the flood, but only delayed.

Jessie flew mercy missions and made survey flights over the recently flooded areas. Through her work in this regard, she was carrying on a noble family tradition. Her great-grandfather, Zheng Yao, so generous to his fellow-villagers, was no less open-handed with those who lived in China's far-off interior. Year after year, whenever the Yellow River overflowed its banks, Zheng Yao's Confucian principles and his great heart obliged him to dispatch mercy ships loaded with grain to those afflicted by the flood. He did this at his own considerable expense, and while it was true that a goodly portion of the old man's fortune eventually evaporated through speculation, a disproportionate amount of his wealth went to the succor of the Yellow River flood victims. As a member of the flood relief commission, Jessie followed in the philanthropic footsteps of her charitable ancestor.

Soon, the longed-for peace began to seem like an illusive dream. Inexorable enemy incursions into China required the removal of nation's capital to the relative safety of Chongqing. Commercial, industrial and financial concerns were also relocated to that interior city, and so, too, were most of Jessie's immediate family, including her two Zheng aunts, Xuean and Yuxiu. Selected as the temporary seat of government because of its location deep in the heart of China, Chongqing was a magnificently situated mountain city. Built on precipitous cliffs, it sprawled over the surrounding rugged hills, and jutted like the prow of a boat into the confluence of the Jialing and Yangtze rivers.

In happier times, it was the embarkation point for water tours of the celebrated Yangtze Gorges, but by the time Jessie arrived to take up her work with the Aeronautical Commission, it had become known as a city of refugees and the terminus of the Burma Road, China's vital land link to much-needed overseas supplies. It also had the unhappy distinction of being dubbed the rat capital of the world. Those who lived in the city during this period have testified to all-too-frequent encounters with the infamous rodents who grew outrageously to the size of beavers.

Throughout the war, aside from occasional hiccups, Chongqing managed to maintain its position as one of the main centers of the nation's air communications. Remarkably, the city's airport, which received flights from all the national carriers, was of a temporary nature. It was located on one of the few flat areas in the region, a long and narrow sandbar that formed each year at a bend in the river. The first time she flew into town, Jessie was amazed to note that one side of the 'airfield' was bordered by rushing waters, and the other by a steep cliff atop which Chongqing was located. The city itself could be reached only by climbing hundreds of broad stone steps that extended up the steep cliffside from the river. Panting coolies ran up and down this Jacob's ladder, lugging arriving and departing passengers to and from the aerodrome in sedan chairs. Each year, the airfield was rendered unusable when it was drowned by the implacable floods of spring, but when the waters receded, its matshed buildings were reconstructed and the airport was back in business. Eventually, some stability was lent to the runways' surfaces when they were overlaid with old tombstones, an expediency that might have seemed sacrilegious had not approval for the project been granted as a necessity of war by Madame Chiang Kai-shek herself.[15]

To Jessie, Chongqing seemed neither altogether Chinese nor altogether Western, but a hybrid of both, with antiquated Chinese shops huddling up against square modern buildings of grey brick. The equally grey remains of recently bomb-flattened buildings clogged the crowded, winding streets, forcing ricksha drivers to divert their vehicles around the detritus. In fact, much of the city lay in ruins from the relentless bombing, and clouds of dust hung in the air, but despite the destruction and the dirty avenues, its residents were fiercely proud of Chongqing and its ability to endure. One of the first things Jessie noticed were the great number of slogans of encouragement that were plastered everywhere; indeed, they were impossible to miss. "Victory in resistance; success in reconstruction!" "If you have strength, give strength; if you have money, give money!" "A good boy goes to war!"

She soon discovered that Chongqing winters were warm and exceedingly moist, and these conditions precipitated a dense fog that blanketed the area like cotton wool from September to late April. Normally regarded as a nuisance, the low cloud and mist was blessed as a godsend in wartime; the poor visibility prevented the enemy from launching its deadly air raids against the city. But when spring arrived and the mists finally cleared, the Imperial Japanese Air Force once more declared open season on Chongqing.

The canny dwellers of the city used the natural geography of the area to defend themselves. They tunneled deep into the surrounding mountains until the hills were honeycombed with winding air raid shelters vast enough to accommodate Chongqing's swollen wartime population. One such shelter was under construction when Jessie arrived. Slated to provide sanctuary for over one hundred thousand souls, the non-stop drilling and hammering of the workers was music to the townspeople's ears.

The city instituted an impressive early warning air raid system, or *jingbao*, that allowed everyone ample time to reach the shelters. Look-outs in outlying districts were deputed to watch for the enemy. Upon learning that Japanese raiders had left their airfields and were airborne, the watchers would alert Chongqing of the probable danger, and the city would hang big red balloons of warning on poles that could be spotted easily throughout the city. When enemy bombers were within a half-hour's flight of Chongqing, the first alarm was sounded, and when they were ten to fifteen minutes away, a second cacophonous alarm—dubbed the 'Urgent' for obvious reasons—was given. By that time, all citizens were expected to be safely sheltered, although Jessie observed that bound-footed women, swaying painfully on their lotus feet, made haste slowly and had the most difficulty reaching the caves in good time.

To impose some sort of order, each citizen was assigned a particular cavern, but of course, in a raid, any shelter would do. Dynamited and then hand-chiseled, the caves were impressive, but Jessie soon found that some of them were often damp and dripping, and she had to step gingerly on the planks that covered the many puddles. In smaller tunnels that had little ventilation and no electricity, lanterns burning non-toxic vegetable oil provided illumination. This dispelled some of the gloom, but the air of close confinement quickly became unpleasant, and like everyone else, Jessie had to fan herself to keep from fainting. When the bombs started to fall, however, the tremendous pressure of the blasts caused gusts of air to whoosh through the caves, and this terrifying phenomenon was even more disagreeable.

With the rest of the evacuees, Jessie sat—or, during night raids—tried to doze on the wooden stools or benches that constituted the only other furnishings of the caves. One of the more telling slogans posted around town advised the citizens of Chongqing to "Sleep While You Can." When it was known that a bomber's moon would light the night skies, Jessie took the slogan's advice and went to bed right after supper to catch some shut-eye before the inevitable raids would drive her and her neighbors to spend yet another sleepless night in the cave, not knowing, until they finally emerged, whether or not their homes and businesses would be intact. Jessie grimly noted that it was almost a badge of honor to receive a direct hit; those unfortunates who lost their homes would joke that they had "won first prize in the aviation lottery." They also professed to be grateful to the Japanese for helping to destroy the noxious rat population with their deadly bombs, but this was just bravado. In truth, they knew that the flattened buildings provided yet additional fertile breeding grounds for the vermin.

In the early days of the bombing, a cavalier disregard for air raid warnings had resulted in the unnecessary demise of many inhabitants of Chongqing. Rickshaw coolies lay lifeless in the streets along with their fares, and they were joined in death by those who recklessly ignored the danger and chose instead to watch the spectacle of the attack.[16] This needless loss of life soon prompted the city to require its citizens either to shelter during the raids, or else be executed outright—local police were invested with extraordinary powers and ordered to shoot on sight those laggards who were still in the streets after the second alarm had sounded. And they did.

When the raiders came, Jessie, too, literally had to run for her life. "Many times I have narrowly escaped," she later recalled from the safety of Canada, observing that more than once she reached the caves just as the missiles began to fall with deadly accuracy. However, she joked with black humor that she and her fellows quickly became accustomed to the banality of war. As she put it, the falling bombs were "just part of our daily bread!"

"They bomb us out," she shrugged, "and we move back in."[17]

Thus, despite the *jingbao* which sounded from morning 'til night in the summer months, and the terrible beatings taken by the city, the bombers only succeeded in stiffening the backbone of the long-suffering citizens of Chongqing. The more irregular their lives became, the more doggedly determined they were to carry on as usual. When the bombing ceased, the townsfolk would emerge blinking from the caves to bury their dead and pick up their lives where they had left off. Newspapers invariably appeared each morning, restaurateurs famously resumed their noodlemaking, and government officials continued to meet and conduct the nation's business. Even after Jessie relocated to the safety of Canada, the doughty citizens of Chongqing and their gritty ability to endure were never far from her thoughts.

Meanwhile, the Chinese Air Force stood squarely between Chongqing and disaster. The air arm of the military operated directly under the supervision of Song Meiling, and as chair of the Aeronautical Affairs Commission, she felt deeply responsible for each and every young man she sent up to protect the skies. She studied all the aircraft at her disposal—Curtiss, Lockheed, Martin, and Boeing ships, as well as craft from Britain, Russia and France—and considered any and all innovations that might improve the fighting chances of 'her boys.'

"She knew every plane and every pilot," reported journalist, Emily Hahn. "Whenever they took off she was down at the field to watch; she climbed the hills to see the battles and was back on the field to tell them about it later when they returned—if they did return."[18]

They were Jessie's boys, too. They were her colleagues in the Chinese Air Force, but she grew up with many of them, and knew the families of all the rest. Their names were synonymous with industry, banking and politics in China. These young lads were the scions of the land, the sons of the nation's wealthy and empowered. Pathetically young—their average age was twenty—they abandoned their overseas university studies in diplomacy or finance, law or engineering, to return to their homeland and take to the skies at this dark hour. Jessie's brother, Zheng Yun, was one of their ranks, having volunteered from the outset.

Unlike Japanese pilots, some of whom were willing to power dive straight into a target to ensure they achieved their objective—killing themselves in the process—Chinese airmen were expected to be more pragmatic. Having far fewer aircraft at their disposal than the enemy (by this point, China's fleet apparently numbered less than two hundred craft compared to Hirohito's thousands), they were advised to avoid immolating themselves and their planes. Their mission was to hit their objective *and* return the aircraft safely to base. Each and every plane was precious, and the boys knew it. There were heart-rending stories of pilots, riddled with enemy bullets, who made a supreme effort to return their aircraft home, and, mission accomplished, promptly succumbed to their wounds and slumped dead over the controls.

It is unlikely that Jessie would have been allowed to participate in operational flying (she was much more valuable to her country alive than dead), but it is likely she would have relished the opportunity, and her training with the RAF would have given her a handsome advantage in any engagement with the enemy. She must have been proud, and even envious, of one of her close relatives, also an airman, who had that privilege. It is probable that this relative was Jessie's daredevil brother, Zheng Yun, but unfortunately, Zheng Yuxiu, who tells the story of the young man's heroics, does not provide his name.

Dr. Zheng recounted with pride that this pilot, her nephew, was flying home one day from a mission when he ran into a swarm of no less than seven Japanese Zeros. These were early days, and China still had no aircraft that could compete with the Mitsubishi Zero in terms of speed and maneuverability. The situation looked bleak for the lone flyer, especially as he had no armaments on board. To survive, he would have to out-fly his aggressors, but even after employing all the aerobatic arts at his command—climbing, spiraling, rolling—he was unable to shake off the enemy pilots who, throughout this deadly aerial ballet, clung to his tail and fired on him continuously. Having run out of tricks, he realized he could only stay alive by out-daring his opponents. He wheeled and turned, flying directly into their midst, and suddenly sent his aircraft into a screaming downward plunge.

On a collision course with planet Earth, and barely two hundred feet from certain death, at the last minute the young aviator coolly pulled out of the dive and continued to fly at low altitude, just skimming the ground and steeply banking his craft until he was flying on one wing. He made for the pass of a canyon so narrow that it could not have admitted his wingtips had he proceeded at level flight, and then flew sideways through its tight and twisting passage. His assailants, who had stuck like glue through his previous aerobatics, had no stomach for this sort of risky business and finally broke off their pursuit. The innovative and wounded airman flew on to his base where he made a crash landing. Remarkably both man and machine survived this grueling encounter intact—more or less. Fifty-one bullet holes were counted in the fabric of his ship.[19]

Zheng Yuxiu went on to relate that, shortly thereafter, this daring aviator, who had already downed many enemy aircraft and was no longer in the first flush of youth, was reassigned to fly as a transport pilot, and was commissioned to ferry men and supplies throughout China in support of the war.

The account of this young man's career dovetails with the flying record of Zheng Yun, who also left operational flying to become a transport pilot, so it is likely that he was the pilot who evaded the Japanese marauders. Tragically, however, it is also known that, in 1943, Jessie's beloved brother died of serious injuries sustained in the crash of his plane on take off from the Lanzhou airfield. Today his name can be found in the annals of Guangdong aviation history as one of those overseas Chinese personnel who died in the line of duty during the War of Resistance against Japan.[20] Zheng Yun fulfilled the solemn vow made by China's young pilots at the ceremony where they received their commission: "I shall live or die for my country."

An extension of the Burma Road had its terminus in Chongqing, and Jessie witnessed first hand the construction of this amazing lifeline that began in Rangoon and zigzagged for a thousand miles through trackless jungle and craggy mountain passes to its ultimate destination. After the enemy blockade of the China seas, this ribbon of red earth became the only route by which supplies and manpower from the outside world could enter the beleaguered country. Jessie took a tour of the primitive motorway and could never forget the sight of her people carving its passage through impossible terrain, battling monsoons and disease, not to mention regular strafing by Japanese fighter planes. The army of workers who died of malaria or mishap on the job were simply buried in the roadside craters left by enemy bombs. Many of these casualties were female.

"I have seen young women working on the Burma Road, digging and hauling stone," Jessie told her audiences in Canada, bearing proud witness to the strength and power of her rugged sisters who clawed at the rocks with their bare hands under the torrid sun. [21]

27. ROMANCE… AND UNFORESEEN CONSQUENCES

In 1938, Jessie received a transfer from Chongqing to the offices of the Commission of Aeronautical Affairs in Hong Kong. After the daily stresses of existence in the bombed-out capital, life in the peaceable Colony (Britain was not yet at war with Japan) came as a bit of a shock.

When she had left Hong Kong the year before, it was recoiling from the initial shockwaves of the conflict, but by the time of her return, it had settled back into a comfortable routine while the war raged at its perimeters. It presented a crazy quilt of contrasts. While a variety of local philanthropic organizations busily dedicated themselves to relief efforts, their fundraisers took the form of genteel garden parties or swank evening entertainments. Anti-aircraft firing practice was carried out at night, but peevish citizens grumbled that these exercises disrupted their slumbers. As a concession to war, Japanese goods were strictly boycotted, but this noble renunciation caused no hardship; store shelves groaned with luxury items. The city was still bursting at the seams with refugees, but many of them were gilt-edged. On any day of the week, displaced Shanghai movie stars and society ladies could be spotted on fashion parade at the Happy Valley race course while the much less fortunate lived nearby in hopeless squalor. Jessie was surprised to encounter a huge shantytown of destitute refugees that had mushroomed just fifty feet away from the gates of the Kai Tak airfield. Houses fashioned out of burlap, tin cans and matting sheltered some ten thousand squatters who shared their fetid streets and fly-infested water wells with dogs, pigs and chickens. The contrast between these foul quarters and the adjoining state of the art airport facility could not have been more dramatic.

Jessie joined a variety of relief organizations and took her turn providing aid for refugees, but having survived the bombing of Chongqing, her sensibilities had undergone a subtle shift. She began to live for the moment. Like everyone else, she plunged into the social whirl, and there was no shortage of pleasurable diversions to occupy her free hours. Dinner dances were popular events in the Colony, and on any evening of the week, couples did the Lambeth Walk to the big band sounds of live orchestras at the Peninsula Hotel or the Gripps. One of the most requested waltz tunes that season was 'Deep Purple,' a dream-like song that everyone in Hong Kong seemed to be humming. The

Lido at Repulse Bay was another romantic nightspot where young lovers danced into the wee hours and then made their way home along a moonlit road lined with Flame of the Forest trees. Jessie loved to dance, and in the company of her cousin, Perry, she attended a number of functions. Her striking appearance at one tea dance drew the admiring attention of a newspaper fashion critic who reported that the aviatrix from Paris wore a dazzling black crepe dress saturated with an all-over floral design. A green enameled watch adorning one small wrist cleverly mimicked a green jade bangle encircling the other.[1]

Jessie's chic turnout had always won rave reviews, but now the press also heralded her professionalism as an officer of the Chinese Air Force. An article printed in the *Da Gong Bao* trumpeted her experimental flying investigations and her yeoman's work with the 'Saving the Nation by Aviation' movement.[2] As one of the fledglings of the Dragon, and at the pinnacle of her success, she was fêted for her achievements and gentility, and admired for her selfless contributions to China's security. There seemed to be no limit to the heights to which her ambition and courage might carry her. And yet, as she made her confident and upwardly mobile passage through the bureaucracy of her nation's defense establishment, there lurked a diversion. We may never know precisely when or where Jessie met the handsome young man who was destined to disrupt the even pattern of her life, but it is possible to reconstruct some of the circumstances surrounding her fateful encounter with Wilfred Bien-tang Seto.

Wilfred Seto was born in Vancouver, B.C., Canada, on August 21, 1914. Tall and handsome, his parents dispatched him to China, likely in 1936, so that their only son would acquire a solid education in the great city of Shanghai. As a sort of reverse 'overseas student,' they also hoped he would imbibe the culture of his ancestral homeland and return to Canada with a fuller appreciation of his ethnic heritage.

Wilfred descended from a highly respected and unusual family. His grandfather, Seto Fangin, had emigrated from China to San Francisco in the early 1860s and eventually found his way north to Victoria, British Columbia, where his son (and Wilfred's father), Seto More, was born. Seto More was a distinguished gentleman, well-known in Western Canada as passenger agent for the Canadian Pacific Railway steamship line. Through his connection with those who booked passage on the legendary Empress ships that linked Canada with the Far East, Seto More had an intimate knowledge of the villages and family histories of all the Chinese who immigrated to Vancouver, or 'Salt Water City,' as it was known to the newcomers. A suave and courtly man, Seto was also well read and regarded as the city's acknowledged expert on the history, art, language and culture of China. Even though he had never set foot in the land of his ancestors, Seto More was accustomed to receiving a steady stream of illustrious visitors—university professors, politicians, diplomats—who beat a path to his door to partake of his knowledge. He also maintained a lively interest in natural history and served for a time as vice-president of the Royal Astronomical Society of Canada. A sensitive artist, he painted in watercolors and was a fine calligraphist.

Wilfred had inherited much of father's refinement, but his mother no less influenced his upbringing. Fanny Lew Seto had been born in Olympia, Washington, and she was celebrated as the first Chinese to graduate from high school in the United States. Wilfred lived with his parents and his sister Geraldine in the family home, located in Vancouver's West End. Atypically for the time, the Setos did not live in Chinatown, but moved easily and largely without prejudice among their white neighbors.[3]

Although the senior Setos valued higher education as a precious jewel, young Wilfred was not a particularly scholarly soul, and during his unsupervised time in China, he made the most of his opportunities by enthusiastically embracing the hedonistic pre-war social life that abounded in its largest cities. With his regal bearing, elegant wardrobe and imposing height (he was six feet tall), Wilfred found himself being admitted to Shanghai's most exalted social circles. Wilfred mixed easily in the rarified world of taipans, self-made millionaires and beautiful women. He acquired a pair of leather riding boots and took up horseback riding. To his delight, he also discovered that he enjoyed considerable success as a ladies' man. However, in August 1937, the Sino-Japanese war suddenly arrived on Shanghai's doorsteps and intruded on his pleasures. During an enemy air raid, Wilfred was injured by a bombing explosion, and, suddenly alive to the injustice of the conflict and the needs of a great city in wartime, he was galvanized to serve for a time with the renowned Shanghai Volunteer Corps, a paramilitary body dedicated to the protection of the Foreign Settlements.

Months later, as life in Shanghai became less tenable, Wilfred quit the city and evacuated to the safety of Hong Kong. He may have continued his education by transferring his credits to the highly respected Lingnan University, temporariy relocated in Hong Kong from the bombed-out city of Guangzhou. Wilfred quickly made himself at home in the Colony and slipped into its social life with ease. By joining a number of special interest groups, he met a variety of new people. There were dinner reunions for ex-members of the Shanghai Volunteer Corps, lively socials convened for Guangdong students and Chinese Canadians, and charitable events organized by aid workers. Wilfred enrolled in the worthy Chinese Youths' Medical Relief Association (CYMRA), and through this organization, he worked to raise funds for the war wounded and refugees. CYMRA also placed him in the company of the Colony's most well to do young heirs and heiresses, giving him access to the upper echelons of Hong Kong's high hat society. Wilfred's natural stylishness served him well in this environment, and he was well received both for his philanthropy and for his public-spirited defense of Shanghai in its hour of need. He became closely involved with the CYMRA's fund-raising activities, which included flag days and dinner dances. In March 1939, the group launched its most ambitious project, the rendering of an American play, *A Debutante Goes to Town*, with an all-Chinese cast. When staged at the Queen's Theater, it won kudos as the most successful amateur musical-comedy show ever staged in Hong Kong. Wilfred received a positive review for his portrayal of a racketeer's henchman.[4]

It was about this time that Wilfred also met a lovely woman with a shy, dimpled smile—very classy, aristocratic, different from all the rest—and he was bowled over by her quiet elegance. The dazzler was Jessie Zheng. For her part, the young aviatrix was no less attracted to Wilfred. Five months older than she, and likewise born under the sign of the Tiger, the Canadian import was a charming and cultured gentleman, possessed of an easy grace. He was also independent and public-spirited. This combination of traits that so closely mirrored her own was compelling, and in the romantic, urgent atmosphere that gripped Hong Kong in those days, the young couple embarked on a passionate love affair. Jessie went up like straw. To her dismay, however, she soon discovered she was carrying Wilfred's child.

She was in quite a predicament. Not only could an out-of-wedlock pregnancy bring dishonor to the Zheng family name, it might also cause her to lose her professional standing as the only woman in her nation's air force. Why she chose to forfeit all for a physical encounter that could have ruined her hard-won status and reputation will never be known. Perhaps she sought a release from the pressures of wartime. Perhaps she fell in love. The next step, however, could not be in doubt. As a devout Roman Catholic, Jessie knew that abortion, considered a grave sin, was out of the question. For the sake of their unborn child, Wilfred would have to marry her. While Jessie's adamant decision was certainly informed by her religious scruples, it is just as likely that the notion of being formally joined to her handsome lover was not altogether repugnant. 'Forever after' was a long time if one's heart were not thoroughly engaged.

It is not clear when Wilfred was made aware of Jessie's condition, but he appears not to have shared her sense of commitment. He booked passage on one of the Empress ships sailing to Canada and arrived back home in Vancouver, safe and sound.

Or so he thought.

Certainly, 'shotgun weddings' have been a constant in the long history of human relations, but in most circumstances, it has been the outraged parent, and not the blushing bride, who has wielded the shotgun. Although Wilfred was now half a world away, Jessie refused to consider that she could be left in the lurch. She made immediate plans to fly to Canada and beard her lover in his lair.

To Wilfred's consternation—and his family's acute embarrassment—Jessie soon arrived in Vancouver and virtually camped on his doorstep, demanding her rights and insisting that he recognize the child she was carrying. Not for nothing was she the niece of Zheng Yuxiu. Outwardly quiet and shy, yet she was shot through with a stubbornly aggressive streak that acknowledged no opposition to her ambitions. Her audaciously overt behavior in this matter elicited a variety of reactions in Vancouver's Chinatown where the scandal was an open secret. Wilfred's parents were mortified by the whole situation, and they received a good deal of sympathy from those who regarded Jessie's conduct as inappropriate and much too forward for a Chinese girl, especially as she was targeting one of the most respected families in the city.

However, there were those who stood in awe of Jessie's unyielding stance.

Peggy Lee, a youthful and fascinated observer of the debacle, recalled that, in an era when women's rights were still in the conceptual stage, she and her girl-friends were deeply impressed by Jessie's obdurate determination to convince her man to do the right thing. This, coupled with the breathtaking accomplishments that studded the career of the young aviatrix, put them solidly in the pregnant woman's corner.[5] Everyone hunkered down to await the dénouement of this closely watched showdown.

Contrary to expectations, however, Wilfred did not marry Flight-Lieutenant Zheng Hanying. Newly returned from China, he was jobless and living at home with his parents; he was certainly in no position to support a bride and a burgeoning family. Even Jessie sagged under the realization that her ambitions for their future were unrealistic. The romance was over, and she was destined to become an unwed mother. However, Wilfred had inherited his father's gallantry. He declared himself willing to acknowledge his responsibility as the father of her unborn child. With this avowal, Jessie was satisfied.

These are the raw facts of how and why Jessie Zheng ended up in Canada. However, the official story that she subsequently put forth for public consumption was unwaveringly lofty and conspicuously lacking in fine detail. It made no mention of Wilfred and her out-of-wedlock pregnancy. She reported that her arrival in Canada coincided with her appointment by the office of the Waijiaobu to a professional assignment abroad.

In 1940, she related, the Foreign Office ordered her to report to the Chinese Consulate-General in Ottawa. Jessie was her nation's ideal foreign representative because she enjoyed fluency in both of Canada's official languages, English and French, and her piloting skills would also prove to be a boon. Traveling by air would expedite her journeys across Canada's vast terrain, distances that were as immense as those of her own homeland. Jessie swelled with pride at the prospect of serving her country overseas at this hour of its utmost need. Once in Canada, she would not use the name 'Jessie,' but would be known exclusively as 'Hanying.' This would remind those she met that she was a proud Chinese national, and it would serve to remind herself of the responsibility she bore to China. Hanying. Heroine of China.

Through her military connections, Jessie explained, the Waijiaobu arranged that she would fly—as a passenger—to Canada. At this juncture of the war, the passage of civilians across the Pacific was severely restricted, but through her diplomatic and military status, she had priority clearance to make the crossing in an armed forces aircraft. Jessie was proud to declare that this flight qualified her to become the first Chinese woman member of the Short Snorters' Club, an exclusive fellowship restricted to those who had made a trans-oceanic crossing in a bomber.[6] Upon her arrival in the nation's capital in the summer of 1940, Jessie acquired another significant 'first'—the distinction of becoming the first Chinese woman to be appointed to Canada in any official capacity. She also claimed to be the only woman in Canada to hold the prestigious FAI international flying license issued through the Royal Aero Club of London, and this provided her with the flexibility to fly, not only throughout her host nation, but also in the United States.

Jessie received a briefing on the political situation that existed in Canada, and China's place within it. At this point in the war, the Canadian government was almost solely preoccupied by the European conflict in which it had been immersed since September 1939. It had relatively little interest in China's desperate struggle with Japan. The Chinese legation could expect a polite audience with Canadian officials, but little tangible aid. China's pleas that Canada immediately cease making shipments of scrap iron to Japan—raw material that was promptly converted into armaments for use against China—also fell on deaf ears. The Canadian government argued that, on the one hand, it desperately needed the profits earned from the sale of the iron to prosecute its war against Germany, and, on the other, it feared to offend the Japanese by stopping the shipments. However, Canada was not alone in its insensitivity to China's problems. The United States was making matters even worse by allowing the sale and shipment of some fifty thousand barrels of crude oil a day to Japan. Ironically, these shipments would provide the Imperial government with the muscle it would need to attack Pearl Harbor in December 1941.

In the face of these frustrating obstacles, there was little the officials of the consulate could do but continue to reiterate their need for help, and to point out China's potential as a bulwark against Communism and Japanese imperialism.

With the Canadian government obdurate and distracted by the situation in Europe, the Chinese decided it might be more profitable to alter their strategy by appealing directly to the citizens of Canada. It was worth a try. The favorable opinion of the latter might force the government to rally around China's banner. Frustratingly, however, the Sino-Japanese conflict received scant publicity in the media, and with their friends and loved ones serving—and dying—in Europe, most Canadians knew little, and cared less, about the war across the Pacific. Chinese officials faced the challenge of somehow turning this attitude around and bringing their nation's predicament to the forefront. At this point, they did not realize they had a champion in their midst, and that Flight-Lieutenant Zheng Hanying, the recently arrived junior diplomat, was shortly destined to capture the hearts and minds of Canadians from coast to coast.

28. ZHENG TAKES VANCOUVER

This then, was Hanying's account of her arrival in Vancouver.

A few months after she had arrived in Canada's capital, Jessie left Ottawa, still cloaked in the snows of winter, to arrive on the West Coast just as Vancouver began to enjoy the first daffodils of spring. The serious housing shortage that would plague those who searched in vain for accommodation in the later years of the war had not yet cramped the city, and she readily found an appropriate suite at the Earlscourt Hotel and Rooms. Located on West Georgia Street at Thurlow, her inexpensive new quarters once had been a gracious old private home, and its small, furnished suites were perfect for her needs. One of the dictums of the diplomatic life was 'travel light.' Personal possessions were pared to a bare minimum to expedite transport in case of last-minute postings.

The Earlscourt was the largest in a string of aging residences that lined the north side of Georgia Street. Postwar, they were rapidly replaced by high-rise office towers, but in those days, the city's West End still retained a gracious, almost pastoral, quality. Although most of its once-grand Victorian mansions had been converted into tumbledown rooming houses, giving much of the area a down-at-heel look, its defenders pointed to the peerless compensations afforded by vistas of blue ocean, snow-capped mountains and spectacular sunsets.

Jessie's residence was ideally situated halfway between the sea-girt rainforest of Stanley Park to the west, and the clutch of imposing downtown office towers and hotels to the east. Since commencement of hostilities in Europe, however, her tree-lined street had begun to lose much of its relaxed and intimate ambience. In fact, Jessie's neighborhood bore unmistakable evidence that Canada was at war. Just down the road from her apartment were clustered the Canadian Government Ordnance and Armouries buildings. These facilities routinely thronged with the military, and to serve their needs, several nearby structures had undergone conversion to soldiers' hostels and recreation quarters. Uniformed servicemen coming and going from these facilities outnumbered the neighborhood's civilian population.

To the west, one of Jessie's most impressive Georgia Street neighbors was the Boeing Aircraft factory. Adjacent to Coal Harbor and near the entrance to Stanley Park, it had been manufacturing aircraft and their parts at this location for over a decade and was now intensely focused on wartime production. By the time of Jessie's arrival, it was turning out Fairey Battle warplanes for Britain. As an experienced pilot, Jessie observed the output of this thriving industrial concern with considerable professional enthusiasm, but as a one-time member of the Aeronautical Commission, whose chief headache had been finding aircraft enough for the chronically under-equipped Chinese Air Force, her interest was also tinged with envy.

Up Georgia Street in an easterly direction, the old Hotel Vancouver at the corner of Granville was the nerve center of the city's military detachments. Once empty and made redundant by the construction of a new hotel bearing the same name at Georgia and Burrard, it now enjoyed fresh life as the province's central armed forces recruiting office and billeting location. It was re-christened Vancouver Barracks for the duration. Uniforms representing every allied country swirled on the streets outside the doors of the Barracks, but Jessie was quick to note that men, not women, wore these uniforms. When she arrived in Vancouver, the federal government was still months away from announcing that it would create women's auxiliaries to the armed forces. Jessie was a rare bird in any crowd, but as a full-fledged representative of her country's military—and a commissioned air force officer to boot—she was unique in Canada. Even after the forces finally permitted the enlistment of Canadian women, they were relegated into their own 'women's divisions,' or WDs, and those who entered the Royal Canadian Air Force (WD) were denied the honor of flying for their country—even the handful enlistees who were already seasoned pilots. The motto of the RCAF (WD) was, 'We Serve That Men May Fly.' There was to be no backing down on this policy, and the restriction against women air force pilots persisted in Canada for the duration of the war.

This was the outline of the story that Jessie provided to anyone who asked—and it was all true—but it carefully omitted any mention of Wilfred and her pregnancy. She gave birth to her child, a daughter, and named the infant Beverley Ann Seto. Although in appearance Beverley remarkably resembled her pretty mother, this was no cause for sentimentality on Jessie's part. She promptly deposited the infant with Wilfred and his parents, and recommenced her work on behalf of her beloved homeland. Predictably, Chinatown was all abuzz with this latest installment of the Zheng v. Seto showdown, and reactions ranged from indignation to amusement. The elder Setos, who had imagined their diapering days were behind them, undertook to care for their young grand-daughter.

As soon as she had delivered her child, Jessie made herself at home in Vancouver by pragmatically joining three local organizations that would fulfill her philanthropic, cultural and practical needs: the Canadian Red Cross, L'Alliance Française, and the Aero Club of British Columbia. Through her relief work in China, Jessie was already a member of the International Red Cross, and she would have found many of the Canadian society's wartime operations familiar territory. The Red Cross was one of the busiest volunteer organizations in Vancouver at any time, but its responsibilities trebled as it tried to meet the needs of troops and civilians overseas. The Vancouver chapter of the Chinese Red Cross was probably initiated at the urging of Zheng Hanying.

L'Alliance Française also enjoyed a healthy presence in China, and in Shanghai, an impressive facility that boasted a wonderful library housed its head-quarters. The Vancouver group was smaller and less thriving, but enthusiastic, and through its regular hosting of social lectures, Jessie had an opportunity to meet with local Francophiles, and to speak the language that she cherished.

However, the flourishing Aero Club of British Columbia was perhaps

Jessie's most important affiliation. It connected her with a support group of similarly minded individuals who loved to fly as much as she did, and provided her with contacts for the rental of aircraft. The local Aero Club was one of Canada's oldest flying clubs, and by the time Jessie joined the organization in the spring of 1941, it had grown enormously busy through its conversion to an official flying school for wartime pilot training. Its instructors were enlisted as aircraftsmen by the RCAF and were assigned to train provisional pilot officers. Ultimately, through its participation in the British Commonwealth Air Training Plan (BCATP), the Aero Club's contribution to the war effort would help to save the federal government some $750,000 in training costs.

The BCATP was an enormous scheme whereby British, Canadian, Australian and New Zealand aircrews received training in Canada for service overseas in Europe. It was the largest single enterprise in Canadian history, perhaps in the history of the world, and it helped to groom twenty thousand aircrews per year for active duty. The amount of cement laid to build the airstrips of the BCATP bases could have built a highway from Vancouver to Ottawa, and Winston Churchill called the plan "one of the major factors, and possibly the decisive factor, of the war."[1] In the lower mainland of British Columbia, the BCATP controlled airfields at Vancouver, Boundary Bay and Abbotsford. When the Aero Club's participation in this plan was announced in the spring of 1940, scores of Vancouverites immediately offered their services to the Club, volunteering to act as office workers, parachute folders and ground staff. By the summer, when it began to operate under the auspices of the Department of National Defense, the Club technically ceased to exist as a private organization, but it decided to carry on as a fraternal and social organization for the duration.

Through her membership in the Aero Club, Jessie came in contact with local aviatrixes. Mrs. Betsy Flaherty, who, at 59 years of age, was thought to be the oldest woman flyer in the world, served on club's board of directors and was also a charter member of Vancouver's famous Flying Seven club. Founded in 1936, the Flying Seven represented Canada's first formal organization of female pilots, and it was dedicated to the promotion of aviation among women in Canada. As more of their sex started to take up flying, the club's numbers very modestly increased from the original seven, but its name remained the same.[2] In a typical display of generosity, Mrs. Flaherty decided to honor the arrival of China's first woman air force officer by entertaining her at a special luncheon of the Flying Seven. Every aviatrix who happened to be present in Vancouver, either resident or visitor, licensed or student pilot, was invited to attend the get-together at the elegant Georgian Club where Mrs. Flaherty was a long-time member. Some of the invitees hailed from Eastern Canada and the United States, and when they gathered on April 21, 1941 to celebrate Jessie's arrival in the city, it suddenly occurred to them that this was likely the largest agglomeration of women pilots that had ever assembled in Canada, and that they were making history. The women were twelve in number.[3]

Jessie was understandably a novelty in their midst (this was underscored by her exotic appearance that day in a chic Chinese outfit), and they were all intrigued to know more about her. Surely, they observed, a 'Chinese aviatrix' was an anomaly, an oxymoron. Jessie conceded that the idea of flying simply would not occur to most nationals of her sex, and if they ever did entertain the notion, their parents would probably lock them in their rooms. However, she proudly acknowledged that her family was of a revolutionary bent and more supportive than most. Jessie also declared that it had been her heart's desire to fly in the service of her government, but her present position was much too demanding.

"It's a great deal of work," she sighed. "I can't even consider flying now. I have more important things to do for China."[4]

What these 'important things' were she did not say, nor did she offer an explanation for her presence in Vancouver. She acknowledged that she had already been living inconspicuously in the city for several months, but her general evasiveness on the subject (likely intended to shield the details of her pregnancy) only fueled speculation that China had dispatched its flying attaché to Canada on some sort of secret mission.

Intrigued by the high-powered Eastern aviatrix and delighted by her company, the clubwomen invited Jessie to go aloft with them. A few days later, she accompanied her new friends to the airport, donned her white flying coveralls (impressively adorned with the splendid wings of the Chinese Air Force), and flew for the first time since she had arrived in Canada. She was invited to become a member of the Flying Seven, and she quickly agreed. Thereafter, she attended as many of the women's Georgian Club meetings and luncheons as her duties permitted.[5]

The Chinese Consulate to which Jessie was assigned had its Vancouver offices in the Standard Building at 510 West Hastings Street. This towering, fifteen-story structure was located in what was then the heart of the city's business district. Today, the structure's impressive marble lobby has been restored to its full ornate grandeur, approximating its wartime appearance. Then, as now, a frieze of large, gilded clocks running along its upper walls draws the attention of the visitor. A timepiece is dedicated to each of the major capitals of the world, and these cities include Hong Kong and Tokyo. As Jessie arrived for work each day, the cheek-by-jowl location of the ticking clocks, alluding to the closeness, in geographical terms, of the two East Asian cities, must have been a sharp reminder of China's vulnerability to attack by its militant neighbor. She vowed to dedicate every minute of her waking hours to her nation's cause.

Thirty-one countries were represented in Vancouver by their consulates. To the layman, the officials who staffed these legations seemingly lived for pleasure, their lives one constant round of banquets, teas and social afternoons. In truth, however, these occasions functioned as opportunities for diplomacy, lobbying and national promotion. The responsibilities that Jessie assumed upon her arrival at the Vancouver consulate are unknown, and when she was asked by the press to describe her special duties, she shrugged and replied, in typically cryptic fashion, "I just like working here."[6] But as the functions of the Chinese consulate were many and varied, it was certainly true that she and her seven colleagues were never at a loss for something to do. In promoting the economic and cultural affairs of its nation overseas, and latterly, China's war agenda, the consulate liaised between its home government and the host country.

The Chinese consulate also shouldered a responsibility shared by few other legations. It had the special task of representing Chinese Canadians to the various levels of local government. Even though many of those whom they represented were born in Canada, or were long-time permanent residents, they were denied the privileges of Canadian citizenship and yet they were saddled with its obligations. Regarded as 'inassimilable' and unable to vote, Chinese Canadians were bereft of civic representation and had no one else to whom they could turn for help. The special status of the Chinese consuls gave them some chance of succeeding with government officials, and there was a history of their acting in this capacity.[7]

With the outbreak of World War II, young Chinese Canadians began volunteering for Canadian military service. This was an especially noble gesture considering their non-citizenship status and the restrictions imposed on their lives and liberty, and the racist deliberations of Vancouver's City Council in February 1941 only served to underscore the rank unfairness of the situation. The councilors met to consider barring Chinese from desirable residential districts where their presence was considered to reduce property values, and these discussions opened just as Jessie arrived in Vancouver. By strange coincidence, it was the immodest behavior of the Seto family that precipitated them.

Wilfred's sister, Geraldine, was engaged to marry Lei Yutang, better known as Tong Louie, an up-and-coming Chinatown businessman. Louie was destined to become titan of one of Canada's largest business empires and a future recipient of the Order of Canada, but these honors lay far in the future. Prior to their marriage in 1941, the pioneering young couple purchased a home on Vancouver's upscale west side, and when a majority of their white neighbors learned of the 'yellow peril' invading their midst, they lost no time in lodging a formal complaint with city hall. They filed a petition, "requesting that actions be taken to prohibit further Oriental penetration in the better residential areas of the City." In response, Vancouver's City Council struck a special committee to consider drafting a by-law that would "restrict Orientals from owing or occupying property for residential purposes in any other than the recognized localities for Orientals."[8] One council member airily swept aside any potential legal protests to this decision by pointing out that, as the Chinese had no civic rights anyway, they certainly could have no legal redress.[9]

Taking up the cause of the local Chinese, Jessie's boss at the Consulate, Consul-General Chunhow H. Pao, waded into the fray and fired off a letter of complaint to Mayor Cornett in which he emphatically protested the proposed legislation, labeling it as "prejudicial, discriminatory, a gross miscarriage of justice," and one that "casts reflection on the national dignity of China."[10] In the midst of this furor, Geraldine and her fiancé were married in early April. In the wedding announcement released to the press, the newlyweds made proud note of their exclusive new address. In the end, wiser heads prevailed at City Hall, and no by-law was created to restrict the movements of Vancouver's Chinese.

Although bigotry continued to bedevil most Asian natives of the city, the Seto family had always lived in the midst of Vancouver's white community, and they took for granted their inclusion in the society at large. Jessie also found that she, too, was more or less immune to the sting of racial prejudice. As an official representative of her country and possessed of a bearing and dignity that came naturally to one born to wealth and power, she moved easily in the white world, and she was received with a politeness and enthusiasm that many of Vancouver's Chinese citizens could not always expect for themselves.

Jessie settled into her new surroundings, becoming attuned to life in Vancouver. Typical of wartime, the news she received from home left her either elated, or deeply saddened. In July 1941, she was overjoyed to learn that her aunt and uncle, Zheng Yuxiu and Wei Daoming, were sailing to San Francisco *en route* to Europe where Dr. Wei had been appointed China's new Ambassador to France. At the same time, she was horrified to learn that some four thousand of her fellow Chongqing citizens had suffocated in an air raid shelter, a fate she might easily have shared.

She sought diversions whenever possible. A long-time fan of the Peking Opera, she had always enjoyed sitting in the darkened theater, munching dried watermelon seeds while the cymbals crashed and stringed instruments wailed. To her delight, she discovered this traditional theater was alive and well in Vancouver's Chinatown, and it even featured occasional guest appearances by artists from China and Hong Kong. Jessie had an opportunity to do some acting herself when the young women members of the Vancouver Chinese thespian community prevailed on her to guest star in a play being broadcast on a local radio station. She was delighted to oblige.

She made friends with her fellow members in the clubs she had joined, involving herself in their social functions, and soon became a well-known woman about town. The newly arrived attaché was lauded for her youthful good looks, fashion sense and flair on the dance floor. And yet, while Jessie's accomplishments and war relief activities received wide exposure in the mainstream Vancouver dailies, the city's Chinese press virtually ignored her. This cold shoulder treatment contrasted sharply with the extravagant coverage that had been lavished on aviatrix, Li Xiaqing, whose arrival in the city less than two years before had been celebrated like the Second Coming. Column after column in the *Chinese Times* had been devoted to exhaustive accounts of Miss Li's charm and flying expertise, but Jessie's arrival in Vancouver received no such coverage, nor could she expect to receive positive publicity at any time thereafter. She had embarrassed a highly esteemed family in the tightly knit community, and out of respect for the Setos, the Chinese media ignored her.

No such stigma attended Jessie's forays into the white world of Vancouver where she was enthusiastically welcomed as a genteel and accomplished woman. Perhaps she had most in common with her new acquaintances in the Flying Seven club. One of these was Mrs. Alma Gilbert. Alma had earned her private pilot's license in 1934 and was working toward her commercial license. A French Canadian, she originally hailed from Québec, so in addition to their shared interest in aviation, she and Jessie were able to converse in French—although Alma's *accent québécois* came as a bit of a surprise to Jessie until she got used to it. Alma and her husband operated Gilbert's Flying Service at Vancouver Airport, and they made their gleaming yellow Aeronca LC (CF-BAT) available to Jessie for her flights.[11] Known as 'The Bat' because of its distinctive registration letters, the Aeronca was already the rental aircraft of choice among the women of the Flying Seven. They had used it in June 1940 to 'bomb' the city with one hundred thousand pamphlets urging Vancouverites to 'Smash the Nazis' and support the Air Supremacy Drive.[12]

The Flying Seven were keen to back the war effort. The previous year, club President, Tosca Trasolini, had announced to the press that, "We'll go over France and drop bombs on the enemy, or we'll stay in Canada and test planes. In fact, we'll do anything."[13] The government failed to take Miss Trasolini up on her offer. In fact, the clubwomen's proposals were regularly rebuffed, but Jessie's presence in their midst may have inspired them to redouble their efforts. A month after Mrs. Flaherty hosted the luncheon to honor the arrival of Miss Zheng, the Flying Seven announced to the press that they would be opening their own Ground School. They rightly anticipated that the government would soon create women's divisions in the armed forces, and they planned to give preparatory flight instruction to young women, who, like Jessie, aspired to enter their country's air force. However, they wrongly supposed that women would be called upon to fly for their country. In late June 1941, the government did indeed announce the creation of women's auxiliaries to the services, but it quashed the notion that they would be allowed to take to the skies for their nation's benefit.

Despite their disappointment, the members of the Flying Seven carried on with the operation of the Ground School, teaching parachute folding and wireless operation to those who were interested, but they also continued to lobby the government to permit women to fly for Canada. On behalf of the club, President Elianne Roberge went to Ottawa to make this appeal in person. She pointed to the example cut by Flight-Lieutenant Zheng Hanying of the Chinese Air Force—an illustration the Canadian government would do well to emulate—but in the end, the appeals of the Flying Seven were ignored.[14]

29. COMMISSIONING

By mid-1941, Jessie had been resident in Canada for several months, but she had consistently maintained a low profile and did not involve herself in flying tours and public speaking. This pattern was soon to change. It is impossible to know if she received orders to ramp up her activities, or whether it was her own idea to lobby for China in the public arena, but her commissioning seemed to dovetail with the summertime arrival in America of her aunt and uncle. *En route* to France, where they were expected to assume the ambassadorship of that country, Zheng Yuxiu and Wei Daoming arrived in the United States just as the Japanese invaded Indochina, sections of which were French protectorates. This development caused the Weis to postpone their trip to Paris. They took up temporary residence in the United States while they awaited clarification of the political situation.[1] It is probable that Jessie took this opportunity to travel south and meet with her relatives and to receive from her dynamic aunt the directives by which she was ordered to win Canada's support for her homeland.

In an effort to raise China's profile in her war of resistance against Japan, Jessie was slated, like her colleagues Li Xiaqing and Hilda Yan, to begin the round of public speaking engagements that would broadcast the plight of the Chinese people to as many potential sympathizers as possible. Initially, she

273

would confine her efforts to Vancouver by addressing a variety of local clubs and organizations, but when she grew more comfortable in her new public role, she would move further afield and make appearances throughout the province of British Columbia and the American Northwest. Ultimately, she would take her message to Eastern Canada.

Over the next month or so, Jessie honed her program. In both English and French, she developed a press kit that included a thumbnail biography and a couple of photographs. Distributing the kit in advance of her appearances would obviate the need for personal interviews and the inevitable probing questions about her private life. On yellow paper, she typed out three set speeches about China's resistance to the enemy that she felt would be appropriate for a variety of audiences. Where necessary, she could tailor these addresses to appeal to the type of organization to which she was speaking, and update them according to current events.[2] Later, Jessie would add additional lectures to the roster, but as she became comfortable speaking extemporarily, she would occasionally abandon a set speech, and be pleasantly surprised by the enthusiastic reception her spontaneous address would invariably receive.

Like her flying colleagues to the south, Jessie now needed a plane at her disposal, ideally, one donated for her use by an aircraft manufacturer. As part of its war effort, the Piper Aircraft Company became interested in sponsoring the 1941 fund-raising campaign of the Canadian Red Cross, and it offered to gift one of its planes—a blood red Cub—to the cause. Piper declared it would be happy to dedicate the aircraft to the Chinese division of the Red Cross in Vancouver if only someone would be willing to retrieve it from its hangar in Hamilton, Ontario. It is likely that Jessie was expected to go east to claim the Cub and, while she was at it, help kick off the Red Cross appeal, but for some reason she was unable to make the trip. One of her Flying Seven friends, Mrs. Rolie Moore Barrett, stepped into the breach. Rolie was a professionally qualified pilot with a commercial license and she agreed to ferry the Cub back to Vancouver. Even better, on her return flight she would touch down at all the major cities in Western Canada to publicize China's plight and appeal for funds.

On September 9, 1941, Rolie flew by commercial carrier to Hamilton, and arrived in that city just as New York-based Li Xiaqing flew into town. Miss Li had been invited to kick off the drive and make a couple of publicity flights in the Cub as part of the Red Cross campaign. A month later, the *Vancouver News-Herald* announced that Rolie had finally taken possession of the designated aircraft, and was "working her way across Canada to Vancouver" in order to raise $100,000 for Friends of the Chinese Relief Campaign.

"Recently installed as first Red Cross Transport aviatrix of Canada," the article declared, "Mrs. Barrett hopes to bring merits of the campaign before enough people to raise the money."[3]

This report was premature. In the end, the Chinese Red Cross and the Piper Aircraft Company were unable to come to an agreement, and three months after she had left, Rolie returned home to Vancouver without the Cub.[4] In her trips to centers outside of the city, Jessie would have to fall back on the Gilbert's yellow 'Bat' to meet her flying requirements.

On the eve of her first speech in Vancouver, Jessie nervously admitted that she had never before addressed a large gathering. Subconsciously, however, she had already absorbed lessons in public speaking from a consummate professional, Song Meiling. On the occasions when she had an opportunity to hear Song deliver a public address, Jessie, the acolyte, attended, not only to her mentor's words, but also to her appearance. She noted that, although Madame Chiang enjoyed wearing Western fashions in private (especially the lovely French frocks that enhanced her petite figure and youthful appearance), she eschewed these foreign glad rags for her speaking engagements and invariably appeared in the *qipao*, the long and slim, slit-sided Chinese sheath that was both representative of her country, and flattering to her form.

Madame Chiang might wear floral print gowns to parties and informal gatherings, but for her public addresses, she chose to appear in solid-colored garments of midnight blue or black. A consummate performer, she instinctively knew that a dark background was an ideal foil to her ivory skin and forced the listener's attention onto her face and voice. As an antidote to this austerity, she declared the quality of her pedigree through the rich fabric and superb cut of her garments, and by the fiery flash of her exquisite jewelry. The only other decoration she allowed herself were the wings of the Chinese Air Force. As Secretary-General of the National Aeronautical Committee, she routinely pinned them atilt above her heart.

Jessie also paid close attention to Song Meiling's speaking style. It tended to place the audience in the palm of her hand. She noted that Madame Chiang would commence any address in a barely audible whisper—a device that effectively stilled a gathering of any size to a breathless hush—and then, as her listeners attentively leaned forward to catch each faint syllable, the pitch of her voice would slowly rise until she reached the patriotic meat of her speech. Thereafter, she would deliver her words in ringing, fervent tones that worked like a tonic on the audience.

Jessie adopted a similar speaking style to great effect, but she also injected a dollop of her own personality into the mix. The obvious sincerity of her remarks carried considerable emotional appeal, and this, coupled with a voice that rose until it literally vibrated with passion and intensity, frequently had the surprising effect of reducing her captivated audiences to tears. In addition, she also possessed a Churchillian turn of phrase and a grandiloquence that gave certain of her one-liners a memorable quality. In other times, they might have been considered melodramatic, but during an impassioned era of global stress and sacrifice, they were highly appropriate.

As for her personal appearance, Jessie was already renowned for her beautiful, classically cut clothing, and had many a dark-hued *qipao* in her wardrobe that was appropriate for public speaking. As time went by, however, she began to appear almost exclusively in her air force uniform, relying on the dramatic effect that the wing-embellished, scarlet tunic afforded. Unlike Song Meiling, she had no important jewels to enhance her appearance, and she fretted over this lack of sparklers until she decided to purchase some significant pieces of expensive jewelry on her own credit.[5] Most notably, these included glittering earrings set with precious gemstones. She wore them even with her uniform. Ornamentation in the form of jewelry or make-up (which she also sparingly applied) was generally forbidden to women wearing the uniforms of their nations, but Jessie was acting more as a diplomat than a military officer, and in this capacity, she was unique among her sex. She overrode both these strictures.

Did she acquire the jewels to give her spirits a psychological boost prior to her grueling round of public speaking, or to symbolize the worth of the country she represented? If the latter, she wasted her money.[6] The people she encountered at her personal appearances considered Jessie herself as the true embodiment of her nation, and this equation worked to her country's advantage. One Vancouverite who had the privilege of hearing her speak fell under her spell and felt compelled to learn more about the woman behind the message. He invited Jessie to join him and his wife for dinner.

"While waiting for her in the lobby of the Georgia [Hotel]," he recalled, "it was still the usual Friday night in Vancouver. Suddenly, however, in walked China. That is about the only way to describe Miss [Zheng], and her company during the entire evening only furthered this feeling."[7]

In October 1941, the Women's Canadian Club asked Jessie to address its members. To her surprise, she arrived at the Hotel Vancouver to encounter a 'standing room only' crowd of almost two thousand women who had gathered to hear her maiden speech. It was a daunting debut for a neophyte speaker, but she showed no sign of nervousness. As she took her place at the podium, flanked on one side by the red ensign of the British Empire, and on the other by the dark blue flag of the Guomindang, Miss Zheng herself appeared to be as remarkable as her message. Attired in a *qipao*, she took possession of the stage and delivered her speech with an undeniable sincerity that tugged at the hearts of her listeners.

Jessie spoke about the unbreakable spirit of her countrymen and women, who, inspired by the leadership of the Generalissimo and his wife, had moved inland *en masse* to rebuild their governments, industries and educational institutions. She told her listeners about the pilgrimage of five hundred students who marched over a thousand miles into the interior to re-establish their university, and she described a massive project that relocated twenty thousand farm families on eighty million acres of land. Just as Song Meiling had advised at the Kuling conference, she looked forward to a postwar world of future prosperity.

"The Chinese industrial cooperative—cooperative road building, cooperative reforestation—is the seed of a new and flourishing industrial system after the war."

The style of her speech marked a change from typical appeals for aid delivered by most representatives of war-beleaguered countries. She avoided trotting out the usual inventory of enemy atrocities and spoke instead about the positive accomplishments of her Chinese brothers and sisters. Rather than beg for pity, she painted a vivid picture of a 'can do' people determined to overcome adversity. As if to engage her listeners even further, she pointed to the similarities between her land and careworn England.

"We the people of China are struggling today with outmoded equipment to preserve the world's oldest civilization," she exclaimed. "Just as Britain stands as the last outpost of democracy in the Atlantic, so Chongqing represents the symbol of democracy in the Pacific." "China," she concluded, "is fighting shoulder to shoulder with the shopkeepers of Britain."[8]

While the version of 'democracy' practiced by China was rather more totalitarian than the one enjoyed by Churchill's 'nation of shopkeepers' (Chiang Kai-shek had already admitted that he would not be granting the franchise to his citizens, even after the war), her audience forgave her, or rather, chose to ignore this sugar coating of the truth. It was not necessarily what Jessie said, but the way she said it, that lingered in the memory. Two years later, an eyewitness still marveled at the upbeat and inspiring quality of that evening's speech.

"Every eye was riveted, for more than an hour, to the tiny figure on the big platform," she recalled, and "every ear was in harmony with the emotional vibrations of the lovely voice of a Chinese girl who spoke English with a French accent from learning our language in Paris while she studied law at the Sorbonne University; every eye was wet when, in ringing tones, after telling of her country's magnificent stand during six years of tragic devastation and horror, she declared that China never had, never could be beaten."[9]

Jessie had launched her career as a speechmaker. Building on her success, she accepted a sudden flurry of invitations to address a variety of associations in the city. These included opportunities to speak in French both to the Alliance Française, and to the francophone students of the University of British Columbia. In Chinatown, she spoke in Cantonese to promote the sale of Aviation Salvation bonds, and to support the work of the Chinese Refugees War Relief committee.[10] In the main, however, Jessie delivered her speeches in English to white audiences. She made one of her most significant addresses to the commissioned and non-commissioned officers of the Royal Canadian Air Force at Jericho Station in Vancouver. With her audience in thrall, she described her elite RAF training in far-off Hong Kong, and her experiences while flying throughout China as an air force officer. This speech marked the beginning of Jessie's warm, semi-professional relationship with the RCAF, both men's and women's divisions, whose representatives respectfully regarded her as a rare and distinguished colleague, and granted her complimentary privileges normally accorded only to senior officers within their own ranks.

Vancouver had always existed somewhat apart from the rest of Canada, isolated from the eastern provinces by vast distances and massive mountain ranges. Vancouverites focused on the war in Europe, and it was to this conflict that they dedicated the lion's share of their labor and resources, but at the same time, they also kept a wary eye cocked on the Pacific. The potential danger posed by Japan's mighty military was omnipresent, and the ocean waves that crashed onto the province's shoreline were a constant reminder that, if the enemy came by sea, the province of British Columbia would be Canada's first line of defense.

The intangible fears of many were finally realized on December 7, 1941 when the Japanese Imperial Air Force bombed the American military base at Pearl Harbor, Hawaii. An outraged Canadian government quickly stepped forward and became the first power in the world to declare war on Japan. The United States, Britain and the twenty-four other allies soon followed suit, but a grateful China swore never to forget Canada's initiative in this matter.[11]

Upon the declaration of war, the Chinese citizens of Vancouver did not even bother to cloak their jubilation. The Japanese attack had finally brought Allied involvement into the conflict in the Far East, and Chinatown rejoiced. Laughing and singing crowds milled in the streets and rushed to read the latest war bulletins pasted up in the windows of the *Chinese Times*. "Now Japan will get a taste of her own medicine!" cried one of the celebrants. This sentiment was widely applauded. For four long years, Chinese Canadians had worried about the fate of their families in China. Surely now the tide would turn.

Overnight, the city went on high alert and stiffened itself for an attack by the Japanese. Two days after the strike on Pearl Harbor, air raid sirens sounded in Vancouver and blackout conditions were ordered for a surprise drill. Shaken citizens scrambled to buy flashlights, blackout curtains, and shields for their vehicles' headlights. "It was the greatest day we ever had," gasped a hardware store employee. "We are right out of everything!" The basement of the steel framed building where Jessie's consulate office was located was declared an official shelter and sported a large, red-lettered sign reading: "A.R.P. AIR RAID SHELTER, Follow the Arrows." The war also brought changes to Jessie's own neighborhood. Just one block away from her apartment, an anti-aircraft gun was installed on West Georgia Street, its snout pointed skyward, ready for anything.

Suddenly, all things Japanese were suspect. Japan's consulate was put under round-the-clock surveillance, and the B.C. Council of Women investigated the possibility that oranges labeled as 'Mandarins' were actually 'Nipponese.'[12] The chief gardener at the city's famed Stanley Park insisted that, contrary to long held belief, the park's vaunted Japanese cherry trees were actually a Chinese species. Chinese Canadian residents of the city were issued with pin-back buttons that declared, "I am Chinese," so they would not be mistaken for the enemy. Invasion, or at least attack, seemed not only inevitable, but imminent. No less a personage than the well-connected Lieutenant Governor of the province, the Honorable W.C. Woodward, declared with assurance, "Make no mistake about it. We will be bombed here, if not in three months, certainly in six."[13] Some even whispered that the government had mined the province's beloved Legislative Buildings in Victoria and planned to blow them up rather than stomach occupation by alien invaders.[14]

Jessie must have been somewhat amused by the near-hysteria and rumor-mongering that suddenly rippled through Vancouver, particularly after the actual horrors she had endured in Chongqing, but she was relieved that, at last, Canada had a keener appreciation of the suffering borne by her own countrymen. For its part, China was suddenly 'hot,' and its consular officials were in high demand, bombarded with questions about their nation's resistance to Japan. It was well known that the Vancouver office received up-to-the-minute cable communications regarding the Far Eastern situation (these arrived via shortwave from San Francisco), and everyone wanted to be kept apprised of the enemy's movements and intents.

Chinese fashions and hairstyles were suddenly chic. The *Ku-kan* or 'courage' coiffeur of China, adapted by Max Factor, began to appear on Western women's heads, and less than a week after Canada's declaration of war on Japan,

Flight-Lieutenant Zheng Hanying was the subject of an illustrated feature article in the women's pages of the *Vancouver Daily Province*. "Chinese Girl Pilot Lives Colorful Life," trumpeted the headline. It was a glowingly positive article—and good publicity for China's cause—but Jessie must have winced when she saw in black and white the usual estimates of her height and weight.[15] However, the article did manage to preserve the most important aspect of her private life; there was no mention of Wilfred or Beverley Ann.

Canadian optimism suddenly plummeted when, on Christmas Day 1941, Hong Kong fell to the Japanese. The Kai Tak airfield where Jessie had learned to fly was the first area to be hit by bombs, and three of the paltry five RAF aircraft stationed there, ostensibly to protect the Colony from invasion, were demolished along with seven civilian aircraft. Two Canadian regiments, the Québec Royal Rifles and the Winnipeg Grenadiers, were among those who fought in vain for the defense of the Crown Colony. The involvement of their own troops made the Far Eastern conflict of more immediate concern to Canadians, especially when it was realized that the survivors of the calamity would be consigned to the dreaded Japanese prisoner of war camps.

As 1941 drew to a close, Vancouverites tuned their radios to the Canadian Broadcasting Corporation's New Year's Eve program that mourned the dead and praised the vigor of China's Chiang Kai-shek. As the Ottawa Peace Tower chimed twelve midnight and the carillon played *Auld Lang Syne*, fervent prayers were offered up for better times in the coming year.

Unfortunately, the New Year of 1942 brought no respite from misfortune. Initially, reports were upbeat, and Jessie cheered to the news that the Japanese were retreating from Changsha, harried by the pilots of the re-born Chinese Air Force who were now bolstered by talented and daredevil American pilots. However, by February 15, the day that kicked off the Chinese Year of the Horse, conditions deteriorated and faces fell upon hearing the report that Singapore had fallen to the enemy. On the heels of this depressing news, the Canadian morale-boosting propaganda machine was stoked into high gear. An Oscar-nominated film, *Inside Fighting China,* appeared in movie theaters, and viewers thrilled to the narration of Canadian actor, Lorne Greene, whose famous 'voice of doom' intoned,

"For more than ten years, China has successfully withstood the barbarous armies of Japan. Struggling under the blows, she withdrew, but would not admit to defeat. Using guerrilla tactics to brilliant advantage, she keeps the enemy engaged while gathering strength to rid the land of the aggressor."

Now that China was her ally, Canada received a series of booster visits by distinguished representatives of the Far East. Generalissimo Chiang Kai-shek's brother-in-law, the Foreign Minister T.V. Song, made a brisk visit to Eastern Canada for a weekend of inspection trips to munitions factories. He and his retinue of highly-placed military leaders left a positive impression on Canadian politicians and business leaders.[16] On February 20, the Chinese ambassador to the United States, the Honorable Dr. Hu Shi, arrived in Vancouver to help kick off the Second Victory Loan, and through his personable charm, he further cemented Canadian goodwill toward China. Dr. Hu paid honor to his hosts by declaring he had cancelled all his engagements and made the onerous three-thousand-mile journey to Vancouver because Canada "was not only China's old friend and new ally, but China's *first* ally."[17] In a national radio broadcast, he lauded Canada's contributions, making special note of its shipments of Bren guns and aircraft to the Orient, consignments that represented some of the first allied war materiel that was being made available to China since the war began. In a private capacity, he was entertained by the Vancouver consulate, and was able to bring Jessie the latest news of her aunt and uncle who were still languishing in Washington, D.C.

On March 8, 1942, in celebration of International Women's Day, the CBC radio carried a fifteen-minute broadcast by Song Meiling. Speaking all the way from Chongqing, Song haughtily disparaged the trademark intolerance of women's rights that was routinely displayed by totalitarian regimes, and then, by contrast, went on to describe the welcome contributions to the war effort that were being made by the women of China. Listening closely to her old boss, Jessie jotted down much new material for her own speeches.

Meanwhile, Jessie was more than ever in demand as a public speaker. Invited to Vancouver Island to address the Victoria branch of the Women's Canadian Club, she gave her speech, 'China Marches On,' to six hundred clubwomen at the Empress Hotel. In a voice trembling with pride, she described how rescue airplanes had saved more than two hundred fifty civilians, airlifting them from Hong Kong just before the Colony fell to the Japanese. She confidently predicted that aviation would reverse her homeland's present misfortunes.

"Wings over China," she cried, "will bring the world to our door and freedom to our skies!"[18]

With the war heating up in the Far East, significant changes were suddenly made to the Chinese legation. China was appointing its first foreign minister, the Honorable Liu Shishun, to Ottawa, and, on March 20, the consulate-general offices were transferred from the nation's capital to Vancouver. This move reflected the West Coast's proximity to the increasingly dangerous situation in the Pacific. The Honorable Shih Chao-ying was installed as the new consul-general in Vancouver, posted to the West from Ottawa where he had served since 1939.[19] Jessie was now at the epicenter of Chinese operations in Canada.

She gave another landmark speech when she was invited to address the Vancouver Council of Women. Again, the papers reported "there wasn't an eye that was dry or a heart that didn't thrill to her plea to 'work together so the victory may the sooner be ours.'" In a voice that throbbed with feeling, Miss Zheng told her tearful listeners that her people "had never once, despite intolerable suffering, thought of compromise or surrender." A frisson passed through the audience when she promised with considerable intensity, "China will launch an attack against the enemy that will drive them back forever to their little islands beyond the seas!"[20]

On July 14, the potent combination of her arrow-straight, diminutive appearance and mighty powers of oratory reportedly brought down the house at the Bastille Day celebrations in Vancouver. After the German occupation of their country, a contingent of the Free French forces had regrouped on Canada's West Coast, and these boys were learning to fly for their country through the BCATP. Like Jessie, their futures were uncertain, and they were far removed from their families and comrades who were suffering under the boot of enemy aggression, but their spirits were rallied by the Chinese aviatrix who addressed them in the beloved language of their homeland. Speaking in ringing tones, she reminded them that, as part of a continuum, they were carrying on the same great principles of *Liberté, Egalité, et Fraternité* that had inspired the Revolution.

"Today, you, the Free French, are upholding that principle," she assured them. "Your courage and your faith have earned for you the admiration of the entire Allied world."[21]

Enormously moved by her words, the emotional crowd erupted in a maelstrom of cheers, whistles and prolonged applause. Plaster was still falling from the ceiling when Jessie resumed her seat.

A few weeks later, she scored yet another triumph when the Vancouver Junior Board of Trade asked her to address its membership. She was the first woman invited to do so. Her speech, entitled 'Japan—The Weakest Link,' was a new one with a new premise arguing that, if the Allies would supply China with the transport and fighter aircraft they needed so desperately, her homeland would at last be able to turn the tide in the Pacific. Defeating the Japanese, she calculated, would have the positive effect of freeing up the Pacific shipping lanes. This victory would allow the United Nations to concentrate their combined forces on the war in Europe, and the inevitable result would be a speedier conclusion to the hostilities. The logic of her speech rang true to the audience.

"Tiny and beautiful," gushed the next day's paper, "the young Chinese girl—the first woman ever to address the Board—drew wave after wave of applause for her sound reasoning and graphic description of China's fight during the past five years."[22]

Again, the same curious phenomenon occurred; her speech brought the audience—this time composed of hardy young men—to tears. Attempting to analyze the emotional effect she had had on them all, the Board's president later deduced that, "It was not facts but her sincerity which caused so much feeling and so many lips to tremble in a gathering of young men and young ideas."[23]

Jessie made many other successful addresses that year, and these included speeches to the National Council for Democratic Rights, the University Women's Club, the Vancouver Women's School for Citizenship, and also to associations further afield on the Pacific coast of the United States.[24] However, despite the brilliance of her appeals, and the warmth with which she was received, she sometimes tended to resemble an automaton with a one-track mind. When praised for her hard work and many accomplishments, Jessie objected.

"I am not interested in doing these things for myself," she insisted. "Everything I do is for my countrymen."[25]

One interviewer reported that he found her gracious and charming, but somewhat stiff and unable to unbend, or, more troubling, unwilling to admit to any failings in her country's political infrastructure. Like a seasoned politician, she skillfully sidestepped his enquiries about China's reported rampant inflation, and refused to address his questions about the overriding hostility that was said to exist between the Guomindang and the Chinese Communists.

"Diplomatically," he reported, "Miss [Zheng] is perfect. To twenty or thirty leading questions, we were carefully and deftly allowed to supply our own answers."

To his mild frustration, he was unable to steer Jessie away from the party line that China desperately needed foreign aid. He began to think that her comparison to a carved ivory statue was highly appropriate. Later, however, he was relieved to discover that she was human after all. He and his wife invited their guest to the cinema (Jessie had asked to see *Mrs. Miniver*), and as she watched the pre-feature cartoon, he noted that the official façade finally cracked and "she laughed just as heartily as we did..."[26]

As far as the interviewer was aware, Jessie was a single woman living alone whose closest family member, a brother, was posted at the Chinese consulate in far-away San Francisco. She never revealed to him that she had much closer relative—her daughter, Beverley Ann—living in the same city.

30. CROSSING CANADA

Jessie had always welcomed a challenge, and it was time to take up a large one on behalf of her nation. It would require all of her energy, charm and courage.

In early September 1942, Dr. Hu Shi, the Chinese ambassador to the United States, received his recall to the Far East, and Jessie's uncle, Dr. Wei Daoming, was appointed as his replacement. Basking in the reflected glory of her uncle's new status, Jessie called a press conference to highlight her familial relationship with the ambassador, and to confide that her aunt had expressed a hope that she and her husband might visit Vancouver sometime in the late spring.[1]

Jessie was also pleased to announce that, within the next few months, she herself would become an 'ambassador of goodwill,' and would be leaving for

Eastern Canada on an extended four-month speaking tour. This trip would augment her local efforts to raise support for China and would "promote a friendly understanding of China's and Canada's common contribution to the cause of the United Nations." She confided that she hoped to include Washington, D.C. on her itinerary where she would spend some time with her aunt and uncle at the Twin Oaks Embassy, but knowing Zheng Yuxiu as well as she did, she predicted that the visit would not be a holiday. Her aunt would likely conscript her for yet additional speechmaking. A busy time lay ahead of her, but she was not complaining.

"It is all for my country," she affirmed. "I shall speak in New York, too, probably for the United China Relief. But it all helps the Allied nations."[2]

Four months was a long time to spend away from her daughter, but Jessie was already little involved in the infant's upbringing. Almost from the outset, tiny Beverley Ann had been taken in and cared for by her grandparents, the long-suffering Setos. As far as Jessie was concerned, the happiness of those around her would have to be postponed during the present emergency when the fate of her homeland was teetering in the balance. She was Zheng Hanying, Heroine of China, and her country needed her.

In addition to raising China's profile, her trip would fulfill another important function. Just as an opening act works to bring the crowd to a fever pitch before the main performer arrives on stage, so Jessie would be the forerunner for Song Meiling, scheduled to make a North American tour in the New Year. From late February to June 1943, Song was slated to embark on a public relations expedition that would take her from one end of the United States to the other, and include a side trip to Canada. This tour was destined to lay the groundwork for America's love affair with China's First Lady that would last for years and result in her being nominated again and again as one of the world's most admired women.

Jessie's junket would have entailed enormous expense. In the United States, the organization known as the Friends of China picked up the tour costs of her flying colleagues, Hilda Yan and Li Xiaqing, and Jessie may have counted on similar aid (Friends of China were active in Canada, too), but most likely the Chinese consular services underwrote her travels. However, there were some opportunities to cut expenses. As a diplomatic representative of an allied nation—and a commissioned air force officer—she was sometimes able to travel in Canadian government aircraft free of charge, and this would have moderated to a large extent the huge costs of an expedition of this nature. However, she confidently hoped that the goodwill accrued from the venture would more than compensate for any expenditure.

She packed as lightly as she could. Her kit included only a dark wool military coat with 'China' sleeve patches, warm winter boots, her new set of jewels, and a few Chinese garments, but on this tour of duty, Jessie's most indispensable garment would be her uniform. She would elect to deliver all her speeches while wearing the scarlet tunic of the Chinese Air Force; its splendid appearance never failed to elicit the desired dramatic effect. She steeled herself for the gruelling pace of the tour—she would be invited to give anywhere from two to three speeches a day—but her sympathetic audiences would be delighted to receive her in their midst. In return, their enthusiasm would fire her energy. While the addresses she made to white organizations would receive impressive press coverage, those delivered to Chinese associations would garner no mainstream publicity whatsoever, so it is impossible to know the exact extent of her efforts in this regard, but the Chinese Canadians that she encountered were enormously proud of her accomplishments—and impressed by the ease with which she moved in the Occidental world.

At 6:00 a.m. on November 28, 1942, Jessie commenced her tour by departing Vancouver for Ottawa via an eastbound flight of the Trans-Canada Airlines.[3] Prior to her departure, she announced that, in addition to visiting the nation's capital, she would make personal appearances in Montréal, Québec, Halifax, Toronto, and other Eastern cities. She also mentioned that she hoped to drop in on major centers in the Prairie Provinces. Jessie was able to fulfil this latter ambition sooner than she anticipated. Several hours into the flight, the TCA pilot had successfully crossed the Rocky Mountains and was *en route* to a fifteen-minute refuelling stop at Kenyon Field in Lethbridge, Alberta, when he suddenly encountered low ceiling weather. He was forced to put down at Fort Macleod, some twenty-eight air miles from Lethbridge. The Macleod airfield belonged to a Flying Training School facility (No. 7 SFTS) where budding Canadian air force personnel were being readied for active duty. When Wing

Commander Brown learned of Jessie's impromptu arrival at the airfield under his command, he hastened over to meet the plane and conduct her to the officers' mess where she was invited to relax and await the clearing of the weather. Grateful for the Wing Commander's gallantry, Jessie was happy to accept his hospitality, especially when the flight ended up being delayed by a couple of hours. As a wartime ally and a fellow air force officer, she likely made quite an impression at the mess. Compared with the neophyte pilots on base, Flight-Lieutenant Zheng was a veteran aviator with operational training and over two hundred fifty flying hours to her credit.

A couple of hours later, her plane was airborne once more and landed at nearby Lethbridge for refuelling. The press had been alerted of the VIP passenger on board, and a representative of the city's newspaper hurried out to the airport to conduct an interview. In the few moments remaining before takeoff, Jessie met with the reporter and went into her official spiel. She forecast that, after the war, with new areas opening up in the aero transportation industry, Chinese women would have a great future in aviation. In addition, the airplane was the tool that would help to knit her vast country together.

"This rapid form of transportation will not only help in the development of China," she predicted, "but will bring the people of the various provinces together in a closer bond of understanding and fellowship."

Then she lightened up and gave the smitten reporter some impressions of her tour of duty in Canada.

"This is my first trip across Canada," she conceded, "and I think it is a wonderful and beautiful country. The people have been most hospitable to me and I feel very much at home, not like a stranger at all."

The remainder of the tour would only confirm this impression. She was about to be bombarded with goodwill.

Jessie arrived late and weary in Ottawa some eighteen hours after she had left Vancouver, but she was cosseted by her colleagues at the new Chinese legation headquarters which, since June, had been located at Glensmere, one of the city's loveliest old mansions. Once the home of former Canadian Prime Minister, Sir Robert Borden, it was sited in a park-like setting on the banks of the frozen Rideau River, and Jessie had a day to relax in this almost rural setting before she began her first public engagement. Fittingly, her premier address was made in the nation's capital to a luncheon meeting of the Ottawa Women's Canadian Club. Jessie paid tribute to her hosts:

"Canada was the first of twenty-seven Allies to rally to the side of China," she gratefully acknowledged, "and we are proud. The Pacific ocean, instead of being a barrier against mutual understanding and aid, has tied our two nations closer together."[4]

Taking her seat at the head table with Lady Byng of Vimy and Lady Perley, she was thanked for her address by Squadron Officer Willa Walker of the RCAF Women's Division. It was also S.O. Walker who also accompanied her that same evening to the Air Force headquarters at Rockcliffe airfield to meet with the RCAF Women's Division based at the No. 7 Manning Depot. After dining with officers in the mess, Flight-Lieutenant Zheng was asked to address the airwomen. She did so, both in French and in English. There was a marked contrast between the audience—a sea of Canadian women in blue who were not permitted to fly for their country—and the red-uniformed Chinese officer who wore the golden wings of the Dragon and spoke so stirringly about her adventures in aviation. On that snowy evening in Ottawa, she recalled for them the exacting RAF instruction she received in tropical Hong Kong, and she described her many hours of flight throughout war-torn China. If the Canadian airwomen were chagrined by the disparity between their restricted circumstances and hers, they did not show it. They listened spellbound to Jessie's tales of life in the CAF and the endurance of her nation. For her part, the aviatrix had nothing but praise for the women of the RCAF (WD).

"It is with admiration that I see you entering one of Canada's famous branches of the armed forces," she declared. "To serve your country is a very high ideal, and I know that all of you will carry on with honor and pride the name of the Royal Canadian Air Force."

The next day at the Institut de Jeanne d'Arc, she addressed the Ottawa Regional Committee of the Fighting French and once again told her audience about the indomitable spirit of the Chinese. This time, she spoke entirely in French—good practice for the upcoming francophone leg of her tour.

On December 4, Jessie took off from Ottawa's Rockcliff Air Force Base in an Avro-Anson Mk II twin-engine trainer of the RCAF and flew to the Saint-Hubert airfield just outside Montréal.[5] She had received an invitation to attend a special event. The first Catalina Amphibian aircraft, known as the Canso by the air force, was set to roll off the assembly line at Saint-Hubert's Vickers plant, and a variety of Canadian and overseas dignitaries—Jessie included—had been asked to witness its christening and test flight. She flew into the base to celebrate the naming of the mighty, two-engine aircraft. The city was shivering under a severe cold spell, the mercury having dipped to its lowest mark in almost a decade, but when Jessie's aircraft taxied to a stop on the snow-covered runway, the sun was shining brilliantly. She jumped down from the cockpit to a warm welcome by Group Captain J.S. Scott, Commanding Officer of the No. 13 Air School of Saint-Hubert.

Jessie was accorded yet another elaborate courtesy. She was invited to inspect an honor guard of the RCAF Women's Division who had met her plane and were standing stiffly to attention on the frozen apron where her aircraft had come to a stop. Still wearing her bulky flying suit and escorted by Group Captain Scott, Jessie carefully carried out the inspection for all the world as if she were accustomed to such honors, and stopped to chat amiably with some of the women.[6]

While she was still in town, the Montréal Chinese Women's Society wasted no time in asking her to address its members. An RCAF staff car and driver were put at her disposal, and Jessie was chauffeured to the women's headquarters in Chinatown where she was greeted with an armful of flowers and a huge banner of welcome in English and Chinese. The clubwomen conducted Jessie to her place of honor at the society's head table, adorned with British and Chinese flags. The wall behind her was crowded with portraits of Dr. Sun Yat-sen and yet more flags and bunting, and as she delivered her address against the colorful backdrop, her audience thrilled to the realization that this representative of China was a member of the Republican inner circle, and had received her commissioning from none other than the Generalissimo himself.

Next day, Jessie and Squadron Officer Willa Walker attended the dedication of the new Canso airplane, and were present in the hangar when Lady Bowhill of the Royal Air Force Ferry Command enthusiastically christened the amphibian with a bottle of champagne, soaking her uniform in the process. The atmosphere in the Vickers' hangar quickly grew warm and hearty, and a great deal of fuss was made over Flight-Lieutenant Zheng Hanying, only woman member of the Chinese Air Force and the Chinese consular corps in Canada. She happily posed for publicity photos with chief executives of the aero industry and the new aircraft's test pilot, E.C.W. 'Ted' Dobbin, a popular aviator who hailed from Vancouver.[7]

The pretty propagandist was in her element in the largely French-speaking province of Québec and she hugely enjoyed her sojourn there. Through her friendship with Alma Gilbert of the Flying Seven, she was already familiar with *l'accent québécois,* and her bilingualism put her in great demand by a variety of service clubs. Two days after she arrived in Montréal, she made a quick trip upriver to the province's capital at Québec City to fulfill additional speaking engagements. She found Vieux-Québec bristling with black cannons, and ringed with crumbling stone ramparts that reminded her of the ancient walled cities of her homeland. It was unlike any Canadian city she had ever visited, and the differences extended even to the Québec newspapers which referred to her as, 'Mlle. Hanyin Tcheng,' using the French version of her name that her Francophile family generally preferred.

While in Québec City, Jessie stayed within the walls of the old town at the Chateau Frontenac, the turreted Canadian Pacific hotel that soared castle-like on a prominence overlooking the frozen St. Lawrence River. (Nine months hence, President Roosevelt, Prime Ministers Churchill and Mackenzie King and Chinese Foreign Minister T.V. Song would meet at the same site to plan the future course of the war.) It was there that she was invited to speak to the local branch of the Cercle des Femmes Canadiennes (Women's Canadian Club), and she appeared in uniform at the podium when she trotted out her old speech, 'China Marches On.' She worked her usual magic, switching easily from French to English and back again, holding her listeners captive by the sincerity of her appeal and the logic of her arguments. Included in the audience was Lady Fiset, wife of the Lieutenant Governor, and Madame Georges Vanier, wife of the future Governor-General. A photo of "*la charmante messagère de bonne entente,*" standing with Lady Fiset and officers of the club, appeared next day in the local papers. As she hobnobbed with Canada's wealthy elite, Jessie was probably glad that she had thought to invest in her sparkling new jewelry.

She hurried back to Montréal where the next day she was guest speaker at a luncheon of the Advertising and Sales Executives Club of Montréal. The

Club had borrowed the big English and Chinese banner of welcome from Chinese Women's Society and affixed it to the head table. Resplendent in her uniform, Jessie sat at the right hand of Mr. W.C. Stannard, president of the Club, and to the left of Lady Bowhill, whom she had met a few days earlier at the christening of the *Princess Alice*. Deeply appreciative of the personal warmth she had encountered in the frosty province, she rose and assured her audience,

"*Tout le peuple du Québec a été charmant et hospitalier envers moi, et je l'en remercie beaucoup.*"

Then in French and English, she told them of her homeland's gratitude to Canada for having become the first of China's allies in the current conflict. She predicted that the consequent friendship, cultivated in the face of a common enemy, would endure even after the war, the positive outcome of which could not be in doubt.

Her popularity snowballed. Out of the blue, Jessie received another invitation to a function at Montréal's Ritz-Carleton Hotel. It was a dinner hosted by the League of Nations Society in honor of Mr. Warwick Chipman, K.C. The Canadian government had recently appointed the Honorable Mr. Chipman as Minister to Chile and, as Jessie also enjoyed consular status, the dinner organizers asked her to address the gathering. Seated at the head table with the city's leading political and religious leaders, Jessie opened her speech in a conventional fashion by wishing the new Minister success in his appointment, but while she had a captive audience, she could not resist putting in a plug for her countrymen. By their resistance, both fallen soldiers and civilians were "making the world a better place for its teeming millions." Jessie was frankly in awe of the stamina and resolve of her fellow countrymen, and she never tired of praising their qualities. Granting an interview to the press, she did her best to explain why she knew the Chinese people would win in the end.

"They will endure any hardship whatever in the hope that China will benefit eventually," she declared. "Their courage and fortitude in some sections of the country, where bare necessities of life have often been unobtainable, is almost unparalleled."[8]

On the morning of December 23, she made an official visit to City Hall to meet the mayor, Adhemar Raynault. Her reputation preceded her, and M. Raynault received Flight-Lieutenant Zheng Hanying as an honored guest of

Montréal. As they chatted together in French, city counselors joined them, as well as the executive of the Montréal Chinese Women's Society and representatives of the Junior Board of Trade. Like other distinguished visitors to City Hall, the mayor invited Jessie to sign the *Livre d'or*, and a photo of this occasion appeared next day on the front page Christmas edition of *La Presse*. All in all, her efforts in the La Belle Province had received excellent coverage, and there were now few who did not know about the pressing needs of the Chinese people.

There is no trace of Jessie's movements after this day and for the remainder of 1942. However, it would be safe to assume that she took this opportunity to fly at last to Washington, D.C. to spend Christmas at the Embassy with her aunt and uncle, where the gregarious Zheng Yuxiu, already regarded as the Capital's most popular hostess, was always delighted to welcome family members into her home.[9]

In the New Year of 1943, Jessie returned to Ottawa to find the capital city all aflutter. Princess Juliana of the Netherlands, who had taken refuge in Canada when the Nazis overran her homeland, had given birth to a daughter, Margriet, on January 19, just two days after Jessie's birthday. By special decree, the Canadian Government had declared that the hospital room occupied by the newborn and her mother would be granted extraterritorial status, a point of law that allowed the child to be born on 'Dutch soil.' All of Ottawa rejoiced over the royal birth and its unusual circumstances, but none more so than the diplomatic community, which took particular interest in the legal niceties of the situation. The Chinese Foreign Minister, Dr. Liu Shishun, celebrated on behalf of his nation by honoring the Minister of the Netherlands with a dinner party, one occupied nation paying tribute to another.

It was a busy month in Ottawa. On January 28, 1943, the Canadian Parliament was set to open, and political representatives converged on the city. Vancouver journalist, Margaret Ecker, was among those present and she reported to her readers that she was suitably impressed by the majesty of the occasion. From her seat high in the House of Commons press gallery, Miss Ecker surveyed all the pageantry, observing the splendid fashions of the women who, she noted, arrived at the opening arrayed mostly in black. She assumed this was intentional—their dark costumes made a striking foil to the deep red carpet of the chamber—but as she scanned the unvarying sea of basic black, her roving eye was suddenly arrested by a bright splash of scarlet in the diplomatic corps gallery. Less than two years before, Miss Ecker had been invited to the all-aviatrix luncheon in Vancouver that honored China's woman military pilot, and she realized at once that the dash of color was the red tunic of the Chinese Air Force being worn by none other than Flight-Lieutenant Zheng Hanying, "China's outstanding girl flier."[10]

Jessie's show-stopping appearance at the opening of the House of Commons was intentional and served to remind Canadian politicians of their obligations to their Far Eastern ally. Indeed, the speech from the Throne made reference to China.

"The government has maintained close relations with the nations with which Canada is united in the common struggle," intoned the Governor-General. "Direct diplomatic representation has strengthened our relations with China." With this official recognition of her nation, Jessie swelled with pride. When she had arrived three years before, the struggles of her homeland had been largely ignored, but by dint of her unceasing efforts and those of her colleagues, Canada had finally become the first of China's Western allies. Jessie never looked for pity for her people, nor did she depict them as losers in a battle against an omnipotent foe. Rather, she continued to insist that China was a self-confident, resourceful nation, well worthy of Canada's respect and support. Her oft-repeated message was finally bearing fruit.

On February 3, 1943, Jessie recommenced her tour, traveled to Toronto and booked herself into the resplendent King Edward Hotel. (Like her mentor, Song Meiling, she had a predilection for expensive lodgings.) She was exhausted, and looked it, but the luxury of the accommodations helped to ameliorate some of her road-weariness. The enthusiasm with which Torontonians took her to their collective bosoms also exhilarated her.[11] The city's thriving Chinese community was thrilled that her arrival coincided with the Chinese New Year. Her appearance in the lucky-colored red uniform was a good omen for the coming year, and seemed to ensure a bright future for the wearer.

A press photographer tagged along as Jessie paid a visit to the Chinese War Relief fund headquarters at 24 Elizabeth Street, and he took a clutch of pictures as she chatted amiably with volunteer workers. Over *yum cha* (or Dim Sum) at a nearby Chinese restaurant, she spoke about the progress China was making in the war. She was free with her praise of Song Meiling.

"Madame Chiang Kai-shek's heart bears all the suffering of her people," she declared with some passion. "The plight of every native of her country is her heartache, too."

She encouraged Torontonians to open their hearts and wallets to aid her appeal.

"Money raised here and cabled to her," Jessie promised, "gives her an opportunity to alleviate suffering, hardship, famine, lack of medical supplies in a thousand different ways."[12]

She also touched on the important martial contributions of guerrilla fighters, in particular, the remarkable efforts of the redoubtable sixty-three-year-old warrior woman, Madame Zhao Hong Wenguo. Also known as 'Madame Mosquito,' China's foremost senior had gained renown for her unnerving ability to appear from nowhere, 'sting' the invaders, and then vanish—apparently into thin air—only to re-emerge elsewhere to maim and harass. Madame Zhao traveled throughout China rallying her countrywomen, both old and young, to become spies and guerrillas in aid of their nation. In October 1938, Jessie had the good fortune to be present when the old woman delivered an electrifying address in Hong Kong. From that day onwards, Madame Zhao occupied a special place in Jessie's heart as an outstanding heroine of China, well worthy of emulation, and the younger woman never tired of extolling the elder's virtues.

Two months into her tour, Jessie had learned to unbend, and she was beginning to veer away from the party line and her usual fixed responses to questions. Uncharacteristically forthcoming, she appeared to be growing more accustomed to meeting with people and handling press interviews. Perhaps exhaustion also caused her to become more garrulous. Rather than harp continuously on 'the cause,' she began to reminisce about her wartime experiences, recounting how she dodged bombs in Chongqing and then flew to Canada in the noisy hull of bomber.

She also spoke of her growing affection for Canada.

"I think," she affirmed over a bowl of tea, "I shall call it my second home."

But while she was in a confiding mood, Jessie did not reveal the extent to which she was already emotionally tied to Canada, that she had given birth to her only child on Canadian soil and that this decisive event could not help but bind her forever to her 'second home.' Perhaps she was implying that she was looking forward to permanent residence in Vancouver after the war, and maybe she intended to assume more responsibility for the raising of her child.

Before she left Toronto, Jessie made a public appearance at Malton airport where she took a test flight in an Anson Avro II and, engulfed by her bulky flying suit, smilingly posed for photos with the delighted pilots of the RCAF. It was one of her good days, and with her face brightened by make-up, she was at her attractive best. Ominously, however, dark hollows had begun to appear around her eyes, and she was even thinner than she had been at the beginning of the tour. With two more months of her trip yet to complete, she confessed that, "I have been working very hard, and now I think I need a rest."[13]

Meanwhile, Song Meiling had begun her landmark tour of America, accompanied for the extent of the excursion by her old friend, Zheng Yuxiu, wife of the ambassador and Jessie's aunt. Madame Chiang had caused a sensation when she addressed the United States Senate on February 18, 1943, and given her success on that occasion, there was a flurry of excitement two days later when the mayor of Vancouver announced that he had invited her to visit the city. Shortly thereafter, however, Vancouver's Chinese community was enormously disappointed to learn that Madame Chiang had declined this invitation on the orders of her doctor who warned against overexertion. Jessie must have been disappointed as well; if Song had visited, Zheng Yuxiu would have been at her side. However, Canadians soon learned that Madame Chiang did not intend to exclude Canada entirely from her itinerary. When the bulk of her coast-to-coast tour of America was over, she promised to make an official visit to the nation's capital.

She was as good as her word. On June 15, 1943, Song Meiling stepped off the train in Ottawa and onto the red carpet in her peep-toe alligator shoes and stunned everyone with her 'striking beauty.' Her reputation in Canada was already exalted, but by the end of her three-day visit, it would be unassailable. She was met at Union Station by Governor General Lord Athlone and his wife, Her Royal Highness the Princess Alice, granddaughter of Queen Victoria. Prime Minister Mackenzie King and one thousand flag-waving Chinese were also on hand to ensure that her welcome to Canada was nothing less than regal. In her capacity as wife of China's Ambassador to Washington, Zheng Yuxiu also accompanied China's First Lady on this leg of the tour, and she was one of those in Madame Chiang's retinue who came in for a full measure of reflected glory. All official representatives of China who were serving throughout the nation, including the Vancouver contingent, traveled to Ottawa to re-pledge their allegiance to their homeland and to debrief Madame Chiang on the situation in Canada. Given Jessie's official status, as well as her professional and familial ties to Madame Chiang and the Ambassador's wife, it would have been surprising if she had not rendezvoused with them on this historic occasion, but no record exists to claim that she did.

31. GATHERING SHADOWS

Madame Chiang's visit to Canada shone a bright spotlight on the dire needs of her homeland. The Japanese had now completely blockaded China, she reported, and her countrymen were running out of money and munitions, not to mention food. Song Meiling claimed that it was almost impossible for the West to appreciate fully the acuteness of her nation's difficulties. The cost of living had skyrocketed and some prices were eighty per cent higher than they had been in 1937. The Japanese had closed down the Burma Road, and goods could enter China only via costly and dangerous air flights over the 'Hump route' of the Himalayas.

Madame Chiang's appeals fell on fertile ground. In an effort to help alleviate the strictures imposed on China by its enemy, the Chinese War Relief Fund kicked off a special drive in August 1943. The optimistic organizers cherished an ambitious goal—they targeted a national quota of one million dollars. In British Columbia, a special ceremony inaugurated the campaign. Consulate representatives and prominent members of Chinatown attended the launch, and seated among the honored guests were Wilfred's parents, but there is no evidence that Jessie was in attendance. Perhaps she was avoiding the Setos; it is equally likely that she may not have felt well enough to attend.

Soon thereafter, there was a changing of the guard at the consulate. In the middle of August 1943, Consul-General Shih Chao-ying, posted to Vancouver the previous April, received a transfer to Johannesburg, and his replacement, the Honorable Li Chao, arrived from the Chinese Legation in Ottawa.

Just as this shift was taking place, Jessie's health began to betray her. For some time, her lungs had harbored the deadly tuberculosis virus; she had even infected her child with the disease. TB, the dreaded 'coughing sickness,' was endemic in China. Some reports estimated that it afflicted as much as seventy per cent of the total population, and it was all too easy to acquire the deadly bacilli in the refugee-laden cities and closely packed air raid shelters. The disease had infected Jessie in her native land, but it was exacerbated by her busy agenda in Canada. The chronic condition soon burst into full flower. The fibrosis that gradually hardened her lungs effectively turned them into unyielding leather, making it ever more difficult for her to draw breath. Even the act of eating became a labor, and her already spare body grew perilously gaunt, and yet, as driven as ever, Jessie endeavored to maintain her punishing schedule of speaking engagements.

The Vancouver Junior Board of Trade invited her to make an address to its members on August 26, 1943. It was a little over a year since she had made her first triumphant speech to the organization, but at this stage in her illness, she could barely speak above a whisper. Although she attended the luncheon and spoke briefly to the assembly, she begged that she be excused due to a bad case of laryngitis, and she declared her intention of returning and delivering her talk at later date. This promise was not to be fulfilled. Jessie's time was running out.

At this point, she must have been fully aware of the debilitated condition of her lungs, yet her obsessive desire to serve China claimed center stage. Jessie continued to appear at her desk at the consulate, but by the end of August, she was too weak to go into work. On September 6, she was in acute respiratory distress, and she was rushed by ambulance to Vancouver's St. Paul's General Hospital.[1] There was little that could be done for her. Successful treatments for tuberculosis were still in the experimental stage, and even if they had been available, Jessie's condition was so far advanced that nothing could have saved her from what was, by this time, galloping consumption.

The day after her admission to hospital, Jessie's fierce spirit finally acknowledged that her weakened body could not survive the crisis. She called for a solicitor and dictated her last will and testament. At this supreme moment, the imperatives of her faith were uppermost in her thoughts. She had saved little money, but directed that her entire estate, including any cash that might be accrued from the sale of her clothing and jewelry, be presented to the French-speaking sisters of the religious order who ran the children's school at Maillard-ville, a francophone village on the outskirts of Vancouver.[2]

She also ordered that all her private papers be burned... with one exception. Jessie singled out her flying license, the document representing that accomplishment of which she was most proud, and requested that it be presented to the Chinese Air Force. Ever mindful of her country's struggle with the enemy, through this last gesture she signified her oneness with her comrades' gallant efforts to oust the invader. And then, thousands of miles from her beloved China and the ministrations of her family, Jessie's restless spirit finally quit her frail form. On September 7, 1943, Jessie Hanying Zheng died at the age of twenty-eight.

In her will, Jessie made no mention of Wilfred, not surprising considering the bitter feelings that likely dominated their relations by this time, but inexplicably, she also made no provision for Beverley Ann. Rather than bequeath the child with some token of her existence, she left all her worldly goods to the nuns of Maillardville. Had she already made some separate provision for her daughter, or was she secure in the knowledge that Beverley would receive loving care and proper upbringing from Wilfred and his parents? She took the answers to these questions to her grave.

Jessie's death was front page news in the local papers. During her brief sojourn in the city, amounting to a scant two and a half years, she had met and addressed thousands of Vancouverites, and her sincerity and passion had won the hearts of many. Early on the Saturday morning immediately following her death, her life was celebrated with a requiem mass at Holy Rosary Cathedral. Mourners packed the church, civilians and military personnel alike, all intent on paying their respects to a remarkable young woman who had lived her brief life beyond conventional expectations, and who had served her country with the last drop of her strength.

As a tribute to Jessie's memory, the Royal Canadian Air Force, both men's and women's divisions, did her one last service and participated in the funeral rites, embellishing her send-off with full military honors. At the end of the mass, a uniformed guard of honor carried her coffin, draped with the flag of China, out into the sunshine and down the steps of the cathedral. As if to give Vancouver a final opportunity to bid farewell to its exotic, gentle visitor, the *cortège d'honneur* marched through the city streets for several blocks to the steady beat of a drum. Then the guards lifted the coffin onto a military truck and proceeded to Burnaby's Ocean View Cemetery for the interment. As a trumpeter sounded the haunting strains of the Last Post, the mortal remains of the only woman pilot in the Chinese Air Force were slowly lowered into the ground. Members of the firing party raised their rifles and fired a deafening three-gun salute into those same blue skies where Jessie had expertly piloted her aircraft.[3]

Wong Foon Sien, the leader of Vancouver's Chinatown, issued an official statement. "The Chinese here mourn the loss of such an able woman," he declared. "It is a great pity that she could not live to see our country win the victory for which she worked so hard."[4]

A few days later, a moving epitaph penned by her journalist friend, Mamie Maloney, appeared in the *Vancouver Sun*:

"Yes, China has lost a fair daughter," she grieved, "and we who knew her have lost a gracious and charming friend. But Hanyin's work will go on. She has thrown the torch and it will be picked up by successive generations of Chinese women, who, like Hanyin, are worthy of the greatest compliment that could be paid a fighting ally—'They just don't know what quitting means.'"[5]

Three days after Jessie's death, organizers of the Chinese War Relief Fund in Vancouver were pleased to announce that provincial contributions to the campaign would likely realize twenty-five per cent more than the anticipated provincial quota of one hundred thousand dollars. In fact, contributions across Canada were well in excess of the fund's original goals. The success of the campaign was Jessie's legacy, and a monument to her unceasing work on China's behalf.

It was to be her only memorial. No stone marks her grave, and there is nothing to indicate, in the scenic cemetery where she is laid to rest with its sweeping lawns and distant view of the sea, that there lie the remains of a supremely modern woman who gave every ounce of her spirit for the people of her native land. The mystery in which she cloaked herself in life robbed her of a lasting remembrance in death.

32. POSTSCRIPT

In the years since Jessie's passing, sweeping changes have altered her world almost beyond recognition. She did not live to see the war's end in 1945 when the enemy were finally driven back to their "little islands beyond the seas." She was saved the ignominious fate of exile that was the lot of other zealous representatives of the Guomindang when Chiang Kai-shek's ruling party lost control of China to Mao Zedong's Communist forces in 1949 and were forced to flee to Taiwan, vowing one day to return to the Mainland.

In 1997, the Crown Colony of Hong Kong, where Jessie received her early education, was released from British control and unified with the People's Republic of China. Kai Tak, the airstrip where Jessie became the first Chinese woman to fly, and which ultimately evolved to become one of the world's most spectacularly—and dangerously—sited airports, was replaced in 1998 by the Hong Kong International Airport at Chek Lap Kok, whose construction and design represent a staggering feat of modern engineering.

Of the principal characters who peopled Jessie's world, Chiang Kai-shek died in Taipei in 1975, and his widow quit their island refuge to relocate to the United States. The charismatic Song Meiling, wartime catalyst to millions of women and one of Jessie's foremost mentors, lived in New York State for the rest of her life, and died there in October 2003 at 106 years of age. For decades one of the most admired women in the world, she and many of her family members were ultimately vilified for their alleged corruption, and denounced for having amassed one of the world's greatest fortunes at a time when millions of Chinese died from starvation. Song's contributions to the war and women's empowerment worldwide go largely unheralded.

In 1946, the Nationalist government recalled Jessie's uncle, Wei Daoming, from Washington to Taipei and installed him as governor of Taiwan. Two years later, he was dismissed from this position, and the Weis left the island in high dudgeon for Brazil, and then Los Angeles, where they licked their wounds in exile. Increasingly disillusioned with the corruption of the Guomindang, Zheng Yuxiu began to distance herself from the party. On December 16, 1959, she died of cancer at the age of sixty-eight and was buried in a Los Angeles cemetery. Even in death, she pays tribute to her longing for China—her headstone faces the East. Shortly afterwards, her husband, who apparently did not nurse the same ill-will for the Nationalists, quit America for Taiwan, and, in 1966, he was appointed foreign minister of the Republic of China. Wei died on May 18, 1978. He had remarried, but in accordance with his last wishes, his remains were interred in Los Angeles with those of his first wife, Zheng Yuxiu.

Wilfred Seto, the father of Jessie's child, enlisted with the Canadian Army, and a month after Hanying's demise, he was dispatched to Europe. Just prior to his embarkation, he attended a farewell dance where he met the woman he would marry, a local Chinese woman named Patricia Lowe. Sent off to Italy, Wilfred served with distinction as a lieutenant in the Seaforth Highlanders (where he was affectionately dubbed 'MacSeto' by his fellow-soldiers), but soon returned to Canada where he ultimately rose to the rank of captain with the No.1 Discrimination Unit in Ottawa. At war's end, he received an honorable discharge. To celebrate the unique wartime contributions made by the military volunteers of Canada's Chinese community— particularly in view of the fact that they held no legal status as citizens—Wilfred became one of those responsible for organizing the nation's only Chinese Canadian veterans' unit, Pacific Unit 280 of the Army, Navy and Air Force Veterans.[cn] For his ongoing contributions to the community, he was one of seven men and women selected to become the first Chinese in British Columbia to receive Canadian citizenship on February 19, 1947.[1]

While Wilfred was serving in the military, his parents continued to care for his daughter, Beverley Ann, in their West End home. After the war, Wilfred married Pat Lowe and the couple moved in with the elder Setos. They gave birth to a son, but Pat raised Hanying's daughter as if she were her own. Wilfred supported his family by operating a wholesale business that imported quality British and Japanese fabrics. He also ran a menswear shop that supplied custom-made suits to discerning clients. In 1960, at the age of forty-five, Wilfred Seto succumbed to a heart attack and was buried in the same cemetery as

Jessie Zheng, but in a different section.

After her father's death, Beverley continued to live with her stepmother and grandparents, and when she graduated from high school, did clerical work for a variety of local firms. In 1964, she accepted a permanent position at Canadian Pacific Airlines (CPA), thereby becoming an employee of the same sprawling transportation corporation for which her grandfather, Seto More, had worked for four decades. In her late twenties, she moved to Montréal, the city where her birth mother had made such an impact in 1942, and worked at the CPA offices as an executive secretary. In the late 1980s, Beverley Ann Seto died in Montréal of multiple sclerosis. She never married.

Today the Zheng family is dispersed from Guangdong's Lequn Cun where patriarch Zheng Yao founded his personal empire, and the remnants of the once-splendid palace compound he built to celebrate his wealth have suffered from neglect. Those crumbling structures that do remain are still objects of fascination, but they have endured a mixed fate. One of them, the long and multi-roofed building known as Qiyun Shushi, served as a Japanese brigade headquarters during the WWII occupation. Postwar, it suffered much abuse, and was converted first into a granary and then a sofa factory. However, a hundred meters away from this structure, the shell of the Zheng Ancestral Hall and its altar within continue to be carefully maintained, and the antique beauty of this building still retains power to awe the curious visitor.

Belatedly recognizing the architectural importance of these structures, as well as the historical significance of the county's favorite daughter, Zheng Yuxiu, a government initiative has been launched to protect the heritage buildings of Baoan County, and the Qiyun Shushi has been named a listed structure. Monies have been allocated to assist in refurbishing the remains of the Zheng family palace.[2]

fig. 1

fig. 2

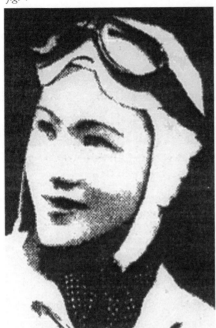

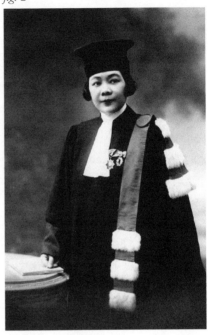

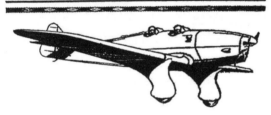

LEARN TO
FLY
COMPLETE TRAINING GIVEN FOR EVERY TYPE OF BRITISH LICENCE BOTH PILOTS AND ENGINEERS.
FOR PROSPECTUS APPLY:—
FAR EAST
FLYING TRAINING SCHOOL, LTD.
Kai Tak Airport.
Hongkong.

fig. 3

女飛行員鄭漢英
日間北上

卒業於本港遠東航空學校之女飛行員鄭漢英女士、最近得接中央當局電邀北上。×××、××××、記者聯鄭女士友人稱、鄭女士自接中央電召後、本擬剋日起程北上參加、惟因料理私務、故暫延遲、至其行期、在短期間內當可北上云、

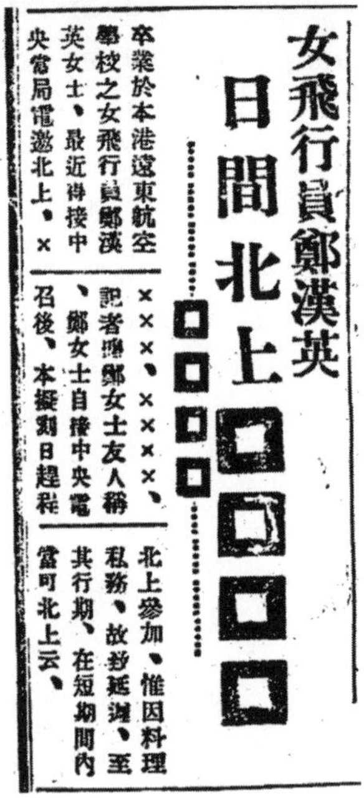

fig. 4

fig. 5

fig. 6

女飛行家
鄭漢英

領得港府飛行執照

鄭漢英女士早歲就讀於國內，後赴法洲逃，得有巴黎大學學位，我已學成歸國，近正在港致力于航空救國工作，領有省港政府飛行執照，並為英國皇家航空俱樂部及法國國際航空學會會員。女士平日對於飛行技術頗多研究，提倡航空救國之著述，亦頗望富云。

fig. 7

fig. 8

fig. 9

fig. 10

fig. 11

fig. 12

fig. 13

fig. 14

fig. 15

fig. 16

fig. 17   *fig. 18*

處捐籌民難兵傷國祖濟救僑華大拿加華高雲駐
Chinese War Refugees Relief Committee
108 Pender St. E.   P. O. Box 249   Vancouver, B. C.

中華民國廿......年......月......日 Date................19......

茲收到....................先生捐助救濟祖國傷兵難民

Received from M

Address

Donation for The Chinese War Refugees Relief Fund

The Sum of...Dollars

                                    Chinese War Refugees Relief Committee

Thank You   N⁰ 902

                        By...................................
                                          經手收銀人

TRANS-CANADA AIR LINES
TRANSCONTINENTAL SERVICE

Miles	EASTBOUND Read Down	Time Zone	Trip No. 2 Daily	Trip No. 4 Daily
0	Lv. **VANCOUVER**............§	PST	6.00AM	5.00PM
469	Ar. **Lethbridge**..................	MST	9.30AM	8.30PM
	Lv. **Lethbridge** ....§	MST	9.50AM	8.50PM
836	Ar. **Regina**......................	MST	11.55AM	10.55PM
	Lv. **Regina**......................§	MST	12.05PM	11.05PM
1169	Ar. **WINNIPEG**	CST	2.55PM	2.00AM
	Lv. **WINNIPEG** ....§	CST	3.15PM	2.15AM
1836	Ar. **Kapuskasing**..............	EST	7.35PM	6.35AM
	Lv. **Kapuskasing**...............§	EST	7.45PM	6.45AM
2104	Ar. **North Bay**	EST	9.25PM	....
	Lv. **North Bay** ....§	EST	9.35PM	....
2291	Ar. **TORONTO**	EST	10.55PM	9.20AM
2656	Ar. **NEW YORK**...............	EST	1.30AM	12.35PM
2291	Lv. **TORONTO** ....§	EST	11.15PM	9.35AM
2519	Ar. **Ottawa**	EST	12.45AM	11.05AM
	Lv. **Ottawa**.....................§	EST	12.50AM	11.10AM
2614	Ar. **MONTREAL**	EST	1.35AM	11.55AM
	Lv. **MONTREAL** ....§	EST	1.45AM	
3058	Ar. **Moncton**	AST	5.10AM	
	Lv. **Moncton** ....§	AST	5.20AM	
3176	Ar. **HALIFAX**	AST	6.15AM	

fig. 19

fig. 20

le 23 décembre 1942.

Visite de Mlle Hanyin Cheng, Lieutenant dans le Corps d'Aviation Chinois.

Fl. Lt. Hanyin Cheng - Chinese Air Force. Chungking. Chine.

G. Yuen   Canton   China

Tilene D. Bain   Verdun   Que.

H. S. Bain   Verdun   Que.

Fred Duck

fig. 21   *fig. 22*

fig. 23

fig. 24

fig. 25

fig. 26

fig. 27

○鄭漢英女士昨患病逝世

鄭漢英女士・年廿九歲・乃中國空軍之唯一女飛行家・又為世界之第一名女子執有駐倫敦皇家航空俱樂部之國際航空憑證者・曾肄業於巴梨大學・領得法律博士畢業證・近日患病・直至昨星期二日一臥不起。聞者莫不惋惜・現定於星期六日上午八點鐘・在此間天主教堂・舉行殯葬儀式。查鄭女士自到雲埠後・向外宣傳頗竭力・其姑丈係駐美京中國大使魏道明云。

In solemn procession, members of the Royal Canadian Air Force march behind the Chinese flag-draped casket of Flight-Lieut. Hanyin Cheng as the woman flyer was carried to her last resting place in Ocean View Burial Park, Saturday. Full military honors were accorded Flight-Lieut. Cheng, only woman pilot in the Chinese Air Force. While the coffin was lowered into the grave a bugler sounded "Last Post," and a firing party fired three volleys.

Photo by Western Air Command.

fig. 28

APPENDIX I

Hilda Yan's Participation at the League of Nations, as Documented in the Minutes of the Meetings.

Sixteenth Ordinary Session of the Assembly, Geneva, Sept. 9 – Oct. 11, 1935
Minutes of the First Committee (Constitutional and Legal Questions)
      Fifth Meeting, September 19, 1935
      Chairman: M. Limburg (Netherlands)

Re: Nationality of Women: Convention on the Nationality of Women concluded on December 26th, 1933, at the Conference of American States at Montevideo: Examination and Adoption of the Draft Resolution submitted by the Drafting Committee

Mme Yen CHEN (China) stated that the Chinese delegation was in full accord with the views put forward by the Irish delegate at the previous meeting. She desired, as representative of a country reputed to be one of the oldest and most conservative, to explain the present status of women in China.

The National Government, formed in 1927, had officially recognized and proclaimed the principle of equality of rights for women, and a resolution had been passed at the National Congress enunciating the guiding principles for national legislation concerning women's rights. Those principles were as follows: equality of rights as between men and women; women's equal right to inherit property; equality of freedom in contracting and dissolving marriage; "same work, same pay" for women workers.

The Legislative Yuan had, during the last few years, enacted a number of laws, and had revised the civil and criminal codes on the basis of the principles set forth in the foregoing resolution. The new civil code, promulgated in 1930, contained important changes in the laws relating to the family and succession, and gave men and women equal freedom in the possession and disposal of property. A far-reaching reform had been made in the laws of succession by a ruling of the Supreme Court, in 1928, according to which a daughter, whether married or not, had the same right as her brothers to inherit the property of her parents. The new Constitutional Pact promulgated by the National Government on June 1st, 1931, declared that all citizens of the Chinese Republic should be equal before the law, without any distinction of sex, race, religion or class, and that the opportunity of education should be offered equally to men and women.

Thus a new jurisprudence had been evolved, tending to create more and more new laws in which women's rights would be further extended. A stimulus had thus been given to Chinese women to prepare themselves for the new opportunities opened to them in the various spheres of national life. Already many women were engaged in the professions—in medicine, law, banking and teaching—and held high political and administrative posts. There were also some women members in the Legislative

Yuan, and women judges in the law courts.

Such was now the legal status of Chinese women, because Chinese men realized that, although women were by nature different by reason of their function of motherhood, that differentiation did not mean inferiority or inequality. Women asked for protection only in the very special case of maternity; other humanitarian and so-called protective laws, when applied to women only, made them feel that they were hedged about with limitations disadvantageous to their possibilities of work. Humanitarian laws were protective and beneficial only when they applied to all human beings, not when they worked to the advantage of only one sex and resulted in unfair competition under the guise of protection.

The fact of the complete legal equality that Chinese women now enjoyed came as a surprise to the Western world; but it was no less surprising to modern China that so many countries in Europe and America granted their women little or no legal status. Mme. Yen Chen felt, however, that there was a genuine awakening of the idea of equality among men and women all over the world. Some countries, it was true, still appeared reluctant, and others seemed to have turned reactionary, either because they were afraid of female competition or by reason of traditional conservatism. That situation, she firmly believed, could not last long, for women would eventually be given the rights to which they were entitled as human beings and as responsible guardians of their sons and daughters.

The countries of the Occident would be well advised to reflect that it was preferable and far more gracious for men to share their legal rights equally and willingly with women than to force all women to become feminists and to wrest that equality from them. There were enough fighters in the world; women might, on the other hand, prove effective peacemakers. Given a fair chance, women, who made up half the population of the world, might help to improve the present state of affairs, might help to achieve the League's aims of peace and collective security.

On behalf of the Chinese delegation, Mme. Yen Chen desired to support the draft resolution submitted by the Irish delegation, to the effect that the question of the status of women should be taken up by the League. China was prepared to assist in any international action that the League might eventually take in regard to the Montevideo Treaty of 1933. She trusted that the Assembly would not only draw the attention of the Members of the League to the Equal Rights Treaty, but that it would also recommend States to accede to and ratify the Treaty as soon as possible.

From the:
League of Nations, Records of the Sixteenth Ordinary Session of the Assembly, *Minutes of the First Committee,* Special Supplement No. 139 (Geneva, 1935), 33-34.

Eighteenth Ordinary Session of the, Assembly, Geneva, Sept. 13 – Oct. 6, 1937
Minutes of the Fifth Committee (Humanitarian and General Questions)
>Fourth Meeting, September 18, 1937
>Chairman: Countess Apponyi (Hungary)
>Lead Speaker: Hilda Yan

Re: Social Questions: Proposal for the Establishment of an Eastern Bureau; Discussion and Appointment of Sub-Committee

Mlle Yen, Hilda (China) wished, on behalf of the Chinese delegation, to endorse the recommendations adopted by the Bandoeng Conference. That conference deserved appreciation for having made practical suggestions. Immediate importance attached to the proposal for the establishment of a Central Bureau in the Far East. As reported by the Commission of Enquiry in 1932, the victims of the traffic in the East were mostly Chinese women and children. The lack of co-ordination between the activities of the Chinese authorities on the one hand, and those of the authorities in foreign settlements and in the colonial possessions of the Western Powers in the South Seas on the other, made the prevention of this traffic by the Chinese Government more difficult and more complicated. The difficulties would largely be removed if a Central Bureau were established for the purpose of distributing information among the competent authorities of the various countries concerned and of acting as a liaison agency so as to secure closer cooperation. Once that Bureau was in full operation, it was to be hoped that the bulletin discussed at the last meeting might also be published in Chinese.

In the opinion of the Chinese delegation, the Bureau must be set up if the other recommendations of the Bandoeng Conference were to be carried out. That had also been the opinion of the Bandoeng Conference itself. It appeared to be shared by the Advisory Committee on Social Questions, and Mlle. Yen felt that the Fifth Committee ought to take the same view.

As to the place at which the Bureau was to be established, both the Chinese delegation to the Bandoeng Conference and the Chinese representative on the Advisory Committee had voiced their desire that primarily concerned Chinese women and children, and the presence of a League Bureau in the country of origin of the traffic would be extremely useful in advising and assisting the Chinese authorities and in promoting closer collaboration with the authorities of the foreign Settlements. Again, from a budgetary point of view, Shanghai deserved preference. The Chinese delegation, however, was not unaware of the claims of some alternative place as a suitable site for the Bureau, and felt that that site should be determined by purely technical considerations. The immediate question before the Committee was to reach a decision in support of the proposal to create the Bureau and to recommend its adoption by the Assembly so that this outstanding recommendation of the Bandoeng Conference might be put into effect without delay.

From the:
> League of Nations, Records of the Eighteenth Ordinary Session of the Assembly, *Minutes of the Fifth Committee,* (Geneva, 1937), 23.

Eighteenth Ordinary Session of the, Assembly, Geneva, Sept. 13 - Oct. 6, 1937
Minutes of the Fifth Committee (Humanitarian and General Questions)
> Eighth Meeting, September 25, 1937
> Chairman: Countess Apponyi (Hungary)

Re: Social Questions: Proposal for the Establishment of an Eastern Bureau: Report of the Sub-Committee: Discussion and Provisional Adoption.

Mlle. YEN Hilda (China) said the Chinese Government had always been in favor of the proposal to set up an Eastern Bureau. The Chinese delegation at the Bandoeng Conference had, however, understood that the Bureau would be under the direction of the League's machinery. She thought other delegations had had the same impression. Her Government having no knowledge of the new proposal [the establishment of an International Bureau], she must reserve the decision as to Chinese participation.

From the:
> League of Nations, Records of the Eighteenth Ordinary Session of the Assembly, *Minutes of the Fifth Committee,* (Geneva, 1937), 49.

APPENDIX 2

MINXIN FILMS of LI DANDAN (LI XIAQING):
Inventory in Chinese (Trad.) & English

WHY NOT HER? (Pure and Noble) - **yu jie bing qing**《玉洁冰清》1926
B+W silent, 70 minutes
Director: Bu Mocang

GOD OF PEACE - **he bing zhi sheng**《和平之神》1926
B+W, silent, 30 minutes
Director: Hou Yao

A POET BY THE SEA/ CAPE POET - **hai jia shi ren**《海角诗人》1927
B+W, silent
Director: Hou Yao

WANDERING SONGSTRESS - **tian shi ge nü**《天涯歌女》1927
B+W, silent, 30 minutes
Director: Bu Mocang

ROMANCE OF THE WESTERN CHAMBER / WAY DOWN WEST - **xi xiang ji**《西厢记》1927
B+W, silent, 56 minutes
Director, Screenwriter: Hou Yao

FIVE VENGEFUL GIRLS – **wu nü fu chou**《五女复仇》1928
Director: Gao Xi Ping

HUA MULAN JOINS THE ARMY – **Mulan cong jun**《木兰从军》1928
Silent, B+W, 3 hr
Directors: Hou Yao, Gao Xiping

REVIVING ROMANCE – **zai shi yin yuan**《再世姻缘》1928
Silent, B+W
Director: Gao Xiping

GLOSSARY

Almost all Chinese proper names and words that appear in the text are cross-referenced in the glossary according to *pinyin* and Wade-Giles transliterations. Their equivalent in simplified Chinese characters is also provided. Names in common usage, such as Chiang Kai-shek or Sun Yat-sen, have not been transliterated into *pinyin*.

Aeronautical Affairs, Nat'l Com. …航空委員會

air raid (jing bao)…警报

Anking (Anqing)…安庆

Anqing (Anking)…安庆

apsara (fei tian xian nü)…飞天仙女

Baishiyi…白市驿

Bao'an county…宝安

Bao Huizhi…飽会秩

Baotou (Paotow)…包头

Beihai (Pakhoi)…北海

Beijing (Peking/Peiping)…北京

bomb (zha dan)…炸弹

Bu Mocang…卜万苍

Cai Chusheng…蔡楚生

Cai Jiguang (Choi Kai-kwong)…蔡继光

cai yu da xun zhang (Order of Brilliant Jade)…采玉大勳章

Canton (Guangzhou)…广州

Cao Yunxiang (Tsao Yun-hsiang)…曹云祥

CATC (Central Air Transport)…中央航空公司

Ceng Zongjian (T.K. Tseng)…曾宗鑑

Central Air Transport Co. (CATC)…中央航空公司

Chang Ching-chiang (Zhang Jingjiang)…张静江

Chang, Laura, Mme TV Song (Zhang Yueqia)…张樂恰

Chang, F.Y. (Zhang Fuyun)…张福运

Chang Wei-chang (Zhang Huichang)…张惠长

Changsha…长沙市

Changzhou (Wuzhou)…梧州

Chen Bingzhang (Chen Ping-tsang, or P.T.)…陈炳章

Chen Ding (Chen Ting)…陈定

Chen Dexie, Col. (T. H. Shen)…沈德燮

Chen, Percy (Chen Pishi)…陈丕士

Chen Pishi (Chen, Percy)…陈丕士

Chen Ruidian, Capt. (Art Chin)…陳瑞鈿

Chen Shaokuan…陈绍宽

Chen Ting (Chen Ding)…陈定

Chen Wenkuan, Capt. (Moon Chin)…陈文宽

Chen, P.T., Ping-tsang (Chen Bingzhang)…陈炳章

Cheng Baishi (Pax Cheng)…郑柏士

Cheng Han-yin, Jessie (Zheng Hanying)…郑汉英

Cheng Hsüeh-an (Zheng Xuean)…郑雪案

Cheng, Jessie, Han-yin (Zheng Hanying)…郑汉英

Cheng Mu-lan, Mary (Zheng Mulan)…郑木兰

Cheng, Pax (Zheng Baishi)…郑柏士

Cheng Tianxin (Emma Ing Chung)…程天信

Cheng Wen-chih (Zheng Wenzhi)…郑文治

Cheng Yun (Zheng Yun)…郑云

Cheng Yü-hsiu, Soumay (Zheng Yuxiu)…郑毓秀

Cheng Yao (Zheng Yao)…郑姚

Chengchow (Zhengzhou)…郑州

Chengdu (Chengtu)…成都

Cheung, Katherine (Zhang Ruifen)…张瑞芬

Chiang Chao-ho (Jiang Zhaohe)…蒋兆和

Chiang Ching (Jiang Qing)…江青

Chiang Kai-shek, Generalissimo (Jiang Jieshi)…蒋介石

Chiang Kai-shek, Madame (Song Meiling)…蒋夫人

Chin, Art, Capt. (Chen Ruidian)…陳瑞鈿

Chin, Moon, Capt. (Chen Wenkuan)…陈文宽

China Aviation League (zhongguo hangkong xie)…中国航空协

China Sun Film Co. (minxin ying pian)…民新

影片

Chinese Youth's Medical Relief Ass'n…中国青年救护团

Choi Kai-kwong (Cai Jiguang)…蔡继光

Chongqing (Chungking)…重庆

Chou En-lai (Zhou Enlai)…周恩来

Chung, Emma Ing (Cheng Tianxin)…程天信

Chungking (Chongqing)…重庆

CNAC (zhongguo hangkong gong si)…中国航空公司

Co Tui, Frank W., Dr. (Xu Zhaodui)…許肇堆

da gong bao (Ta Kung Pao)…大公报

da yue jin (Great Leap Forward)…大跃进

Deng Xiaoping (Teng Hsiao-ping)…邓小平

Dong Daqiu…董大酋

Du Yueh-sheng (Du Yuesheng)…杜月笙

Du Yuesheng (Tu Yueh-sheng, Big Ears)…杜月笙

Eurasia Aviation Corp. (ou ya hang kong gong si)…欧亚航空公司

Fang Zhenwu, General…方振武

Far East Flying Training School (yuan dong hang kong xue)…遠東航空學

fei ma zhui di (Pursing the Enemy on Horseback)…《飞马追敌》

Feng Ling…冯玲

Feng Shan, Gen'l…将军凤山

Five Vengeful Girls (wu nü fu chou)…《五女复仇》

Foreign Office (Waijiaobu)…外交部

fu huo de mei gui (Reviving Rose)…《复活的玫瑰》

Fujen Catholic University…輔仁大學

gai ge zhong guo hang kong de jian yi (Suggestions to Reform Chinese Aviation)…改革中国航空的建议

Gang of Four (si ren bang)…四人帮

Gansu (Kansu)…甘肃

Gao Qianping…高倩萍

Gao Xiping…高西屏

God of Peace (he ping zhi shen)…《和平之神》

Gong Louli (Lully Goon)…宫露丽

Goon, Lully (Gong Louli)…宫露丽

Great Leap Forward (da yue jin)…大跃进

Green Gang (Qing Bang)…青帮

Gu Weijun, Dr. (Wellington VK Koo)…顾维钧

Guangzhou (Canton)…广州

Guangdong (Canton province)…廣東

Guilin (Kweilin)…桂林

Guo Bingwen (P.W. Kuo)…郭秉文

Guomindang (Kuomintang)…国民党

Guo Taiqi (Quo Tai-chi)…郭泰祺

hai jiao shi ren (Poet by the Sea)…《海角诗人》

Haichow (Haizhou)…海州

Haizhou (Haichow)…海州

hang kong jiu guo (Saving the Nation by Aviation)…航空救国

hangkong wei yuan hui (Nat'l Com. of Aero. Affairs)…航空委員會

Hangchow (Hangzhou)…杭州

Hankow (Wuhan)…武汉

Hangzhou (Hangchow)…杭州

He Desheng (Ho Tak-sang)…何德生

he ping zhi shen (God of Peace)…《和平之神》

He Xiangning…何香凝

Hing, Leah (Li Fenglin)…李凤麟

Homantin Hill, No. 1…何文田山道一號

hongqiao jichang (Hungjiao airfield)…虹桥机场

Hoo, Victor Chi-tsia (Hu Shize)…胡世泽

Hsiao Chi-Yung (Xiao Jirong)…萧继荣

Hsiung Hsi-ling (Xiong Xiling)…熊希龄

Hsü Jun (Xu Run)…徐润

Hsü Tsung-han (Xu Zonghan)…徐宗汉

Hu Die (Butterfly Wu)…胡蝶

Hu Mei, Dr. (Edward H. Hume)…胡美

Hu Shi, Dr. (Hu Shih)…胡适

Hu Shize (Victor Chi-tsai Hoo)…胡世泽

Hua Mulan Joins the Army (Mulan cong jun)…《木兰从军》

Huang Guiyan (Virginia Wang)…黄桂燕

Huang Huilin (Mme Wellington Koo)…黄蕙兰

Huang Liushuang (Anna May Wong)…黄柳霜

Huang Xing (Huang Hsing)…黄兴

Huanghuagang Uprising…黄花岗起义

Hume, Edward H., Dr. (Hu Mei)…胡美

Hungjiao airfield (hongqiao jichang)…虹桥机场

Ichang (Yichang)…宜昌

Jiang Jieshi, Gen. (Chiang Kai-shek)…蒋介石

Jiang Qing (Chiang Ching)…江青

Jiang Tingfu (Tsiang Ting-fu)…蒋廷黻

Jiang Zhaohe (Chiang Chao-ho)…蒋兆和

Jiangwan District, Shanghai (Kiangwan)…江湾，上海

Jiemu Yao (Wooden Yao)…界木姚

Jin Wensi (Wunsz King)…金问泗

Jinan (Tsinan)…济南

jingbao (air raid)…警报

Jiujiang (Kiukiang)…九江

Kansu (Gansu)…甘肃

Kiangwan District, Shanghai (Jiangwan)…江湾，上海

King, Wunsz (Jin Wensi)…金问泗

Kiukiang (Jiujiang)…九江

Kong Xiangxi (H.H. Kong or Kung)…孔祥熙

Kung, H.H., Dr. (Koong Xiangxi)…孔祥熙

Kunming…昆明

Koo, Wellington V.K. (Gu Weijun)…顾维钧

Koo, Wellington, Mme.(Oei Hui Lan)…黄蕙兰

Kuo, P.W. (Guo Bingwen)…郭秉文

Kuomintang (Guomindang)…国民党

Kweilin (Guilin)…桂林

Lai Man-wai (Li Minwei)…黎民伟

Lam Chor-chor (Lin Chuchu)…林楚楚

Lanchow (Lanzhou)…兰州

Lanzhou (Lanchow)…兰州

Le-ch'ün ts'un (Lequn cun)…樂群村

Lee Chin-yee (Li Jinyi)…李晋一

Lee Ching-chun (Li Qingchun)…李庆春

Lee Dan-dan (Li Dandan)…李旦旦

Lee, Frances E (Ou Yangying)…欧阳英

Lee, Hazel (Li Yueying)…李月英

Lee Pei-ji (Li Peiji)…李沛基

Lee Tzu-shih (Li Zishi)…李紫石

Lee Ya-ching (Li Xiaqing)…李霞卿

Lee Ying-sheng (Li Yingsheng)…李应生

Lei Yutang (Tong Louie)…雷鈺堂

Lequn cun (Le-ch'ün ts'un)…乐群村

Li Dandan (Lee Dan-dan)…李旦旦

Li Feng Lin (Leah Hing)…李凤麟

Li, George (Li Yixiang)…李颐祥

Li Yueying (Hazel Lee)…李月英

Li Jinyi (Lee Chin-yee)…李晋一

Li Minwei (Lai Man-wai)…黎民伟

Li Peiji (Lee Pei-ji)…李沛基

Li Qingchun (Lee Ching-chun)…李庆春

Li Xiaqing (Lee Ya-ching)…李霞卿

Li Yixiang (George Li)…李颐祥

Li Yingsheng (Lee Ying-sheng)…李应生

Li Yueying (Hazel Lee)…李月英

Li Zishi (Lee Tzu-shih)…李紫石

Liang Bi…良弼

Liang Long (Lone Liang)…梁龙

Lieu, O.S. (Liu Hongsheng)…刘鸿生

Lim Kho-seng, Robt, Dr (Lin Kesheng)…林可胜

Lin Chuchu (Lam Chor-chor)…林楚楚

Lin Kesheng, Dr (Lim Kho-seng, Robt)…林可胜

Lin Pengxia…林鹏侠

Ling Long (Ling Lung)…玲珑

Liu Chieh (Liu Kai)…刘锴

Liu Hongsheng (O.S. Lieu)…刘鸿生

Liu Kai (Liu Chieh)…刘锴

Liu Pei-chuan (Liu Peiquan)…刘沛泉

Liu Peiquan (Liu Pei-chuan)…刘沛泉

Liu Shishun (Liu Shih-shun)…刘师舜

Liuzhou (Longchow)…柳州

Lone Liang (Liang Long)…梁龙

Longchow (Liuzhou)…柳州

longhua jichang (Longhua Airfield)…龙华机场

Louie, Tong (Lei Yutang)…雷鈺堂

Low, Anna B. (Mrs. Lu Zuoqia)…爱娜·彼·卢

Lu Zuoqia, Mrs. (Anna B. Low)…卢佐洽

Longhua Airfield (longhua jichang)…龙华机场

Luoyang…洛阳

longhua lieshi lingyuan (Martyrs' Cemetery, Longhua)…龙华烈士陵园

Luo Qia (Law Kar)…羅卡

Ma Bangji, Capt. (Albert Mah)… 马邦基

Ma Shaoji, Capt. (Cedric Mah)… 马绍基

Mah, Albert, Capt. (Ma Bangji)…马邦基

Mah, Cedric, Capt. (Ma Shaoji)…马绍基

Manzhouli (Manchouli)…满洲里

Maoming…茂名

Martyrs Cemetery, Longhua…龙华烈士陵园

Mei Lanfangg (Mei Lan-fan)…梅兰芳

Mei Zhen Hua Ji…美珍华记

Minxin Film Company, or China Sun (minxin ying pian)…民新影片

modern woman (xin nü xing)…新女性

mulan cong jun (Hua Mulan Joins the Army)…《木兰从军》

Mukden (Shenyang)…沈阳

Nanchang…南昌

Nanjing (Nanking)…南京

Nanning…南宁

Nat'l Comm. Aeronautical Affairs…航空委员會

Oei Huilan (Mme. Wellington Koo)…黄蕙兰

Order of Brilliant Jade (Cai Yu Da Xun Zhang)…采玉大勳章

Ou Yangying (Mrs. Frances E. Lee)…欧阳英

ouya hangkong gongsi (Eurasia Aviation Corp.)…欧亚航空公司

Pakhoi (Beihai)…北海

Paotow (Baotou)…包头

Peach Garden Oath (taoyuan san jieyi)…桃园三节义

Peng Jia Zhen…彭家珍

Poème du Bout du Monde (hai jiao shi ren)…《海角诗人》

Poet by the Sea (hai jiao shi ren)…《海角诗人》

Pure and Noble (yu ji bing qing)…《玉洁冰清》

Pursuing the Enemy on Horseback (fei ma zhui di)…《飞马追敌》

Qi Yun Shu Shi…绮云书室

Qian Tai (Tsien Tai)…钱泰

Qing Bang (Green Gang)…青帮

Qingdao (Tsingtao)…青岛

Quan Jiyu…权基玉

Quo Tai-chi (Guo Taiqi)…郭泰祺

Reviving Romance (zai shi yin yuan)…《再世姻缘》

Reviving Rose (fu huo de mei gui)…《复活的玫瑰》

Romance of the Western Chamber (xi xian ji)…《西厢记》

La Rose Ressuscitée (fu huo de mei gui)…《复活的玫瑰》

Ruan Lingyu…阮玲玉

Salt Water City (Vancouver, B.C.)…咸水埠

San Min Zhu Yi…三民主义

Saving the Nation by Aviation (hang kong jiu guo)…航空救国

Seto More (Situ Mao)…司徒旄

Seven Sisters Constellation…星级七姐妹

Shen, T.H., Colonel…沈德燮

Shanghai…上海

Shaoguan (Shuikwan)…韶关

Shenyang (Mukden)…沈阳

Shi Zhaoji, Dr. (Sze Sao-ke)…施肇基

Shuikwan (Shaoguan)…韶关

si ren bang (Gang of Four)…四人帮

Situ Mao (Seto More)…司徒旄

Sian (Xi'an)…西安

Sinkiang (Xinjiang)…新疆

Song Ailing (Soong Ai-ling)…宋蔼龄

Song Faxiang (Far-san T. Sung)…宋发祥

Song Meiling (Soong Mei-ling)…宋美龄

Song of the Fisherman (yu guang qu)…《渔光曲》

Song Ziwen (T.V. Soong)…宋子文

Southwestern Aviation Corporation (xi nan hang kong gong si)…西南航空公司

Suchow (Suzhou)…苏州

Suggestions to Reform Chinese Aviation (gai ge zhong guo hang kong de jian yi)…改革中国航空的建议

Sun Yat-sen (Sun Zhongshan)…孙中山

Sun Zhongshan, Dr. (Sun Yat-sen)…孙中山

Sung, Far-san T. (Song Faxiang)…宋发祥

Suzhou (Suchow)…苏州

SWAC (xi nan hang kong gong si)…西南航空公司

Sze Sao-ke, Alfred, Dr. (Shi Zhaoji)…施肇基

Ta Kung Pao (da gong bao)…大公报

Tan Baoshen (Tan Pao-shen)…谭保慎

Tan Pao-shen (Tan Baoshen)…谭保慎

tao yuan sa jie yi (Peach Garden Oath)…桃园三节义

Tcheng Han-ying, Jessie, Flt.-Lt. (Zheng Hany-ing)…郑汉英

Tcheng Pai-fong (Zheng Baifeng)…郑白峯

Tcheng Yü-hsiu, Soumay, Dr. (Zheng Yuxiu)…

郑毓秀

Teng Hsiao-ping, (Deng Xiaoping)…邓小平

Three Outstanding Yans (yan shi san jie)…颜氏三杰

tian ya ge nü (Wandering Songstress)…《天涯歌女》

Tianjin (Tientsin)…天津

Tientsin (Tianjin)…天津

Tsang, Hélène (Zhang Qianying)…张倩英

Tseng, T.K. (Ceng Zongjian)…曾宗鑑

Tsiang Ting-fu (Jiang Tingfu)…蒋廷黻

Tsien Tai (Qian Tai)…钱泰

Tsinan (Jinan)…济南

Tsingtao (Qingdao)…青岛

Tongmenghui…同盟会

Tu Yueh-sheng (Du Yuesheng)…杜月笙

Waijiaobu (Foreign Office)…外交部

Wandering Songstress (tian ya ge nü)…《天涯歌女》

Wang, C.T., Thomas (Wang Zhengting)…王正廷

Wang Chonghui (C.W. Wong)…王宠惠

Wang Jingwei…汪精卫

Wang Renmei…王人美

Wang, Virginia (Huang Guiyan)…黄桂燕

Wang Ying…王莹

Wang Zhengting, Dr. (C.T. Thomas Wang)…王正廷

Wanhsien (Wanhsien)…万县

Wanxian (Wanxian)…万县

Way Down West (xi xiang ji)…《西厢记》

Wei Daoming, Dr. (Wei Tao-min)…魏道明

Weng Wenhao…翁文灏

Why Not Her (yu ji bing qing)…《玉洁冰清》

Wong, Anna May (Huang Liushuang)…黄柳霜

Wong, C.W. (Wang Chongwei)…王宠惠

Wooden Yao (Jiemu Yao)…界木姚

wu nü fu chou (Five Vengeful Girls)…《五女复仇》

Wu Teh-chen (Wu Tiecheng)…吴铁城

Wu Tiecheng (Wu Teh-chen)…吴铁城

Wu, Butterfly (Hu Die)…胡蝶

Wuchang Qiyi (Wuchang Uprising)…武昌起义

Wuchang Uprising (wuchang qiyi)…武昌起义

Wuhan (Hankow)…武汉

Wuzhou (Changzhou)…梧州

xi xiang ji (Romance of the Western Chamber/Way Down West)…《西厢记》

Xiang township…西乡

xinan hangkong gongsi (Southwestern Aviation Corp.)…西南航空公司

Xi'an (Sian)…西安

Xiao Jirong (Hsiao Chi-Yung)…萧继荣

Xie Ang (Angelo Xie)…谢昂

xin nü xing (modern woman)…新女性

Xinjiang (Sinkiang)…新疆

Xiong Xiling (Hsiung Hsi-ling)…熊希龄

Xu Mulan (Hsü Mu-lan)…徐慕兰

Xu Peilan…徐佩兰

Xu Peixuan…徐佩萱

Xu Run (Hsü Jun)…徐润

Xu Yingying…許盈盈

Xu Zhaodui, Dr. (Frank Co Tui)…許肇堆

Xu Zonghan (Hsü Tsung-han)…徐宗汉

Xue Jinhui…薛锦回

Yale-in-China Institute (Yali)…雅礼大学

yali daxue (Yale-in-China Institute)…雅礼大学

Yan Deqing, Dr. (Strong Teh-ching Yen)…颜德庆

Yan, Dorothy Xiangya (Yen Hsiang-ya)…颜湘雅

Yan Fuqing, Dr. (Yen Fu-ching)…颜福庆

Yan, Hilda Yaqing (Yen Ya-tsing)…颜雅清

Yan Huiqing (Yen Wei-ching)…颜惠庆

Yan, Julia Qinglian…颜庆连

Yan Nansheng…颜楠生

Yan Yaqing, Hilda (Yen Ya-tsing)…颜雅清

Yan Yongjing…颜永京

Yan Zi (Yen Tzu)…颜子

Yan Xiangya, Dorothy (Yen Hsiang-ya)…颜湘雅

Yan, Hilda Yaqing (Yen Ya-tsing)…颜雅清

Yan, Strong Deqing, Dr (Yen Teh-ching)…颜德庆

Yan Huiqing (Yen Wei-ching)…颜惠庆

Yang Jinxun…杨瑾珣

Yan Kaihui…杨开慧

Yan Youyin (Mme. Kuangson Young)…严幼韵

Yang Guansheng (Kuangson Young)…杨光泩

Yans, 3 Outstanding (Yan shi san jie)…颜氏三杰

Yen, Dorothy Tsiang-ya (Yan Xiangya)…颜湘雅

Yen Fu-ching, F.C., Dr. (Yan Fuqing)…颜福庆

Yen, Hilda Ya-tsing (Yan Yaqing)…颜雅清

Yen Teh-ching, Strong, Dr. (Yan Deqing)…颜德庆

Yen Tsiang-ya, Dorothy (Yan Xiangya)…颜湘雅

Yen Tzu (Yan Zi)…颜子

Yen Wei-ching, W.W., Dr. (Yan Huiqing)…颜惠庆

Yen Ya-tsing, Hilda (Yan Yaqing)…颜雅清

Yichang (Ichang)…宜昌

Yingkou (Yinkow)…营口

Yinkow (Yingkou)…营口

yuan dong hang kong xue
    (Far East Flying Training School)…遠東航空學

Young, Kuangson (Yang Guansheng)…杨光泩

Young, Kuangson, Mme. (Yan Youyin)…严幼韵

YWCA, Shanghai (Shanghai Nü Qing Nian Hui)…上海女青年会

yu guang qu (Song of the Fisherman)…《漁光曲》

Yu Junji, Dr. (Yu Tsune-chi)…于焌吉

Yu Tsune-chi, Dr. (Yu Junji)…于焌吉

Yu-pin, Paul, His Eminence (Paul Yubin)…于斌

zai shi yin yuan (Reviving Romance)…《再世姻缘》

zha dan (bomb)…炸弹

Zhang Geng…张庚

Zhang Fuyun (Chang, F.Y.)…张福运

Zhang Huichang (Chang Wei-chang)…张惠长

Zhang Jingjiang (Chang Ching-chiang)…张静江

Zhang Ruifen (Katherine Cheung)…张瑞芬

Zhang Qianying (Hélène Tsang)…张倩英

Zhang Yueqia (Mme T.V. Song, Laura Chang)…張樂恰

Zhao Hong Wenguo (Mme. Mosquito)…赵洪文国

Zheng Ancestral Hall…郑氏宗祠

Zheng Baifeng (Cheng or Tcheng Pai-fong)…郑白峯

Zheng Baishi (Pax Cheng)…郑柏士

Zheng Hanying (Cheng Han-yin, Jessie)…郑汉英

Zheng Mulan (Mary)…郑木兰

Zheng Wenzhi (Cheng Wen-chih)…郑文治

Zheng Xuean (Cheng Hsüeh-an)…郑雪案

Zheng Yao (Cheng Yao)…郑姚

Zheng Yuxiu (Tcheng Yü-hsiu, Soumay)…郑毓秀

Zheng Yun (Cheng Yun)…郑云

Zheng, Jessie Hanying (Cheng Han-yin)…郑汉英

Zhengzhou (Chengchow)…郑州

zhongguo hangkong gongsi (CNAC)…中国航空公司

zhongguo hangkong xie (China Aviation League)…中国航空协

zhongguo qingnian jiuhu…中国青年救护团

Zhonghua (China) magazine…中华

Zhonghua Minguo (Chung-hua Min-kuo)…中华民国

Zhou Enlai (Chou En-lai)…周恩来

Zhou Xuan…周璇

Zhu Bingru…朱冰如

zi mei hua…《姊妹花》

CHRONOLOGY

HILDA YAN (1906-1970)

1906   Born in Jiangwan to Yan Fuqing and Chow Siu-ying

1910   Father graduates with a degree in medicine from Yale University

Moves with parents to Changsha, Xiang where father is surgeon at a US mission hospital

1916   Enrolled at Rye Seminary in Rye, NY while father attends Harvard Medical School

1917   Enrolled at McTyeire School, Shanghai, China

1921   Leaves McTyeire for USA where father studies Public Health Medicine at Harvard

1922   Attends Smith College (Class of 1926) as university cultural exchange student

1924   Leaves Smith College, returns to China with family

1925   Graduates from Yale-in-China Institute, Changsha, with bachelor's degree

1927   Weds Chen Bingzhang who is connected with the National Ministry of Finance

1928   Gives birth to a son, William

Board member: YWCA, Shanghai Women's Club, Nat'l Child Welfare League

1932   Gives birth to a daughter, Doreen

1935   Accompanies ambassador uncle, Yan Huiqing, to Moscow as hostess of China's Embassy

Makes maiden address to League of Nations' First Committee on status of women

1936   Divorces husband and returns to Shanghai as Miss Hilda Yan

Wins a government job in Nanjing

1937   Appointed to League of Nations committee to reduce traffic of women & children

Attends League's Conference on Traffic of Women and Children, Bandoeng, Java

Attends coronation of King George VI and his consort Elizabeth in London, England

In Shanghai, helps Li Xiaqing organize flying club for Chinese women

Studies welfare of women and children in Europe

Takes flying lessons in Rome and earns a solo flying license

Marco Polo Bridge incident marks beginning of Sino-Japan war

Attends 18th League Assembly in Geneva to endorse Bandoeng resolutions

Lends support to League's condemnation of Japan invasion

Shanghai is invaded by enemy forces

Hilda relocates to New York to study welfare of women and children

1938 Begins flight instruction at Roosevelt Field, NY, and graduates same year

Lives in Washington, D.C. and New York City and is engaged in public speaking

Learns her father is installed as director of China's National Health Administration

Serves on executive of a variety of relief and social organizations

Makes plans to fly throughout USA for China refugees with Li Xiaqing

1939 Begins a projected three-month solo flying tour of Eastern U.S. in Turner-Porterfield

Crashes her aircraft in Prattville, AL and is hospitalized

Continues speaking and touring but travels by automobile

Becomes involved with ABMAC and Bowl of Rice Chinese charities

Attends Institute of Public Relations meeting, Virginia Beach, VA

Ex-husband, Chen Bingzhang, remarries

1940 Relocates to Hong Kong where her family has fled from the war in China

1941 Pearl Harbor, HI, bombed by Japan; USA enters the war, becomes China's ally

Hilda is trapped in Hong Kong when it falls to the Japanese

1942 Interned in Hong Kong, but escapes to Free China and returns to America

Attends Institute of Pacific Relations conference in Mont Tremblant, Québec

1943 Inquires about renewing pilot's certificate, but does not follow through

Continues fund-raising for China relief

1944   Impressed by Bahá'í teaching that the human race is one, enrols as a Bahá'í

Attends Bretton Woods monetary conference

Attached to Chinese delegation at Dumbarton Oaks to form United Nations

1945   Attached to Chinese delegation at San Francisco Conference

Serves on Chinese delegation to the U.N.

1946   Serves as public liaison officer, U.N. Dept. of Public Information

Lectures throughout the United States on behalf of the U.N.

Becomes increasingly involved with promotion of the Bahá'í & the new world order

1947   Assists Eleanor Roosevelt in drawing up the Declaration of Human Rights

1948   Oversees Bahá'í community's inclusion as non-governmental organization at U.N.

Marries U.N. worker and intellectual, John Gifford Male, of Wellington, NZ

Son William and daughter Doreen relocate from China to NYC

1949   Revolution in China brings Communist party to power

1950   Uncle Yan Huiqing dies in Shanghai

1951   Application to enter New York School of Social Work is rejected

Serves as an accredited observer for the Bahá'í U.N. Committee

Husband John is investigated by FBI for un-American activities

1954   Hilda and John relocate to South Norwalk, CT

1955   Hilda volunteers as amateur occupational therapist at Fairfield State Hospital

Application to enroll in occupational therapy course is rejected

Lobbies for revision of U.N. Charter

The Males buy extensive property at Mahurangi Harbor on NZ's North Island

1956   Hilda enters into studies for a degree in library science at Columbia University

1958   Graduates as a librarian; works at Brooklyn library

1959   Divorced from John Male

1970   March 18 - dies in New York City of occlusive coronary arteriosclerosis

LI XIAQING (1912-1998)

1912   April 16 - Born in Hong Kong to revolutionary family; known by nickname, 'Dandan'

Accompanies parents to Paris; father Li Yingsheng studies at the Sorbonne

1916   Family returns to Guangdong from Paris

Mother dies of tuberculosis

Father remarries; Dandan lives with grandmother, Xu Mulan, in Hong Kong

1918   Attends St. Stephen's School, Hong Kong

1922   Father opens Shanghai jewelry shop; is involved with 'Big Eared' Du Yuesheng

Revolutionary grandmother, Xu Mulan, dies of illness in Shanghai

Dandan enrolls at McTyeire School

1925   Li Yingsheng goes into partnership with Li Minwei of Minxin Film Co.

1926   Dandan quits school to become a Minxin movie actress

Appears in *Why Not Her* and *God of Peace*

Plays lead role in *A Poet from the Sea*

1927   Stars in *Wandering Songstress*

Plays supporting role in *Romance of the Western Chamber*

1928   Plays supporting role in *Five Vengeful Girls*

Stars as the lead in *Hua Mulan Joins the Army*

Plays a supporting role in *Reviving Romance*

Father withdraws her from film; sends her to England to continue her education

Hereafter known as Li Xiaqing

1929   Weds Zheng Baifeng, a secretary to the League of Nations

1931   Travels widely through USSR, France, Germany, Italy, Switzerland

Gives birth to son, Pax

Mukden Incident – Japan invades Manchuria

1932   Travels to China to visit family

Returns to Geneva, gives birth to daughter, Mary Mulan

1933   Takes flying lessons in Tiger-Moth at Geneva's Cointrin-Ecole d'Aviation

1934   Earns Brevet I, Aéro-Club de Suisse, the first woman to win pilot's license in Geneva

1935   Awarded Brevet II

Relocates to USA while husband & children go to Shanghai

Takes professional flying lessons at Boeing School of Aeronautics, Oakland, CA

Falls out of aerobatic plane and parachutes into San Francisco Bay

With bail-out, becomes first Chinese woman member of the Caterpillar Club

Becomes first woman to graduate from Boeing School of Aeronautics

Returns to China

1936   Takes up residence in Shanghai; becomes involved with Aviation League

Awarded a government flying license; demonstrates government aircraft

Serves as the only woman flight teacher in Shanghai

First Chinese woman to perform aerobatics in China skies

With Hilda Yan, forms a club for women who wish to study aviation

1937   In government aircraft, flies throughout China to inspect all airfields

Tours China's civil air routes prior to writing a book on aviation

Co-pilots Eurasia Aviation Corporation's Junkers tri-motor

Flies commercial routes for Southwestern Aviation Corporation

Sets women's distance flying records in China

Earns Hong Kong commercial pilot's license

Living in Shanghai when Sino-Japanese hostilities commence

Grounded, she organizes & funds a Red Cross hospital

On Hirohito's black list, flees Shanghai for Hong Kong

1938   Makes plans to fly throughout USA on behalf of refugees

Regularly travels by rail from Hong Kong to Canton to help relocate refugees

CNAC's *Kweilin* aircraft downed by enemy fighters; civilian passengers killed

Xiaqing travels to USA via *China Clipper* to raise American awareness of war

Uses own jewels as collateral to finance flights

1939   Lost in dense fog for three hours flying Pittsburgh-New York

Flying Stinson SR-9B *Spirit of New China,* begins tour of US for refugee relief

Appears in Hollywood movie, *Disputed Passage*, with Dorothy Lamour

Learns of Hilda Yan's plane crash in Alabama

Switches to Stinson Racer SR-5E in Chicago

Arrives NYC having flown 10,000 miles and visited almost 40 cities

Attends National Air Races at Cleveland, OH

Participates with Hilda Yan in New York City Bowl of Rice fund-raiser

1940   Flies *Estrella China* Beechcraft C17R to Caribbean, Central & South America

Safely flies 18,000 miles

Participates in Hollywood charity fair for China Relief at home of Mary Pickford

Joins aviatrix Ruth Nichols to help promote Relief Wings air ambulance service

1941   Assists pioneer aviatrix Ruth Nichols as she raises funds for Relief Wings

Helps First Lady Eleanor Roosevelt choose a *qipao* for Song Meiling

Goes on staff at United China Relief (UCR)

Visits Canada for an intensive four-day promotion of the Chinese Red Cross

Flies UCR's-Aeronca Superchief 65 LB on a tour of Ohio & New England states

Pearl Harbor is attacked by Japanese air forces, and the USA enters the war

1942   Promotes the Red Cross with Anna May Wong in New Orleans

Begins intensive round of UCR speaking engagements & personal appearances

Appears in Times Square with Hollywood stars; makes appeals on radio and NBC-TV

1943   Begins the year with a variety of public appearances

Becomes the subject of a bubble gum card and a 'True Aviation' comic book story

Song Meiling arrives in US for her historic tour of America

In the fall, Xiaqing tours Pennsylvania, Ohio, New York

1944   Flies Pan-Am to South America & the Caribbean on fund-raising tour

Extends her tour from three or four months to eight

Arrives back in USA having won many large cash gifts for Chinese relief

Rampant inflation in China gobbles up the worth of Xiaqing's efforts

U.S. WASP, Li Yueying, dies in plane crash; may have been confused with Li Xiaqing

1945   World War II ends

1946   Requests priority clearance from USAAF Transport Command to return to China

Receives permission to fly to Shanghai via Clipper "in the national interest of the US"

Relocates to Hong Kong; retires

1950   Receives Hong Kong private pilot's license

For the next decade, flies for sport and pleasure throughout South East Asia

1963   Is granted Hong Kong Special Purpose License

1966   Spends some time in USA and applies for pilot's license

Adhering to FAA regulations, takes flying lessons & is granted a license

1971   Father Li Yingsheng dies in Shanghai

Xiaqing & husband, George Li, take up permanent residence in the United States

1993   Ex-husband, Zheng Baifeng, dies in US

1997   Attends handover of Hong Kong Colony from Britain to China

1998   January 24 - dies in Oakland, CA, of respiratory disease at 85 years.

ZHENG HANYING (1915-1943)

1915   January 17 – born in Guangdong province

Her powerful aunt, Dr. Zheng Yuxiu, is an early mentor

1920s Attends school in Hong Kong

331

c1933   Studies at the Sorbonne, University of Paris, France

Takes some courses in England

1936   Graduates from the Sorbonne with degree in law

Returns to China; visits parents & Aunt Zheng Yuxiu in Shanghai

Relocates to Hong Kong

1937   Becomes 1st Chinese woman to attend Hong Kong's Far East Flying Training School

Elder brother, Zheng Yun, also a student at FEFTS, chastised for 'foolish escapade'

Sino-Japanese hostilities erupt

Is appointed to the National Aeronautical Commission, Chongqing

1938   Relocates to Hong Kong to train as cadet for Chinese Air Force

Receives commission from the Generalissimo, serves as only woman in the CAF

Holds international flying license (FAI) through Royal Aero Club of London

Attends Song Meiling's first women's conference in Kuling

Provides flood relief when river levies are broken to halt progress of Japanese

Becomes an authority on Red Cross work

1939   Granted Hong Kong Government flying license

Meets overseas student, Wilfred Seto, of Vancouver

1940   Discovers she is pregnant by Wilfred Seto

Flies to Canada as a passenger aboard a bomber to confront Wilfred

Becomes only Chinese woman member of the 'Short Snorter' club

Becomes 1st Chinese woman appointed to Canada in an official capacity

Gives birth to daughter, Beverley Ann Seto

1941   Works as attaché at Vancouver's Chinese Consulate

Joins Aero Club of B.C., Canadian Red Cross, and l'Alliance Française

Rents Aeronca LC CF-BAT from Gilbert Aero Service, Vancouver Airport

Becomes a member of Vancouver's Flying Seven club of women air pilots

Helps to organize Vancouver branch of the Chinese Red Cross

Makes first public address to two thousand members of the Women's Canadian Club

Addresses UBC French students and Alliance Française in French language

1942   Travels to Victoria, B.C.; addresses Victoria Women's Canadian Club

Achievements noted in Britain's *Flight* magazine

Addresses Vancouver Local Council of Women & Natl Council for Democratic Rights

Rallies Vancouver contingent of Free French on Bastille Day

Becomes first woman invited to address Vancouver Junior Board of Trade

Uncle Wei Daoming, husband of Zheng Yuxiu, is appointed Ambassador to USA

Hanying Describes China to Vancouver Women's School of Citizenship

Addresses University Women's Club on women's role in postwar reconstruction

Departs on four-month speaking tour of Eastern Canada via TCA

Addresses women's groups, Free French, & RCAF Women's Division in Ottawa, ON

Attends launching of first made-in-Canada PBY aircraft, Saint-Hubert, PQ

Speaks to cercle des femmes canadiennes in Québec City

Addresses variety of groups in Montréal, PQ

Received by mayor of Montréal; signs *Livre d'or*

1943   Wearing CAF uniform, attends opening of Canadian Parliament in Ottawa

Makes whirlwind tour of Toronto, ON, for Chinese War Refugees Relief

Returns to Vancouver

Madame Song Meiling visits Ottawa; her retinue includes Zheng Yuxiu

Brother Zheng Yun dies in airplane crash

An ailing Hanying turns down invitation to speak to Vancouver Jr. Board of Trade

September 7 – dies in Vancouver of tuberculosis

Funeral with full military honors given by RCAF; burial in local cemetery.

ENDNOTES

INTRODUCTION

1 Sterling Seagrave, *The Soong Dynasty* (New York: Harper & Row, 1985), 387.

2 Ibid., 315.

Part 1: HILDA YAN (颜雅清): LIFE OF THE HEART

2. LIBERAL STRAINS

1 Hilda was rather cavalier about her birth date, and when asked to supply it, provided a variety of dates. According to her grandson, in the late 1960s she said that she had consulted a reference book and found out that she was born on January 17 according to the Gregorian calendar, and her family celebrated her birthday on that date until her death. She never mentioned the year, although her son had '1904' put on the grave marker. Her death certificate states that her birth date was November 29, 1905. Hilda was also accustomed to taking anywhere from five to ten years off her age.

2 At this time, the Yans were the only family in China all the members of which had received their education overseas. This included the boys' sister, Julia Yan (Yan Qinglian), who took a post-graduate course in the United States at the Virginia Female Institute, Staunton, Virginia. Julia graduated in about 1904.

3 The Shanghai natives were the Misses Quong Han and Yong-hing Lee. Rye Seminary was later known as Rye Country Day School. Coincidently Rye, NY was also the birthplace of George Putnam who would one day marry American aviatrix, Amelia Earhart.

4 "Connecticut Girls Take Part in College Affairs," *Hartford Courant*, March 19, 1923.

5 The State of Connecticut authorized the College to grant degrees. Hilda was lucky she attended Yali when she did. The school had only begun to allow the registration of women students in 1922, and three years later, it was obliged to turn them away due to housing difficulties. (In 1928, Yali received funding to build a women's dormitory, and then began a fresh campaign to recruit women students.) In 1926, the year after Hilda's graduation, the school temporarily closed its doors when revolutionary unrest drove the teachers away from the campus.

6 Edward H. Hume, *Doctors East Doctors West: An American Physician's Life in China* (New York: W.W. Norton & Co. Inc., 1946), 265-66.

7 Ibid., 266. By 1927, all Americans had withdrawn from Yali and Hunan province as the political unrest increasingly put their lives in danger.

8 Hilda Yen Male, South Norwalk, CT, to Rachel A. Dowd, Recording Secretary, Yale-in-China Association, New Haven, CT, March 20, 1955; Yen, Hilda (1950-1956); Yale-in-China Series II, New Haven Office Subject Files, 1901-1975; Yale-China Association, Record Unit 232; Manuscripts and Archives, Yale University Library, New Haven, CT. Her Yali teachers were Dr. Woodbridge Bingham, Mr. C. Lester Walker, Rev. William J. Hail (Dean), Mr. Daniel S. Sandford, Dr. Kenneth Rose and

Francis S. Hutchins. George D. Vaill, Executive Secretary, Yale-in-China Association, New Haven, CT, to Hilda Yen Male, South Norwalk, CT, March 29, 1955, Ibid.

9   The Shanghai Women's Club, often criticized for being too 'high hat' and exclusive, had its origins as a committee of women organized by Dr. C.T. Wang to entertain a foreign goodwill mission to China in 1919. By the 1930s, it had become an activist organization, promoting social welfare and raising civic and national consciousness. It also liaised with twenty or so Shanghai women's organizations, both foreign and Chinese, to promote civic improvement projects. During the war of resistance against the Japanese, the Shanghai Women's Club became active in war relief, comforting the wounded and caring for refugees.

10 In the mid-1930s, Jiang Qing, who enjoyed some fame as a movie actress, moved to Shanghai and became associated with the YWCA. She taught singing, acting and reading to its poorest members. It is said that, in 1934, the Y posted bail for her when she was arrested for being an activist.

11 Kong was one of the richest men in China, and was married to Song Ailing, sister of Mesdames Chiang Kai-shek (Song Meiling) and Sun Yat-sen (Song Qingling). A very personable fellow, nevertheless Kong was regarded by some as having a poor grasp of financial matters, a decided handicap for a Minister of Finance, and it is likely that his Ministry was propped up by his personal secretary, P.T. Chen. Ironically, acting on a postwar tip that Dr. Kong had illegally benefited by a specious bond scheme, P.T. conducted a personal investigation of his boss's financial dealings and discovered several irregularities. These were reported to Kong's brother-in-law, Generalissimo Chiang Kai-shek, but apparently no punitive action was taken.

12 When the school was bombed by the Japanese in 1932 and classes moved temporarily into St. John's University, Yan Fuqing once again started from scratch and worked unceasingly to rebuild his school. The government was only able to allocate 160,000 Yuan for its reconstruction, while the actual cost was projected at one million. Yan personally raised the additional amount.

3.   LIFE UNDER THE SOVIET STAR

1   Yan Huiqing, *Yan Huiqing Ri Ji* [The Diaries of Yan Huiqing] Shanghai shi dang an guan yi. (Beijing: Zhongguo dang an chu ban she, 1996), February 16, 1935.

2   On February 19, 1935, Yan Huiqing reports in his diary that his wife declared her opposition to Hilda's going to a foreign country. This was a surprising outburst from a woman who had once lived in France for several years in the company of her diplomat brother. It was there that she learned to speak and write the French language, and her cosmopolitan upbringing was one of the reasons Yan Huiqing considered her a suitable life partner. Ibid., February 19, 1935.

3   "Charming Hostess," *North-China Daily News*, February 19, 1935.

4   At the Moscow Film Festival, *Song of the Fisherman* or *Yu Guang Qu* (1934) won an award. Produced at Lianhua studio and directed by Cai Chusheng, it was the first Chinese film to win a prize outside of China. Choi Kai-kwong, director, & Law Kar, script. *Lai Man-wai: Father of Hong Kong Cinema*. DVD. Feature-length docu-

mentary. Hong Kong: Dragon Ray Motion Pictures, Ltd., 2001.

5   Among those reported to have traveled to Moscow were Dr. Chiao Hsiang-tsung, Yan Huiqing's personal physician; Mr. and Mrs. K.Y. Chow, delegates of the Chinese film industry; Mr. Chang Peng-chun, theater educator; Mr. Yu Shang-hang, dramatist; Mr. C.Y. Chow, manager of the Star Motion Picture Company; M. Wu Kang, staff member of the Embassy in Moscow; Mme. Wu Nanru, wife of the Chinese *charge d'affaires* in Moscow; Mme. Hsu Tseng-nien, wife of a Chinese consul-general in Russia; and M. Tien Kwan-chi, Chinese consul-general in Vladivostock, and his wife. "Group of Prominent Chinese Departs for Russia via Vladivostock," *China Weekly Review*, February 23, 1935.

6   While they were traveling through Russia, they received word that Ruan Lingyu, China's most famous movie actress, had committed suicide on March 8, 1935. Ruan's death was widely mourned, but with her passing, Butterfly Wu (Hu Die), then en route to Moscow, became the undisputed foremost star in the Chinese movie pantheon.

7   Anthony Eden, *The Eden Memoirs: Facing the Dictators* (London: Cassell, 1962), 145.

8   Hu Die was appearing in *Zi Mei Hua* at the Moscow International Film Festival.

9   Yen Hui-ch'ing, *East-West Kaleidoscope, 1877-1946: An Autobiography* (New York: St John's University Press, 1974), 212-3.

10   Yan, *Yan Huiqing Ri Ji*, May 4, 1935.

11   The First Committee of the Sixteenth Ordinary Session of the Assembly was chaired by M. J. Limburg of the Netherlands, and the Chinese delegates to this Committee were listed as His Excellency Quo Tai-chi, Liang Lone (substitute); Liu Chieh (substitute); and Hilda Yan Chen (substitute). League of Nations, Assembly, *Minutes of the First Committee* (Geneva, 1935), 6.

12   Ibid., 33-34.

13   "Women's Voice: Madam Hilda Yen Chen's Speech at Geneva," *Hong Kong Telegraph*, Sept. 20, 1935.

14   Zheng was the aunt of aviatrix Zheng Hanying, and the aunt of Zheng Baifeng, who was the ex-husband of aviatrix Li Xiaqing.

15   The Chinese delegates to the 1935 League of Nations assembly were: Son Excellence le docteur W.W. Yen, Ambassadeur à Moscou; Son Excellence M. Quo Tai-chi, Ambassadeur à Londres; Son Excellence le docteur V. Hoo Chi-tsai, Envoyé extraordinaire et Ministre plénipotentiaire à Berne; Secretaire general—Secretary-General: Son Excellence le docteur Hu Shih-tse; Suppléants—Substitutes: Son Excellence M. T.Y. Lo; Son Excellence M. Wunsz King; Son Excellence le docteur Tsien Tai; Délégués adjoints—Assistant Delegates: M. Liang Lone; M. Hsiao Chi-Yung; M. Wu Nan-Ju; Conseillers techniques—Experts: Le docteur K.S. Weigh; M. Tan Pao-Shen; M. Liu Chieh; M. Chen Ting; M. Lou Che-Ngan; M. Pao Hua-Kuo; Mme. Hilda Yen Chen; M. Fang Paotchung; M. Yu Kien-Wen; M. H.C. Sung; M. Hsieh Ching-Kien; M. Yen Youngson; M. Woo Kwang-han; M. C.Y. Cheng; M. F.C. Tien; M. Tsao Kou-pin. League of Nations, Assembly, *Records, Index* (Geneva, 1935).

16   Mona Yung-ning Hoo, *Painting the Shadows: The Extraordinary Life of Victor Hoo* (London: Eldridge & Co., 1998), 33.

17 Yan, *Yan Huiqing Ri Ji*, March, 8, 9 & 15, 1936.

4. SEXUAL SLAVERY AND THE LEAGUE OF NATIONS

1 *Ling Long*, no. 291, (1937), 1908.

2 "Men and Events: To facilitate research…" *China Weekly Review*, September 12, 1936.

3 Song Meiling was the first woman to serve on the Chinese Child Labor Commission. This body was linked to the League of Nation's International Labor Office.

4 Shortly after it was built in the early 1920s, the *Carlotto* became the first Italian naval vessel to steam up the Yangtze to Chongqing. Six years after Hilda dined on its decks, its crew scuttled the boat to avoid its falling into the hands of the enemy, but the Japanese raised her from the riverbed and refitted her. In the early 1950s, she saw service under the government of the People's Republic of China.

5 "Two Women Attend Conference," *North-China Daily News*, January 14, 1937.

6 Just four months later, Amelia Earhart flew into Bandoeng on June 21, 1937 as part of her round-the-world flight. She rested there for three days before tackling the remainder of her tour. Less than two weeks later, the aviatrix was reported missing and presumably lost somewhere over the Pacific. Her fate has not been satisfactorily determined.

7 China's other delegates included Mr. Far-san T. Sung, the Chinese Consul-General in Batavia and his wife; Miss Kwang Jui Wu of the Hsiang Shan Children's Home in Beijing; Mr. Hsiung Hsi-ling, former Premier of China, and his wife, who were representing the Chinese World Red Swastika Society; and Dr. H.C. Chen. The Conference ran from February 2-15. Association for Moral and Social Hygiene in India, *Notes on the Conference of Central Authorities in Far-Eastern Countries Convened by the League of Nations, at Bandoeng, Java, in February, 1937* (Delhi: Delhi Printing Works, May 1937); *North-China Herald*, March 10, 1937, p. 412.

8 Hilda presented the following statistics to the Fourth Meeting of the Conference of Central Authorities in Eastern Countries on February 5, 1937:

- It is estimated that there are about fifty Japanese and Korean brothels in the Settlement, the majority being located in the Hongkow district.

- According to the French report, there does not exist a single foreign brothel in the French Concession. There is evidence, however, of extensive casual prostitution.

- There are approximately one thousand, non-Chinese prostitutes in the International Settlement and probably half of this number belongs to the Slavonic race.

- The French authorities estimate that there are 270 clandestine prostitutes operating in the French Concession. The majority of these women has parents but the latter are sometimes out of employment or receive inadequate salary to assure their existence.

- There are thirty-one licensed dance-halls in the International Settlement and eighteen registered and supervised dance-halls in the French Concession, but, according to some independent investigations, there are nearly 100 dance-halls operating in Shanghai.

- Estimates of the number of girls employed as taxi-dancers vary from 2,300 to 5,000. Of these 2,300 dancers, about 96% are estimated to be Chinese, with Russians, Portuguese, Japanese, Koreans, Eurasians, Filipino and Jewish making up the other 4%. This is significant with reference to the position of Russian women who were previously supposed to constitute the majority engaged in this occupation.

- Two opinions taken as to the extent to which these women engage in prostitution give the following percentages:

  -According to one, foreign taxi-dancers engaging in prostitution, about 50%, Chinese 65% to 70%

  -According to the other one, at least 60% of the dancers are either casual or regular prostitutes, no distinction being made between foreigners and Chinese.

League of Nations, Traffic in Women and Children, Conference of Central Authorities in Eastern Countries, Bandoeng (Java), February 2nd to 13th, 1937, *Minutes of Meetings*. IV. Social, 1937, iv, 10 (Geneva: December 1937), 33-34.

9   Association for Moral and Social Hygiene in India, 14.

10 While the Conference was in full swing, Hilda's maternal uncle and brilliant scholar statesman, Dr. Cao Yun Xiang (Y.S. Tsao), died in Shanghai on February 8, 1937 at fifty-six years of age. During his lifetime, he had tried unsuccessfully to interest Hilda in the Bahá'í faith.

11 By the time Hilda's tour of duty in Europe ended, she had visited every European nation but Finland, Spain and Portugal.

12 Yan, *Yan Huiqing Ri Ji*, April 11, 1937.

13 The Special Mission departed Shanghai for London on April 2, 1937 via the *s.s. Victoria*. Some three weeks after attending the Coronation, H.H. Kong and his entourage, including P.T. Chen, P.W. Kuo and Kuangson Young, left London for the 97th League of Nations Council in Geneva, and then made their way to Germany. On June 11, 1937, they met with Hermann Goering in his capacity as Plenipotentiary of the Reich's Four Year Plan, and on the 13th, they lunched with Adolf Hitler at his mountain retreat in Berchtesgaden. On June 16, they sailed in the *Queen Mary* to the U.S. to meet with American political and economic leaders. They set sail for England aboard the *Normandie* on July 14, arrived at Dorchester on July 19, and remained in Europe and Geneva until the end of September. The delegation did not return to China until October 1937. "Dr. H.H. Kung Honored in Belgium and Germany, Leaves Europe for U.S.A.," and "Hitler Receives Dr Kung, and Presents him with an Autographed Photo," *China Weekly Review*, June 19, 1927; "Dr Kung Arrives in London From U.S.: Hopes for Peace in China," *China Weekly Review*, July 24, 1937.

14 Those listed as representing China in the Abbey were Dr. H.H. Kong, who was named Special Ambassador and Chief Delegate to the Coronation of King George VI and Queen Elizabeth of Great Britain; Admiral Chen Shaokuan, Deputy Del-

egate; Dr. Weng Wenhao, Secretary-General; and Counsellors T.K. Tseng, F.Y. Chang, Dr. P.W. Kuo. Also invited were Lieutenant-General Y.C. Kwei, Military Attaché; Rear Admiral S.H. Lin, Naval Attaché; Colonel T.H. Shen, Air Attaché; and Quo Tai-chi, Chinese Ambassador to the Court of St James. "Dr. H.H. Kung Represents China at the British Coronation," *China Weekly Review*, May 15, 1937.

5. A WAR OF RESISTANCE

1   China Ministry of Information, *China Handbook: 1937-1943* (NY: Macmillan, 1943), 333. General Chennault claimed that there were only 91 aircraft fit for combat. Claire Lee Chennault, *The Way of a Fighter: The Memoirs of Claire Lee Chennault*, ed. by Robt Hotz (NY: GP Putnam's Sons, 1949), 38.

2   The groom, Franklin Lieu, was son of wealthy industrialist and renowned philanthropist, O.S. Lieu (Liu Hongsheng). The bride was a recent graduate of the University of Shanghai.

3   Zhang Qianying (Hélène Tsang) was the artistic, raised-in-Paris daughter of wealthy diplomat, Zhang Jingjiang, and one of five sisters known as the 'five golden blossoms.' She made a name for herself as a fashion designer. Born in 1910, and a good friend of both Yan girls, as well as aviatrix Li Xiaqing, she had been retained by Dorothy Yan to outfit her wedding. In 1936, Hélène opened an atelier in Shanghai's Park Hotel and named it 'Tsingyi' for her diminutive. After her lovely gowns began to be worn by Shanghai socialites and the Chinese American actress, Anna May Wong, her business began to skyrocket. Billed as China's first modern dress and gown designer, she relocated to New York City in 1938 where she re-established her design company. In 1946, she married eminent physiologist, Dr. Lin Kesheng (Robert Khoseng Lim), who had been responsible for the introduction of the mobile first aid units of Medical Relief Corps during the Sino-Japanese war. The Red Cross organizations of America and China, and the ABMAC sponsored these units.

4   "Equal Status Clauses Sought by Organization Delegates," *Christian Science Monitor*, November 3, 1937.

5   Chinese delegates to the Fifth Committee included Dr. Tsien Tai, Dr. Victor Hoo, Liu Chieh, Chen Ting, and Mlle. Hilda Yan.

6   League of Nations, Assembly, *Minutes of the Fifth Committee* (Geneva, 1937), 23. Hilda also spoke briefly at the eighth meeting on September 25, 1937.

7   Freda White, "China and Spain Ask for Judgment," *Headway* (October 1937), 191.

8   Yen Hui-ch'ing, *East-West Kaleidoscope*, 258.

9   "Chinese Woman Flies Plane," *Christian Science Monitor*, December 30, 1937.

10   She was also deemed physically qualified to train for a commercial certificate.

11   At the time, Roosevelt Field was one of the busiest airports in America. During World War II, it was used by the military. The airfield was closed in 1951, and its remains lie under a shopping mall.

12   "China Needs Medical and Food Supplies," *Lima News* [Lima, OH], April 29, 1938.

13 O.P. Hebert was the president of Safair Flying School, as well as a one-time representative of the Curtiss-Wright Corporation. He had already tutored at least one Chinese student of aviation, Kar Lee of New York, who, under Hebert's supervision, learned to specialize in aerobatics. Shortly after the commencement of Sino-Japanese hostilities, Kar Lee sold his plane and departed for the Far East to join the Chinese Air Force.

14 Hope Ridings Miller, "Mmes. McNary, Tydings Entertain with 'At Home': Miss Hilda Yen with Miss Wong," *Washington Post*, February 11, 1938.

15 Hilda made one of her first entrees into Washington society at a tea and cakes gathering thrown by the Chinese Embassy on January 20, 1938. There she met John Hall Paxton, second secretary to the American Embassy in Nanjing, who was tottering about on crutches. He was recovering from injuries he sustained as a passenger on the American gunboat, the *USS Panay*. On December 14, 1937, Japanese bombers attacked and sank the *Panay* on the Yangtze River, but Japanese diplomats quickly smoothed over the incident and claimed the strike had been unintentional. On Christmas Eve, Japan tendered a formal apology to President Roosevelt, and it was accepted.

16 Ibid.

17 In 1946, Bishop Yubin (1901-1978) became Archbishop of Nanjing, and in 1969, he was elevated to the post of Cardinal. While he was in Washington during WWII, his credentials included his positions as Vicar Apostolic of Nanjing, Special Envoy of the Chinese National Government Relief Commission, Delegate of the Associated Philanthropic Societies of Shanghai, and Co-Founder and Director of the Catholic War Relief Association in China.

18 "1,500 Unite Here in Mass Peace Plea," *Washington Post,* May 17, 1938.

19 After Miss Matsui, whose real name was Ayako Ishigaki, stood onstage at Hilda's side and urged a boycott of her country, U.S. State department officials so feared for her safety that they provided her with personal protection against possible assassination attempts. In 1940, Miss Matsui wrote the best-seller, *Restless Wave: An Autobiography*.

20 "Chinese War Refugees to Get $5,000 From Benefit Function," *Washington Post*, March 1, 1938.

21 "China Needs Medical…" *Lima News*, April 29, 1938.

22 The 1939 air tours later undertaken by both Hilda and Li Xiaqing would not have been possible without the aid of Friends to China. Others who served on the Washington executive of this society were Mrs. Charles L. McNary, Mrs. Hamilton Fish, Mrs. Sol Bloom, Mrs. Ralph Brewster, Mrs. George Barnett, Mrs. Robert Woods Bliss, Mrs. William L. Breese, Mrs. Mark Bristol, and Mrs. Frederick Brooke. Also involved were Mrs. Dwight Davis, Mrs. John Allan Dougherty, Mrs. Rufus Mather, Mrs. Mason Gulick, Mrs. George Thorpe, Mrs. Gifford Pinchot, and Mrs. Arthur Ringland.

23 The Chinese Women's Relief Association of New York formed a special wartime committee known as the Women's Committee for Civilian Relief in China. Mrs. C.H. Wang also served as its president.

24 Yan, *Yan Huiqing Ri Ji*, March 1-2, 1938.

25 Ronald K. Chen, Berkeley Heights, NJ, email to author, July 9, 2002.

26 Yan, *Yan Huiqing Ri Ji,* April 1, 1938.

6. AID TO CHINA

1 Yan Huiqing also did wartime service as a member of the People's Political Coun-cil. *Biographical Dictionary of Republican China,* eds. Howard Boorman & Richard C. Howard (NY: Columbia University Press, 1967), IV: 52a.

2 *Chinese Year Book* (Shanghai: The Commercial Press), 1937/38, 663.

3 NC-20706, serial number 324. Its wingspan was 32 feet, and its range 340 miles. aerofiles.com

4 While on tour, Hilda announced to reporters that the aircraft was a 'Porterfield-Turner.' For a detailed description of this aircraft, see "Porterfield-Turner 2-place 50 hp Model 50," *Aero Digest,* July 1939, 117.

5 This same naming of the two planes, as well as the similarities of the two women's first names, was likely the reason why the Chinese press wrongly confused Li Xiaq-ing with Yan Yaqing, assuming that they were one and the same person.

7. MAY DAY

1 Miss Yan apparently did not refuel before she left Mobile. Barring mechanical mal-function or a miscalculation of the fuel actually on board, a full tank would have given her sufficient gas to fly about 340 miles. The aerial distance from Mobile to Birmingham is only 216 miles.

2 "Aerial Tour for China Lands Pilot in Hospital," *Montgomery Advertiser,* May 2, 1939.

3 Ibid. She had deep cuts that required numerous stitches. An early report also claimed she had sustained a badly broken nose and two broken teeth. "Chinese Aviatrix Hurt in Plane Crash," *Dunkirk [NY] Evening Observer,* May 2, 1939. Miss Yan's grandson recalls that she had at least one single false tooth, presumably a re-sult of the crash.

4 "Chinese Mercy Flyer Crashes," *San Francisco Chronicle,* May 2, 1939; "Hilda Yen Injured as Plane Crashes," *Washington Post,* May 2, 1939; "End of Goodwill Tour," *Victoria Daily Colonist,* May 21, 1939. The news of the crash that arrived in China was somewhat garbled. The *China Weekly Review,* an American-owned newspaper published in Shanghai, reported on May 6, 1939 that she was seriously injured in the smash-up, and the Hong Kong edition of the *Da Gong Bao* (May 8, 1939) got it wrong altogether, and claimed that Li Xiaqing was the victim of the accident.

5 Yan, *Yan Huiqing Ri Ji,* May 1-8, 1939.

6 "Gov. Dixon Visits Injured Aviatrix: Pretty Chinese Girl Showing Rapid Recovery," *Birmingham Age-Herald,* May 3, 1939.

7 "Miss Yen's Crash a Dramatic Reminder of Her Mission," *Birmingham News,* May 3, 1939; "A Chinese Girl," *Birmingham Age Herald,* May 3, 1939.

8   Hu Shi was China's Ambassador to the United States from 1938 to 1942 when Dr. Wei Daoming suddenly replaced him. Wei was husband of feminist lawyer Zheng Yuxiu, and uncle by marriage of aviatrix, Zheng Hanying.

9   The United Council for Civilian Relief published a list of the worth of one American dollar in China: One Dollar: Will buy enough quinine to cure one person of malaria; Will immunize fifty people against cholera; Will immunize fifty people against the bubonic plague; Will immunize fifty people against typhoid; Will sterilize a day's drinking water for 1000 people; Will provide enough tannic acid for 2000 burn cases; Will feed a child for one month. United Council for Civilian Relief in China archive, in possession of author.

10 "Miss Yen Thinks Russo-German Pact Will Be 'Helpful' to China," *Daily Kennebec Journal*, August 28, 1939.

8. AMERICAN BUREAU FOR MEDICAL AID TO CHINA

1   Dr Xu Zhaodui (Frank Wang Co Tui, 1897-1984) was a physician, surgeon and medical research scientist who, postwar, lobbied for science and technology development in the Far East. Born in Fujian province, he went to the Philippines as a young lad and obtained his B.A. and M.D. degrees at the University of the Philippines. He interned in Chicago, 1923-1925, and went on staff as professor at the NY University College of Medicine. Among his many affiliations, he was a member of the American Association of the Advancement of Science, American Pharmacological Society, Fellow of the NY Academy of Medicine and the NY Academy of Sciences.

2   By 1941, $800,000 had been raised in America and went toward the purchase of much-needed items. The 'wish list' was always in flux, but an inventory of the most urgent requirements was regularly airmailed to the ABMAC via Pan-Am Clipper, and the requested items were transported into China as quickly as possible. One typical cargo that arrived in Chongqing via the Burma Road consisted of truck ambulances, bubonic plague vaccine, and poison to kill the rat population that carried the plague in the first place. The drug, Sulfathiazole, just one year old and dubbed 'the magic bullet' for its curative properties, was also much in demand for the treatment of dysentery and blood poisoning. ABMAC, open letter, typed transcript. February 12, 1941. ABMAC, December 1940-June 1941; United Service to China, Seeley G. Mudd Manuscript Library, Princeton University, Princeton, N.J.

3   Dr. Hume himself was fully involved with China relief, serving as assistant treasurer of the ABMAC, chair of its organization committee, and a member of both its medical committee and needs & disbursements committee.

4   "More of Chungking Bombed," *New York Times*, May 13, 1939; "American Missions Bombed," *New York Times*, May 16, 1939.

5   The United Council for Civilian Relief in China was a union comprised of three prominent Chinese relief organizations: Dr. Xu's American Bureau for Medical Relief to China, Col. Theodore Roosevelt Jr.'s China Emergency Civilian Relief, and Mrs. C.H. Wang's Women's Committee for Civilian Relief in China. Hilda was closely associated with all three organizations. Theodore Roosevelt Jr. became the United Council's National Chairman and he oversaw an army of volunteers who

helped coordinate the organization's efforts. To achieve a degree of coordination among all the Bowl of Rice parties, 800 letters of appeal were sent to city mayors throughout North America, 520 to committee chairmen, over 700 to newspapermen and radio station managers, 256 to editors of religious publications, 2089 to executive heads of local chambers of commerce, 375 to heads of women's clubs, 288 to men's clubs and organizations, and 15 to radio commentators. Communities were advised that Bowl of Rice parties could take the form of dinners, teas, dances, theater parties or any other appropriate activity at the discretion of the local organizers. The first Bowl of Rice events, held in 1938, netted $178,362.37, the total proceeds of which were targeted for relief work in China. United Council for Civilian Relief in China archive, in author's possession.

6   On November 9, 1939, the New York Bowl of Rice event was held at the Hotel Pierre, 5th Ave. at 61st St.

7   The Institute of Pacific Relations grew out of a tentative suggestion in 1919 that representatives of the Young Men's Christian Associations (YMCA) located in the Pacific Rim might wish to hold a conference to promote understanding and peaceful relations. Australia hosted the first meeting on May 31, 1923, but a meeting held the next year broadened the scope of the conference and moved the focus away from the YMCA. The first true meeting of the Institute was held in July 1925 in Hawaii, and was attended by representatives from Australia, Canada, China, Korea, Japan, New Zealand, Philippines and the U.S.A.

At the 1939 meeting in Virginia Beach, Adam von Trott zu Solst (1909-1944) was in attendance as a German observer. Although American authorities suspected him of being a Nazi stooge, von Trott became a participant in the von Stauffenburg Conspiracy that sought to assassinate Adolf Hitler. Von Trott had been to China, and then to America, to seek foreign help with the resistance he was trying to mount against the Nazi leader. However, he received no support and returned to Germany with empty hands. When the attempt to assassinate Hitler failed in 1944, he was executed for his role in the conspiracy.

8   Marcus Mervine, an American observer living in Tianjin, wrote a report entitled, "Japanese Concession in Tientsin and the Narcotic Trade," that appeared in the February 11, 1937 *Information Bulletin* published by the Council of International Affairs, Nanjing. This report claimed that narcotics were being employed by Japan as an instrument of national policy designed to weaken and debauch the Chinese race.

9   The Chinese delegates were delighted to have the opportunity of meeting at this historically significant location, but Hilda was more impressed to learn that they would be staying just sixty miles north of Kill Devil Hill, the site of the Wright Brother's first flight, the thirty-fifth anniversary of which was just weeks away.

10   Yan, *Yan Huiqin Ri Ji*, December 6, 1939.

9.   RETURN TO THE FAR EAST

1   Adet, Anor & Mei-mei Lin, *Dawn Over Chungking* (New York: Da Capo Press, 1975, c1941), 1.

2   Ibid., 9.

3   Yan Huiqing sailed from San Francisco.

4   P.T. Chen also married a third time, but the marriage ended in divorce.

5   Yan Fuqing apparently resigned on account of poor health in mid-April ("Health Administration Director Chosen," *North-China Herald,* April 24, 1940), but a month later, he left Hong Kong for the United States "to study the organization and equipment of the American hospitals with the object of improving Chinese hospitals." *China Weekly Review,* June 1, 1940.

6   Ibid.

7   Yan, *Yan Huiqing Ri Ji,* May 13, 1941.

8   The Chinese title in pinyin was *Mei Zhou Hua Qiao Yi Wan Fan Yun Dong.*

9   "World Leadership in U.S. Hands," *Maryville Daily Forum,* February 18, 1944.

10 He reported that the occupying officer in charge of his detention was a decent fellow who allowed him to go for walks and to visit with his friends. The Japanese did try to tempt him to work with its occupying government, but he stoutly refused. It was during this period of enforced inactivity that Dr. Yan translated into English his *Stories of Old China.* He hoped the book would "enable foreign friends to better understand the Chinese people." He was released on May 5, 1942 and later declared he had no serious complaint to make regarding his treatment. Yen Hui-ch'ing, *Stories of Old China,* translated by W.W. Yen (Hong Kong: Commercial Press, 1974), foreword.

11 "World Leadership…" *Maryville Daily Forum.* In May, Hilda's father had left Hong Kong for Shanghai, where he was importuned by Wang Jingwei and urged to support the puppet regime that was doing the bidding of the occupying forces in China. Wang was considered to be one of the heroes of the 1911 Revolution, but in March 1940, he agreed to be installed by the Japanese as 'premier' of China. For this treachery, he was widely despised as a collaborator. Desperate to prop up his administration, Wang tried to lure respected public figures to join his cabinet, and knowing that Yan Fuqing's support would lend legitimacy and luster to his government, he used a variety of threats and inducements to persuade the eminent physician to enter his service as chief health officer. Yan, however, adamantly refused to cooperate, and spent the remainder of the war years working for the people of China while maintaining as low a profile as possible. The Japanese had underestimated the hatred that most Chinese would harbor for Wang. In the streets, kneeling clay statues were made of Wang and his wife, and passersby were invited to desecrate them.

12 Ibid.

13 The ultra chic Madame Song, or 'La Chang' as she was known in New York and Washington, was one of the world's ten best-dressed women. She was dubbed China's 'Minister of Goodwill' for her charm and personable manner.

14 First Lady, Eleanor Roosevelt, indignantly resigned from the D.A.R., and invited Miss Anderson to perform instead at the Lincoln Memorial. She accepted and sang before an audience of 75,000. The performance was broadcast to a million listeners. In 1944, Miss Anderson received an honorary degree in music from Hilda's

alma mater, Smith College.

15   In February 1943, she was guest speaker at Women's Service Guild of Christ Methodist Church meeting, Park Ave. & 60th Street. Her topic was, 'A Chinese Looks at World Unity.' "To Talk on World Unity," *New York Times*, February 14, 1943.

10.   "COMING OF AGE OF THE ENTIRE HUMAN RACE"

1   Later in life, Hilda also found some measure of serenity through the practice of Transcendental Meditation, or T.M., a path to peace propounded by the Maharishi Mahesh Yogi, a controversial figure who gained international recognition in the late 1960s as guru to various celebrities of the day, including the Beatles. T.M. was touted as a technique for gaining relaxation and eliminating stress, with all the positive accretions, including world peace, emanating from these ideals. This promise proved an irresistible magnet to Hilda, as it did to many others who looked to the East for spiritual guidance during this era.

2   "Peace Depends on Religion, Baha'is Told by Hilda Yen," *Grosse Pointe News*, August 16, 1945.

3   "Chinese Diplomat Attacks 'Loopholes' in Charter," *The Lima News*, July 1, 1945. Within the first five years or so of the establishment of the United Nations, there was a good deal of interest in the need for a revision of the U.N. Charter, but the outbreak of the Korean War took the spotlight off this issue.

4   Ibid.

11.   JOHN GIFFORD MALE

1   From 1943 to 1945, John Male served New Zealand with the Field artillery, 8th Reinforcements, Second Expeditionary Force, and rose from the rank of private to sergeant in Field Intelligence. Beverley Simmons, "Keeper of the Curtains," in *Fairburn and Friends*, ed. Dinah Holman and Christine Cole Catley (Dunedin, Cape Catley, 2004), 131, 134.

2   John Male's first wife was Mabel Walton, by whom he had a son and a daughter.

3   Upon his premature death in 1957, Fairburn was hailed by the writer Frank Sargeson as "one of the most extraordinary men born in the southern hemisphere."

4   Various email communications between the author and Janis Fairburn, Dinah Holman, and Corin Fairburn Bass, daughters of A.R.D. Fairburn resident in New Zealand and Australia, August 2005.

5   "Lost Jewels' Value Disputed in Court," *Washington Post*, May 18, 1949.

6   William Chen received his B.Ch.E. from the Massachusetts Institute of Technology, and his Ph.D. from the Brooklyn Polytechnic Institute. After his sister, Doreen, received her M.D., she studied traditional Oriental medicine and returned to the United States as an acupuncturist. Just as her grandfather, Yan Fuqing, had taken Western medicine to the East, so Doreen brought Eastern medicine to the West.

7   Simmons, "Keeper of the Curtains," 134. The FBI file on Male was based on the testimony of a former Communist party member who "advised that she had heard

subject describe himself as a liberal and progressive. She stated that he was quite openly pro-Russian and had stated that he has always been a socialist, a non-conformist, a person who believes that an artist is a man above all others. Informant stated that MALE does not always follow the CP [Communist Party] line and on occasion has heard him attack Russia." The same report states, "This Informant advised that MALE married HILDA YEN, a Chinese who is from a wealthy family, and was educated at Wellesley College. Informant stated that recently MALE and his wife have joined the Bahai group, an international religious organization." US Dept of Justice, Federal Bureau of Investigation, File: Male, John Gifford. Office Memorandum, US Govt., to Director FBI, from SAC New York, May 19, 1952.

8   Both Henry and Anita Willcox descended from America's so-called First Families. Henry's forebears arrived on the Mayflower, and his Puritan ancestor, William Bradford, was governor of the first colony of New England. Anita descended from Roger Williams, founding rebel of Rhode Island and proponent of the brotherhood of all mankind. After World War II, Henry Willcox became the largest postwar builder of housing in the State of New York, and Anita was a successful magazine illustrator, but the couple fell into disfavor with the State Department when they made an unauthorized trip to Communist China in 1952. Their liberal views (and large personal fortunes) inspired them to support the victims of McCarthyism, and to promote their vision of America as the 'land of the free.'

9   John G. Male Archives, Special Collections Manuscripts Division, Auckland City Library, Auckland, NZ.

10   Simmons, 128.

11   George D. Vaill, Executive Secretary, Yale-in-China Association, New Haven, CT, to the School of Library Service, Columbia University, New York City, NY, July 10, 1956; Yen, Hilda (1950-1956), Yale-in-China Series II. New Haven Office Subject Files, 1901-1975; Yale-China Association.

12.   ENDINGS

1   Ronald Chen, email to author, July 12, 2002.

2   Of the prominent notables that peopled Hilda's life, H.H. Kong, P.T.'s old boss, was buried at Ferncliff in 1967, and a year after Hilda's death, so was T.V. Song. Much later, the cemetery also became the burial site of Wellington Koo (1988) and Song Meiling (2005).

3   Hilda became an American citizen in the early 1960s, and, with her deep pacifist convictions, claimed full right to be opposed to her adopted nation's involvement in the Vietnam War.

Part II: LI XIAQING (李霞卿): PROFILE OF A LEGEND

15. REVOLUTIONARY TO THE CORE

1   Xu Mulan was born Xu Peilan, and Xu Zonghan's birth name was Xu Peixuan. Their father-in-law, Li Qingchun, was from Haifeng, and it is believed he occupied the important post of Haifeng Minister of Customs for the Qing Government.

2   These included sisters, Xu Zonghan and Xu Peiyao, brothers, Xu Shaoqiu and Xu Shenbo, and sister-in-law, Li Peishu.

3   Lee Ya-ching, with Elsie McCormick Dunn, [untitled] (unpublished manuscript. n.d.), 15.

4   Pax Cheng, Hercules, CA, to author, faxed transcription. January 13, 2005.

5   A little more than a decade later, her niece, Li Xiaqing, would visit these same countries to raise funds for China in its war of resistance against the Japanese.

6   It was when the bones of the ancestors were disinterred that the black jade medallion, the existence of which had long been rumored, was discovered adorning the remains of an early Li grandmother. It was removed and so passed down through the ages to successive members of the Li family. Pax Cheng, interview by author, transcribed notes, Hercules, CA. March 1, 2005,

7   Dandan's mother was fragile, but noted for her courage. She and her mother-in-law, Xu Mulan, often risked their lives carrying gunpowder in their quilted jackets for use by the revolutionaries. On one occasion, the women received a dangerous assignment that required their traveling together to Hong Kong to pick up a consignment of identical watches marked with the character 'Liberty.' These timepieces were to be distributed among their fellow-revolutionaries so that, through possession of these watches, they could identify those who belonged to their secret society. They secured the watches without incident and returned by ship to Guangzhou. Preparatory to passing through customs, Mulan and her daughter-in-law secreted the watches inside their jackets, but, as they descended the ship's gangplank, they realized with horror that each watch was ticking loudly. They foresaw their being searched, arrested and forced to endure horrible deaths by torture, but suddenly, Xu Mulan began to laugh uproariously at the remembrance of a street entertainer whom they had witnessed that afternoon in Hong Kong. Noisy behavior was considered most unseemly for a dignified matron of high social standing, and passers-by were doubly shocked when Xu's daughter-in-law also chimed in, but they little knew that the women's raucous laughter was intentional and served to drown out the tell-tale ticking. The ruse succeeded, and they managed to pass through customs without being searched. Lee Ya-ching, with McCormick Dunn, [untitled], 17-18.

8   Dandan was not totally without playmates. She had a young stepsister, Li Biqi (李碧琪) or Betty (Deng), who was an affectionate supporter throughout her life. She also had a stepbrother, Li Jincheng (李金城).

9   Lee Ya-ching, with McCormick Dunn, 6.

16. STAR OF THE SILVER SCREEN

1   A few examples of ruled 'actress notepaper' still survive. The headers of each page feature portraits of popular 1920s Chinese movie stars, one of which is Li Xiaqing.

2   Pax Cheng, interview by author, March 1, 2005.

3   According to Martin, his store was called Mei Zhen Hua Ji. Brian G. Martin, *The Shanghai Green Gang: Politics and Organized Crime, 1919-1937* (Berkeley: University of California Press, 1996), 54. Li Yingsheng lavished his daughter with some of the spectacular jewels that passed through his hands during this period.

4   The title, *yu ji bing qing,* when translated into English (literally, 'pure as jade, clean as ice') was also rendered as *Pure and Noble.*

5   Choi Kai-kwong, director, & Law Kar, script, *Lai Man-wai: Father of Hong Kong Cinema,* DVD. Feature-length documentary (Hong Kong: Dragon Ray Motion Pictures, Ltd., 2001). The company did not return to the civilized comforts of Shanghai until the end of February 1928.

6   The maimed director was Gao Xiping. *Diary of Lai Man-wai* [Li Minwei Ri Ji. Bian Ding Li Xi], collated by Lai Sek, trans. Ma Sung (Hong Kong: Hong Kong Film Archive, 2003), 12.

7   Yuan Xiaojuan, "Di yi ge kua chu guo men de nü ying xing" [Beginnings of a native movie star], R*en Min Zheng Xia Bao,* July 27, 2001.

8   "If you met her, you would take her for a young girl. But on the screen, she is the embodiment of grace, passion and energy…" However, this same reviewer was somewhat dismayed by the length of the feature (3½ hours, including an interlude of song and dance), and recommended that it be edited judiciously before being distributed to the art houses of Europe and America.

    English translation of an excerpt from "Un Admirable Film Chinois: Mu-Lin, amazoné chinoise, incarnée avec un talent prestigieux par Melle Li Dandan," *Le Journal de Shanghai* (clipping, exact date unknown, circa 1928), a copy of which was supplied to the author by Law Kar of the Programming Section of the Hong Kong Film Archive, Hong Kong.

9   *Diary of Lai Man-wai,* 12.

10   Li Minwei notes in his diary: "1/4/1928 - Li Yingsheng marries Xu Yingying at Maiyang Road, Shanghai." Ibid.

11   His misgivings about the finances of the company were well founded. Shortly after he left the partnership, Li Minwei was unable to manage financially on his own and, when pressed by his creditors, was obliged to ask Li Yingsheng to lend him $2,000. Ibid.

12   Yuan Xiaojuan, "Di yi ge kua chu guo men de nü ying xing."

13   *Diary of Lai Man-wai,* 12.

14   "Avenue Pavilion: An All-Chinese Film," *Times* (London), September 23, 1929. There is no evidence that Li Yingsheng brought copies of *Hua Mulan Joins the Army* with him to Europe.

15   Jay Leyda, *Dianying: Account of Films and the Film Audience in China* (Cambridge, Mass:
      MIT Press, 1972), 70. The French transliteration of the names of other two films,
      both directed by Hou Yao, are also given as *Le Poème du Bout du Monde* and *La Rose
      Ressuscitée* which was produced by Li Yingsheng. *Le Cinéma Chinois,* sous la direc-
      tion de Marie-Claire Quiquemelle et Jean-Loup Passek, textes de Geremie Barmé
      (Paris: Center Georges Pompidou, 1985), 12. During WWII, director Hou Yao was
      arrested by the Japanese, and, refusing to admit he was a member of the Resistance,
      was covered with black paint and subsequently suffocated to death. *Diary of Lai
      Man-wai*, 24.

16   Leyda, *Account of Films*, p. 70.

17   "Nü Fei Xing Jia: Li Xiaqing Fang Wen Ji," *Ling Long* 291 (1937) 1908-1903 [page
      numbering runs from right to left]. Translated from the Chinese by Xie Ang, De-
      cember 2003.

18   Zheng Baifeng's birth name was Zheng Yulau.

19   The marriages of eminent diplomats Gu Weijun (Wellington Koo) and Hu Shize
      (Victor Hoo) were arranged by Zheng Yuxiu, but Gu eventually divorced his glam-
      orous and fabulously wealthy wife, Huang Huilan (Huilan Oei). Hu Shize and his
      wife, who did not divorce, were nevertheless unhappy together and, according to
      their daughter, lived a great deal apart. Mona Yung-ning Hoo, *Painting the Shadows:
      The Extraordinary Life of Victor Hoo* (London: Eldridge & Co., 1998). While Zheng
      Yuxiu preferred to arrange 'marriages of state' that would work to the benefit of
      China, she was always conscious that her matchmaking also tended to establish un-
      breakable bonds between her and the betrothed couple, a special relationship that
      she might be able to exploit at some future time. Accustomed to taking advantage
      of personal connections, she sometimes overstepped the mark, as in 1931 when she
      was disbarred by the Shanghai Bar Association for her alleged use of political influ-
      ence in legal cases that fell into her practice. At the time, she was living in Nanjing
      where her husband was serving as mayor of the city.

20   While attending the Sorbonne in early 1920s, Zheng took under his wing a young
      and impoverished overseas student named Deng Xiaoping. The two men corre-
      sponded throughout their lives, even after Deng became leader of the People's
      Republic of China in the late 1970s.

21   Pax Cheng, Weatherford, TX, telephone conversation with author, transcribed
      notes. March 30, 2006.

17. "ISN'T FLYING THE TOP OF EVERYTHING?"

1   François Durafour (1888-1967), who was at Cointrin airfield between 1919 and
      1939, flew air mail in his single-passenger Caudron-G3 (F-ABDO) between Paris
      and Geneva. In 1921, Durafour landed on Mont-Blanc (4,650 m.) in F-ABDO and
      took off again, establishing a world record. Jean-Claude Cailliez, Meyrin, Switzer-
      land, email communication to author. November 26, 2005.

      The Moth aircraft in which Xiaqing flew secondarily and later took her lessons was
      likely de Havilland Tiger-Moth, c/n 5041 (CH-359 / HB-OKA). Cailliez to author,
      email communication. November 23, 2005.

2   Inga Arvad, "Glamorous Flying Ambassadress at Home in Either East or West," *Vancouver Daily Province*, March 13, 1943.

3   The école was manned by two flight instructors, one of whom was 'le capitaine' Marcel Weber (1896-1975), who also managed the Genève-Cointrin airfield until 1937. Tall, strong and energetic, Weber began to teach flight in 1927. His colleague was Charles Bratschi (1907-2004), who succeeded M. Weber as Cointrin's manager. A small man, Bratschi likewise displayed a vibrant energy, and offered his first flight lessons in 1932. Cailliez to author, email communication. November 23, 2005.

4   Li Xiaqing, typed speech, untitled, n.d., 4. In the possession of the Li Xiaqing family.

5   Cheng Naishan, "Li Xiaqing: Cong zhu ming ying xing dao quan neng fei xing yuan," *Shanghai Lady* (Shanghai: Wen hui chu ban she, 2003).

6   *Aéro-Revue*, March 1934. Although she was the first woman to receive a brevet in Geneva, she was not the first to obtain a flying license in Switzerland. J-C Cailliez claims that at least three women earned pilot's licenses respectively in 1913, 1914 and at some point in the 1920s. Cailliez to author, email communication. April 26, 2005.

7   Training aircraft at the Boeing school included Boeing 203 and 81 Trainers; a Stearman Trainer with J6-5; Boeing & Stinson Trainers with Lycoming engines; Boeing 40-C and B's with Pratt & Whitney Wasp engines; Hornets with blind landing apparatuses; a Hamilton 8-place monoplane with Wasp engine; and a Ford tri-motor Transport with 3 Wasp engines (VFR, IFR). William B. Stout, "Aviation Training at the Boeing School," *Aero Digest* (June 1935): 23.

8   Later, she lived much closer to the Oakland aerodrome at International House, Berkeley. She also claimed to have taken a few courses at the Berkeley University of California campus. Nina Varian, "Pretty Chinese Flyer Wins Boiseans' Hearts," *Idaho Statesman*, May 23, 1939.

9   Gregg was one of the first flight instructors in the U.S. Army, and in the early years, he flew out of almost every army airfield in America. In 1916, he won his transport license. In 1923, he worked as a test pilot for an aircraft factory in southern California before he once more returned to teaching flight and took a position at the Boeing School. Shortly after he instructed Xiaqing, he became a pilot for United Air Lines.

10 Xiaqing initially reported that her safety belt had broken or snapped open, but later she may have admitted that she might have forgotten to fasten it. "Chinese Girl Aviatrix Saved by Parachute," *San Francisco Chronicle*, May 16, 1935.

11 Ibid.

12 Chief pilot, Roger 'Tex' Marley, and Lieutenant Harry Sartoris were responsible for her rescue.

13 "Chinese Girl Aviatrix…," *San Francisco Chronicle*, May 16, 1935; and Elsie McCormick, "Notes on the Life Story of Lee Ya-ching," unpublished, n.d. In possession of Li Xiaqing family.

14 The first Chinese member of the Caterpillar Club was probably Mr. Tang Pao-sun, who parachuted from his spinning aircraft at the Central Aviation School in Hang-

zhou, China in the summer of 1933. *Flight*, September 28, 1933.

15 She was also a member of the National Aeronautic Association of the U.S.A.

16 This number, and the feat it represented, was dear to her heart. She would later request its reinstatement in 1938 and 1966 when reapplying for a U.S. pilot's license.

18. RETURN TO CHINA

1 This was an exaggerated claim. Others of her sex had already flown, particularly in South China in the 1920s when private flying had been permitted, but Xiaqing was certainly China's most publicized and highly qualified woman pilot. She was possibly the first to receive government certification. Notably, China's early aviatrixes included the wife of air pilot Bao Huizhi, and Xue Jinhui, wife of celebrity aviator Zhang Huichang, as well as the Misses Wang Guifeng, Zhu Mufei, and Quan Jiyu. (Miss Quan was born in Korea of Chinese-Korean parentage). These women were all flying in China in the 1920s. In 1919, Annie Lee flew in Saskatoon, SK, and Huang Huilan (Mme. Wellington Koo) flew in Europe, as did Yuan Mingjun in the late 1930s. China's prominent aviatrixes in the 1930s included the British-trained Lin Pengxia, Ruthie Tu, Cheh Su-jen and Yang Jinxun, as well as Huang Waicheng, who trained in France and was reported by the press to be the first woman granted a flying license from the Military Affairs Commission ("Chinese Woman Aviator Secures Flying License," *China Weekly Review*, February 16, 1935, 398). See also, "Cantonese Aviators Welcomed in the South," *North-China Herald*, February 16, 1929. As well, more than a dozen Chinese American women were flying in the USA prior to 1940. The following list, compiled by Guan Zhongren and the author, may be incomplete: Mrs. Lu Zuoqia (Anna B. Low); Mrs. Li Peifen née Ou Yangying (Mrs. Frances E. Lee); Gong Louli (Lully Goon); Louise Woo; Aitu Desheng; Zhang Ruifen (Katherine Cheung); Rose Lok (Mrs. Edward N. Jung); Li Yueying (Hazel Lee); Wang Guifeng (Virginia Wong); Zhang Qianying (Hélène Tsang); Ruth Chinn; Li Fenglin (Leah Hing); Cheng Tianxin (Emma Ing Chung); Hop Hee Dunne; and Dr. Margaret Chung. Dr. Maggie Gee took flying lessons in 1942. Guan Zhongren, *Zhogguo Fu Nu Hang Kong Guo Chen* (Canton, China: Guangdong sheng Zhongshan tu shu guan : Guangdong sheng fu nü lian he hui ; [Enping xian]: Enping xian zheng Xia wen shi zu, 1988) 89, 146-7. Mr. Guan was in the process of preparing an update of his 1988 work, but he died in 2004 before it could be published.

2 Li Xiaqing, typed speech, untitled, n.d., 8.

3 Twenty souls were taken up for five-minute flights in the club's two aircraft, named *Fleet* and *National Salvation*. *China Journal*, March 1936.

4 *China Weekly Review*, March 21, 1935. *Ling Long* magazine's announcement of her divorce referred to her, not as Li Xiaqing, but as the actress and aviatrix, Li Dandan. "Yi tan li hun…" *Ling Long* 231 (1936): 930.

5 Pax Cheng, interview by author, transcribed notes. Hercules, CA. March 2, 2005.

6 Peter Doo, London, UK, to Li Xiaqing, Oakland, CA, transcript in the hand of Peter Doo. May 1935. In the possession of the Li Xiaqing family.

7 Among his more lucrative business deals, during World War II, Doo sold barrels of wood oil to the United States where it was used to manufacture wartime explosives.

He and Xiaqing also managed at least one business together.

8 Peter Doo, location unknown, to Li Xiaqing, April 5, 1937, transcript in the hand of Peter Doo, in the possession of the Li Xiaqing family.

9 The first woman to enroll was Yang Jinxun and the second was 22-year-old Cheh Su-jen, but there is no evidence that Cheh continued with her training. In early 1937, thirty students graduated, including Yang, who used to roller skate to her lessons at the aerodrome. Information from Shanghai Public Library's digital library and "Chinese Aviatrix: Second Woman Pupil At Shanghai Aviation School," *South China Morning Post*, July 3, 1936.

10 Adhering to the Chinese method of age calculation, wherein the individual is already reckoned to be one year old on the day he or she is born, the Generalissimo's age included the lunar year for 1887, the year of his birth.

11 "Shanghai Notes: China's Air Effort," *North-China Herald,* October 28, 1936.

12 "Nü fei xing jia: Li Xiaqing fang…," *Ling Long* 291 (1937), 1905.

13 Alternate title of publication: *Gai Ge Zhongguo Hang Kong De Jian Yi = Suggestions to Reform Chinese Aviation.*

14 Apparently, the book was later published and then purchased by Friends of China for free distribution to the Chinese public.

15 Eurasia was a domestic airline company controlled by the Chinese government and co-owned by Germany's Lufthansa whose airline connected China with Europe.

16 Flug-Kapitän Walther Lutz was one of the most accomplished commercial pilots flying in China, and Xiaqing would have benefited enormously from having the opportunity of flying with him. After a fruitful career with Deutsche Lufthansa, for whom he logged 380,000 km, Walther Lutz arrived in China in 1931 to fly for the Eurasia Aviation Corporation, or Luftverkehrsgesellschaft Eurasia, an airline jointly owned by the Chinese Government and Lufthansa. In December 1931, he made a successful test flight from Shanghai to the remote Xinjiang border in the northwest provinces to inaugurate a new route, and, in the process, he discovered from the air a lost and long buried 2,000-year-old city. Prior to the opening of the line, this area was accessible only by a three-month cart and train journey. A few months later, and while flying the same aircraft, he attempted to pioneer the opening of another line to Semipalatinsk, but crashed, wrecking the airplane, yet receiving no injury to himself. On June 13, 1933, he safely ferried the second of Eurasia's Junkers W/34 aircraft from Berlin to Shanghai, helping to inaugurate the new seven-day Europe-to-China air connection. In 1935, he left for to Germany but returned to China in 1936, ferrying one of Eurasia's new Junkers JU/52 tri-motor cabin planes via Athens and India to Shanghai. It was shortly after this time that Xiaqing was given leave to fly with Lutz in the JU/52. In April 1937, having flown over one million kilometres (620,000 km of these in China), Kapitän Lutz was awarded a medal and made Member No. 1 of an new Eurasia club known as "The Select Company of Men Who Have Flown One Million Kilometers." The club was established exclusively to accommodate the honor bestowed upon him.

In 1937, with the outbreak of war in China, flying became dangerous, even for the pilots of commercial aircraft who were supposed to enjoy immunity from aggression. In September 1938, a number of Japanese aircraft attacked a Eurasia tri-motor flown by Lutz and the machine sustained several bullet holes in the wings and gas tank. With fuel streaming from one wing, Lutz increased his speed and out-flew his attackers. He was credited with saving the plane and his passengers. A year later, his luck ran out when, in November 1940, his Eurasia Junkers was attacked again by three Japanese airmen during a raid on Kunming. With his aircraft aflame, he was forced to land in a rice field where his plane continued to be strafed by enemy flyers. The machine was completely destroyed and Lutz received three wounds, one of them in the face. His crew was also injured. In January 1941, he returned to Germany to have his injuries treated by a specialist. It is believed that he survived WWII and continued to fly with Lufthansa.

In December 1941, China declared war against Germany, and confiscated the Eurasia Aviation Corporation. It fell under the sole ownership of China. In 1943, China reorganized the airline as the Central Air Transport Company, or CATC.

17 "Gay Chinese Miss Daring Stunt Flier," *Toronto Daily Star*, September 9, 1941.

18 Ian D. Johnson, *China's First International Airline, the Southwestern Aviation Corporation: Shi Nan Hang Kong Gong Se: or The People's Aviation Company for the Five Provinces* (unpublished, 2004), 21. The SWAC's lines were:

   (1) Guangzhou-Wuzhou-Nanning-Longzhou-Hanoi

   (2) Guangzhou-Leizhou Bandao-Beihai

   (3) Guangzhou-Wuzhou-Guilin-Liuzhou-Nanning

   (4) Leizhou Bandao-Beihai-Hanoi

19 While in South China, she applied for, and received, Hong Kong flying license no. 84 on March 30, 1937. It gave her leave to fly 'all types' of British Flying Machines in the Colony.

20 "Nü fei xing jia…" *Ling Long* 291 (1937), 1905. Translation by Angelo Xie.

21 Ibid. The intrusion of war would cause her dream of flying to Europe from China to remain unfulfilled.

22 Xiaqing's woman student flyer, Yang Jinxun, also applied to become an air force pilot and received a similar rebuff. Two Chinese-American aviatrixes, Hazel Yueying Li and Virginia Guiyan Huang, arrived in Shanghai from Portland, Oregon to join the Chinese Air Force, but were denied the privilege.

   However, Xiaqing was not entirely earthbound at this time. She flew—as a passenger—aboard the personal aircraft of China's First Lady, Madame Chiang Kai-shek, to various centers to help rally the citizenry in support of aviation. Upon the commencement of hostilities, all civilian flying was prohibited.

23 The Belgium Radium Institute furnished the hospital with three doctors, six nurses and an operating room, while the Red Cross supplied the medicines and dressings. Boy and girl scouts, as well as Buddhist monks, acted as stretcher-bearers and continually risked their lives to bring the wounded from the battle fronts to the hospital. Xiaqing helped coordinate the programs that trained men to nurse the soldiers and prepare their food. On average, the hospital cared for two hundred day patients with another twenty arriving surreptitiously by night. The facility was located in the

International Settlement, a supposedly neutral territory, and this stricture meant that all patients had to be smuggled in for treatment. Li Xiaqing, typed speech, untitled, n.d., 9.

24   Pax Cheng, Hercules, CA, telephone interview by author, transcribed notes. January 3, 2005.

25   Elsie McCormick, "Notes on the Life of Lee Ya-ching," n.d.

26   Peter Doo, location unknown, to Li Xiaqing, location unknown, transcript in the hand of Peter Doo. May 15, 1938. In possession of Li Xiaqing family. Canadian-born 'Pat' Patterson was a good friend to Xiaqing, whom he met at the Longhua airfield, and Chen Wenkuan (Moon Chin) reports that before she won her flying license, Patterson took her aloft many times and allowed her to take the controls. As a representative of Consolidated Trading Co. Ltd., Patterson was responsible for selling American aircraft to the Aeronautical Commission and was therefore well known to Madame Chiang who chaired this body. He was also an outstanding pilot in his own right. On October 29, 1936, in honor of the Generalissimo's fiftieth birthday, Patterson traced the Chinese character 'shou' (壽) or 'longevity' in the sky to honor the 'Gimo' (this was a rehearsal for the actual celebrations two days later), and this occasion represented the first time sky-writing in Chinese had been attempted in Shanghai. However, Pax Cheng reports that the 'shou' was an intimate term generally bestowed on the beloved, so the honor actually represented a social blunder.

27   C.W. Wong, or Wang Chonghui, served as minister of foreign affairs from 1937 to 1941. T.V. Song succeeded him. Xiaqing's son Pax Cheng recalls that Wong was affectionately known to his family as 'uncle' (his exact relation is unknown), and despite Peter Doo's assumption that little help would be had from him, the statesman was a staunch supporter of all members of the Li family throughout his lifetime, to whom he rendered extraordinary aid.

28   "Chinese Aviatrix Leaves," *Hong Kong Daily Press*, October 15, 1938.

19. RETURN TO THE NEW WORLD

1   After he came under attack by the Japanese, the pilot of the *Kweilin* brought the aircraft safely down, half on the shore of a river and half in the water, and he ordered his passengers out of the sinking plane. As these civilians fled to safety, they were deliberately and repeatedly strafed by the enemy flyers. It is thought the Japanese had received word that Dr. Sun Fo, the son of modern China's revered founder, Sun Yat-sen, would be on board the plane, and he was likely the target of their depredations. Ironically, Sun Fo was not among the passengers; he had taken an earlier flight by a different airline.

2   One of her fellow-passengers was Catherine Bond, wife of CNAC's organizational manager, William L. 'Bondy' Bond. She was flying on to Washington, D.C. to see her eighteen-month-old son.

3   Several typhoons created general havoc in the Pacific region and complicated the flight. At Guam, Miss Li and her fellow-passengers were obliged to transfer from the *China Clipper* to the *Philippine Clipper* before continuing on to Alameda. The *Phil-*

ippine Clipper had recently encountered troubles of its own. Some 400 miles before it had reached the island, one of its motors had gone dead, a surprising development that suddenly pitched the flying ship close to the ocean. Capt. A.E. Laporte quickly regained control and proceeded to fly onwards on three engines. After a week's layover at Guam to effect repairs, the *Philippine Clipper* was ready once more to transport passengers.

4   These included a letter of introduction from William D. Pawley, aircraft representative and president of the Hong Kong and Shanghai Bank, Hong Kong, and a letter to J.S. Allard, President of the Curtiss-Wright Export Corporation in the U.S. whom she intended to visit, if necessary, to acquire a plane.

5   Xiaqing also expressed her appreciation for the support Miss Wong had given her. "You have always encouraged me to do something in the way of aviation," Xiaqing wrote in the same letter, "and you have always given me such fine support that I am again taking up your good suggestion, this time for the cause of our country." Xiaqing apparently considered Anna May Wong, born and bred in Los Angeles, to be a fellow countryman. Li Xiaqing, Kowloon, HK, to Anna May Wong, Los Angeles, CA, typed transcript. September 6, 1938. In the possession of the Li Xiaqing family.

6   Among the jewels that traveled with her and is not included in this assessment was a necklace presented to her by her father. It came from the hoard of a maharaja, and its central pendant was a ruby the size of a pigeon's egg. During the war, when she was unable to return to China, she pawned the necklace and was able to live off the proceeds for several years. It eventually ended up in a museum. Pax Cheng, March 2, 2005.

7   "Men and Events: Miss Lee Ya-ching, Chinese aviatrix…" *China Weekly Review*, December 3, 1938. However, Xiaqing was not the pilot of the plane. Popular California aviator and barnstormer, Harry Sham, flew her to Los Angeles.

8   "Robinsons Fete Visitor," *LA Times*, December 4, 1938.

9   The seventeenth century Chinese princess, Mirrah (it is more likely she was Indo-Chinese or Indian, and may not have been of royal birth), was kidnapped by pirates who conveyed her to Manila where she was sold in slavery to a ship's captain, Miguel de Sosa. In about 1622, de Sosa brought her to Puebla, Mexico to work as his servant. After her master's death, Mirrah went into the service of a priest. She converted to Christianity and took the name Catarina. An exceedingly pious woman, she apparently had holy visions and performed several miracles. Many folk legends became attached to her memory. Catarina is considered the inspiration for the Mexican 'La China poblana' costume and other national symbols, from the Mexican flag to the Mexican hat dance.

10 Jacqueline Cochran, Indio, CA to Beatrice Edgerly, Tucson, AZ, typed and signed communication, August 23, 1965. Cochran, Jacqueline: Papers 1932-75, General File Series, 1932-1975, Dwight D. Eisenhower Library, Abilene, TX. To Li Xiaqing's delight, she and Cochran traveled at 220 miles per hour. Helen Worden, "Hong Kong Girl Here Plans Flights Across US to Solicit Funds to Aid War Victims in China," *New York Herald-Tribune*, March 18, 1939.

11 In 1946, Pope Pius XII named Paul Yubin Archbishop of Nanjing, but in 1949,

when Mao supporters took the city, the pope ordered him to evacuate to Taiwan. Yubin became an implacable foe of the Chinese Communists who condemned him to death in absentia. In 1969, Pope Paul VI named him a Cardinal of the Roman Catholic Church. Upon the death of the pope in August 1978, Cardinal Yubin journeyed to Rome to attend the pontiff's funeral and to participate in the papal elections. He himself was one of 115 cardinals eligible to be elected as pope, but on August 16, he died in his hotel room of a heart attack. Subsequently, when the newly elected pope, John Paul I, died after only thirty-three days in office, there were rumors that the pontiff's death had occurred under mysterious circumstances, particularly when details of the death were contradictory and several notable Italians were murdered shortly thereafter. In light of these events, Yubin's death was re-examined, but although conspiracy theories abound, no theory of evil doing has ever received official support.

12   The Stinson's registration number was NC-17174, serial # 5155, and it came with a 245 hp Lycoming engine. Its range was 610 miles, ideal for the long hauls she would be making on her tour. However, she did not finish her expedition with this aircraft. At the beginning of June, with only three weeks to go until the end of the tour, she secured a different plane from Walter Beech, a Stinson Racer SR-5E. It was an older, less expensive model with a shorter range, and again, she used her jewels as collateral to obtain the use of it.

13   Worden, "Hong Kong Girl..."

14   O. Kathleen Kohan, "Flying Emissary," *Far East.* vol. 3, no. 3 (March 1940); Varian, "Pretty Chinese Flyer..." Miss Li gave her height as five feet, four inches.

15   "China Woman Flyer Here," *Los Angeles Times,* April 20, 1939; "Petite Chinese Girl Flyer Reaches City," *Vancouver News-Herald,* May 12, 1939; Ruth Taunton, "China Girl Flier Arrives Here to Plead for Aid Against Japanese," *San Diego Union,* April 17, 1939; Varian, "Pretty Chinese Flyer…"

16   Varian.

17   "Dainty Chinese Aviatrix Seeks Aid for China," *Vancouver Sun,* May 12, 1939.

18   Robert Reeds, "Pretty Chinese Girl Flier Likes All Men—To Look At," *Toronto Daily Star,* March 25, 1939.

19   Varian.

20   Sidney Li, Washington, D.C., to Li Xiaqing, Miami, FL, March 30, 1939, transcript typed and signed by the Bishop's personal secretary, Sidney F. Li, in the possession of the Li Xiaqing family.

21   In Portland, Oregon, Chinese American aviatrix Li Fenglin (Leah Hing) was at the airport to meet her plane when Xiaqing arrived on May 6, and to express her sincere wish that one day the two of them might have an opportunity of flying together. Leah Hing, Portland, OR, to Li Xiaqing, location unknown, transcript in the hand of Leah Hing. May 11, 1939. Li Xiaqing family.

22   "Aviatrix Appeals to Salt Lake to Aid Chinese War Refugees," *Salt Lake Tribune,* May 24, 1939.

23   She also made an impressive debut as a stunt pilot. Her role naturally required that she fly an aircraft, and to this end, she was conducted to a small cow pasture ringed

with hills. In size, it was barely eight hundred by three hundred feet, with no margin for error, and she was asked to land and take off from this improvised airfield. Conditions were far from ideal for a 'touch and go,' but Xiaqing acquiesced, and while the cameras rolled, she expertly did the job, three times in all.

24 Sidney Li, secretary to Bishop Paul Yubin, Washington, DC, to Li Xiaqing, Chicago, IL, transcript in the hand of Sidney Li. May 31, 1939. Li Xiaqing family. Mr. Li begins his letter by stating, "I am sorry I was not able to tell you the actual cause of Miss Yen's accident in Alabama through the phone last night as it is such a long story and cannot be finished in a few words…"

25 NC13865, serial no. 9239A. aerofiles.com

26 She had already appeared as a fashion model on October 7, 1938, just a week before she left Hong Kong for America. In company with other society women, she took part in a pageant at the Hongkong Hotel convened by the Hong Kong Women's National Relief Association. The show provided a chronological display of Chinese fashion throughout the ages, and Xiaqing, appropriately clad as The Future, was one of the highlights. "The climax of a highly entertaining evening was reached when Miss [Li Xiaqing], the aviatrix, appeared on the floor in a gown of futuristic design. She was dressed in a streamlined creation of brown with designs of phoenix and dragons, which left the assembly gasping with amazement." Rosette, "Gorgeous Gowns Seen in Mannequin Parade," *Hong Kong Daily Press*, October 8, 1938.

20. FLYING DOWN TO RIO

1 A description of ABMAC is given in a discussion of various China Emergency Relief Committees operating in America, dated February 12, 1941:

"The American Bureau for Medical Aid to China was organized by Frank W. Co Tui [Xu Zhaodui], Chinese scientist, who gives about half his time to it. His Board consists mainly of American medical men of importance and he has an elaborate fund raising activity which he conducts without employment of paid fund raisers, his central device for raising money being the so-called Rice Bowl parties, which are social functions held in large hotels or clubs nationally.

"Theodore Roosevelt, Jr. is one of his active Board members. The Bureau is supposed to have a semi-official link to the Government of Free China and devotes money which it raises to the purchase of medical supplies in this country which are sent into Free China over the Burma Road and elsewhere; they have done a splendid money raising job, apparently an excellent job of getting medical supplies, hospital equipment, drugs, etc. and have thus far, they state, raised about $800,000 in the past year and a half or two years."

ABMAC open letter, typed transcript. February 12, 1941; ABMAC, December 1940-June 1941; United Service to China, Seeley G. Mudd Manuscript Library, Princeton University, Princeton, N.J.

2 Ibid. "Vitamins for the Chinese War Orphans" undated.

3 Kohan, "Flying Emissary."

4 Ruth Nichols reported that she was the next person to borrow the plane for her

Relief Wings program, and she recalled that Xiaqing "was somewhat unhappily familiar with the plane…" Ruth Nichols, *Wings for Life: The Story of the First Lady of the Air* (New York: Lippincott Co., 1957), 273-4.

5   "Li Xiaqing: jiang zuo nan mei fei hang," *Xiang Gang Hua Zi Ri Bao,* March 27, 1940.

6   Guan Zhongren, "Patriotic Aviatrix Li Xiaqing" (translated by Pan Zhongming) *Women of China.* July 1990, 40.

7   Dr. Xu Zhaodui (Co Tui) reported that from January 1, 1940 to November 1, 1940, ABMAC raised $483,255.31. Letter. Dr. Co Tui, vice-president, ABMAC, to Dr. B.A. Garside, Executive Vice President, United China Relief, Inc., December 21, 1940; ABMAC, December 1940-June 1941; United Service to China.

Although the Bowl of Rice parties were responsible for the lion's share of this total, it is likely that Li Xiaqing's lucrative tour of South America would have accounted for a large proportion of that amount. In America, Xiaqing also participated in the Bowl of Rice extravaganzas, lending her undeniable celebrity appeal to the success of these events.

8   China's famous intellectual, Eugene Chen, who was father of Xiaqing's good friend Percy, had been born in Trinidad where he was raised and eventually practiced law before arriving in China, apparently ignorant of any Chinese dialect, to take the country's political system by storm.

9   Guan Zhongren, "Patriotic Aviatrix," 40.

10   Miss McCormick was an American poet and journalist who had lived for some time in Shanghai, and she won a readership as the author of a couple of successful, tongue-in-cheek impressions of the Orient, *Audacious Angles on China,*(1923) and *Unexpurgated Diary of a Shanghai Baby* (1923). For the Li Xiaqing project, Miss Mc-Cormick secured the services of prominent literary agent, Barthold Fles.

21. RELIEF WINGS & UNITED CHINA RELIEF

1   The other Relief Wings women were aviators Jane Hyde and Mercedes Ormston. Ruth Nichols, *Wings for Life,* 273.

2   Ibid.

3   Ibid.

4   Talbot Lake, "Miss Lee Seeks Funds in U.S. To Aid China," *Hayward Daily Review* [Hayward, CA], February 4, 1941.

5   The UCR was composed of the American Bureau for Medical Aid to China (AB-MAC), the China Emergency Relief Committee, the China Aid Council, American Committee for Chinese War Orphans, the Church Committee for China Relief, the American Committee for Chinese Industrial Cooperatives (Indusco, Inc.), and the Associated Boards for Christian Colleges in China (ABCCC).

6   In tone and style, the fragmentary account that exists closely resembles the nostalgic early chapters of the biography of her ex-husband's aunt, Zheng Yuxiu. Entitled *A Girl From China (Soumay Tcheng),* Zheng's book was written by Bessie Van Vorst in 1926, and first appeared in the French language before it was translated

into English.

7   "Chinese Pilots Called Better Than Japanese," *Vidette-Messenger* [Valparaiso, Indiana], June 20, 1941.

8   Lee Ya-ching, with McCormick Dunn, 6-7.

9   One young Chinese Canadian girl who was fascinated to witness her operatic performance was Patricia Lee of Toronto, a future aviator and a member of the Ninety-Nines International Organization of Women Pilots. She would also become a volunteer co-pilot for HopeAir, a charitable organization dedicated to arranging air transportation for Canadians in financial need who require medical treatment or diagnosis not available in their home communities. Patricia Lee, Toronto, ON, telephone interview by author, transcribed notes, January 9, 2003.

10 Marian Cadwallader, Director of the UCR's Speakers and Entertainment Department, to Mr. Mueller, January 19, 1942, office memorandum. Lee Ya-ching 1942-1944; United Service to China Archives, Seeley G. Mudd Manuscript Library, Princeton University, Princeton, N.J.

11 The Aeronca 65LB had registration number NC-36631 and serial number LB 16711. It had a 65 hp Lycoming engine. According to the factory production logbook, this particular aircraft was completed on September 11, 1941. John Houser, Aeronca, Inc., letter to author, August 30, 2002.

12 As part of her test flight, she flew to Mitchel Field at Mineola, Long Island, to watch a football game for China relief played between the troops of Fort Monmouth and Fort Hancock. Before she left, Xiaqing signed a form releasing the UCR from any liability in the event of an accident while flying the Aeronca.

13 UCR office memorandum. Robert Hamill of Kneeland Moore, to Messrs B.A. Garside and Douglas Auchincloss, UCR, October 21, 1941. Financial: Aeronca Airplane, 1941-1943; United Service to China Archives.

14 She more or less stopped using the Aeronca to get around. Flights of more than fifty miles from the home hangar required the submission of a mountain of registration forms and the acquisition of expensive insurance policies. Despite the munificence of the gift, the maintenance and housing of the aircraft became a financial burden. The UCR decided to sell it and donate the proceeds to China relief. At the end of April, the Civil Air Patrol tendered an offer to buy the aircraft for $1,100, but the UCR turned it down when Xiaqing advised that the offer was too low. Meanwhile, the UCR continued to pay exorbitant hangar and mechanical upkeep fees (there is some evidence that they were being gouged by the hangar owner), and probably wished they had not taken her advice. In December 1942, Edgar H. Bauman of Trans-America Airports Corporation bought the aircraft for $1,250. Xiaqing had logged some fifty hours of flight time in the aircraft.

15 Marian Cadwallader, to Li Xiaqing, typed schedule. August 27, 1942. Lee Ya-ching 1942-44; United Service to China Archives.

16 Marian Cadwallader to Li Xiaqing, typed memorandum. August 28, 1942. Lee Ya-ching 1942-44; United Service to China Archives.

17 This was not the only time that an artist sought to capture her likeness in a three-dimensional format. Ruth Yates created a plaster cast of her head in severe Art Deco

360

style, and it was shown at the Women Artists Show held in Boston, MA in January 1942. Likewise, Boris Lovet-Lorski, a Lithuanian American sculptor, also cast her bust in white plaster.

18   Marian Cadwallader to Li Xiaqing, typed schedule. September 14, 1942. Lee Ya-ching; United Service to China Archives.

19   Leonard Lyons, "Broadway Signboard," *Washington Post*, August 29, 1942.

20   As the subject of War Gum card number 101, printed by Gum Inc. of Philadelphia, Xiaqing was dubbed 'China's First Girl Pilot.' "The first girl to win her pilot's license from the Chinese government," noted the card, "was Miss Lee Ya-ching. She came to America as a special Ambassador of Good Will. Her mission was one of making appeals for the relief of China's war refugees. With jet black hair, Miss Lee, whose full name means 'Glow-After-Sunset,' flew from city to city to tell her story: There are more than two million refugee children in China. Forty-seven orphanages have already been established but the needs are still very great. Her flaming red monoplane is called 'The Spirit of New China.' She admires and somewhat resembles her great leader, Mme. Chiang Kai-shek. Miss Lee's next assignment is to return to her homeland on a mission of mercy to fly medical supplies to the interior of China."

21   Arvad, "Glamorous Flying Ambassadress at Home..." *Vancouver Daily Province*, March 13, 1943.

22   "Flying for Victory," *True Aviation Picture-Stories*, no. 3 (March/April 1943).

23   While in New York, Chen Wenkuan visited fellow Chinese-American pilot, Chen Ruidian (Art Chin), of Portland, Oregon, who was shot down in flames and sustained horrific burns while flying for China. Chen Ruidian was undergoing skin grafts at Columbia-Presbyterian Medical Center's burn unit courtesy of the Chiang Kai-sheks. The community of Chinese pilots was a relatively small one, and Xiaqing also knew and visited Chen.

24   Moon Chin (Chen Wenkuan), interview by author, transcribed notes. Hillsborough, CA, February 28, 2005.

25   "No. 1 Girl Flyer: Miss Lee Ya-ching," *Chicago Tribune*, March 30, 1943.

22. SOUTH AMERICA REPRISED

1   In her 1939 contract with Walter Beech, this brooch was one of the jewels she agreed to put up for security in case of loss or damage of her borrowed aircraft. The previous year, it had been assessed and described as: "Platinum and Diamond, long effect, with Airplane Wings paved with diamonds, set with 1 Center Diamond, and 10 Diamonds in Round Cluster Center, 38 Diamonds in Wings, Old Mine Cut." It was assessed at $375.00. J.C. Fergusson, Los Angeles CA, typed assessment. November 28, 1939. Li Xiaqing family.

2   Before embarking, she learned of the death of her great aunt, Xu Zonghan, on March 8, 1944. This intrepid woman had also toured South and Central America on China's behalf.

3   She would have flown via one of Cruzeiro do Sul's four DC-3s that the president

had purchased in America in 1943. Before that date, Cruzeiro was a German company going by the name Syndicato Condor. WWII interfered with the directors' operation of the firm and they withdrew, handing it over to the Brazilians. American DC-3s duly replaced the German Junkers aircraft, but many felt this was a cosmetic change only, and the company was suspected of having deep ties to the Gestapo.

4   "Lee Ya-ching: Luz de Crepusculo," *A Noite* [Rio de Janeiro], 11 July 1944. According to Seagrave, Song Meiling and her sister Ailing were also in Brazil in July 1944, taking a rest cure on Brocoió, one of the islands in Rio de Janiero's harbor. Xiaqing likely rendezvoused with them at this time. Seagrave, *The Soong Dynasty*, 413.

5   Ibid.

6   Alex Curiel, of Morris E. Curiel & Sons, S.A., Caracas, Venezuela, to Li Xiaqing, typed letter. May 3, 1944. Lee Ya-ching, 1942-1944. United Service to China Archives.

23. BLUE SKIES

1   J.H. Oldham, American Vice-Consul, to US Air Transport Command, US Air Naval Transport Service, typed and signed Priority Certificate. April 29, 1946. Li Xiaqing family.

2   "Li Xiaqing nü shi: jia ji biao yan," *Xiang Gang Gong Shang Ri Bao*, September 12, 1958.

3   Pax Cheng, Hercules, CA, interview. March 2, 2005.

4   Xiaqing's first-born daughter, Mulan, married Herman Wolfson of Connecticut.

5   With the Communist takeover of the Mainland in 1949, Du Yuesheng fled to Hong Kong, but he knew he was dying. He summoned Li Yingsheng and asked his old friend to take possession of his remains and return them to China for burial when the Nationalist regime re-took control of China.

6   Li Yingsheng was tipped to receive a knighthood from the Queen until it was rumored that he had collaborated with the enemy during WWII. Li was unavoidably required to work with the Japanese occupiers of the Colony, as were all persons of high office, but as a devoted Chinese patriot, he steadfastly refused to collaborate. Nevertheless, the rumor stuck and Li was denied the honor. Pax Cheng, Hercules, CA, interview. March 2, 2005.

Part III: ZHENG HANYING (郑汉英): UNEASY SPIRIT

24. INTRODUCTON

1   Blanche E. Holt Murison, "Hanyin Cheng of China," *Saturday Night* (November 28, 1942), 30.

25. ORIGINS

1   The *South China Morning Post* stated that Jessie and her brother, Zheng Yun, "belong to a family with no other children, and which therefore can justly claim to have given both to the service of China's further aviation development." ("Chinese Girl Flier: First to be Aviation Student in This Colony," *SCMP*, February 6, 1937). However, after she went to Canada, Jessie declared to reporters on at least two occasions that she had four brothers: "Her four brothers are also in government service (one in the consulate at San Francisco) and they, too, took the oath of service for the duration." (Ben V. Williams, "We Want To Go To China," *Forward*, vol. 9, no. 11 [August 1942]: 3); and also, "The Chinese airwoman who received her commission as a Flt.-Lieut. from Generalissimo Chiang Kai-Shek has four brothers, the one in the air force, two with the Chinese government and one is a Chinese Consul in the United States" ("Flt. Lieut, Hanyin Cheng Predicts Great Future for Chinese Women in Aviation," *Lethbridge Herald*, November 30, 1942). Pax Cheng recalls a 1945 meeting with a cousin named Cheng Bao Huao who was serving at the Chinese consulate in San Francisco, but it is not known if this was Jessie's brother. In her memoirs, Jessie's aunt, Zheng Yuxiu, writes that when she evacuated to Chongqing during WWII, "Some of my relatives were with me, notably one of my brother's sons. When my second brother died some years earlier, I had undertaken to care for his children—four boys and two girls. (One of them was in the Law School of the University of Shanghai until that city had to be evacuated, and another one has been in the Consulate-General at San Francisco for some time.) This particular boy had been crazy about flying since he was a young sprout of eighteen." Mme Wei Tao-ming, *My Revolutionary Years* (NY: Charles Scribners' Sons, 1943), 225. Zheng Yuxiu goes on to recount that (like Zheng Yun) her nephew became a commercial pilot before the war and then joined the Chinese Air Force. Aside from the mention of two girls in the family, Zheng Yuxiu's account dovetails with Jessie's. In accordance with traditional Chinese custom, it is also possible that Jessie's father had at least two wives and two sets of children.

2   Tang Dongmei, *Chuan Yue Shi Ji Cang Mang: Zheng Yuxiu Chuan* (Zhong guo she hui chu ban she, 2003), 4-7.

3   Ibid., 353. On January 26, 1912, Peng Jiazhen assassinated Liang Bi, general of the palace guards and a royal court hardliner, by means of a bomb, and voluntarily lost his own life in the attack. This assassination is regarded as one of the precursors of the emperor's abdication, and Peng is considered a martyr of the Revolution. Bessie Van Vorst (McGinnis), *A Girl from China (Soumay Tcheng)* (New York: Frederick A. Stokes Co., 1926), 138-141.

4   Zheng Yuxiu was clearly a persuasive character and she got results. Upon addressing a girls' school in China on the eve of her return to post-graduate studies in

Europe, she so inspired the young women in her audience that they resisted the protests of their parents and sailed with Zheng to Paris in order to continue their education abroad. Zheng also undertook to supervise them for the duration of their studies overseas.

5   It is not known for certain what degree Jessie obtained, or if she continued her university education upon her arrival in China. An article in the *South China Morning Post* stated that she held a bachelor's degree in science (*SCMP*, February 3, 1937), but when she began her speechmaking in Canada, several reports claimed she held a Bachelor of Arts, and at least one declared she held a Master of Arts degree in law. It is unlikely that she had time to earn a graduate degree; the confusion may have arisen because the University of Paris used the term *maître* or 'master' to describe its undergraduate degree holders.

26. WINGS FOR CHINA

1   "Fashion Show Tea," *North-China Herald*, November 11, 1936.

2   "Flt. Lieut. Hanyin Cheng Predicts…," *Lethbridge Herald*, November 30, 1942.

3   "Aviation Progress in Hongkong," *North-China Herald*, June 27, 1934.

4   Lord Malcolm Douglas-Hamilton was not the eldest son. His brother, Lord Douglas Douglas-Hamilton succeeded to the title in March 1940.

5   Others also availed themselves of the RAF expertise on offer at the Far East Flying Training School. The Guangzi (Kwangsi) Air Force, one of the pre-war air forces of the southern provinces, had its own aviation school in Liuzhou, but some of its cadets took preliminary flight instruction at the FEFTS. "Canton Air Force: Demonstration of Latest Tactics," *Hong Kong Daily Press*, September 11, 1934.

6   Hong Kong Historical Aviation Association, *Wings Over Hong Kong: An Aviation History, 1891-1998*, Cliff Dunnaway, ed. (HK: Pacific Century Publishers, 1998), 110.

7   "Hong Kong Defense," *Flight,* January 9, 1941.

8   Two outrageous incidents reinforced the potential dangers involved. On August 24, 1938, the CNAC's Douglas DC-2 passenger liner *Kweilin* had just taken off from Kai Tak, and was skimming over the Pearl River delta near Macao, when it was deliberately machine-gunned by lurking Japanese aircraft. After the pilot made a forced landing on the water, the Japanese continued to strafe the plane until fourteen passengers, including two women and two children, were killed. Two weeks later, one of the passenger planes of the Eurasia Aviation Corporation also came under fire and was forced down on the Kwangtung-Kwangsi border. On this occasion, there was no loss of life. Despite the hostilities, the two airlines carried on with their operations, but they would fly in and out of Kai Tak only after the sun had set and before it had risen. When the moon was full, the pilots would postpone their flights until clouds hid its light.

9   "Nü Fei Hang Yuan Zheng Hanying: Ri Jian Bei Shang," *Xiang Gang Gong Shang Ri Bao*, August 21, 1937. The news article announcing her invitation to travel north is studded with squares and crosses, as were many news items of the day that alluded to the Japanese invasion. Israel Epstein, editor of the *Hong Kong Daily Press* in the late 1930s, explains the reason for these typographical symbols: "…the Hong Kong

government was very nervous about angering Tokyo. In the Chinese language press of the colony, explicit references to Japanese aggression and war atrocities were not allowed (the forbidden adjective was replaced with an 'X')." Israel Epstein, *My China Eye: Memoirs of a Jew and a Journalist* (San Francisco: Long River Press, 2005), 115.

10 "Nü Fei Hang Jia: Zheng Hanying," *Da Gong Bao*, June 2, 1939.

11 The semi-fitted, below-hip tunic, cut in red gabardine wool and with slightly extended padded shoulders, closed with six gold buttons. It had no epaulettes, but on each upper shoulder-sleeve was sewn a dark patch embroidered with white letters that read, 'China.' The gold wire (bullion) wings patch, applied over the heart, was centered with the 'blue sky, white sun' symbol of Nationalist China. Jessie wore the accompanying navy blue skirt with sheer hose, but alternatively she wore a black skirt that also fell just past her knees, and black hose. For summer wear, she was issued with a white, tailored, below-hip uniform jacket with collar that she wore over a *qipao* and with spectator shoes. The jacket had the same 'China' shoulder-sleeve patches, gold buttons and gold wire wings. When she made her cross-country tour of Canada, she wore a navy blue, knee-length winter coat of heavy wool with gold button closure and sleeves with vent and gold button trim. She pinned a small wings badge to her left collar.

12 Several years later, an equally impressed Mao Zedong would appropriate the Chiang's stone house for his own use, and, from this sylvan setting, would launch his economic initiative, the Great Leap Forward.

13 Mme Wei, *My Revolutionary Years*, 214.

14 Ibid., 215.

15 In 1943, New York-based W.L. Van Dusen, public relations director for Pan-American Airways, expanded on the story of Chongqing's tombstone-reinforced runways in an interview given in Vancouver. He explained why, despite being bombed three hundred times, the unique airport was still able to operate: "The secret is that the runways are made of tombstones. The airport is situated on a small island in the Yangtze River and in the wet season can be high and dry one day and the next day be under 40 feet of water. This caused much trouble until an old Chinaman interested the boys in the tombstones. Well, the first set of tombstones that were laid down cost the company $11 (Mexican) per fong (about 100 square feet). After a year of war in China, the price jumped to $17 per fong. By 1941, says Van Dusen, when trouble with the Japs necessitated night flying and in turn called for longer runways, another 250 feet of tombstones was added making the runway 2400 feet long and that addition was made at a cost of $240 per fong." Later additions were needed, and the original contractor, whose price by then had risen to $1,334 per fong, was persuaded under protest to accept $1,260 per fong. (Jack Meek, "Skylines," *Vancouver Sun*, April 6, 1943) Not long after, a large and more permanent military airfield was constructed at Baishiyi located on a flat stretch of land some seventeen miles of rough road outside of Chongqing.

16 "Chungking Bombed Daily," *North-China Herald*, June 5, 1940.

17 "Chinese Airwoman Tells of Country's Crying Need," *Toronto Daily Star*, February 4, 1943.

18   Emily Hahn, *The Soong Sisters* (NY: Doubleday, 1941), 263.

19   Mme. Wei, *My Revolutionary Years*, 225-7.

20   Guan Zhongren and Patti Gully, ed., *Wu Yi Hua Qiao Yu Zhongguo Hang Kong* [Overseas Chinese from the Five Counties and Chinese Aviation], Yi zhe: Xie Ang. [Translated by Angelo Xie] (Xiao dui: feng ru meng huang jian yun lu zhao jin lu wen cong, 2003), vol. 1, 368.

21   "Pretty Chinese Girl Flier Working Hard for Victory: Flight-Lieut. Hanyin Cheng Has Title of 'Ambassador at Large': On Speaking Tour," *Toronto Daily Star*, February 5, 1943.

27. ROMANCE... AND UNFORESEEN CONSEQUENCES

1   Rosette, "Tea-Dance Season Re-Opens: Beautiful Frocks," *Hong Kong Daily Press*, October 3, 1938.

2   "Nü Fei Hang Jia: Zheng Hanying," *Da Gong Bao*, June 2, 1939.

3   Leigh Seto, son of Wilfred and Patricia (née Lowe) Seto, interview by author, transcribed notes. Vancouver, BC, January 26, 2005.

4   A couple of news articles list one of the chorus members as 'Jessie Chan.' Jessie Zheng was stationed in Hong Kong at this time, and it is likely that this was she. It may be that she and Wilfred met on the set. "Splendid Show at Queen's: A Debutante Goes to Town," *Hong Kong Daily Press*, March 2, 1939; "Another Good Performance: Charity Play is a Distinct Success," *Hong Kong Daily Press*, March 3, 1939. The English-language press routinely provided variations on the spelling of her family name (these included Cheung, Tsang, Tcheng) and even the Chinese press made mistakes, referring to her as Chen (陈).

5   Peggy Lee (née Wong), interview by author, transcribed notes. Vancouver, BC, January 24, 2005.

6   The Short Snorter Club probably had its origins in the British military, and referred to a 'short snort' or alcoholic drink. It required that airmen collect paper currency of the country they had visited and join them together end to end, accordion-style. Some 'snorters' consisted of many bills and stretched to a distance of several feet. When in a bar, anyone could demand that the snorters be produced, and whoever held the shortest length of bills would be required to buy a round of drinks. Typically, fellow passengers who had also made the flight were invited to autograph the bills.

28. ZHENG TAKES VANCOUVER

1   *The Canadians at War: 1939/45* (Montreal: Reader's Digest Association, Canada, 1976), vol. 1, 85-88.

2   The original members of the Flying Seven were Betsy Flaherty, Alma Gilbert, Rolie Moore, Jean Pike, Tosca Trasolini, Margaret Fane, and Elianne Roberge. It is not known if Jessie met Jean Pike, who was working at the Alhambra airport in Oakland, CA, but she knew all the others. The club provided support and friendship for women pilots, and got its start in 1936 when an American women's flying club

refused to grant entry to its members. In 1935, Margaret Fane had lunched with Amelia Earhart in Burbank, CA, and requested that Canada's women pilots be allowed to join the Ninety-Nines, but Earhart demurred, feeling that the Canadians were too few in number and too scattered. When Fane returned to Canada, she became instrumental in forming the Vancouver Flying Seven, which, by 1941, expanded to include women pilots in other provinces. After WWII, the club folded its wings; there were enough Canadian women pilots that gaining acceptance in the Ninety-Nines was no longer a problem.

3   Original members of the Flying Seven in attendance at the Georgian Club were:

-Miss Elianne Roberge, President (licensed PQ, 18 Oct. 1930; commercial PQ, 27 Oct. 1932)

-Mrs. Elizabeth Flaherty (licensed BC, 19 Dec. 1931)

-Mrs. D. Barrett (Rolie Moore Barrett Pierce, licensed BC, 7 Oct. 1935, commercial, 19 Jul. 1939)

-Mrs. Alma Gilbert (née Gaudreau) (licensed BC, 7 Apr. 1934, commercial BC, 26 Sept. 1941)

Subsequent members of the Flying Seven in attendance:

-Miss Beryl Armstrong (licensed BC, 21 Oct. 1940)

-Miss Pat Gray (licensed 25 Sept. 1941)

-Miss Betty Waller, Vancouver

Others: -Miss Margaret Ecker, Vancouver

-Mrs. Victor York, Vancouver

-Miss Rohama Lee, Los Angeles

-Mrs. Victor Fox, Toronto Flying Club

-Zheng Hanying, Hong Kong Flying Club

"Social World," *Vancouver News-Herald,* April 24, 1941; "Women Flyers Are Luncheon Guests," *Vancouver Daily Province,* April 22, 1941.

4   "Chinese Girl Pilot Visiting Vancouver," *Vancouver Daily Province,* April 22, 1941.

5   "Girl Pilots Ask Ferry Job to Aid Air Training Work," *Toronto Daily Star,* August 25, 1941

6   "Flying 'Diplomat' Makes Her First Speech Today," *Vancouver Sun,* October 29, 1941.

7   After the arrival of Chinese gold prospectors and laborers in late nineteenth-century Canada, a clutch of laws were passed to restrict these immigrants' activities. Act for the Protection of Women and Girls (1919), Act to Amend the Qualification and Registration of Voters (1871/1875), Act to Restrict and Regulate the Immigration of Chinese (1885), and the Act to Regulate the Employment of Chinese and Japanese (1897) were just a few of the restrictions imposed on Orientals to ensure they would not prosper, and their numbers would not increase. Under the Exclusion Act of 1923, Canada refused to allow Chinese immigrants into the country, other than students and members of the diplomatic community, until 1947 when

the law was repealed.

8   Vancouver, BC. City Council and Office of the City Clerk fonds – Clerk's Office. *Orientals in better residential districts*. Minutes of the Meeting of the Building, Civic Planning and Parks Committee's Special Committee, February 3, 1941. City of Vancouver Archives, Vancouver, BC.

9   "Orientals Protest: Chinese Would 'Feel Badly' About Restriction, Says Consul," *Vancouver Daily Province*, February 4, 1941.

10   Vancouver, BC. City Council and Office of the City Clerk fonds – Clerk's Office. *Consuls*. Letter from Chunhow H. Pao, Chinese Consul-General, to J.W. Cornett, Mayor of Vancouver, February 4, 1941. City of Vancouver Archives, Vancouver, BC. The house in question was located at 5810 Highbury Street, Vancouver, BC. The bride, like her husband, was a graduate of the University of British Columbia, and the young couple received support from the University Women's Club, which sent a letter to city hall stating that it was unwise, unfair and intolerant to restrict the residence of any race. "Women's Club Objects to Zoning Chinese," *Vancouver Sun*, February 11, 1941.

11   The Aeronca LC, CF-BAT (C/N 2046), was a two-place, side-by-side, low wing monoplane built in 1936-37 as Aeronca's answer to the Boeing P-26. With its vivid yellow livery and sporty wheel pants, CF-BAT was a popular favorite at the Vancouver Airport, and it flew locally for many years postwar. While providing a history of CF-BAT, aviation historian, Douglas E. Anderson, describes its special appeal. "As a young airport visitor leaning on the green picket fence, I recall the thrill of seeing that bright yellow monoplane rolling on scoffed donuts over the apron, its propeller ticking over slowly and 'big' radial oblique against a sky forever blue. It was undoubtedly the star of the show with a supporting cast of red and yellow Fleets, gleaming silver Luscombes and high-wing Aeroncas in blue and yellow, green and yellow, black and yellow." After sustaining considerable damage in a ground accident, in 1955 it was donated to Oakalla Prison in Burnaby, BC, to serve out its days as an instructional aircraft for inmates learning aero mechanics. Douglas E. Anderson, "Poor Man's P-26: The Aeronca LC," *CAHS Journal*, vol. 14, no. 4, 126.

12   Unfortunately, the women were not allowed to fly lower than 3,000 feet, and their altitude, combined with a strong wind, drove many of the 'bombphlets' out to sea ("Vancouver Woman Fliers Drop 'Pamphlets' on City, *Vancouver Sun*, June 20, 1940). The City of Vancouver Archives has preserved one of the pamphlets. On September 15, 1939, the Flying Seven put their aeronautical expertise at the disposal of their country. In their letter to Ottawa, they pointed out that two of their members had commercial pilot's licenses, and the others held private licenses. They proposed that, among other duties, they might serve as flying instructors or coast guards. On October 7, Ottawa notified them that their proposal was receiving careful study, but it is recounted that when the government realized the Flying Seven was a club of women, it turned down their offer. Nevertheless, for the duration, the clubwomen did not cease in their efforts to be of some service to Canada in a flying capacity.

13   "Flying Seven: Vancouver Women Pilots Offer to Go Over France—Bomb Enemy," *Winnipeg Free Press, June 15, 1940.*

14   "Women's War Work: Girl Pilots Ask Ferry Job to Aid Air Training," *Toronto Daily*

Star, August 25, 1941.

29. COMMISSIONING

1 In addition, with the establishment of the collaborationist Vichy Government in the south of France, there was some question as to which entity served as the legally constituted government of that country. The Weis wintered in Washington where Wei Daoming served as an Embassy staff person until suddenly, in September 1942, the incumbent ambassador, Hu Shi, was dismissed and Wei was nominated to succeed him.

2 The speeches were entitled, 'China Marches On,' 'Resistance and Reconstruction in China,' and 'China and Canada, Two Great Peoples, One Great Purpose.' A variation on this last title was 'China and Canada, Bulwarks of Democracy.' A popular later speech was entitled, 'Japan—The Weakest Link.'

3 "Day by Day: Aviatrix," *Vancouver News-Herald*, October 11, 1941.

4 Joyce Spring, *Daring Lady Flyers: Canadian Women in the Early Years of Aviation* (Porter's Lake, N.S.: Pottersfield Press, 1994), 100.

5 The jewelry cost CAD $1,975.00. At the time of her death, she still owed $1,033.75 on the gems, plus $89.50 in interest.

6 Madame Chiang's visit to Canada in June 1943 was well documented and included exhaustive descriptions, not only of her attire, but also of her jewels, important accoutrements of the well-dressed woman. "Her jewelry consisted of tiny round earrings of black onyx outlined by tiny diamonds and on her right hand she wore a matching ring," reported the *Ottawa Evening Citizen* on June 15, 1943, and a few days later, "a glittering diamond brooch was fastened to the neck of her dress and as she moved her hand the light caught the smouldering tones of a gigantic sapphire." (*Ottawa Evening Citizen*, June 18, 1943). Media focus on prominent women's gemstones was likely the goad that caused Jessie to invest so heavily in jewels to complement her appearance while on her own tour.

7 Williams, "We Want To Go To China," *Forward*, 3.

8 Ibid.; "Consul Attaché Speaks on China," *Vancouver News-Herald*, October 30, 1941.

9 Mamie Maloney, "In One Ear," *Vancouver Sun*, September 14, 1943.

10 The Chinese War Relief committee was Canada's answer to America's United China Relief, and there were branches located throughout Canada in the major cities and smaller towns. Monies collected would be remitted in pounds sterling to China's Ministry of Finance (and later, care of the Ministry of Finance, to the account of the incorruptible Mme. Sun Yat-sen, Song Chingling). Funds were routed through the Bank of China in New York. Letter from G. Kwong, Vernon Committee for Chinese War Relief, Vernon, BC, to Mr. T. K. Bulman, Vernon, BC, January 5, 1945, transcription typed and signed, copy in author's possession.

11 When China's ambassador to the U.S., the Honorable Hu Shi, made a radio address to Canadians from Vancouver, he declared, "It is a historical fact that Canada was the first power to declare war against Japan. The first day that the Japanese at-

tacked Pearl Harbor, Canada declared war on Japan, more than half a day before the United States declared war." "No Doubt of Ultimate Victory Dr. Hu Shih Tells Canadians," *Vancouver Daily Province*, February 20, 1942.

12 On May 4, 1942, the RCMP removed the Japanese consul, Ichiro Kawasaki (of the famous manufacturing family), his young family and staff from the Vancouver consulate at 3351 The Crescent, and put them aboard a train that conveyed them to New York. From there, they traveled by ship to Lisbon and then Africa where they were exchanged for Canadian consular staff who had been stationed in Japan when the war began.

13 "Woodward Flays Complacency in Board of Trade Address," *Vancouver Sun*, March 21, 1942.

14 Gwen Cash, *A Million Miles from Ottawa* (Toronto: Macmillan, 1942), 35.

15 The reporter estimated her height at five feet, two inches, and her weight at one hundred ten pounds. "Chinese Girl Pilot Lives Colorful Life," *Vancouver Daily Province*, December 12, 1941.

16 On May 18, 1942, a Chinese aeronautical delegation would make another good impression at the week long Ottawa Air Training Conference of the allied united nations. Major-General T.H. Shen, senior officer of the Aeronautical Commission in the U.S. and commander of the Chinese Air Forces training in America, received rousing applause from the delegates of the fourteen participating nations when he rose to make his address. He declared that, although China had built a number of air bases from which aircraft could take off and bomb Tokyo, and that she had expert pilots who could do the job, she had no planes.

17 "Dr. Hu Shih Speaks Here: Canada China's First Ally," *Vancouver Daily Province*, February 20, 1942.

18 "Courage, Suffering of Chinese Outlined by Visiting Speaker," *Victoria Colonist*, March 4, 1942. In March 1918, her aunt Zheng Yuxiu had also visited Victoria, BC. She was *en route* to the Paris Peace Conference where she was destined to play a historic role. Her brief sojourn in the provincial capital received wide coverage in the press.

19 In addition to receiving her first Chinese Foreign Minister, Dr. Liu Shishun, Canada also welcomed Fong Gat-shun, the first Chinese consul stationed in Toronto. The territory covered by the Toronto consulate extended eastward to the Atlantic.

20 "China Speaks—and Vancouver Women Thrill to Her Story," *Vancouver Sun*, April 14, 1942.

21 "Chinese Girl 'Steals the Show' of the Fighting French," *Vancouver News-Herald*, July 15, 1942.

22 "Sound Strategy to Beat Japs First...," *Vancouver News-Herald*, July 31, 1942. Jessie could not take credit for this strategy. Her remarks echoed those of Song Meiling who told Henry Hopkins: "the two wars against Germany and Japan can both be won, but that the way to do it is to put all our strength into defeating Japan." Robert E. Sherwood, *Roosevelt and Hopkins* (NY: Harper & Brothers, 1948), 660-61.

23 Williams, "We Want To Go To China," 10.

24 "Chinese Girl Flier To Speak in East," *Vancouver Sun,* November 24, 1942.

25 "Chinese Girl Lives Colorful Life," *Vancouver Daily Province,* December 12, 1941.

26 Williams, "We Want To Go To China," 3. Mr. Williams' questions to Miss Zheng were as follows: "To our enquiries about the tremendous financial inflation now current in China, we received only a deprecatory shrug, and the answer that inflation existed only in the larger cities, and did not materially affect the war effort, and the Chinese need help. To the more important questions of lack of cooperation and even hostilities between the Guomintang (National Party of Chiang Kai-shek) and Kungchangtang (Chinese communists mostly supplied and armed by Russia), she claimed China's complete oneness against the Nipponese, and that China still needed help. Asked for her opinion on a sweeping Chinese guerilla offensive, which the United Nations wish them to stage since in that type of fighting the Chinese have few equals, Miss Cheng asked if the Chinese should fight with their bare hands, and still emphasized China's need for arms and equipment."

30. CROSSING CANADA

1 The Weis never made this visit. "Chinese Envoy to U.S. May Come Here," *Vancouver Sun,* September 26, 1942.

2 "Chinese Flyer to Tour East," *Daily Province,* November 25, 1942; "Chinese Woman Pilot Now Ambassador For Her Country," *Daily Province,* September 26, 1942.

3 Ibid. The Vancouver-Ottawa flight took some 16-18 hours, departing at 6:00 am and arriving at 12:35 am next morning, and cost $220.40, plus 15% transportation tax. Jessie flight was likely made via a new Lockheed Lodestar 1808A. There were six stops for refueling and taking on new passengers: Lethbridge, AB; Regina, SK; Winnipeg, MB; Kapuskasing, ON; North Bay, ON; and Toronto, ON. TCA's trans-continental flight was only a few years old. Inaugurated on April 1, 1939, its first woman passenger had been Hanying's friend, Elizabeth Flaherty of the Flying Seven. Mrs. Flaherty also bought the first TCA ticket sold. She made the trip aboard a twin-engine, 10-passenger Lockheed 14H2 (CF-TCA) that had a top speed of 210 mph, and a maximum altitude of 17,000 feet. Oxygen masks were required over the Rocky Mountains. However, Flaherty's flight stalled in Ottawa due to heavy snows and the passengers had to proceed to Montreal by train. When Jessie made the flight, she went only as far as Ottawa, but after she reached this initial destination, she flew throughout the East via RCAF aircraft. After she made her maiden speech to the RCAF officers at Jericho Beach, she maintained close ties with Canada's airborne military, and the formal wartime alliance of China and Canada further cemented this relationship. As a result, she enjoyed *carte blanche* privileges and the air force allowed her to catch rides on any planes that happened to be flying to her destination.

4 "Chinese Girl Flier Impressive In Address before Ottawa Club," *Ottawa Evening Citizen,* December 2, 1942.

5 The Avro Anson's registration number was 8401.

6 Jessie's landing and her inspection of the honor guard were filmed by the National Film Board whose cameraman was also on hand to take moving pictures of the

christening of the amphibian aircraft. The plane was named the *Princess Alice* after the wife of the Governor General.

7 Photos of Jessie attending the event appeared in the January 1943 edition of *Canadian Aviation* magazine and the *Toronto Daily Star*, December 5, 1942.

8 "Only Woman in Chinese Air Force Visits Canada," *Toronto Daily Star*, December 21, 1942.

9 Jessie's Christmas visit with her aunt and uncle in Washington would have been brief; on December 27, Drs. Wei Daoming and Zheng Yuxiu flew to Chicago where the men's and women's bar associations in that city had invited them to address their members.

10 Margaret Ecker, "Fashion Spotlight on Hats as Parliament is Opened: Women Choose Black as Contrast to Rug," *Globe and Mail*, January 29, 1943. On May 9, 1945, Vancouverite Margaret Ecker went on to become the only woman to witness the German and allied signing of the peace treaty at Reims in Europe. Formerly a *Vancouver Sun* editorial staff member, she was present at the signing in her capacity as Canadian Press correspondent overseas. The event was so momentous that she reported she "didn't once think" about the historic significance of her presence.

11 "Pretty Chinese Girl Flier Working Hard for Victory," *Toronto Daily Star*, February 5, 1943.

12 "Chinese Airwoman Tells of Country's Crying Need," *Toronto Daily Star,* February 4, 1943.

13 "Pretty Chinese Girl Flier…," *Daily Star*, February 5, 1943.

31. GATHERING SHADOWS

1 She was attended by Dr. Edward B. Gung, one of three Chinese doctors then practicing in the city.

2 When she drew up her will, Jessie could not recall the name of the order of nuns to whom she wished to leave her estate, but it was later established that she was referring to Les Soeurs de l'Enfant Jésus (Sisters of the Order of the Child Jesus), and it was to them that the monies were remitted. Her barrister, Thomas Dohm, and Mrs. Louise Pearl Forsyth, a woman who lived in the same Georgia Street boarding house as Jessie, witnessed her signing of the will. Mrs. Peggy Lee recalled that, a few weeks after Jessie's death, an Englishman representing Miss Zheng's estate made the rounds of Chinatown trying to sell her dresses and shoes. There were many items of excellent quality—Paris fashions, as well as silken Chinese gowns from Shanghai covered in fine embroidery, some of them likely the stylish creations of couturier Zhang Qianying (Hélène Tsang)—but although these stunning items generated considerable interest, most women were disappointed to discover they were unable to squeeze into the lovely, but too petite, garments. Peggy Lee, interview by author, January 24, 2005, Vancouver, BC.

3 Flying Officer A.B. Wilkinson led the RCAF funeral parade of fifty-one men and eight officers, three of whom were women officers of the RCAF Women's Division. "Air Force Funeral: RCAF to Honor Hanyin Cheng," *Vancouver Sun*, September 10, 1943. Burnaby, the site of the interment, was a suburb of Greater Vancouver.

4 "Chinese Woman Pilot Dies Here," *Vancouver Daily Province*, September 9, 1943.

5 Mamie Maloney, "In One Ear," *Vancouver Sun,* September 14, 1943.

32. POSTSCRIPT

1 Wilfred Seto enrolled in the Canadian Officers' Training Corps (COTC) at the University of British Columbia. The COTC trained university undergrads for officer commissions in the Canadian Army reserves. In April 1942, he actively campaigned for the formation of a Chinese Canadian Battalion to serve in the Pacific arena, but he found no official enthusiasm for the notion. In October 1943, the month following Jessie's death, Lt. Wilfred Seto was sent overseas to join Vancouver's Seaforth Highlanders regiment stationed in Italy. Upon arrival, however, his brigadier told him that it was unlikely any men put under his command would be willing to take orders from a Chinese officer, and he would make a more effective contribution to the war effort if he joined Pacific Command. Seto returned to Vancouver where he attended the S-20 Japanese Language School, graduating in 1945. Sent to Ottawa with the rank of captain, he served at the No.1 Discrimination Unit, rendering Japanese wireless messages into English. Marjorie Wong, *The Dragon and the Maple Leaf: Chinese Canadians in World War II* (London, ON: Pirie Pub., 1994), 72, 73, 91, 106, 107fn, 110. Leigh Seto, interview by author, transcribed notes, Vancouver, BC, May 2, 2006.

2 Larry Wong, "February 19, 1947: First Chinese become Canadian Citizens," *The Beaver*, February-March 2003, 49.

373

BIBLIOGRAPHY

ARCHIVES, LIBRARIES, COLLECTIONS AND PRIVATE PAPERS

Aero Club of British Columbia, Pitt Meadows, BC

L'Aéro-Club de Genève, Genève, Switzerland

Aeronca Inc. Archives, Middletown, OH

Autauga-Prattville Public Library, Prattville, AL

Auckland City Library Special Collections, Auckland, NZ

Bibliothèque de l'Université Laval, Collections spéciales, Ville de Québec, PQ

Burnaby Public Library, Burnaby, BC

British Columbia Archives, Victoria, BC

British Columbia Vital Statistics Agency, Victoria, BC

Chinese Canadian Military Museum, Vancouver, BC

City of Richmond Archives, Richmond, BC

City of Vancouver Archives, Vancouver, BC

Cochran, Jacqueline: Papers 1932-75, Dwight D. Eisenhower Library, Abilene, KS

Hong Kong Film Archive, Hong Kong

Hong Kong Historical Aircraft Association, Hong Kong

Irving House/New Westminster Museum and Archives, New Westminster, BC

Kwong, G., Vernon, BC, to T.K. Bulman, Vernon, BC, 5 January 1945. Transcription typed and signed. Copy in possession of author, Vancouver, BC

Li Xiaqing private papers, family of Li Xiaqing, Weatherford, TX

Mobile Public Library, Mobile, AL

National Archives of Canada, Ottawa, ON

National Film Board, Montréal, PQ

Office des Nations Unies à Genève, Genève, Switzerland

Philadelphia Public Library, Philadelphia, PA

Salt Lake City Public Library, Salt Lake City, UT

San Francisco Public Library, San Francisco, CA

State of Alabama Department of Archives and History, Montgomery, AL

Toledo–Lucas County Public Library, Toledo, OH

United Service to China Archives. Seeley G. Mudd Library. Princeton University, Princeton, NJ

United Council for Civilian Relief in China, Bowl of Rice Campaign, 1939, Author's collection

US Department of Justice, Federal Bureau of Investigation, Washington, DC

US Department of Transportation, Federal Aviation Administration, Oklahoma City, OK

University of British Columbia Special Collections, Vancouver, BC

University of Washington Special Collections, Seattle, WA

Vancouver Public Library Special Collections, Vancouver, BC

Ville de Montréal Section des archives, Montréal, PQ

Western Canada Aviation Museum, Winnipeg, MB

Yale-China Association. Yale University Library Manuscripts and Archives, New Haven, CT

INTERVIEWS

Chen, Doreen, Queens Village, NY. Telephone interview by author, 2002

Chen, Ronald K., Berkeley Heights, NJ. Email communications to author, 2002, 2006.

Cheng, Pax, Hercules, CA. Interviews by author, 1-3 March 2005.

Chin, Moon, Hillsborough, CA. Interview by author, February 28, 2005.

Choi Kai-kwong, Hong Kong. Email communications to author, August 14, 16, 2003.

Dunnaway, Cliff, Hong Kong. Email communications to author, various dates 1999-2005.

Fairburn, Janis, Auckland, NZ. Email communications to author, August 13, 17, 2005.

Fairburn Bass, Corin, Sydney, AU. Email communication to author, August 17, 2005.

Holman, Dinah (née Fairburn), Auckland, NZ. Email, postal communications to author,

August 2005.

Johnson, Ian D. Surrey, England. Email communications to author, various dates, 2003-06.

Law Kar, Hong Kong. Email, postal communications to author, August 2003.

Lee, Dan, Vancouver, BC. Interview by author, September 26, 2004.

Lee, Patricia, Toronto, ON. Telephone interviews by author, January 9, 2003.

Lee, Peggy, Vancouver, BC. Interviews by author, January & February 2005.

Mah, Albert, Montreal, PQ. Telephone interview by author, March 2, 2001.

Mah, Cedric, Edmonton, AB. Email communications to author, 2001-2006.

Robertson, Renée (née Lym), San Francisco, CA. Interviews by author, March 2005.

Seto, Leigh, Vancouver, BC. Interview by author, January 26, 2005, May 2, 2006.

Wei, Linda (née Hsu), Hercules, CA. Interview by author, March 2, 2005.

Wilson Owen, Kim, Prattville, AL. Email & postal communications to author, 2002.

Wong, Larry, Vancouver, BC. Email communication to author, January 16, 2006.

NEWSPAPERS AND PERIODICALS

Aero Digest

Aéro-Revue

Aviation

Beaver

Birmingham Age-Herald

Canadian Aviation

Chicago Tribune

China Journal

China Mail

China Weekly Review

Chine illustrée (China illustriert/China illustrated) (Geneva, Switzerland)

Christian Science Monitor

Da Yi Gong Bao [Chinese Times] (Vancouver, BC)

Da Gong Bao (Hong Kong & Chongqing, China)

Daily Kennebec Journal (Augusta, ME)

Dallas News

Forward

Le Droit (Ottawa, ON)

Gazette (Montreal, PQ)

Grosse Pointe News

Grosse Pointe Review

Halifax Herald

Hartford Courant

Hong Kong Daily Press

Hong Kong Telegraph

Huaqiao Ribao

Idaho Statesman

Izvestia

Journal de Shanghai

Lethbridge Herald

Life Magazine

Lima News (Lima, OH)

Ling Long

Los Angeles Times

Maryville Daily Forum (Maryville, MI)
Mobile Press Register
Montgomery Advertiser
Modesto Bee and News-Herald
New York Herald-Tribune
New York Times
North-China Daily Herald and Supreme Court and Consular Gazette
North-China Daily News
Ottawa Evening Citizen
Photoplay and Movie Mirror
Popular Aviation
Prattville Progress
Pravda
La Press (Montreal, PQ)
Movie-Radio Guide
New York World-Telegram
Renmin Zheng Xie Bao
Salt Lake City Tribune
San Diego Union
San Francisco Chronicle
San Francisco Examiner
San Francisco News
Seattle Daily Times
Shanghai Evening Post
Soleil (Quebec, PQ)
South China Morning Post
Times (London, UK)
Toledo Blade
Toronto Globe & Mail
Toronto Daily Star
Vancouver Daily Province
Vancouver News-Herald
Vancouver Sun
Victoria Daily Colonist
Victoria Times
Vidette-Messenger (Valparaiso, IN)

Washington Post

Xinhua Ribao (Chongqing, China)

Xianggang Gongshang Ribao

Xianggang Huazi Wanbao

Zhong Hua (China Pictorial)

BOOKS AND ARTICLES

"Aero Club of BC." *West Coast Aviator Magazine* (April 1999), 8:5.

Aerofiles, aerofiles.com

Anderson, Douglas E. "Poor Man's P-26: The Aeronca LC." *Canadian Aviation Historical Society Journal* vol. 14, no. 4. 126.

Arvad, Inga. "Glamorous Flying Ambassadress at Home in Either East or West," *Vancouver Daily Province*, March 13, 1943.

Association for Moral and Social Hygiene in India. *Notes on the Conference of Central Authorities in Far-Eastern Countries Convened by the League of Nations, at Bandoeng, Java, in February, 1937.* Delhi: Delhi Printing Works, May 1937.

Biographical Dictionary of Republican China. Edited by Howard Boorman & Richard C. Howard. NY: Columbia University Press, 1967.

The British Columbia and Yukon Directory. Vancouver, B.C.: Sun Directories, 1941-43.

Cailliez, Jean-Claude. "Quand Lindbergh Alaquait à Gèneve." *La Feuille Volante* 90 (novembre 2004), 7-9.

The Canadians at War: 1939/45. vol. 1. Montreal: Reader's Digest Association (Canada), 1976.

Cash, Gwen. *A Million Miles from Ottawa.* Toronto: Macmillan Co. of Canada Ltd., 1942.

Chen, Percy. *China Called Me: My Life Inside the Chinese Revolution.* Boston: Little, Brown, 1979.

Chen, Lawrence M. "Aviation in China." In *Information Bulletin*, May 1, 1937, by the Council of International Affairs, 255-274. Nanking: Council of International Affairs, vol. iii, no. 12.

Chen Leyda, Si-lan. *Footnote to History.* Edited by Sally Banes. New York: Dance Horizons, 1984.

Cheng Naishan. "Li Xiaqing: Cong zhu ming ying xing dao quan neng fei xing yuan," *Shanghai Lady.* Shanghai: Wen hui chu ban she, 2003.

Chennault, Claire Lee. *Way of a Fighter: The Memoirs of Claire Lee Chennault.* Edited by Robert Hotz. New York: G.P. Putnam's Sons, 1949.

Chiang, May-ling Soong. *China in Peace and War.* With a preface by Charlotte Haldane. London: Hurst, 1940.

_____. *China Shall Rise Again, by May-ling Soong Chiang (Madame Chiang Kai-shek):*

Including Ten Official Statements of China's Present Progress. New York and London: Harper & Bro., 1941.

_____. *We Chinese Women: Speeches and Writings during the First United Nations Year [by] Mayling Soong Chiang (Madame Chiang Kai-shek) February 12, 1942 - November 16, 1942.* New York: John Day Co., 1943.

China Ministry of Information. *China Handbook: 1937-1943.* NY: Macmillan Co., 1943.

China Yearbook 1938/39. Tientsin: Tientsin Press Ltd., 1939.

Chinese Year Book. Shanghai: The Commercial Press. 1935- (vol. 1-7).

Choi Kai-kwong, director, & Law Kar, script. *Lai Man-wai: Father of Hong Kong Cinema.* DVD. Feature-length documentary. Hong Kong: Dragon Ray Motion Pictures, Ltd., 2001.

Le Cinéma Chinois. Sous la direction de Marie-Claire Quiquemelle et Jean-Loup Passek, textes de Geremie Barmé. Paris: Centre Georges Pompidou, 1985.

The Diary of Lai Man-wai. Collated by Lai Sek, translated by Ma Sung. [Li Min Wei Ri Ji. Bian Ding Li Xi]. Hong Kong: Hong Kong Film Archive, 2003.

Eden, Anthony. *The Eden Memoirs: Facing the Dictators.* London: Cassell, 1962.

Epstein, Israel. *My China Eye: Memoirs of a Jew and a Journalist.* San Francisco: Long River Press, 2005.

Exley, David J. "John G. Male." *Association of Former International Civil Servants (New York) Quarterly Bulletin* vol. xxxiv, no. 3 (July 2003): 31-32.

"Flying for Victory," *True Aviation Picture-Stories.* New York: Parents' Magazine Press no. 3 (March/April 1943).

Gilkey, George R. *The First Seventy Years: A History of the University of Wisconsin-La Crosse, 1909-1979.* La Crosse, WI: University of Wisconsin-La Crosse Foundation, 1981.

Guan Zhongren. "Patriotic Aviatrix Li Xiaqing." Translated by Pan Zhongming. *Women of China* July 1990: 38-40.

_____. *Zhongguo Fu Nu Hang Kong Guo Chen* [Study on Chinese Women Aviators, 1915-1949]. Canton, China : Guangdong sheng Zhongshan tu shu guan : Guangdong sheng fu nü lian he hui ; [Enping xian]: Enping xian zheng xie wen shi zu, 1988.

Guan Zhongren, and Patti Gully, ed. *Wu Yi Huaqiao Yu Zhongguo Hangkong* [Overseas Chinese from the Five Counties and Chinese Aviation], vol. 1 & 2. Yizhe: Xie Ang. [Translated by Angelo Xie]. Zhongguo hangkong shi yan jiu hui, Guangdong sheng enping shi zheng xie wen shi wei yuan hui, 2003.

Hahn, Emily. *China to Me: A Partial Biography.* Philadelphia: Blakiston Co., 1944.

_____. *The Soong Sisters.* New York: Doubleday, 1941.

Hart, Scott. "Feminine Bravery: Men, Women Share China's Combat Duty," *Washington Post.* February 18, 1943.

Hauser, Ernest. "T.V. For Victory." *New Republic,* January 26, 1942.

Henderson's City Directory, Vancouver, 1941, 1942, 1943.

Hong Kong. *Report of the Medical Department for the Year 1937.*

Hong Kong Historical Aircraft Association. *Wings Over Hong Kong: An Aviation History, 1891-1998.* Edited by Cliff Dunnaway. Hong Kong: Pacific Century Publishers, 1998.

Hoo, Mona Yung-ning. *Painting the Shadows: The Extraordinary Life of Victor Hoo.* London: Eldridge & Co., 1998.

Hume, Edward H. *Doctors East Doctors West: An American Physician's Life in China.* New York: W.W. Norton & Co. Inc., 1946.

Jackson, Beverley. *Splendid Slippers: A Thousand Years of an Erotic Tradition.* Berkeley, CA: Ten Speed Press, 1997.

Jennings, Dean S. "The Fighting Chinese." *Popular Aviation* vol. xxvi, no. 3 (May 1940).

Johnson, Ian D. *China's First International Airline, the Southwestern Aviation Corporation: Shi Nan Hang Kong Gong Se: or The People's Aviation Company for the Five Provinces.* Unpublished CD, 2004.

Kohan, O. Kathleen. "Flying Emissary." *Far East* vol. 3, no. 3 (March 1940).

Koo, Wellington, Mme. *Hui-lan Koo: An Autobiography.* As Told to Mary Van Rensselaer Thayer. New York: Dial Press, 1943.

_____. *No Feast Lasts Forever.* With Isabella Taves. New York: Quadrangle/New York Times Book Co., 1975.

Lake, Talbot. "Miss Lee Seeks Funds in U.S. To Aid China," *Hayward [CA] Daily Review,* February 4, 1941.

Lash, Joseph P. *Eleanor: The Years Alone.* With a foreword by Franklin D. Roosevelt, Jr. New York: Norton, 1972.

Lau, Theodora. *The Handbook of Chinese Horoscopes.* Twenty-fifth Anniversary Fifth Edition. New York: HarperCollins, 2005.

League of Nations. Assembly. *Records, Index.* Geneva, 1935.

_____. Assembly. *Minutes of the First Committee.* Geneva, 1935.

_____. Assembly. *Minutes of the Fifth Committee.* Geneva, 1937.

_____. Council. *Report on the Work of the League.* Geneva, 1935-1938.

_____. Official Journal, Special Supplement No. 174. *Records of the Eighteenth Ordinary Session of Assembly: Minutes of the Committees: Minutes of the Fifth Committee (Humanitarian and General Questions).* Geneva, 1937.

_____. Traffic in Women and Children. Conference of Central Authorities in Eastern Countries, Bandoeng (Java), February 2nd to 13th, 1937. *Minutes of Meetings IV. Social.* 1937, IV, 10. Geneva, December 1937.

Leary, William M. *Dragon's Wings: The China National Corporation and the Development of Commercial Aviation in China.* Athens: University of Georgia Press, 1976.

Lent, Melba. "Many Chinese Women Hear Talk by Madame Chiang," *Winnipeg Free Press,* June 17, 1943.

Leong, Karen J. *The China Mystique: Pearl S. Buck, Anna May Wong, Mayling Soong, and the Transformation of American Orientalism*. Berkeley: University of California Press, 2005.

Leyda, Jay. *Dianying: An Account of Films and the Film Audience in China*. Cambridge, MA: MIT Press, 1972.

Lin, Adet, Anor Lin and Meimei Lin. *Dawn Over Chungking*. New York: John Day Co., 1941. Reprint, New York: Da Capo Press, 1975.

Lyons, Leonard. "Broadway Signboard," *Washington Post*. August 29, 1942.

_____. "New Yorker," *Washington Post*. February 18, 1939.

Martin, Brian G. *The Shanghai Green Gang: Politics and Organized Crime, 1919-1937*. Berkeley: University of California Press, 1996.

McCormick Dunn, Elsie. "Notes on the Life Story of Lee Ya-ching." Unpublished manuscript. n.d.

Meek, Jack. "Skylines," *Vancouver Sun*. April 6, 1943.

Miller, Hope Ridings. "Mmes. McNary, Tydings Entertain With 'At Home': Miss Hilda Yen with Miss Wang," *Washington Post*. 11 February 1938.

_____. "Mrs. Garner Steps Out To Southerners' Tea," *Washington Post*. April 29, 1939.

Nellist, George F., ed. *Men of Shanghai and North China*. 2nd ed. Shanghai: The Oriental Press, 1935.

Murison, Blanche E. Holt. "Hanyin Cheng of China," *Saturday Night,* November 28, 1942.

National Spiritual Assembly of the Baha'is of the United States and Canada. *The Baha'i World:* A Biennial International Record Prepared Under the Supervision of the National Spiritual Assembly of the Baha'is of the United States and Canada with the Approval of Shoghi Effendi. New York City: Baha'i Publishing Committee, 1926; 1968-1973.

Ng Wing Chung. *The Chinese in Vancouver, 1945-1980*. Vancouver: UBC Press, 1999.

Nichols, Ruth. *Wings for Life: The Story of the First Lady of the Air*. New York: Lippincott Co., 1957.

Pan, Lynn. *Sons of the Yellow Emperor: A History of the Chinese Diaspora*. New York: Kodansha International, 1994.

Perrault, E.G. *Tong: the Story of Tong Louie, Vancouver's Quiet Titan*. Vancouver: Harbour Publishing, 2002.

Pride, Harry. *Life with the Moores of Hart House: Pioneer Days on Burnaby's Deer Lake*. Burnaby, BC: City of Burnaby Community Heritage Commission, 2002.

Reeds, Robert. "Pretty Chinese Girl Flier Likes All Men—To Look At." *Toronto Daily Star*, March 25, 1939.

Render, Shirley. *No Place For A Lady: The Story of Canadian Women Pilots, 1928-1992*. Foreword by Punch Dickins. Winnipeg: Portage & Main Press, 1992.

Rosette. "Gorgeous Gowns Seen in Mannequin Parade." *Hong Kong Daily Press*, October 8, 1938.

_____. "Tea-Dance Season Re-Opens: Beautiful Frocks." *Hong Kong Daily Press*, October 3, 1938.

Seagrave, Sterling, and the editors of Time-Life Books. *Soldiers of Fortune*. Alexandria, VA: Time-Life Books, 1981.

Seagrave, Sterling. *The Soong Dynasty*. New York: Harper & Row, 1985.

Selle, Earl Albert. *Donald of China*. New York: Harper, 1948.

Sherwood, Robert E. *Roosevelt and Hopkins*. NY: Harper & Brothers, 1948.

Simmons, Beverley. "Keeper of the Curtains." In *Fairburn and Friends*, ed. Dinah Holman and Christine Cole Catley, 126-135. Dunedin, NZ: Cape Catley, 2004.

Smith, E.G. "China's Spirit Sets Example, Mr. King Notes." *Globe and Mail*, July 8, 1942.

Snow, Edgar. *Journey to the Beginning*. New York: Random House, 1958.

Song Meiling. "Wings Over China." *Shanghai Evening Post*, March 12, 1937.

Spring, Joyce. *Daring Lady Flyers: Canadian Women in the Early Years of Aviation*. Porter's Lake, N.S.: Pottersfield Press, 1994.

Stout, William B. "Aviation Training at the Boeing School." *Aero Digest* (June 1935): 23.

Tang Dongmei. *Chuan Yue Shi Ji Cang Mang: Zheng Yuxiu Chuan* [Exceeding the expectations of her era: the biography of Zheng Yuxiu]. Zhongguo she hui chu ban she, 2003.

Taunton, Ruth. "China Girl Flyer Arrives Here to Plead for Aid Against Japanese." *San Diego Union*, April 17, 1939.

Tcheng Soumé (Wei Yü-hsiu). *Souvenirs d'Enfance et de Révolution. [Par] Soumé Tcheng;* transcrits par B. van Vorst. Paris: Payot & Cie, 1920.

Tcheng Yulau. *La Collaboration Technique Entre La Chine et La Société des Nations.* February, 1935.

Thomas, Harry J. *The First Lady of China: The Historic Wartime Visit of Madame Chiang Kai-shek to the United States in 1943.* [NY]: International Business Machines Corp., 1943.

Thomas, Lowell and Rexford W. Barton. *Wings Over Asia: A Geographic Journey By Airplane.* Philadelphia: John C Winston Co., 1937.

Tong, Hollington Kong. *Chiang Kai-shek, Soldier and Statesman; authorized biography by Hollington Tong.* Shanghai: The China Publishing Company, 1937.

Van Vorst, Bessie (McGinnis). *A Girl from China (Soumay Tcheng).* New York: Frederick A. Stokes Co., 1926.

Varian, Nina. "Pretty Chinese Flyer Wins Boisean Hearts." *Idaho Statesman*, May 23, 1939.

Walters, F.P. *A History of the League of Nations.* London: Oxford University Press, 1967

Wei Yü-hsiu (Tcheng). *My Revolutionary Years: The Autobiography of Madame Wei Tao-ming.* New York: Charles Scribner's Sons, 1943.

White, Freda. "China and Spain Ask for Judgment." *Headway* (October 1937): 190-91.

White, Theodore Harold and Annalee Jacoby. *Thunder Out of China.* New York: William Sloane Assoc., 1946.

Wiethoff, Bodo. *Luftverkehr in China: 1928-1949: Materialien zu Einem Untauglichen Modernisierungsversuch.* Wiesbaden: Otto Harrassowitz, 1975.

Who's Who in China, 1918-1950: with an index. Compiled by Jerome Cavanaugh. Hong Kong: Chinese Materials Center, 1982.

[Williams, V. Ben.] "We Want to Go to China," *Forward.* Vancouver: Vancouver Junior Board of Trade, vol. 11, no. 1 (Aug. 1942).

Wong, Larry. "February 19, 1947: First Chinese become Canadian Citizens," *Beaver* vol. 83 issue 1 (February-March 2003): 49.

Wong, Marjorie. *The Dragon and the Maple Leaf: Chinese Canadians in World War II.* London, ON: Pirie Publications, 1994.

Woodsworth, Charles James, and the Canadian Institute of International Affairs. *Canada and the Orient: A Study in International Relations.* Toronto: Macmillan, 1941.

Worden, Helen. "Hong Kong Girl Here Plans Flights Across U.S. To Solicit Funds to Aid War Victims in China." *New York World-Telegram,* March 18, 1939.

Wyman, Keith. *Aeronca, Inc.* (August 1, 2002).

Xie Qizhang. *Meng Yingji—Wo De Dian Ying Ji Yi* [Dream photo album: my movie memory]. [Beijing]: Beijing tu shu guan chu ban she, 2005.

Yan Huiqing. *Yan Huiqing Ri Ji* [The Diaries of Yan Hui Qing]. Shanghai shi dang an guan yi (Translated by Shanghai Archives). Beijing: Zhongguo dang an chu ban she, 1996.

Yan Zhiyuan. "mian huai zu fu yan fu qing" Biography of Yan Fu Qing by his grandson. http://www.rwfd.fudan.edu.cn/spirit/xiren/yanfuqing.htm Accessed March 6, 2005

Yee, Paul. *Chinatown: An Illustrated History of the Chinese Communities of Victoria, Vancouver, Calgary, Winnipeg, Toronto, Ottawa, Montreal and Halifax.* Toronto: James Lorimer & Co. Ltd., 2005.

_____. *Saltwater City: An Illustrated History of the Chinese in Vancouver.* Vancouver: Douglas & McIntyre, 1988.

Yen Hui-ch'ing. *East-West Kaleidoscope, 1877-1946: An Autobiography.* New York: St John's University Press, 1974.

_____. *Stories of Old China.* Translated by W.W. Yen. Hong Kong: Commercial Press, 1974.

Yuan Xiaojuan. "Di yi ge kua chu guo men de nü ying xing" [Beginnings of a native movie star]. *Ren Min Zheng Xie Bao,* July 27, 2001.

Zheng Hanying. *Actualites Canadiennes No. 24: Aviatrice Chinoise.* 2 min., National Film Board, 1943. videocassette.

INDEX

A

ABMAC. *see* American Bureau for Medical Aid to China
Aero Club of British Columbia, 266, 267
Aéro-Club de Suisse, 138, 139
Aeronautical Affairs, Commission on, 159, 245, 250, 254, 257
Aeronca, LC (the 'BAT'), 272, 275, 368 n.11
  Super Chief, 189, 360 (n.11, n.12, n.14)
Aéroport de Genève-Cointrin, 136, 137
air raids, 56, 73, 79–80, 251–53, 259, 279–280
Alameda, CA, 142, 355 n.3
Alice, Princess, Countess of Athlone, 297
Allard, John S., 356 n.4
l'Alliance Française, 266, 278
American Airlines, 187
American Bureau for Medical Aid to China (ABMAC), 53, 72–73, 175, 177, 180, 182, 343 n.2, 358 n.1, 359 (n.7, n.5)
American Red Cross, 163
Anderson, Marian, 83–84, 345 n.14
Andrews, Joe, 64–65
Anjou, René d', 35
Arden, Elizabeth, 58, 203
Armstrong, Beryl, 367 n.3
Arvad, Inga Marie, 195–96
Athlone, Earl of (Governor General), 297
atomic bombs, 89, 202
Avro
  626 Trainer, 239
  631 Cadet, 239
  Anson Mk II, 289, 296
  Avian biplane, 145

B

Bahá'í faith, 85–86, 89, 90, 95, 100, 339 n.10
Bandoeng Conference, 39–40, 46, A–I, 338 n.7
Bankhead, Tallulah, 74–75
Barrett, Rosalie (Rolie) Moore, 274–75, 366 n.2, 367 n.3
Bastille Day, 283–84
'BAT.' *see* Aeronca, LC (the 'BAT')
Beech, Walter, 58, 174, 357 n.12
Beechcraft, Staggerwing C17R, 178, 179, 183, 358 n.4
Bendix Transcontinental Air Race, 164
'Big Eared' Du. *see* Du Yuesheng
Bloody Saturday, 45
Boeing Aircraft Factory, 265

Boeing School of Aeronautics, 139–44, 146, 154, 204, 205
  trainer aircraft, 139, 351 n.7
Borden, Robert, 288
Bowhill, Dorothy, Lady, 290, 292
Bowl of Rice fundraisers, 72, 74–75, 182, 343 n.5, 344 n.6, 359 n.7
Bratschi, Charles, 351 n.3
Bretton Woods Conference, 86-87
Briondi, Signor, 41
British Commonwealth Air Training Plan (BCATP), 267, 283
  Fort Macleod, AB, 287
  Saint-Hubert, PQ, 289–90
Brooke-Popham, Robert, 243
Brown, Mannifrank, Wing Commander, 288
Buck, Pearl Sydenstricker, 72
Buenos Aires, Argentina, 180, 200
Bullitt, William Christian, Jr., 30
Burma Road, 250, 256, 297
Butterfly Wu. *see* Hu Die (Butterfly Wu)
Byng of Vimy, Marie Evelyn, Lady, 289

C

Cadwallader, Marian, 185–86, 188, 192, 193
Caitlin, Hoyt, 95
Canada, 258–59, 281, 282, 293-94
  Air Training Conference, 370 n.16
  Chinese Canadians
    face racism, 269–70, 367 n.7
    granted citizenship, 302
    in armed forces, 270
    Song Meiling's visit and, 296–97
    status of, 269–70
  relief to China. *see* Chinese War Relief Fund
  Sino-Japanese War and, 263, 279, 282
Canadian Pacific Airlines (CPA), 188, 303
Canadian Pacific Railway (CPR), 258
Canadian Red Cross Society, 187, 266.
Canton. *see* Guangdong and Guangzhou
Cao Yunxiang, 85, 86, 339 n.10
Capra, Frank, 163
Caribbean, 177, 180–81, 199
Catarina, Princess of Mexico, 164, 356 n.9
Caterpillar Club, 144
Caudron G-3, 136, 350 n.1
Cercle des femmes canadiennes, 291. *see also* Women's Canadian Club

Chambliss, Joe, Mr. & Mrs., 63
Changsha, China, 14–15, 18, 19, 20, 281
Chaplin, Charlie, 134
Cheh Su-jen (Chen Suren), 353 n.9
Chek Lap Kok airport, 301
Chen Bingzhang (first husband of Hilda Yan), 20–21, 22, 336 n.11
    attends British coronation, 42–3
    awarded Order of Brilliant Jade, 42
    death, 102
    Hilda Yan and, 23, 42, 75, 76, 77, 81, 92
        marriage to, 20–21, 22
        concern for, 67
        divorced by, 34
        post-divorce relations with, 35, 36
        affection for, 100
    IPR delegate, 75, 76
Chen, Doreen Guofeng (daughter of Hilda Yan), 23, 44, 92, 101, 346 n.6
Chen, Eugene, 157, 359 n.8
Chen, P.T. see Chen, Bingzhang
Chen, Percy, 157, 158, 359 n.8
Chen, Ronald K. (grandson of Hilda), [41, 54, 100]
Chen Ruidian (Art Chinn), 361 n.23
Chen Wenkuan (Moon Chin), 197, 355 n.26
Chen, William (son of Hilda Yan), 22, 92, 101, 346 n.6
Cheng. see also Zheng.
Cheng, Pax. see Zheng, Baishi
Chevy Chase Women's Club, 51
Chiang Kai-shek, 23, 44, 127, 145, 151, 165, 236, 246, 247, 278, 282, 290, 301
    50th birthday celebrations, 36–37, 151–52, 238, 353 n.10
Chiang Kai-shek, Madame. see Song Meiling
Chieri sisters, 149
child welfare, 247. see also trafficking in women & children
    Hilda Yan's study of, 41, 50
Child Welfare Association, National, 22, 38
Chin, Moon. see Chen, Wenkuan
Chin, Tom & Rose, 62
China, 121. see also Chinese Air Force
    Constitution and civil laws, A–I
    Dumbarton Oaks and, 87
    embargo on, lifted, 46
    fashionable in North American, 84, 280–81
    flooding, 56, 249, 250
    inflation in, 200–201, 297
    League of Nations participation, A–I
    Liberation, 92, 93, 301
    National Relief Commission, 58

Northern Expedition, 129–30
Hong Kong handover, 207, 301
Resistance and Reconstruction, 55, 248, 277–78
Sino-Japanese War and, 43, 243, 247, 259, 264, 280–81, 297
    Canada's attitude toward, 263, 264, 279
    effect on civilians, 55, 72–73, 177
Soviet Union and, 24, 27, 33, 87
supports aviation, 37, 151
China Aid Council, 163
China Aviation League, 145–46, 151
China Civilian Relief Committee, 73, 164
China Emergency Relief Committee, 72, 186, 358 n.1, 359 n.5
China Flying Club, 147
China National Aviation Corporation (CNAC), 36, 161, 197, 239
China National Aviation Reconstruction Association, 151, 171–72
Chinese Air Force (CAF), 4, 49, 201, 228, 230, 245, 254, 258, 265, 268, 275, 281, 291, 299
    'Bloody Saturday' and, 45
    Zheng Hanying commissioning in, 246
Chinese aviatrixes. see women in aviation
Chinese Canadians. see Canada
Chinese Communists, 23, 92, 93, 94, 236, 285, 301, 357 n.11, 362 n.5, 371 n.26
Chinese Consulates. see also Chinese Embassies
    New York, NY, 191
    Ottawa, ON, 262, 283, 298
    San Francisco, CA, 285, 363 n.1
    Vancouver, BC, 228, 264, 269–70, 280, 282, 283, 297, 298
Chinese Embassies, 28, 29, 49, 50-51, 65, 69, 286, 293. see also Chinese Consulates
Chinese Red Cross, 54, 55, 79–80, 228.
    Emergency Hospital No. 24, 157, 158
    Vancouver branch, 266, 274
Chinese War Relief Fund, 278, 294–95, 297–98, 300, 369 n.10
Chinese women aviators. see women in aviation
Chinese Women's Club, 22, 27, 35, 27, 77, 83, 149, 157, 336 n.9
Chinese Women's Relief Association, 53, 72
Chinese Women's Society, Montréal, 290, 293
Chinese Youth's Medical Relief Association (CYMRA), 260
Chinn, Art, 361 n.23
Chipman, Warwick, 292
Chongqing, 48, 57, 67, 72, 77, 81, 193, 250–54, 257, 271, 280, 295, 365 n.15

Index

Chow Siu-ying (mother of Hilda Yan), 12, 37
Churchill, Winston Spencer, 267, 278, 291
Cierva, autogyro, 241
Cioppa, Genaro, 38–39, 47
Civil Aeronautics Administration, 84
CKS. *see* Chiang, Kai-shek
Cleveland, OH, 71, 176, 189
Clipper air ships, 75, 77, 161, 239–40, 355 n.3
Co Tui, Frank. *see* Xu, Zhaodui
Cochran, Jacqueline, 57, 58, 75, 164, 176, 195, 204,
    356 n.10
Cointrin École d'Aviation, 136, 137, 169, 351 n.3
Colbert, Claudette, 163
Collier, Constance, 163
Columbia University, 98, 99
communism. *see* Chinese Communists
concubines, 121, 122, 124, 132, 134, 207, 231
coronation, King George VI, 42–3, 339 n.14
Cruzeiro do Sul, 199, 361 n.3
Curtiss-Wright, 254, 341 n.13, 356 n.4
    Hawk 111-type, 37, 115
    Wright Sedan, 54

D

Damita, Lili, 193
Dantas, José Bento Ribeiro, 199
Daughters of the American Revolution, 83, 345 n.14
de Havilland
    Hornet Moth, 239
    Tiger Moth, 136, 350 n.1
Declaration of Human Rights, 90
Del Rio, Dolores, 163
Deng Xiaoping, 350 n.20
Disputed Passage, 173, 176, 181–82, 357 n.23
Dixon, Frank M., 67
Dobbin, E.C.W. (Ted), 291
Dong Daqiu, 145
Doo, Peter, 149–50, 156, 159, 352 n.7
Doolittle, James H., 197
Douglas, DC-2 *(Kweilin),* 161, [355 n.1], 364 n.8
    DC-3, 361 n.3
Douglas-Hamilton, Malcolm, 239, 364 n.4
Du Yuesheng (‚Big-Eared' Du), 127, 135, 206, 362 n.5
Dumbarton Oaks Conference, 87
Dunn, Elsie McCormick, 182, 186, 359 n.10
Dunn, Irene, 193
Durafour, François, 136, 350 n.1

E

Earhart, Amelia, 58, 71, 335 n.3, 338 n.6, 366 n.2
Eastern Air Lines, 200

Ecker, Margaret, 293–94, 367 n.3
Eden, Anthony, 29
Elizabeth Arden cosmetics, 202
Elizabeth II, Queen of England, 206
Elizabeth, Queen consort of George VI, 42–3
Elkins, H.R., 192
embassies. *see* Chinese Embassies
Empress of Asia, s.s., 244
Ermanno Carlotto, 39, 338 n.4
Estrella China, 178, 179, 183, 358 n.4
Ethiopia, 235
Eurasia Aviation Corporation, 154, 239, 353 (n. 15,
    n.16)
extraterritoriality, 18–19, 83, 293

F

FAA. *see* United States Federal Aviation Administration
Fabray, Nanette, 193
FAI. *see* Fédération Aéronautique Internationale (FAI)
Fairbanks, Douglas, 58
Fairburn, A.R.D. (Rex), 91, 96, 98, 346 n.3
Fairey Fox, 239
Fairfield State Hospital, 98
Fane, Margaret, 366 n.2
Fang Zhenwu, 129, 130
Far East Flying Training School (FEFTS), 237–44,
    364 n.5
    training aircraft, 239
Farid-es-Sultaneh, Princess, 75
Farley, James, 58
FBI. *see* Federal Bureau of Investigation (FBI)
Federal Bureau of Investigation (FBI), 96, 97, 346 n.7
Fédération Aéronautique Internationale (FAI), 244
FEFTS. *see* Far East Flying Training School (FEFTS)
Feng Ru, 229
Fengshan, General, 120
Fighting French Forces, 289
Film Fun, 176
Fingesten, Peter, 194
Fiset, Zoé-Mary-Stella, Lady, 291
Flaherty, Elizabeth (Betsy), 267, 272, 366 n.2, 367 n.3,
    371 n.3
Fleet, trainer, 54
Flood Relief Commission, 249
Floyd Bennett Field, 166, 18
Flushing Airport, 174, 189
Flying Seven, 267–68, 272–73, 291, 366 n.2, 367 n.3,
    368 n.12
    Ground School, 273
Flynn, Errol, 163
Ford tri-motor aircraft, 139

Fox, Victor, Mrs., 367 n.3

France, 271, 283. *see also* Free French Forces

Free French Forces, 283–84

Friends of China, 53, 187, 189, 286, 341 n.22

Fritz, Bernadine, 162, 163

Fritz, Chester, 163

Fujien Catholic University, 58

G

Gable, Clark, 187

'Gang of Four,' 23, 100-01, 102

Gao Xiping, 349 n.6

Garner, John Nance, 52

Ge Cijiang, 128

Geneva, Switzerland, 31–32, 33, 37, 41, 45, 49, 133, 135ff, 339 n.13, 350 n.1, 351 n.6

George (Hilda Yan's lover), 75

George VI, King of Great Britain, 42–3

Gibson, Jack, 187

Gilbert, Rose-Alma Gaudreau, 272, 291, 366 n.2, 367 n.3

glossary, English to Chinese, 319–24

Gong Louli, 352 n.1

Goo Weijun. *see* Koo, Wellington

Gray, Pat, 367 n.3

Green Gang, 127, 135

Greene, Lorne, 281–82

Gregg, Leroy B., 141–42, 351 n.9

Gu Weijun. *see* Koo, Wellington

Guangdong, 120, 122, 154, 156, 159, 229, 230, 232, 242–3, 244, 256, 260, 303

    as Cradle of Aviation, 229

Guangxi Air Force, 364 n.5

Guo Daiqi (Quo Tai-chi), 337 n.15, 339 n.14

Guomindang, 93, 94, 118, 126, 172, 277, 285, 301, 302

H

Hamilton, ON, 187, 274

Hayes, Helen, 189

He Desheng, 242–43

Hebert, O.P., 49, 341 n.13

Hepburn, Katharine, 75

Hill of the Yellow Chrysanthemum, 119

Hilsz, Maryse, 237

Hing Leah, 352 n.1, 357 n.21

Hitler, Adolf, 29, 235, 339 n.13

Hong Jiaming (Hung Kai-ming), 239

Hong Kong, 77–78, 79, 80, 144, 158, 196, 201, 204, 240, 257–59, 289

    airlifts from, 282–83

    Chinese war refugees in, 47

    handover, 207, 301

    refugees and, 93, 244

    Sino-Japanese War, and effects on, 243

    under attack, 79–80, 281

Hong Kong Flying Club, 242

Hong Kong Volunteer Defense Corps, 239

Hoo, Victor. *see* Hu Shize (Victor Hoo)

Hou Yao, 350 n.15

Howard, John, 173

Hu Die (Butterfly Wu), 26, 29, 126, 128

Hu Shi, 282, 285, 337 n.15, 343 n.8, 369 (n.1, n.11)

Hu Shize (Victor Hoo), 33, 41, 337 n.15, 340 n.5, 350 n.19

Hua Mulan Joins the Army, 128, 129–131, 147, A–II, 349 n.14

Huang. *see also* Wang; Wong

Huang Xing, 119, 121

Hume, Edward (Lotta), Mrs., 72

Hume, Edward Hicks, 19, 72, 343 n.3

'Hump' air route, 81, 297

Hungqiao airfield, 150

Hurst, Fanny, 58

Hutchins, Francis S., 336 n.8

Huxley, Aldous, 163

Hyatt, Thaddeus, 192

Hyde, Jane, 359 n.1

I

IMF, 87

Institut de Jeanne d'Arc, 289

Institute of Pacific Relations (IPR), 344 n.7

    Mont Tremblant meeting, 83

    Virginia Beach meeting, 74, 75–76

International Exhibition of Chinese Art, 33–4

International Monetary Fund (IMF), 87

International Red Cross Society, 55

IPR. *see* Institute of Pacific Relations (IPR)

Irving Air Chute Co. Ltd., 144

isolationism, 30, 74–75, 78

Italy, 35, 41, 47, 76, 135, 136, 235, 302, 373 n.1

J

Japan. *see also* Sino-Japanese War

    aggressions of deplored by League of Nations, 46

    blockade of China, 250, 297

    Canada declares war on, 279, 282

    Consulate in Vancouver, 278, 370 n.12

    imperialism of, 4, 57, 234, 235, 263

    internment camps of, 80, 281

Japanese Imperial Air Force, 251, 255, 279

    aero capabilities, 44, 186, 255

attack on *Kweilin,* 161, 355 n.1, 364 n.8
bombs Pearl Harbor, 79, 191, 267, 279
spares Aviation League HQ, 145–46
Jèze, Gaston, 235
Jiang Jieshi. *see* Chiang Kai-shek
Jiang Qing, 23, 336 n.10
Jiang Tingfu, 36
Jiangwan, 12, 45
Juliana, Princess of the Netherlands, 293
Junkers, 354 n.16, 361 n.3
    JU-52, 154, 353 n.16
    Junior A50, 145
    W-34, 353 n.16

K

Kai Tak airport, 161, 204, 238, 239, 241, 242, 257, 281,
    301, 364 n.8
Kawasaki, Ichiro, 370 n.12
Keller, Helen, 58, 69
Kennedy, John F., 195
Kenyon College, 11
Keynes, John Maynard, 87
Kieran, John, 58
King, Mackenzie, 291, 297
Kinney, Wiley, 192
Kong Xiangxi (H.H. Kong), 23, 34, 42, 44, 68, 87, 336
    n.11, 339 n.14, 347 n.2
Kong Xiangxi, Madame. *see* Song Ailing
Koo, Wellington, 45, 46, 87, 347 n.2, 350 n.19
Koo, Wellington, Madame (Oei Huilan), 58, 149, 349
    n.19, 352 n.1
Kuling women's conference, 247–49, 277
Kung, H.H. *see* Kong Xiangxi (H.H. Kong)
Kung, H.H., Madame. *see* Song Ailing
Kuo Teh-chuan, 67, 71, 176
Kuomintang. *see* Guomindang
Kwangchowwan (Leizhou Bandao), 147
Kweilin, 161, 355 n.1, 364 n.8

L

Lady of the Tropics, 173
Lai Man-wai. *see* Li Minwei
Lamarr, Hedy, 173
Lamour, Dorothy, 173, 176, 182
Laval, Pierre, 29
League of Nations, 39, 235, 337 n.15, 339 n.13, 340
    n.5
    Eighteenth Assembly, 45–6, A–I
    fails to avert Sino-Japanese War, 47
    First Committee, 32–33, A–I
    Hilda Yan, appointed to, 1, 31-34, 38

Nine Power Conference, 46
    shortcomings, 46-47, 82
    Sixteenth Assembly, A–I, 337 n.11
    traffic of women & children, 39, 41, 46, A–I, 338
        (n.7, n.8)
    Yan Huiqing and, 31, 33
    Zheng Baifeng and, 135
Lee. *see also* Li
Lee, Annie, 352 n.1
Lee, Patricia, 360 n.9
Lee, Peggy, 262, 372 n.2
Lee Ya-ching. *see* Li Xiaqing
Lehman, Herbert H., 189
Leizhou Bandao (Kwangchowwan), 147
Lenroot, Katherine Fredrica, 50
Leopold of Austria, Archduke & Archduchess, 75
Lequn Cun, Guangdong, 230–31, 303
Lethbridge, AB, 287, 288
Lewis, Joe E., 184
Lewis, Mary, 190
Lewis, Nancy, 190
Li. *see also* Lee
Li Biqi or Betty Li Deng (sister of Li Xiaqing), 348 n.8
Li Chao, 298
Li Dandan. *see* Li Xiaqing
Li Fenglin (Leah Hing), 352 n.1, 357 n. 21
Li, George Yixiang, 204, 205, 206
Li, Hazel Yueying, 201, 246, 352 n.1, 354 n.22
Li Jincheng, 348 n.8
Li Jinyi, 118
Li Minwei, 126, 127, 129, 130, 131, 132–33, 349 (n.6,
    n.10, n.11)
Li Peiji (uncle of Li Xiaqing), 117, 119, 120
Li Qingchun, 118, 348 n.1
Li, Sidney, 67, 358 n.24
Li Xiaqing, 65
    as actress Li Dandan, 3, 116
    characterized, 127, 130, 131–32
        deplores moviemaking, 134
        fame, 126, 128, 131-32, 133, 134
        films of, 126, 127, 128–31, A–II
        thwarts thieves, 130–31
    as aviatrix
    aerobatics, 140–44, 152, 180, 205–06
        air shows, 71, 152, 165, 176, 180, 184, 204
        authors Chinese aviation history, 154, 353 n.14
        aviation in China &, 146-7, 150, 154-55, 202
        Chinese Air Force, rejected by, 156–57
        visits Canada, 187-88, 272, 274
        distance flights, 139, 146, 154, 155, 181
        early yearnings to fly, 116–17

Eastern US flying tour, 189–90
Eurasia Aviation Corporation and, 154
falls from stunt plane, 141–44, 150, 351 n.10
first US flying tour, 56-60, 166–75
    groundwork for tour, 161–62
    Hilda Yan, touring with,164, 166–67
    jewelry used as collateral, 162, 163, 174,
        357 n.12
    Song Meiling's approval of, 159–60
    tour completed, 70, 174
and flying club for women, 37-38, 153
flying in fog, 147, 155, 165–66, 173
flying lessons, Geneva, 136–38, 169
    Boeing School, 138–44, 154, 179, 204
hours logged, 187, 197
love of flight, 117, 136–37, 148, 167, 205–06
pilot's licenses, 138-39, 144, 146, 197,
    204-05, 242, 351 n.6, 352 n.1, 354 n.19
as 'pop' art subject, 194, 195, 196, 361 n.20
Relief Wings and, 183–85, 186
'retires' from flight, 203, 204
South American tours, 178–81, 198, 199-200
Southwestern Aviation Corp. (SWAC), 154–55,
    156
teaches flight, 147, 150-51
autobiography, 182-83, 186, 359 n.6
arrivals in U.S., 139, 162, 204
birth, 116, 120-21
Bishop Yubin and, 56, 165, 167, 171, 175
black market and, 203
blacklisted by Hirohito, 158
characterized, 3, 134, 135–36, 146, 158, 181–82,
    198–99, 200, 202-03, 204, 206
    conceals emotions, 124–25, 127, 149, 206
children of, 135, 136, 139, 149, 169, 190, 206
courage of, 130-31, 137, 143-44, 158, 171, 205-06
death, 208
premature death rumors, 201
Disputed Passage, 173, 176, 181–82, 357 n.23
education of, 124, 125–26, 132, 133, 351 n.8
family history of, 116, 117–123, 348 (n.6, n.1)
Hong Kong and, 125, 144, 161, 174, 182, 196
    attends 'handover,' 207
    earns B license, 354 n.19
    resident of, 158, 203-04
husbands of,
    Hsu, [202]
    George Yixiang Li, 204, 205, 206
    Zheng Baifeng, 134–36, 137-38, 139, 148–49,
        150, 181, 207, 352 n.4
jewelry, 162, 163, 174, 176, 180, 349 n.3, 356 n.6,

357 n.12, 361 n.1
men and, 149, 169, 202
mother of, 119–120, 121, 123, 149, 348 n.7
mothering skills of, 149, 206
names of, 58, 121, 200
patriotism of, 116, 117, 133, 136, 148, 156, 181, 185
Peter Doo, 149–50, 159, 352 n.7
physical appearance, 59, 127, 155, 163, 166, 168-69,
    172, 175-76, 195, 198, 205, 206, 357 n.14
related to Zheng Hanying, 237
social life of, 194–95
United China Relief, 185ff, and 'special gifts,' 190,
    191, 200
tours of Eastern states, 189, 192, 193-94, 197
    itineraries, 192, 193–94
    South American tour of 1944, 198, 199-200
    takes a break, 197
US Customs and, 188, 201–02
war work, 186 (see also Li, Xiaqing, United China
    Relief)
    Bowl of Rice participant, 75, 176, 359 n.7
    Disputed Passage, 173, 176, 181–82, 357 n.23
    fashion model, 176, 358 n.26
    hospital work, 157, 354 n.23
    orphanage operator, 157
    Peking Opera actress, 188
    radio station operator, 157
Li Yingsheng (father of Li Xiaqing)
    and Peter Doo, 150
    as entrepreneur, 123, 127, 131, 150, 200
    as father, 124, 132, 134, 137, 178, 349 n.3
    characterizations of, 206–07
    concubines of, 124, 132, 207, 349 n.10
    death, 206–07
    decorated, 206–07, 362 n.6
    movie mogul, 126–27, 132–33, 349 (n.11, n.14)
    revolutionary activities, 118–120
    underworld activities, 127, 135, 326 n.5, 349 n.3
Li Zishi (grandfather of Li Xiaqing), 118, 124
Liang Bi, 363 n.3
Liang, Lilian, 77
Lieu, Franklin, 38, 44
Lim, Robert Khoseng. see Lin Kesheng
Lin Chuchu, 127, 128
Lin Kesheng (Robert Khoseng Lim), 340 n.3
Lin Yutang family, 35, 77
Lindbergh, Charles, 48
Lingnan University, 258, 260
Littoria airport, 41
Liu Changhua, 231
Liu Chieh, 337 n.15, 340 n.5

Liu Peiquan, 154–55
Liu Shishun, 283, 293, 370 n.19
Lockheed, 12A, 199
   Lodestar 1808A, 371 n.3
Lodge, Henry Cabot, Mrs., 53
Longfield, G.P., 239
Longhua airfield, 37, 147, 150, 151, 197, 355 n.26
Louie, Tong (Lei Yutang), 270–71, 368 n.10
Lovet-Lorski, Boris, 360 n.17
Lutz, Walther, 154, 353 n.16
Lyons, Leonard, 194

M
Mackie, Jean, 240
Mahoney, Daniel, 184
Mahurangi Harbour, NZ, 98
Maillardville, BC, 299
Maine Aero Rendezvous, 71
Male, John Gifford (second husband of Hilda Yan),
   as stepfather, 92–93
   background of, 91, 346 n.1
   buys New Zealand property, 98
   death, 102
   FBI investigation of, 96, 346 n.7
   Hilda Yan, marriage to, 91
   divorce & remarriage, 100, 102
   love of the sea, 96, 97
   hurricane 97
Maloney, Mamie, 300
Malton Airport, 187
Manchukuo, 235
Manchuria, 44, 60, 83, 136, 137, 235, 249
Mao Zedong, 92, 93, 235–36, 301, 365 n.12
Marco Polo Bridge, 43, 156, 243
Margriet, Princess of the Netherlands, 293
Marley, Roger ('Tex'), 351 n.13
Matsui Haru (Ayako Ishigaki), 51, 341 n.19
McCormick, Elsie (Dunn), 182, 186, 359 n.10
McTyeire School for Girls, 16–17, 125–26
Mei Lanfang, 26, 27–29
Meredith, Burgess, 194
Metro-Goldwyn-Mayer, 172–73
Mexico, Princess of (Catarina), 164
MGM. *see* Metro-Goldwyn-Mayer
Miami All-American Air Maneuvers, 184
Ministry of Foreign Affairs. *see* Waijiaobu
Minxin Film Company, 126, 127, 131, 132, 133, 172,
   A–II
Mitusbishi, Zero, 255
Mobile, AL, 62
Mont Tremblant, PQ, 83

Montgomery, AL, 62, 63, 67, 69, 74
Montréal, PQ, 287, 290, 291–92, 303
Moore, Rolie. *see* Barrett, Rosalie (Rolie) Moore
Morgenthau Jr., Henry, 87
Moscow, USSR, 26–30, 33, 36, 50
Mosquito, Madame, 295
Moth. *see* de Havilland Tiger-Moth
Mottahedeh, Mildred, 85
Mukden Incident, 43, 136, 234
Mulan. see Hua Mulan Joins the Army
Mussolini, Benito, 47, 235

N
Nanjing, 25, 36, 48, 50, 146, 154
Naples, Italy, 41
National Aeronautic Association, 352 n.15
National Air Races, 71, 176
National Concert and Artists' Corporation, 198
National Council for Democratic Rights, 284
National Relief Commission, 55, 58
National Women's Advisory Committee, 248
Nehru, Jawaharlal, 74
Netherlands, 39, 76, 126, 293
New Haven, CT, 17, 95, 192
New York City, NY, 58, 70–71, 75, 76, 174, 180, 181,
   189, 196
   Brooklyn library, 99
   World's Fair, 58, 73, 74, 175
New York School of Social Work, 95
New Zealand, 91, 96, 98–99, 100, 102, 267
Newark, NJ, 165, 174
Nichols, Ruth, 183–84, 186, 358 n.4
Nine Power Conference, 46
Northeast Harbor, ME, 71
Nosworthy, Taxi, 64–65

O
O'Toole, Barry, Monsignor, 58, 60, 69
Oakland, CA, 138, 139, 140, 149, 204, 205, 208
Oberon, Merle, 163
Oei Huilan. *see* Koo, Wellington, Madame
Order of the Child Jesus, 299, 372 n.2
Order of the Eastern Star, 53
Ormiston, Mercedes, 359 n.1
Ottawa, ON, 262, 267, 281, 283, 288, 293–94, 302
Ou Yang, 127

P
Pan-American Airways, 199, 200, 239
Panay, U.S.S., 341 n.15
Paris Peace Conference, 233, 370 n.18

Paris, France, 123, 133, 134, 136, 137, 233, 234–36, 236, 237, 258, 273, 350 (n.1), 363–64 (n.4)

Parkway Village, Queens, NY, 91–92

Patterson, Allen Lonsdale ('Pat'), 159, 355 n.26

Pawley, William D., 356 n.4

Pearl Harbor, 79, 80, 191, 263, 279, 369 n.11

Peking Opera, 188, 271

Peng Jiazhen, [232], 363 n.3

People's Liberation Army (PLA), 92

Perkins, Jeanne Bayly, 40

Philadelphia, PA, 59, 166, 174, 190, 194

Pickford, Mary, 182

Pike, Jean, 366 n.2

Piper Aircraft Company, 274, 275
    Piper Cub, 187

Pittsburgh, PA, 165, 174

Pius XI, Pope, 165, 356 n.11

PLA. see People's Liberation Army (PLA)

Poet by the Sea (Poeme de La Mer), 128, A–II

Point Judith, RI, 97

Polytechnic Institute of Brooklyn, 92, 346 n.6

Porterfield 35-W, 60, 61, 62–65, 66, 69, 167, 342 n.4

Porterfield Aircraft Corporation, 58, 60

Powell, William, 163

Prattville, AL, 63ff, 85, 100, 173

President Coolidge, s.s., 144

President Harrison, s.s., 74

Pursuing the Enemy on Horseback, 131

Putnam, George, 335 n.3

Puyi, Emperor of China, 235

Q

Qiyun Shushi (Zheng family schoolhouse), 231, 303

Québec City, PQ, 287, 291

Québec Royal Rifles, 281

R

Rajputana, s.s., 244

Rathbone, Basil, 163

Raynault, Adhemar, 292–93

RCAF. see Royal Canadian Air Force

Red Cross Society. see American Red Cross, Canadian Red Cross, Chinese Red Cross

'Resistance and Reconstruction,' 55, 248, 369 n.2

Relief Wings, 183–84, 186

Reviving Romance, 128, A–II

Rice Bowl fundraisers. see Bowl of Rice fundraisers

Rio de Janiero, Brazil, 180, 199–200, 362 n.4

Roberge, Elianne, 273, 366 n.2, 367 n.3

Robinson, Edward G., 163

Rockefeller, John D., III, 189

Rogers, Ginger, 163

Romance of Airways in China, 154, 353 n.14

Romance of the Western Chamber, 126, 128–29, 133, A–II

Romero, Cesar, 163

Roosevelt Field, 48, 49, 54, 179, 340 n.11

Roosevelt, Eleanor, 83, 90, 186, 345 n.14

Roosevelt, Franklin Delano, 185, 197, 291, 341

Roosevelt, Theodore, Jr., 58, 72, 343 n.5, 358 n.1

Rose of Pu-chui. see Romance of the Western Chamber

Royal Aero Club, London, 228, 244, 263

Royal Air Force (RAF), 79, 239, 246, 278, 281, 289, 290, 364 n.5

Royal Canadian Air Force (RCAF), 229, 266, 267, 278–79, 289, 296, 371 n.3, 372 n.3
    refuses women pilots, 273

Royal Canadian Air Force, Women's Division (RCAF WD), 266, 289, 290

Royal Dutch Airlines (KLM), 199

Ruan Lingyu, 126, 337 n.6

Russell, Rosalind, 182, 187

Russia. see Soviet Union

Rye Seminary, 16, 335 n.3

S

Sachs, Nadine, 194

Safair Flying Services, 48, 54

San Francisco Conference, 87–88

San Francisco, 77, 87, 161, 204, 240, 258, 271, 280

Santiago, Chile, 180

Sartoris, Harry, 351 n.12

Sassoon, Victor, 21–22

'Save the Nation Thru Aviation,' 117, 144, 172, 245

Scott, James Stanley (J.S.), 290

Seaforth Highlanders, 302, 373 n.1

Seldenberg, Norman, 93

Service Flying Training Schools,
    No.13 Saint-Hubert, PQ, 290-91
    No.7 Fort Macleod, AB, 287-88

Serviços Aéreos Cruzeiro do Sul, 199, 361 n.3

Seto family, 258-9, 261, 270, 272, 297–98, 299, 303

Seto, Beverley Ann (daughter of Zheng Hanying), 266, 281, 285, 286, 299, 302, 303

Seto Fangin, 258

Seto, Fanny Lew, 259, 286

Seto, Geraldine, 259, 270–71, 368 n.10

Seto More, 258–59, 286

Seto, Wilfred Bien-tang, 266, 281, 299
    meets Zheng Hanying, 260, 366 n.4
    acknowledges Zheng's child, 265
    and Canadian citizenship, 302
    as Canadian army serviceman, 302, 373 n.1

in China, 258–61
    background, 258–59
    death, 302–03
Sever, s.s., 26, 27, 36
Seversky, 164
SFTS. *see* Service Flying Training School
Sham, Harry, 356 n.7
Shanghai, 4, 11, 16, 20, 21, 24, 55, 94, 96, 126, 127,
    129, 135, 145, 182, 202, 236, 259, A-I
    celebrates CKS birthday, 36–37, 151
    Bloody Saturday, 45
    Sino-Japanese War and, 121, 156, 157, 158, 244
Shanghai Flying Club, 145, 150-51, 237, 238, 352 n.3
Shanghai Medical College, 20, 23, 36, 103, 336 n.12
Shanghai Volunteer Corps, 259, 260
Shearer, Norma, 163
Shen, T.H., 339 n.14, 370 n.16
Shi Zhaoji. *see* Sze, Alfred Sao-ke
Shih Chao-ying, 298
Short Snorters' Club, 263, 366 n.6
Showalter, Max, 193
Shu, Lillian, 74
Sino-Japanese War, 44, 45, 256
    beginning of, 43, 156, 243
    and China's need for allies, 74
    deplored by League of Nations, 46
    effect of on Chinese civilians, 55–56
    in Shanghai, 156–58
    in Hong Kong, 79–80
Situ. *see* Seto
Smith College, 17–18
Smith, P.H., 239
Soeurs de l'Enfant Jésus, Les, 299, 372 n.2
Song family, vilified, 301
Song, Ailing (Madame H.H. Kong), 17, 44, 362 n.4
Song, Charles ('Charlie') Jones (Song Jiashu), 17
Song Meiling (Madame Chiang Kai-shek), 5, 44, 83,
    182, 186, 228, 247, 248, 282, 347 n.2, 354 n.22,
    369 n.6, 370 n.22
    chairs Aeronautical Affairs Commission, 159, 178,
        245, 254, 276
    and Chongqing airfield, 250–51, 362 n.4, 365 n.15
    approves Li Xiaqing's flying tours, 159, 177
    as role model, 275–76, 301
    Hilda Yan works for, 81
    Kuling women's conference, 277
    nepotism and, 245, 246
    North American tour, 81, 84, 196–97, 286, 296–97
    Zheng Yuxiu and, 233, 297
Song Qingling (Madame Sun Yat-sen), 17, 75, 177,
    336 n. 11

Song, T.V. *see* Song Ziwen
Song, T.V., Madame. *see* Zhang Yueqia (Laura Chang)
Song Ziwen (T.V. Song), 82–83, 87, 159, 282, 347 n.2
Sorbonne University, 3, 123, 127, 134, 233, 234, 235,
    278, 350 n.20, 364 n.5
South America, 177–81, 197–200, 362 n.4
South Western Aviation Corporation (SWAC), 154–55,
    242, 354 n.18
Soviet Union, 24–30, 76, 87, 135, 160, 179
    and Moscow's Chinese Embassy, 24–34
    at Dumbarton Oaks Conference, 87
    Hu Die in, 26, 29
    Mei Lanfang in, 26, 27–29
    Moscow Film Festival, 26, 29
    war with China averted, 24
Spirit of New China, Porterfield 35-W, 58, 60, 61, 62–65,
    66, 69, 166, 342 n.1
    Stinson Reliant SR-5E, 174, 357 n.12
    Stinson Reliant SR-9B, 58–59, 165, 166, 170, 174,
        176, 357 n.12
St. John's College, Shanghai, 12, 44, 336 n.12
St. Stephen's mission school, 125
Stalin, Joseph, 24, 30
Stannard, W.C., 292
Stearman trainer aircraft, 139
Stillwell, Joseph, 193
Stinson, Reliant
    SR-5E, 174, 357 n.12
    SR-9B, 58, 165, 166, 170, 174, 176, 357n.12
    trainers, 139
Studio 28, 133
Sun Fo, 355 n.17
Sun Yat-sen, 1, 3, 79, 117, 119, 121, 126, 172, 177, 229,
    233, 290, 355 n.1
    'Saving the Nation Through Aviation,' 117, 144,
        172, 245
Sze, Alfred Sao-ke, 53
Sze, Mai-mai, 53

T
Taiwan, 93, 301, 302, 356 n.11
Tamiroff, Akim, 173
Tang Pao-sun, 351 n.14
Taylor, George, Dr., 65–66
Tcheng Soumay. *see* Zheng Yuxiu
Thaden, Louise, 176
Tjibadak, s.s., 39
Toledo, OH, 189–90
Tongmenghui, 118
trafficking of women & children, 38, 39, 41, 46, A-I,
    338 (n.7, n.8).

Trans-Canada Airlines (TCA), 287–88
Trans-Siberian Express, 27
Trasolini, Tosca, 272, 366 n.2
Tsang, Hélène Tsing-ying. *see* Zhang Qianying
Tucker, Sophie, 184
Turner, Roscoe, 60, 167
Twentieth Century Fox Film Corp., 193

U

UCR. *see* United China Relief (UCR)
UN. *see* United Nations (UN)
Un-American Activities Committee, 96
United Airlines, 139
United China Relief (UCR), 84, 188, 193, 198, 286
    and 'special gifts,' 190, 191, 200
    donations affected by inflation, 200–201
    gifted with Aeronca Super Chief, 189
    launching of, 185, 359 n.5
United Council for Civilian Relief in China, 343 (n.9, n.5)
United Nations (UN), Advisory Services, 91
    Bahá'í and, 86
    Declaration of Human Rights, 90
    foundation of, laid at Dumbarton Oaks, 87
    Human Rights Division, 90, 91
    post-war creation of, envisioned, 83
    Public Information, Department of, 86, 89, 90
United Nations Charter, 87–88, 89, 98
United States,
    at Dumbarton Oaks Conference, 87
    attitude to Sino-Japanese War, 57, 263
    impressions of China, 2, 185
    State Dept. assists aviatrixes, 57
    Un-American Activities Committee, 96
    World War II and, 75, 191
United States Air Force Air Transport Command, 202–03
United States Bureau of Air Commerce, 48
United States Federal Aviation Administration, 204–05
United States National School of Law, 51
United States Naval Reserve Base, Alameda, 142–43
United States Senate, 296
University of British Columbia, 278, 372 n.1
University of Harvard, 16, 17, 18, 85
University of Liverpool, 17
University Women's Club, 53, 284, 368 n.10
USSR. *see* Soviet Union

V

Vaill, George D., 99, 336 n.8
Vallon, René, 4

Vancouver Council of Women, 283
Vancouver Junior Board of Trade, 284, 298
Vancouver Women's School for Citizenship, 284
Vancouver, BC, 228, 258–59, 283. *see also* Chinese Consulates, Vancouver, BC
    Bastille Day celebrations in, 283–84
    Chinatown, 171-72, 261–62, 266, 272, 278
    Chinese War Relief Fund kick-off, 297–98
    in wartime, described, 264ff, 279–80
    invites Madame Chiang to visit, 296
    Li Xiaqing visits, 168, 170, 171–72, 272
    racism in, 269–71, 368 n.10
Vanier, Georges, Madame, 291
Vesuvius, Mount, 41
Vickers, Catalina amphibean (PBY), 290
Victoria, BC, 258, 280, 282, 370 n.18
Virginia Beach, VA, 74
von Sternberg, Joseph, 163
von Trott zu Solst, Adam, 344 n.7

W

Waijiaobu (Ministry of Foreign Affairs), 31, 135, 262
Walker, Willa, 289, 290
Waller, Betty, 367 n.3
Walton, Mabel, 346 n.2
Wang. *see also* Huang; Wong
Wang, C.H., Mrs., 58, 341 n.23, 343 n.5
Wang, C.T. *see* Wang Zhengting
Wang Chonghui (C.W. Wong), 160, 355 n.27
Wang Jingwei, 345 n.11
Wang Zhengting (C.T. Wang), 49, 336 n.9
    family of, 49, 50–1
War of Resistance Against the Japanese. *see* Sino-Japanese War
War Refugees Relief Committee, 56, 59, 67, 72
Ward, Dorothy Lee, 184
Washington, D.C., 49ff, 69, 83, 139, 167, 286, 293
Way Down West. see Romance of the Western Chamber
Weber, Marcel, 351 n.3
Wei Daoming, 228, 234, 271, 273, 282, 285, 293, 301–02, 343 n.8, 369 n.1
Welch, G. Harold, 192
Welles, Orson, 194
Wells, H.G., 182
white slavery. *see* trafficking of women & children
White, William Allen, 58
Whitney, Cornelius Vanderbilt ('Sonny'), 178, 183
Why Not Her, 127, A–II
Wilkie, Wendell, 197
Wilkinson, A.B., 372 n.3
Willcox, Henry and Anita, 97, 347 n.8

Index

Williams, V. Ben, 371 n.26
Wilmette, IL, 85–86
Winchell, Walter, 191
Windsor, Edward, Duke of, 184
Winnipeg Grenadiers, 281
Winstone, Martha Catherine, 100, 102
women. *see also* concubines.
at risk, 39–40, 46, 121, A-1, 338 (n.7, n.8)
  encouraged by Song Meiling, 178, 245
  equality for, urged by Hilda Yan, 32–33
  Institute of Women's Education, 121
  status of, at League of Nations, 46, A–I
  Women's Internat'l Association of Aeronautics, 174
women in aviation, 37-38, 153, 174, 176, 237, 351 n.6,
    352 n.1, 353 n.9, 359 n.1. *see also* Flying Seven
Women's Canadian Club, 277–78, 282–83, 289, 291.
Women's International Association of Aeronautics,
    174, 176
Wong. *see also* Huang; Wang
Wong, Anna May, 35, 72, 162, 182, 191, 356 n.5
Wong, C.W. (Wang Chonghui), 160
Wong Foon Sien, 300
Woodward, W.C., 280
World Center for Women's Archives, 73
World's Fair, 58, 73, 74, 175
Wu, Butterfly. *see* Hu, Die
Wu Nanru, 27, 31, 337 (n.5, n.15)
Wu Tiecheng, 145, 151, 156, 243
Wuchang Uprising, 117

X

Xiangya Medical School, 14, 16, 18, 20
Xu Mulan (grandmother of Li Xiaqing), 117–18, 121,
    128, 125, 188, 348 (n.1, n.7)
Xu Peiyao, 121, 348 n.2
Xu Run, 117
Xu Yingying, 132, 349 n.10
Xu Zhaodui (Frank Co Tui), 72, 175, 343 n.1, 358 n.1,
    359 n.7
Xu Zhaodui (Frank Co Tui), Mrs., 53
Xu Zonghan, 117, 119, 121, 178, 348 (n1, n2) 361 n2

Y

Yale University, 12, 13, 14, 15, 21, 72, 85, 335 n.5
Yale-in-China, 14, 16, 18, 19, 72, 99, 335 n.8
Yali. *see* Yale-in-China
Yan Deqing, Strong (uncle of Hilda Yan), 14
Yan Fuqing (father of Hilda Yan), 3, 12–20, 44, 72–73,
    78, 95, 345 (n.5, n.11)
  concern for Hilda, 42, 53, 78, 65–66
  education of, 12-13, 16

in America, 13, 16, 19, 90
Mao Zedong and, 94
as Minister of Health, 55, 72-73
vilified & rehabilitated, 100–03
Shanghai Medical College, 20, 23, 36, 103, 336 n.12
directs Shanghai's Rescue/Defense Committee, 53
Xiangya Medical School, 14, 16, 18, 20
Zhou Enlai and, 94
Yan Huiqing, W.W. (uncle of Hilda Yan), 22, 33, 75, 76,
    79, 337 n.15, 344 n.10
as Ambassador to USSR, 14, 23–4
decision to retire, 33,34, 35, 36
concern for Hilda, 41–42, 53–54, 67, 78
death, 94
deplores isolationism, 30–1
enlists Hilda's help in USSR, 25
and Hilda's divorce, 34
Hong Kong, 77–78
Hu Shize and, 33
in Hong Kong, 47
and Institute for Pacific Relations, 74
International Red Cross Society, 55
League of Nations, 31, 33
Mao Zedong and, 94
as Premier of China, 3
Yan, Julia (Yan Qinglian), 335 n.2
Yan Nansheng, 74
Yan, Victor (brother of Hilda Yan), 16, 101
Yan, William (brother of Hilda Yan), 16, 101
Yan Xiangya, Dorothy (sister of Hilda Yan), 16, 38,
    44, 78, 101
Yan Yaqing, Hilda, 95, 96, 175, 237, 337 n.15, 340 n.5,
    346 n.15
affiliations, 53
  National Child Welfare Association, 38, 39
  Young Women's Christian Association, 38,
    69–70
as aviatrix, 53-54
  airshows, 71
  flying club for women and, 38, 153
  flying lessons, Littoria, Rome, 41
    Roosevelt Field, NY, 48–49, 54
  plans to fly for China, 47–48, 84, 153
  U.S. flying tour, 56–57, 59, 61, 62
    crash in Prattville, AL, 63–64, 67, 70, 173,
      342 n.4, 358 n.24
    fan mail, 70
    injuries, 64–66, 67, 68, 342 n.3
    sponsors, 58
    wins wings, 54, 164
  birth, 12, 335 n.1

characterized, 2, 10, 50-51, 53, 101–02
children of, 22, 23, 37, 44, 50, 92-93, 95, 153, 346
n.6
climbs Mt. Vesuvius, 41
conferences.
Bandoeng, 39–40, 46, A-I, 338 n.7
Institute of Pacific Relations, 74, 75-76, 83
Bretton Woods, 86-87
Dumbarton Oaks, 87
San Francisco, 87-88
death, 101
death of father, Yan Fuqing, 102–03
death of uncle, Yan Huiqing, 94–95
education of,
Rye Seminary, 16
McTyeire School for Girls, 16-17
Walnut Hill School, 17
Smith College, 17-18
Yale-in-China, 18-19
School of Library Service, 99
FBI and, 346 n.7
finances of, 31, 92
health problems, 78, 79, 100
Hong Kong and, 77–81
internment in, 80–81, 88
hurricane and, 97
husbands,
Chen Bingzhang, 20, 34, 100, 153
John Male, 91ff, 100
ideologies of, 31, 81, 82, 86, 96, 347 n.3
internationalist outlook, 30-31, 41, 47, 78, 85
Japanese citizens not to blame for war, 70
colonialism deplored, 83, 88
isolationism, opposition to, 74–75, 78
lawsuit of, 93
League of Nations, 31ff, 51, 153, A-I
as delegate to coronation, 42–3
critical of, 82
Secretariat member, 34
status of women and, 32–33, 45–46, A–I
traffic of women & children, 39, 41, 46, A-I,
338 (n.7, n.8)
Li Xiaqing and, 37-38, 56-61, 70, 71
as librarian, 99, 101
Lilian Liang and, 77
lovers & admirers of, 41–2, 54, 100
'George,' 75, 76
Song Ziwen, 82–83
Moscow, Embassy chatelaine at, 28–31
mothering, 25, 36, 50, 93
occupational therapist volunteer, 98

physical appearance, 10, 20, 59, 60, 66, 83, 90, 94
popularity of, 10, 20, 21, 38, 47, 49-51
Sino-Japanese War, 44, 45, 48-49, 77-81
social work, interest in, 19–20, 95
Song Meiling and, 81
spirituality of, 68–69, 71, 88, 346 n.1
atomic bomb and, 89
Bahá'í faith, 85–86, 89, 90, 95, 100
Daoism, 100
Tallulah Bankhead and, 74–75
travels of, 16, 17, 18, 47, 81-82, 91
United Nations and, 86, 87, 89-92, 95
Bahá'í and, 86
critical of U.N. Charter, 87–89, 98
Declaration of Human Rights and, 90
Department of Public Information and, 89, 90
addresses mini UN Assemblies, 90
United States citizenship and, 347 n.3
war work, 53
aid for Bishop Yubin's refugees, 56, 58, 59-60
assistant to Song Meiling, 81
Bowl of Rice, participation in, 74–75
as fashion model, 52, 74, 75, 176
radio broadcasts of, 73
See also Yan, Hilda Yaqing, as aviatrix, U.S.
flying tour
wedding of sister Dorothy, 44-45
Zhang Qianying (Hélène Tsang), and, 39, 43, 44, 75
Yan Yongjing, 11, 12
Yan Zi, 11
Yan Zujing (grandfather of Hilda Yan), 11, 12
Yang Guangsheng (Kuangson Young), 149, 195, 339
n.13
Yang Guangsheng (Yan Youyin), Madame, 149
Yang Jinxun, 151, 246, 352 n.1, 353 n.9, 354 n.22
Yang Kaihui, 93
Yates, Ruth, 360 n.17
Yogi, Mahesh, Maharishi, 346 n.1
York, Victor, Mrs., 367 n.3
Young Men's Christian Association (YMCA), 92, 344
n.7
Young Women's Christian Association (YWCA), 23,
38, 40, 69, 139-40, 336 n.10
Young, Kuangson. *see* Yang Guangsheng (Kuangson
Young)
Yu Junji (Yu Tsune-chi, James), 174, 201
Yuan Shikai, 233
Yubin, Paul, Bishop, 50, 56, 58, 59, 60, 72, 165, 167,
171, 175, 341 n.17, 356 n.11
YWCA. *see* Young Women's Christian Association

Index

Z

Zamoyska, L.I., Countess, 194

Zanuck, Darryl, 163

Zero, Mitsubishi, 255

Zhang Jingjiang, 340 n.3

Zhang Qianying (Hélène Tsing-ying Tsang), 39, 43, 44, 75, 176, 237, 340 n.3, 352 n.1

Zhang Yueqia (Laura Chang), 44, 83, 345 n.13

Zhao, Madame (Mme. Mosquito), 295

Zheng family palace, 231, 303

Zheng Baifeng (1st husband of Li Xiaqing), 134-35, 145, 150, 169, 181, 350 n.18
  careers of, 207
  characterization of, 134
  considers Li Xiaqing 'dead,' 148, 152, 207
  death of, 207
  reaction to divorce, 148–49
  related to Zheng Yuxiu, 134, 237, 337 n. 14

Zheng Baishi or Pax Cheng (son of Li Xiaqing), 135, 136, 149, 169, 190, 206

Zheng Hanying, Jessie, Flight-Lieutenant, 3
  admiration for Chinese people, 292
  affiliations, 228, 242, 248-49, 266
  as attaché, 262-64, 268, 269, 294, 371 n.26
  as aviatrix, 267–69, 288
    Aeronautical Affairs Commission, 245, 250, 257, 265
    and Chinese Air Force, 228, 246, 254, 258, 299
    air force uniform of, 246, 276, 287, 365 n.11
    FEFTS flight training, 240–42, 243–44
    Flying Seven and, 267–69, 272, 291
    International Flying License, 228, 244, 263
    love of flight, 241
    RCAF and, 273, 278–79, 287–88, 289, 290, 296, 296, 300
    Song Meiling &,245, 275-76, 286, 295, 297
    Waijiaobu and, 262
    wins wings, 244
  attends Catalina christening, 290–91
  birth and childhood, 229–30
  burial arrangements, 300–01
  Burma Road, 256
  characterized, 3, 228, 268, 269, 277, 284-85, 286, 288, 295–96, 301
  child of, Beverley Ann Seto, 266, 281, 285, 286, 299, 302, 303
  Chongqing, dug in at, 251–53
  death of, and funeral, 299-01
  Eastern Canada tour, 285–96
    Montréal, 290, 291–93
    Ottawa, 262, 287, 288-89, 293, 294, 296-97

    Québec City, 291
    Toronto, 287, 294–96
    Washington, D.C., 282, 286, 293
  education of, Sorbonne University, 234, 364 n.5
  family of, 230-34, 250, 285, 363 n.1. see also Zheng Yun.
  francophone, 236, 266, 272, 278, 283, 289ff
  impressions of Canada, 288, 296
  jewelry of, 276–77, 299, 369 n.5
  at Kuling women's conference, 247-49
  languages spoken by, 228, 236
  last will and testament, 299
  legacy of, 300
  and Li Xiaqing, 237, 238, 242, 246, 272, 273, 286
  National Flood Relief Commission worker, 249
  personality, 268, 269, 284–85, 287
  physical appearance, 228, 241, 246, 259, 260, 276, 277, 296, 298, 370 n.15
  political views of, 235, 236, 285
  pregnancy, 260–62, 266, 268
  in radio play, 271
  speeches, 273, 275-79, 282-84, 289ff, 369n.2
  speaking style, 276, 278, 284, 289, 291
  in Vancouver, 264ff
  Wilfred Seto and, 258, 260-62, 266, 281, 299, 366 n.4

Zheng Yun, 230, 238, 242, 254, 255, 256, 363 n1

Zheng, Mary Mulan (daughter of Li Xiaqing), 135, 149, 169, 190, 362 n.4

Zheng, Pax. see Zheng, Baishi

Zheng Wenzhi, 231

Zheng Xuean (aunt of Zheng Hanying), 231-32, 250

Zheng Yao (great-grandfather of Zheng Hanying), 230–31, 250, 303

Zheng Yun (brother of Zheng Hanying), 230, 238, 241, 242-43, 254, 255-56, 363 n.1

Zheng Yuxiu (aunt of Zheng Hanying), 3, 228, 230, 231, 232–34, 236, 238, 242, 245, 246, 250, 255, 271, 273, 285, 293, 359 n.6, 363 (n.1, n.4), 369 n.1, 370 n.18
  accompanies Mme Chiang to Ottawa, 296-97
  as marriage broker, 134, 148, 237, 350 n.19
  at Kuling women's conference, 248–49
  death, 302
  drafts laws of China, 32–33, 34, 234

Zhou Enlai, 94

About the Author

Patti Gully is a graduate of the University of Winnipeg. She holds a BA in Arts with emphasis on English, Religious Studies, and Classics. She also holds an MLIS from the University of British Columbia. She is the co-Author of the two-volume book: *Overseas Chinese from the Five Counties and Chinese Aviation* (*Wu yi huaqiao yu zhongguo hangkong*).

INFCW 926
       .2913
       G973

GULLY, PATTI.
    SISTERS OF HEAVEN

CENTRAL LIBRARY
12/08